S0-GQE-946

The Development of Albert Camus's Concern for Social and Political Justice

The Development of Albert Camus's Concern for Social and Political Justice

"Justice pour un juste"

Mark Orme

Madison • Teaneck
Fairleigh Dickinson University Press

Associated University Presses
2010 Eastpark Boulevard
Cranbury, NJ 08512

The paper used in this publication meets the requirements of the American National Standard for Permanence of Paper for Printed Library Materials Z39.48-1984.

Library of Congress Cataloging-in-Publication Data

Orme, Mark, 1968–
The development of Albert Camus's concern for social and political justice : "justice pour un juste" / Mark Orme.
p. cm.
Includes bibliographical references and index.
ISBN-13: 978-0-8386-4110-1 (alk. paper)
ISBN-10: 0-8386-4110-5 (alk. paper)
1. Camus, Albert, 1913–1960—Political and social views. 2. Justice in literature. I. Title.
PQ2605.A3734Z723135 2007
848′.91409—dc22 2006017918

PRINTED IN THE UNITED STATES OF AMERICA

For my mother and in memory of my father

Contents

Acknowledgments

I WOULD LIKE TO THANK PROFESSOR TERRY KEEFE OF THE DEPARTment of European Languages and Cultures at Lancaster University in the United Kingdom for his supervision of the original research on which the present book is based. My thanks are also due to the personnel at the various centers where I have conducted my research: the libraries of the Universities of Lancaster, Leicester, and Central Lancashire (United Kingdom); the British Library in London; the Taylor Institution in Oxford; and the Bibliothèque Nationale, the Bibliothèque Publique d'Information, and the Bibliothèque Fonds Albert Camus at L'Institution Mémoires de l'Édition Contemporaine (L'IMEC) in France. I would also like to acknowledge the financial assistance from the British Academy which has enabled me to prepare the present study.

In addition, I would like to thank the editors and publishers of the following journals for permission to use material published therein in the present study: *Australian Journal of French Studies* (Monash University), in respect of my article "'[L]'enfance dont il n'avait jamais guéri'? The Perception of Injustice in the Formative Years of Albert Camus" (37 [2000]: 72–90) (incorporated into chapter 1); *Essays in French Literature* (French Studies, Department of European Languages and Studies, The University of Western Australia), with regard to my article "Justice and the Quest for Origins: Sensitivity to Suffering as a Social Phenomenon in Albert Camus's *écrits de jeunesse*" (38 [2001]: 111–28) (also absorbed into chapter 1); the *Série Albert Camus,* published under the aegis of *La Revue des Lettres Modernes* (Lettres Modernes Minard), in connection with my chapter "*L'Homme révolté:* vers une justification éthique de la justice" (*AC19,* 91–122) (based on chapter 7); *French Studies Bulletin* (Oxford University Press), in respect of my piece "Realising 'la vraie justice': A Note on Albert Camus's Moral Transparency" (informing chapter 8); and *Modern & Contemporary France* (Carfax Publishing, Taylor & Francis Ltd.: http://www.tandf.co.uk), in connection with my article "*Retour aux sources:* Crisis and Reappraisal in Albert Camus's Final Pronouncements on Justice" (11 [2003]: 463–74).

The following names deserve special recognition for their assistance, encouragement and support throughout the preparation for, and writing of, this book: Pierre Le Baut; Professor Martin Blinkhorn; Lyndon Davies; Mohammed Farooq; colleagues in the Department of Languages and International Studies at the University of Central Lancashire in Preston and the generation of students there with whom I have discussed my interest in Camus in recent years; Thelma Goodman; Professor Edward Hughes; Peter James; John Shaw; Dr. Christine Margerrison; Annie Morton; Dr. Lyndsay Newman, Martine Ollion and her colleagues at L'IMEC; Françoise Poudevigne; Professor Malcolm Quainton; the late Roger Quilliot; Professor Robert Roeming; Susan and Géry Schneider; Donna Taylor; the late Professor Philip Thody; Philippe Vanney; Professor David Walker; Professor Chris Williams; and Farida, Hayet, and Sabrina Zeghiche.

Finally, and most important of all, an immense debt of gratitude is owed to my family and my parents, without whose support over the past few years this study quite literally could not have been written.

Mark Orme
Preston, England: March 2006

Abbreviations

THE FOLLOWING ABBREVIATIONS WILL BE USED IN THIS BOOK. WHERE possible, I have drawn on available English translations of Camus's works, making occasional modifications when deemed appropriate. All other translations are my own.

- *C1:* Camus, Albert. *Carnets I (mai 1935–février 1942).* Paris: Gallimard, 1962.
- *C2:* Camus, Albert. *Carnets II (janvier 1942–mars 1951).* Paris: Gallimard, 1964.
- *C3:* Camus, Albert. *Carnets III (mars 1951–décembre 1959).* Paris: Gallimard, 1989.
- *CA1:* Camus, Albert. *Carnets: 1935–1942.* Translated by Philip Thody. London: Hamish Hamilton, 1963.
- *CA2:* Camus, Albert. *Carnets: 1942–1951.* Translated by Philip Thody. London: Hamish Hamilton, 1966.
- *CAC: Camus à "Combat": éditoriaux et articles d'Albert Camus 1944–1947.* Edited by Jacqueline Lévi-Valensi. Cahiers Albert Camus 8. Paris: Gallimard, 2002.
- *CAL: "Caligula": version de 1941 suivi de La Poétique du premier "Caligula".* Edited by A. James Arnold. Cahiers Albert Camus 4. Paris: Gallimard, 1984.
- *Corr: Correspondance Albert Camus / Jean Grenier (1932–1960).* Edited by Marguerite Dobrenn. Paris: Gallimard, 1981.
- *Corres: Albert Camus / Pascal Pia: Correspondance, 1939–1947.* Edited by Yves Marc Ajchenbaum. Paris: Fayard / Gallimard, 2000.
- *CP: The Collected Plays of Albert Camus.* Translated by Stuart Gilbert, Henry Jones, and Justin O'Brien. London: Hamish Hamilton, 1965.
- *E:* Camus, Albert. *Essais.* Edited by R. Quilliot and L. Faucon. Bibliothèque de La Pléiade. Paris: Gallimard, 1965.
- *EK:* Camus, Albert. *Exile and the Kingdom.* Translated by Justin O'Brien. Harmondsworth, UK: Penguin, 1974.
- *EX: Albert Camus: éditorialiste à "L'Express" (mai 1955–*

février 1956). Edited by Paul F. Smets. Cahiers Albert Camus 6. Paris: Gallimard, 1987.

- *FC: Fragments d'un combat, 1938–1940. "Alger républicain", "Le Soir républicain."* Edited by André Abbou and Jacqueline Lévi-Valensi. Cahiers Albert Camus 3. 2 vols. Paris: Gallimard, 1978.
- *FM:* Camus, Albert. *The First Man.* Translated by David Hapgood. London: Hamish Hamilton, 1995.
- *HD:* Camus, Albert. *A Happy Death.* Translated by Richard Howard. Harmondsworth, UK: Penguin Books, 1973.
- *JV:* Camus, Albert. *Journaux de voyage (1946–1949).* Edited by Roger Quilliot. Paris: Gallimard, 1978.
- *MH:* Camus, Albert. *La Mort heureuse.* Edited by Jean Sarocchi. Cahiers Albert Camus 1. Paris: Gallimard, 1971.
- *MS:* Camus, Albert. *The Myth of Sisyphus.* Translated by Justin O'Brien. Harmondsworth, UK: Penguin Books, 1988.
- *OFOO: Albert Camus: œuvre fermée, œuvre ouverte? Actes du colloque du Centre Culturel International de Cerisy-la-Salle, juin 1982.* Edited by Raymond Gay-Crosier and Jacqueline Lévi-Valensi. Cahiers Albert Camus 5. Paris: Gallimard, 1985.
- *PC: Le Premier Camus suivi de Écrits de jeunesse d'Albert Camus.* Edited by Paul Viallaneix. Paris: Gallimard, 1973.
- *PH: Le Premier Homme.* Cahiers Albert Camus 7. Paris: Gallimard, 1994.
- *RRD: Resistance, Rebellion and Death.* Translated by Justin O'Brien. London: Hamish Hamilton, 1961.
- *SEN:* Camus, Albert. *Selected Essays and Notebooks.* Edited and translated by Philip Thody. Harmondsworth, UK: Penguin Books, 1979.
- *TF:* Camus, Albert. *The Fall.* Translated by Justin O'Brien. Harmondsworth, UK: Penguin, 1986.
- *TO:* Camus, Albert. *The Outsider.* Translated by Stuart Gilbert. Harmondsworth, UK: Penguin, 1975.
- *TP:* Camus, Albert. *The Plague.* Translated by Stuart Gilbert. Harmondsworth, UK: Penguin Books, 1960.
- *TR:* Camus, Albert. *The Rebel.* Translated by Anthony Bower. Harmondsworth, UK: Penguin Books, 1971.
- *TRN:* Camus, Albert. *Théâtre, Récits, Nouvelles.* Edited by Roger Quilliot. Bibliothèque de La Pléiade. Paris: Gallimard, 1962.
- *YW: The First Camus / Youthful Writings.* Translated by Ellen Conroy Kennedy. London: Hamish Hamilton, 1977.

The *Série Albert Camus,* published under the auspices of *La Revue des Lettres Modernes,* will be abbreviated as follows:

- *AC1: Albert Camus, 1: "autour de 'L'Étranger'"*. Edited by Brian T. Fitch. La Revue des Lettres Modernes 170–74. Paris: Lettres Modernes, 1968.
- *AC2: Albert Camus, 2: "langue et langage"*. Edited by Brian T. Fitch. La Revue des Lettres Modernes 212–16. Paris: Lettres Modernes, 1968.
- *AC4: Albert Camus, 4: "sources et influences"*. Edited by Brian T. Fitch. La Revue des Lettres Modernes 264–70. Paris: Lettres Modernes, 1971.
- *AC5: Albert Camus, 5: "journalisme et politique. L'Entrée dans l'histoire (1938–1940)"*. Edited by Brian T. Fitch. La Revue des Lettres Modernes 315–22. Paris: Lettres Modernes, 1972.
- *AC7: Albert Camus, 7: "Le Théâtre"*. Edited by Raymond Gay-Crosier. La Revue des Lettres Modernes 419–24. Paris: Lettres Modernes Minard, 1975.
- *AC9: Albert Camus, 9: "la pensée de Camus"*. Edited by Raymond Gay-Crosier. La Revue des Lettres Modernes 565–69. Paris: Lettres Modernes Minard, 1979.
- *AC10: Albert Camus, 10: "nouvelles approches"*. Edited by Brian T. Fitch. La Revue des Lettres Modernes 632–36. Paris: Lettres Modernes Minard, 1982.
- *AC11: Albert Camus, 11: "Camus et la religion"*. Edited by Brian T. Fitch. La Revue des Lettres Modernes 648–51. Paris: Lettres Modernes Minard, 1982.
- *AC12: Albert Camus, 12: "la révolte en question"*. Edited by Brian T. Fitch. La Revue des Lettres Modernes 715–19. Paris: Lettres Modernes Minard, 1985.
- *AC13: Albert Camus, 13: "études comparatives"*. Edited by Raymond Gay-Crosier. La Revue des Lettres Modernes 904–10. Paris: Lettres Modernes Minard, 1989.
- *AC14: Albert Camus, 14: "le texte et ses langages"*. Edited by Raymond Gay-Crosier. La Revue des Lettres Modernes 985–92. Paris: Lettres Modernes Minard, 1991.
- *AC15: Albert Camus, 15: "textes, intertextes, contextes autour de 'La Chute'"*. Edited by Raymond Gay-Crosier. La Revue des Lettres Modernes 1123–32. Paris: Lettres Modernes, 1993.
- *AC16: Albert Camus, 16: "'L'Étranger': cinquante ans après". Actes du Colloque d'Amiens, 11–12 décembre 1992, sous la direction de Jacqueline Lévi-Valensi.* Edited by Ray-

mond Gay-Crosier. La Revue des Lettres Modernes 1259–65. Paris: Lettres Modernes, 1995.

- *AC17: Albert Camus, 17: "toujours autour de 'L'Étranger'"*. Edited by Raymond Gay-Crosier. La Revue des Lettres Modernes 1310–16. Paris: Lettres Modernes Minard, 1996.
- *AC18: Albert Camus, 18: "la réception de l'œuvre de Camus en U.R.S.S. et en R.D.A."*. Edited by Raymond Gay-Crosier. La Revue des Lettres Modernes 1472–77. Paris: Lettres Modernes Minard, 1999.
- *AC19: Albert Camus, 19: "'L'Homme révolté': cinquante ans après"*. Edited by Raymond Gay-Crosier. La Revue des Lettres Modernes. Paris: Lettres Modernes Minard, 2001.
- *AC20: Albert Camus, 20: "'Le Premier homme' en perspective"*. Edited by Raymond Gay-Crosier. La Revue des Lettres Modernes. Paris: Lettres Modernes Minard, 2004.

The Development of Albert Camus's Concern for Social and Political Justice

Introduction

> If, amongst the many contemporary authors who have spoken about justice in their work, I have chosen Albert Camus, it is not just because he is one of the most outstanding writers of our time, but also because his entire work is governed by an intellectual honesty and an unfailing generosity which gives him the right to speak about justice.
>
> —M. Devismes, *La justice selon Albert Camus*

"THE NOTION OF JUSTICE IS OVERPOWERING," NOTES JULES ROMAINS in *Men of Good Will.* "One drop is enough."[1] The ideal of justice has, indeed, preoccupied innumerable philosophers, political scientists and moral theorists over the ages. From Plato to Rawls, justice has been—and continues to be—conceived of as a cornerstone of moral inquiry. And yet, fundamental to this timeless ethical process lies the fact that the term "justice" commands no single definition; the concept is interpreted differently by different thinkers. Plato, in *The Republic* (ca. 375 BC), points up the problems of understanding justice in any other context than that of society at large and, in dialogue with Socrates, he proceeds to formulate the idea of a "just state" on the principle of collective stability, whereby each individual agrees to undertake a task to the best of his/her ability in the interests of securing a general consensus.[2] Aristotle, unlike his tutor, deems justice primarily a value in relation to human behavior. Most notably, he distinguishes between "distributive justice"—the allocation of goods and services to social groups—and "rectificatory justice"—the punishment and/or compensation for injuries and unfair exchange—and posits that justice requires that individuals be treated equally until and unless relevant differences dictate otherwise.[3] Jeremy Bentham formulates justice in terms of "the greatest happiness of the greatest number," while another nineteenth-century Utilitarian, John Stuart Mill, posits that maximum aggregate benefit is the moral code determining human action.[4] For his part, John Rawls bases his *Theory of Justice* on the notion of moral reciprocity, that is, the need for humans to cooperate with one another on the ground of consolidating complementary interests within a given community.[5] Clearly, the ideal of justice is a wide-ranging moral precept, transcending many theoretical and conceptual boundaries.

Albert Camus is a man whose life is devoted to justice. Following the writer's untimely death in January 1960, André Malraux paid eloquent tribute to a lifelong moral crusade, remarking that "for more than twenty years, the work of Albert Camus was inseparable from an obsession with justice."[6] René Ménard, writing in the *Nouvelle Revue Française,* similarly spotlighted the moral vitality of a Camus whose existence was entrenched "in an obsession with moral rigor and humane justice."[7] Later, Camus's *maître* Jean Grenier remembered his protégé as a man "with a passion for justice and truth."[8] A recent special edition of *Europe* bears witness to the ongoing pertinence of Camus, deemed "a player in the modern world."[9] Camus himself, however, always played down the significance of such accolades, insisting that he was merely preoccupied with the plight of his fellow human beings in a world conditioned by moral uncertainty.[10] Be that as it may, currently—nearly fifty years since the writer's death—the ideal of "Camus Le Juste" continues to resonate, and critics are generally of one mind in pointing up the prominence of justice in Camus's moral understanding.[11] "Few values," observes one recent commentator, "are as contradictory and polysemous as that of justice in his [Camus's] work."[12] Yet the task of establishing the content of Camus's views on justice has not yet been sufficiently taken on. The aim of this book, then, is to explore the reality of Camus as a man imbued with the ideal of justice, as exemplified in the whole range of his nonfictional writings that relate to the subject, against the background of the historico-political and moral challenges of the mid-twentieth century. As we shall discover, Camus's consideration of the concept underwent significant changes in the different phases of his life and under the pressure of variable external events.

Chronological in character, this study will seek to evaluate the evolution of Camus's lifelong preoccupation with justice by concentrating on the development of his concern for the concept as expressed in a range of nonfictional genres (essays, journalism, articles, speeches, notebooks, correspondence, etc.). The decision to focus on the writer's nonfiction, rather than on his fiction and theater, as a principal (but, granted the absence of relevant texts at various key stages, not entirely exclusive) working tool is justified by two fundamental factors. First, the analysis of *fictional* texts raises additional problems of interpretation over and above those posed by nonfictional writings. While, in the case of fiction, the reader is required to "distill" an author's meaning by engaging in a process of interpretation with a given text, this is not so necessary in the case of nonfiction, where a writer can be said to be speaking on his/her own behalf. I am mindful that the distinction between "fact" and "fiction" is far from clear-cut in the realm of modern literary theory and that it relates in fact to the more general debate surrounding the question "What is Literature?", a full account of which obviously cannot be charted here. Yet while it may be argued that all texts require a degree of interpretation on the part of the reader in order to be "understood," one should note that, as its name implies, "nonfiction" is rooted in reality and, as such, is distinct from the world of the *creative* artist. In his *souvenirs,* Grenier observes that "when Albert Camus spoke about his work he did so with a detachment which contrasted with the attachment he showed to his ideas."[13] I would read this as saying that "his ideas" are primarily to be found in Camus's nonfictional output where, by comparison with his imaginative works, he is more likely to be writing in his own name.[14] Correspondingly, scrutinizing the nonfiction will enable us to explore the development of Camus's attitude toward justice in a context where the need for interpretation is kept to an absolute minimum. I propose only to draw on Camus's fiction and theater, as and when appropriate, in the interests of providing extra illustrative material of an issue under discussion.

A second reason for focussing on the nonfiction lies in the opportunity this affords the present writer to expose a facet of Camus which has been relatively overlooked by the critical activity surrounding, most notably, *The Outsider* (1942), *The Plague* (1947), and *The Fall* (1956). Moreover, the recent publication of *The First Man* (1994), described by one commentator as "a literary event unparalleled in recent memory," has returned Camus's name to the forefront of the contemporary French literary agenda.[15] Against this backdrop, it is particularly apposite to shed light on an aspect of Camus's work that has been hitherto overshadowed by elucidations of the canonical texts.

My interest in this book will primarily be with the sociopolitical domain, with a view to assessing the complexities and emphases of Camus's concern for justice operating within, rather than beyond, the realm of lived experience. This approach is in keeping with the precedent set by Camus himself when, in *Combat* on October 1, 1944, he spotlights the need "not to add to the overwhelming misery of our condition any purely human forms of injustice" (*E,* 1528). It should be noted from the outset that it is in his nonfiction that Camus generally engages with the sociopolitical manifestations of justice, by which I incorporate the socioeconomic, political, institutional, and constitutional modes of the ideal.[16] Some preliminary definitions of these principal terms of reference will be useful. Socioeconomic justice is associated with the alleviation of destitution and the welfare of the least prosperous members of society. It is closely bound up with the interests and aspirations of the weak, the oppressed and the exploited members of a given community, much in keeping with the view of Joseph Joubert who claims that "justice is the right of the weakest."[17] As we will see, Camus's concern for socioeconomic justice is especially evident in his formative experiences of politics and journalism. A fundamental component of the language of legitimacy, political justice can be formulated in terms of the minimal demands for the vindication of political power. A political system may be deemed just when it possesses integrity and when the principles underscoring that integrity are not compromised by considerations of gain, desire, or passion. Camus's interest in the principles determining political justice comes into sharp focus, as we shall discover, in his various responses to totalitarian regimes. It is through the principle of law that institutionalized justice apportions and harmonizes conflicting desires and claims in social interaction. The institution of justice serves to settle disputes arising from the virtues or faults of individual actions—hence the notion of "just deserts"—and its practice implies treating individuals as being responsible for their behavior, praising or punishing them in accordance with their conduct. Camus's engagement with this aspect of justice finds particular expression in his capacity as *chroniqueur judiciaire* at *Alger républicain* and in his personal obsession with the codified practice of capital punishment. Constitutional justice, finally, is usefully defined as a yardstick by which to measure the moral accountability of a given social order. The extent to which governmental organizations are representative of their electorate and whether statutory laws adequately respect the rights and civil liberties of individuals are crucial factors in this manifestation of the concept. Camus's intuitive commitment to liberal democratic values provides a vehicle for refining his understanding of such matters. In fleshing out his responses to these various types of justice, the present study will focus on the idea of Camus as a man *en situation* who, as he himself makes clear in *Actuelles II* (1953), opposes perceived injustice in all its various guises in primarily a personal and practical capacity:

> As artists, we perhaps do not need to intervene in the affairs of the century. But as human beings, we do. The miner who is exploited or shot,

> the slaves of the camps and the colonies, the army of persecuted people throughout the world all need everyone who is able to speak to end their silence and not to distance themselves from them. . . . From my first articles to my last book, I have written so much, and perhaps too much, only because I cannot stop myself from being drawn to the side of those, whoever they are, who are humiliated or degraded. (*E*, 802–3)

The first chapters of the book aim to account for the origins of Camus's engagement with the concept of justice. Chapter 1 assesses the writer's formative years to gauge the extent to which his general preoccupation with the idea arises from a personal sense of injustice, induced by the character of his own particular childhood experience. The chapter then proceeds to examine how far the young Camus's sensitivity to suffering as a social phenomenon, an idea necessarily fundamental to the pursuit of justice, is borne out by his youthful writings. In the absence of an appropriate textual platform on which to voice his emerging moral views, chapter 2 explores how Camus's formative understanding of social and political justice first finds concrete expression in his early experiences of politics and theater. Here, we will see for the first time a key ethical problem that impacts on Camus's consideration of justice: the fragile relationship between politics and morality, and the question of whether the morally desirable end of a revolutionary protest can justify the use of morally ambivalent means.

Chapters 3 and 4 concentrate respectively on Camus's responses to matters of justice relating to the human experience and the political structures of French colonialism, with special reference to Algeria. As he dons the mantle of self-styled revolutionary in his quest for human betterment on behalf of persecuted and oppressed categories within colonial society, we shall meet further significant themes, not least the tension between Camus's vision of social justice and the moral question of charity; the link between institutionalized justice and the issue of punishment; and the nascent awareness of a dialectical association between justice and freedom. However, with regard to the political edifice of colonialism, we will see how Camus's underlying engagement with justice, i.e., his objective not to allow practical objectives to be marred by politico-ideological prejudices, becomes frustrated by a set of historical circumstances in which he is himself implicated.

How the forces of history now begin to impact on, and come into conflict with, Camus's concern for justice becomes further apparent in chapter 5, which deals with the writer's response to the prospect and actuality of the Second World War. The changing historical circumstances in which Camus now finds himself force a rethinking of his earlier view of justice in more collective terms. It is significant the extent to which Camus uses the ideal of justice as he proceeds from a position of "pacifism" to one of "resistance." A key issue that we will explore here is the dilemma between justice and ethics in the political arena.

Chapter 6 examines how continuing moral complexities in the postwar period on the international scale further impinge on Camus's moral sensibility. His fixed view of justice during the war now makes way for an ethic that seeks to strike a balance between the conflicting claims of justice *and* freedom. Highlighting the opposing views of justice as retribution and justice as mercy, the issue of the purge in France will come under investigation, as will Camus's debates on justice and tyranny, and justice and totalitarianism, exposing as they do the whole question of violence in relation to revolutionary justice. This will lead us to an assessment of Camus's alternative to the *politique des blocs* as he attempts to formulate a blueprint for a justice of international tolerance based on, and immersed in, democratic principles in the quest for global security.

The culmination of Camus's postwar moral reasoning and a text in which he would invest considerable time and energy, the pivotal and polemical *The Rebel* (1951) is examined in chapter 7 through the lens of justice. By means of an investigation of the politics of authentic revolt, we will confirm the importance, for Camus, of the idea of equivalent and appropriate relations in the means/end dichotomy. In revolutionary protest, justice and freedom are thus formulated by the writer as relative and interdependent moral values that require proximate ends to be obtained by means consonant with human ability.

The deep psychological impact made upon Camus by the hostile reception of his "Essay on Revolt" draws into question the merits of a project that he maintained to be his most important work. Compounded by the pressures of history which, henceforth, increasingly impact on his concern for justice, Camus's troubled moral psychology in the 1950s is at issue in chapter 8. Here, we will discover how, in his continuing attempt to reconcile the conflicting demands of justice and freedom, Camus eschews the language of political idealism and embraces that of moral transparency, a transparency that comes under severe pressure, however, in the context of the Algerian War. The chapter goes on to demonstrate how, as the pressures of history become increasingly overwhelming for Camus at both a personal and professional level, he embarks on a "scaling-down process" of his whole attitude toward justice, perhaps with a view—and here we must enter the realm of speculation due to the tragedy of Camus's premature death—to reinvigorating his then-frustrated moral sensibility. As we will see, Camus's final utterances on justice mark a return to the personal nature of his preoccupation characteristic of his formative years in Algeria, so that there can be seen to be a cyclical aspect to his overall engagement with the concept.

This book is the first in-depth account in English of the chronological development, as expressed in his nonfiction, of Camus's concern for justice as a moral problematic within the sociopolitical sphere. Although justice is a central theme in Camus's work, most of the existing studies that deal with the concept, such as the projects of Aleida Joanna Gehrels and Maxime Pierre Meto'o, do so in relation to the imaginative writings without considering the significance of the idea in Camus's nonfiction.[18] Other titles addressing moral issues pertaining to the nonfiction, including the work of Tanju Tuzun and Azzedine Haddour, touch on wider areas of justice but do not account for the particular interest Camus accords the concept.[19] This study will, accordingly, adopt a developmental methodological approach to the whole issue of Camus's intellectual preoccupation with justice, and will analyze how an underlying consistency to act on behalf of disfranchised and impoverished categories in the general quest for human betterment, modified by the pressures of changing (historical and personal) circumstances, ultimately emerges as a guiding and unifying thread.

Building on existing scholarship, this book intends to open new lines of inquiry. While in the ever-increasing Camus bibliography (expertly maintained by Robert Roeming and Raymond Gay-Crosier), the writer's fiction and theater continue to attract the lion's share of critical interest, more and more commentators are now being alerted to the pertinence of the nonfictional corpus.[20] The early studies of, notably, Henry Bonnier, Georges Hourdin, and Paul Ginestier were instrumental in drawing attention to the significance of Camus as an intellectual with a social conscience.[21] These works are now, however, somewhat dated: since their publication, a range of primary and biographical texts have appeared—*The First Man* and Olivier Todd's *Albert Camus, une vie* spring immediately to mind here—which contain important and relevant new information, making a reassessment of the issues explored by those early studies a worthwhile and, indeed, now necessary undertaking.[22] Pierre-Henri Simon, Emmett Parker, and, more recently, Bernard East, Susan Tarrow, and Jeanyves Guérin have all spotlighted Camus's nonimaginative writings as a platform on which to engage in moral and political debate.[23] Many of these, and other, pivotal studies touch on the broader question of justice in Camus's thought. For Simon, for instance, the ideal is formulated in terms of "a human order where *we* will *all* be happy," a view shared by East who submits that "justice for Camus is inseparable from happiness."[24] Other commentators point up the humanitarian potential of Camus's vision of social justice. Thus, Raymond Gay-Crosier holds that what Camus seeks is "a form of justice which measures up to human beings," while André Abbou considers that what Camus desires is "a human justice which takes into account both principles and people whilst neglecting neither."[25] This is a quest also fundamental to the thesis advanced by Emmett Parker's seminal account of Camus as *artiste engagé,* recently reformulated by Jeanyves Guérin as *l'artiste en citoyen.* To these eminent titles should be added two further recent publications: Paul Smets's *Albert Camus: ses engagements pour la justice et la justesse,* and Denis Salas's *Albert Camus: la juste révolte,* both of which provide a splendid conspectus of the writer's *raisons de lutter.*[26] A full list of those critical works relating, however modestly, to Camus's consideration of justice is included in the bibliography and will be acknowledged as appropriate in the course of this book. While readily acknowledging the pertinence of such works addressing Camus's "moral" situation, the present study offers a different angle in relation to his understanding of sociopolitical justice. It seeks to assess the density and resonance of Camus's developing views on the concept, as articulated in his nonfiction, against what is a particularly turbulent backdrop of changing historical and personal circumstances. In accordance with Camus's own aim to "[seek] only for reasons to go beyond [nihilism]" (*SEN,* 145; translation amended), what follows, then, is an attempt to analyze and illustrate the complexity, subtlety and intellectual honesty of what Simone de Beauvoir once deemed "that just man without justice."[27]

1

Justice, Injustice, and the Search for Origins

The man that I would be if I had not been the child I was!

—Camus, *Carnets: 1942–1951*

AT THE TIME OF HIS DEATH, ALBERT CAMUS WAS ENGAGED IN AN important process of retrospective self-analysis. *The First Man,* the work that, by Camus's own admission, was to have become "the novel of [his] maturity," was, after much strenuous effort, now finally beginning to take shape.[1] The project looked set to fill in the gaps in a story that, in effect, had already been traced out in Camus's earlier autobiographical writings (in particular, *Betwixt and Between* and *Nuptials,* two collections of youthful essays which originally appeared in Algeria in 1937 and 1939 respectively). Recently published for the first time, the unfinished manuscript of *The First Man* bears eloquent testimony to the fact that, at the very end of his life, Camus was reflecting on his childhood days: looking back at his formative years in Algeria as the source of his next literary creation.

Interestingly, plans to write a work of this sort are already in place as far back as 1946, at which point, in his private notebook, Camus outlines his intention to produce a "Novel on Justice" (*CA2,* 89): a project envisaged as an experiment in self-justification.[2] By the same token, preparations for the important preface to the republished edition of *Betwixt and Between* (which appeared in Paris in 1958; *E,* 5–13; *SEN,* 17–27) may, upon a scrutiny of the *Carnets,* be traced back to the end of 1949.[3] That preface, too, testifies to a desire on the part of the mature Camus to return to his roots and so reassess his Algerian past. The focus on his formative years, then, is a matter that, with increasing intensity, preoccupies Camus for much of his adult life.

Now, given the (quite understandable) absence of firsthand accounts, conceived and written at the time, of his early years in Algeria—Camus was already in his early twenties when he set about writing *Betwixt and Between* and *Nuptials*—this preoccupation with the (i.e. his) past is potentially a very useful source in attempting to establish the beginning of Camus's sensitivity to justice, in that it may reveal how he himself later conceived the origins of his interest in the concept. However, although such a reevaluation of his formative years in this context is of clear interest and importance, we obviously cannot afford to neglect the fact that whenever Camus, in later years, comments on his early life, he does so retrospectively. In other words, he reconstructs, from a vantage point somewhere in the future, experiences that may seem sincere, but that are actually being filtered with the overall effect of producing a subjective portrait of the past. Correspondingly, when scrutinizing later writings in which Camus reconstructs his past, one must not assume that what appears in such texts necessarily gives a precise portrayal of an earlier reality. On the other hand, retrospective writings of this kind deserve to be analyzed, since they at least give Camus's account of what he wants to present as the defining aspects of his formative years. As such, an examination of these texts may provide us with evidence as to how Camus himself conceives the origins of his concern for justice. Thus, with these few preliminary precisions and qualifications in mind, we can now proceed with the task of exploring the extent to which the source of what was to go on to become a passion for justice on his part can be attributed to the particular type of upbringing Camus himself experienced. Given that pursuing justice is intricately linked to perceiving injustice, it will be useful to examine how far the writer's preoccupation with justice arises from a personal sense and fear of injustice, induced by the character of his own childhood experience.[4]

"Half-way between poverty and the sun"

It is well known that Camus spent the first seventeen years of his life growing up in and around Belcourt: a poor, lower-working class, and rather dangerous suburb of Algiers that was home to a diversity of races and nationalities. Located on the rue de Lyon, the family home—Camus's father having been killed during the First World War while his son was still an infant—comprised Albert, his brother Lucien, his mother, grandmother, and uncle, all of whom lived together in a three-roomed flat, where food and clothing were scarce and basic commodities like electricity and running water lacking.[5] In his later preface to *Betwixt and Between,* Camus would publicly acknowledge that they had lived "with very little money"

(*SEN,* 18) and that they "lacked almost everything" (*SEN,* 19).[6] Moreover, the essays themselves in that collection provide an invaluable insight into the nature of Camus's formative years, played out "half-way between poverty and the sun" (*SEN,* 18). In one, "Between Yes and No," written between 1935 and 1936, he recollects his childhood home with poignant emotion: "I think of a child living in a poor district. That district, that house! There were only two floors, and the staircases were unlit" (*SEN,* 39). In another, "Irony," also dating from 1935–36, he contrasts the strange inertia of his mother ("quiet, deep, impenetrable and still like the sea," in Morvan Lebesque's memorable phraseology) with the domineering presence of his maternal grandmother (a figure who, as Camus would later tell Carl Viggiani, raised him "quite brutally").[7] This consolidates the sense of psychological claustrophobia surrounding the family home in general:

> There were five of them living in the same apartment: the grandmother, her younger son, her elder daughter and the daughter's two children. The son was almost dumb; the daughter, an invalid, thought with difficulty, and of the two children one was already working for an insurance company while the other was continuing his studies. At seventy, the grandmother still ruled over all these people. . . . The old woman would wait until there were visitors and would then ask, looking at him [i.e. Albert Camus] severely, "Whom do you like best? Your mother or your grandmother?" She enjoyed it more when her daughter herself was there. For in every case the child would always reply "My grandmother", with a great upsurge of love in his heart for his ever silent mother. (*SEN,* 35)

Granted, then, the emotional turmoil underlying what one critic refers to as "this sad and sordid life," one could justifiably assume that Camus may have felt bitter about his situation in this formative phase of his existence, harboring, perhaps, private feelings of resentment or despair (emotions preluding a sense of injustice) as he learned "the difficult knowledge of how to live" (*SEN,* 72).[8] Yet Camus's own utterances on his childhood do not appear to bear out this supposition. Conversing with Viggiani in 1958, he described his upbringing in Belcourt as "a childhood full of curiosity, silence, energy—and emotion."[9] And, conceding in an earlier interview "his fair share of difficult experiences," Camus nonetheless goes on to view his childhood in a generally favorable light: "The world wasn't hostile to me to begin with. I had a happy childhood" (*E,* 1338).

Camus's (later) reminiscences about his early years are equally upbeat. The highly autobiographical *The First Man,* notably, with its eloquent evocation of "*the riches and joys* of poverty" (*FM,* 210; my italics) at the heart of Cormery-Camus's "poor *and happy* childhood" (*FM,* 104; my italics), further testifies that Camus looks back on his early life in Algeria with affection rather than hostility, almost as though one were the counterpoise of the other.[10] And, in "Return to Tipasa" (1953), he likewise recalls the happiness of his early life in Algeria: "Brought up first of all in the spectacle of beauty, which was my only wealth, I had begun with fullness" (*SEN,* 148).

However, a sequence from Camus's notebook dating from mid-1946 and intended for the aforementioned "Novel on Justice" offers a somewhat different perspective of these childhood years: "Novel. Poor childhood. 'I was ashamed of my poverty and of my family (But they are monsters!). And if today I can talk about it with simplicity it is because I am no longer ashamed of this shame and no longer despise myself for having felt it. I experienced this shame only when I was sent to the *lycée.* Before then, everyone was like me and poverty seemed to me the very air of the world. At the *lycée,* I learned how to compare.'" (*CA2,* 91). Of course, as the word "novel" makes clear, these remarks relate to a projected work of fiction and not, as we might perhaps presume, to an autobiography proper. As such, Camus may well be drawing on imaginary material (as opposed to, or as well as, his own biography) as a basis for the planned narrative. Assuming, however, that Camus is speaking here on his own behalf, what needs to be emphasized is that when obliged to recognize the real social impoverishment underpinning his own family's situation, the young Albert finally becomes aware of the (social) injustice of his personal circumstances and a sense of shame ensues. (In *The First Man,* Cormery-Camus similarly experiences "all at once the shame and the shame of having been ashamed" (*FM,* 159; translation amended) when the *lycéen* Jacques is forced to reflect on the impoverished nature of his social background for what, demonstrably, is the first time in his life. This emotional crescendo comes about as a direct result of the child's sudden awareness of comparisons and contrasts in operation at a social level: issues which occasion Cormery to view his own family's status in an acutely sensitive new light (*PH,* 187–88; *FM,* 159–60). In other words, the humiliation experienced due to the character of his own social background sensitizes the young Albert Camus to the imbalances existing within society at large and which are working against his own family. Correspondingly, Camus's disclosure, in the *Carnets,* that "I should have needed a heart of exceptional and heroic purity not to suffer from those days when I saw on the face of a richer friend the surprise which he could not manage to hide at the sight of the house where I lived" (*CA2,* 91), can, as David Sprintzen suggests, be perceived as an expression of the young Camus's "anguished sensitivity": a clear articulation of his emotional frustration in the face of social impoverishment.[12]

It is perhaps useful to recall at this juncture that, while it was customary for young students to visit one another's domiciles, Camus himself rarely invited friends back to Belcourt, on the grounds, first, of not exposing to his peers the confused emotions privately expressed in the *Carnets;* and, secondly, of not subjecting his family to the probing questions of others. Indeed, according to Lottman, Camus would even go so far as to inform university colleagues that his mother was living in Oran and suffering from a mental disorder as a ruse to prevent any unwarranted visits from his peers.[13]

Further psychological anguish underlies a concomitant extract from the *Carnets,* where Camus again ponders over his childhood emotions: "Yes, I did bear the world a grudge, as is common. And if, up to the age of 25, I always felt fury and shame at the memory of this grudge, it was because I refused to be common. While nowadays I now know that I am common and, finding this neither good nor bad, I think about something else" (*CA2,* 91). Significantly, Camus evokes here the rather stronger sensations of "*fury* and shame": sensations that, *prima facie,* could not unreasonably be construed as expressing a private sense of injustice on the part of the writer or, at least, the prelude to such a sense. Yet, on reflection, these remarks reveal that Camus—assuming, of course, that Camus is the enigmatic narrator here—is (paradoxically) both aspiring *and* refusing to emulate his (socially advantaged) peers; the ambivalent nature of such comments obviously puts their credibility in question. An earlier entry in the *Carnets,* where Camus once more appears to be reminiscing about his formative experience, is no less ambiguous: "The pain of not having everything in common and the misfortune of having everything in common" (*CA1,* 47).

Whatever the true nature of Camus's childhood emotions as expressed in such puzzling remarks, it is clear (as the aforementioned citation from the *Carnets* confirms) that there is no necessary correlation between having felt temporarily ashamed of one's individual circumstances and having a prolonged hostile attitude toward them. While there is some evidence to suggest that the young Albert Camus has an elementary awareness of the social inequalities impacting on his own situation (whence the youthful emotions of "fury and shame"), he does not go on to perceive his family, as poor as it may be, with disdain. On the contrary, writing in the *Carnets* in mid-1950, Camus formulates the value derived from his family in terms of personal prestige: "With them I have felt neither poverty, nor deprivation nor humiliation. Why not say it: I have felt and still feel my nobility. When I am with my mother, I feel that I am of a noble race: one that envies nothing" (*CA2,* 167). Earlier, thinking in a similar vein, he had noted: "how can you make people understand that a poor child can feel ashamed without feeling envious" (*CA2,* 112), a view later reiterated in the preface to *Betwixt and Between* (*E,* 8; *SEN,* 20) and *The First Man* (*PH,* 188; *FM,* 160).[14] It seems permissible to infer that, in the face of grim reality, Camus turns to the natural simplicity of his family circle, uncontaminated as it is by selfishness and materialist aspirations, as a haven from adversity.

The idea that the severity of poverty can be compensated for by focusing one's attention on other, simple and unaffected, pleasures can be discerned through the pages of the retrospective preface to *Betwixt and Between.* There, any sentiment of private bitterness on Camus's part stemming from his formative years is compensated for by what he calls "the radiance and warmth which shone over [his] childhood" (*SEN,* 18), which the young Camus embraced with "a kind of rapture" (*SEN,* 18).[15] A sense of harmony with the natural world around him in this way offsets any sense of disharmony surrounding Camus's own situation: "Poverty, first of all, was never a misfortune for me: it was radiant with sunlight" (*SEN,* 18).[16] As he had earlier elucidated in "Nuptials at Tipasa" (1937), one of the essays from the celebratory *Nuptials,* the feeling at one with the world helps Camus to banish his own harsh reality: "I love life with abandon and wish to speak of it with freedom: it makes me proud of my human condition. Yet people have often told me: there's nothing to be proud of. Yes, there is: this sun, this sea, my heart leaping with youth, the salt taste of my body, and the vast landscape where tenderness and glory merge in blue and yellow" (*SEN,* 72).

The notion of unrestrained happiness in evidence here is also apparent in *A Happy Death* (1971), Camus's posthumously published novel actually composed between 1936 and 1938. Indeed, such is the unconfined nature of Mersault's pursuit of happiness in that narrative that he quite lucidly breaks the law and openly condones injustice—Mersault steals from, and murders, the paraplegic Zagreus—in his quest for success. Surely Germaine Brée is right when she submits that "the deliberate act of violence, at the start of the adventure, is in one of its dimensions a measure of young Camus's revolt against the numbing effect of poverty."[17] Not for the only time here does Camus discharge on to an imaginative schema ("a screen in front of his private life," as Lionel Dubois calls it) some of his own anxieties and apprehensions.[18] As he concedes in the *Carnets* in August 1937, "I sometimes need to write things which I cannot completely control but which therefore prove that what is in me is stronger than I am" (*CA1,* 24).

In another noteworthy text from *Nuptials* ("The Desert," written in late 1937 following a voyage to Italy), Camus empathizes with the inhabitants of the cloister in San Francesco, near Florence. Like himself, these monks live a paradoxical yet distinguished life:

> I had stood for a long time in the little courtyard overflowing with red flowers, sunlight and black and yellow bees. In a corner stood a green watering can. Before going there I had visited the monks' cells, and seen their little tables each adorned with a skull. Now, this garden bore witness to their inspiration. I had turned back towards Florence, down the hill which led towards the town lying open with all its cypress trees. I felt that this splendour of the world, these women and these flowers offered a kind of justification for these men. I was not sure that they were not also the justification for all those people who know that an extreme level of poverty always rejoins the wealth and luxury of the world. Between the life of these Franciscans, enclosed among columns and flowers, and the life of the young people of the Padovani beach in Algiers, who spend the whole year in the sun, I felt that there was a common resonance. (*SEN,* 97; translation amended)

Implicit in this "common resonance" is that social hardship can be compensated for by developing a union with the world and a oneness with nature. Such a notion has all of the characteristics of a retrospective view, in that it seems unlikely that the child Camus thought in terms of compensation. As Camus, then aged twenty-four, observes in "Death in the Soul," another of the essays from *Betwixt and Between* written with the memory of his rather depressing visit to Prague (in 1936) still very much in mind, "in the same way that I took *a long time* to realize my attachment and love for the world of poverty in which I spent my childhood, *it is only now* that I can see the lesson of the sun and of the countries which witnessed my birth" (*SEN,* 54; my italics). Be that as it may, retrospective obervations of this kind can yield useful truth-claims, for the "compensation" view is entirely predicated on the point that Camus *did* experience a rudimentary sense of social injustice regarding his personal circumstances as a child or, at least, as was suggested earlier, a sense of inequalities which he saw to be working against his own family—hence the young Albert's feeling of shame when forced to reflect on his situation and his ignorance as to whether one might be able to justify or explain this state of affairs. Whatever the truth of this, it is clear that, for Camus, taking refuge in the joys of the Mediterranean to counteract the rigors of reality is a gesture of defiance in the face of adversity, rather than an act of denial.

Confirmation of this last claim is provided by the 1953 essay "The Sea close by" (one of the collection of lyrical texts published in 1954 under the title *Summer*), where Camus acknowledges a clear correlation between sensing a communion with the "excess of nature's blessings" (*SEN,* 81) around him in Algiers and maintaining a positive attitude toward his own humble origins: "*I grew up in the sea and poverty was sumptuous, then I lost the sea and found all luxuries grey and poverty intolerable*" (*SEN,* 155).[19] The natural combination of sun and sea overlooking his childhood can, then, be conceived of as Camus's private answer to the general problem of social inequality affecting his formative years. Embracing these elements offsets any feelings of despondency or disillusionment toward reality that he might otherwise have experienced. As he was to point out in the retrospective preface to *Betwixt and Between,* only when forced to leave his beloved Algeria for "the ghastly suburbs of our towns" (*SEN,* 19) would Camus really recognize what he calls "the final and most revolting injustice of all . . . : the double damnation of poverty and ugliness" (*SEN,* 19). Once Algeria's "radiance and warmth" (*SEN,* 18) makes way for France's "cold suburbs" (*SEN,* 19), Camus would come into contact with "real misery" (*SEN,* 19).

A further important feature of Camus's formative years is his experience of tuberculosis. For present purposes, the contraction of that illness is particularly pertinent since it necessarily occasioned a strong emotional reaction on the part of Camus that may shed some more light on the origins of his perception of injustice. Camus himself later explained to Viggiani that he initially fell victim to tuberculosis in December 1930, attributing the disease to what he called "too much sport. Tiredness. Too much exposure to the sun. Spitting of blood."[20] "It is easily imaginable," notes Jacques Delarue, "that a growing adolescent right in the middle of puberty, overworked by the preparation of difficult examinations and, what is more, poor and undernourished as a result, can be an easy prey for the disease."[21] The disease brought to an abrupt end Camus's passion for physical recreation and, in the long term, it would destroy all of his ambitions of embarking on a career in academia.

Writing in his notebook in November 1942, Camus observes that "illness is a convent which has its Rule, its fasts, its silences and its inspirations" (*CA2,* 26). This "pedagogic" configuration of illness has great resonance in the case of Camus's own "metaphysical" medical condition, in that important lessons are deemed to have been learned through personal experience of the affliction.[22] "I am not cured," he thus explains to fellow *tuberculeux* Guy Dumur in correspondence dated January 3, 1944, "because I was not courageous at the start and because I cut corners everywhere I could. Today, I have to make a far greater effort, every day, to keep my distance and to make useful a body which, otherwise, would enslave me entirely" (*E,* 1668–69).

It is curious that, rather than a personal sense of injustice toward his medical condition, which one might perhaps expect given the serious nature of the disease, Camus experiences here a sense of regret, tempered with a lack of will, in not—in its early manifestations at least—having had the courage to take his illness seriously.[23] On the basis of this evidence, then, more than mere indifference (which implies a lack of attention to, without denying the presence of, the ailment), it can be argued that Camus was initially carefree with regard to what, elsewhere, he rather oddly called his "fortunate illness" (*SEN,* 174). As he would later (1950) point out to Jean Grenier, acknowledging the painful reality of his condition was anathema to Camus, over whom illness held no sway: "The only constant worry is that I am not cut out for illness. I'm accustomed to it, but not very well, I think. And I am champing at the bit" (*Corr,* 167).[24]

An examination of other relevant textual evidence may help us to clarify the young Camus's perception of his sudden change in health. In an unpublished "Fragment" of "Between Yes and No" reconstituted by Roger Quilliot in the Pléiade edition of the collected works, Camus—without resentment—highlights his mother's apparent indifference to his disease:

> One thing which he had never been clear about was the peculiar attitude of his mother at the time of a fairly serious illness which affected her son. During the initial symptoms and the very many instances of spitting of blood, she was hardly frightened at all; admittedly she showed signs of concern—but those which any normal sensitive human being

has toward the headache which is afflicting one of her close relatives. . . . Yet she was not ignorant of the serious nature of his disease but she carried around with her in this way her surprising indifference. On reflection, what was even more surprising was the fact that he had never thought of reproaching her for it. A tacit understanding united them. (*E*, 1214)

Assuming that these remarks accurately portray the mother's reaction to her younger son's condition, Camus's lucid acceptance of her impassive response to his illness is, on the one hand, surprising, shocking even, and, on the other hand, completely in accordance with the "tacit understanding [which] united them" and the "attachment [i.e., between the mother and her son] so powerful that no silence could undermine it." (*E,* 1215).[25] "This mutual conviction," to borrow the phraseology of Marcia Weis, "does not stem from a thought process but rather from a common primordial and intuitive source of knowledge" uniting mother and son.[26] Much ink has been poured over the issue of Camus's ambivalent relationship with his mother and we do not need to dwell on the matter unnecessarily here; suffice it to say, Camus's bond with his mother was fraught with emotional intensity.[27] What should be stressed here is the point that the perspicuous recognition of his mother's apparent indifference to his first attack of tuberculosis consolidates the view that Camus himself was initially undaunted by the disease.

It will come as no surprise that Camus was only rarely to speak publicly about his contraction of tuberculosis. Rightly or wrongly, Patrick McCarthy suggests that this reluctance to broach the subject can be explained by the fact that the young Albert was "too proud to reveal what he considered a weakness. To be poor was already bad, to be ill was unforgivable."[28] For his part, Jacques Lemarchand (who later worked alongside Camus at *Combat*) attests to his colleague's embarrassment regarding the affliction: "Of his illness, I only heard him say one thing. . . . Once, at the end of an hour's work, he raised his head and said 'it's humiliating'. And he left."[29] Viewed in this perspective, the following remarks on his condition, published in the retrospective preface to *Betwixt and Between* in 1958, are doubly significant, since they not only lend a public voice to his private thoughts on his tuberculosis, but also articulate an obstinacy on Camus's part to defy the disease:

when a serious illness temporarily deprived me of that natural vigour which for me transfigured everything, in spite of the invisible infirmities and new weaknesses which this illness brought me, *I knew fear and discouragement but never bitterness.* This illness certainly did add new fetters, and these were the hardest to bear, to those which were already mine. But in the last resort, it encouraged that freedom of the heart, that slight detachment from human concerns, which has always saved me from resentment. (*SEN,* 20–21; my italics)

While the considerable psychological impact on Camus of his affliction must not be ignored, it is clear from the preceding citation that Camus harbours no sense of personal injustice toward the state of his health.[30] Indeed, in spite of the severity of his condition, Camus retains a positive attitude, tellingly recorded in a communication with Jean Grenier from August 1934: "It's true that my physical state leaves much to be desired. But I want to get better" (*Corr,* 19). Significantly, some twenty years later, Camus's refusal to allow his medical condition to dictate the terms of his existence would remain equally resolute: "Recuperate at all costs. I need my strength. I do not want life to be easy for me but I want to be able to square up to it if it is difficult" (*C3,* 146). And, judging from a note for *The First Man* (*PH,* 315; *FM,* 252), such stoicism was, had he lived, also to have been incorporated into Camus's *magnum opus.*

Further support for the claim that Camus confronted his condition with stubborn optimism (as opposed to perceiving it in terms of a personal injustice) is provided by writings contemporaneous with the young man's convalescence from his first attack of tuberculosis. "Mediterranean," for instance, a poem written in October 1933, is a paean to the Mediterranean *joie de vivre* against the backdrop of a looming death: "Oh, antiquity impelling us! / Mediterranean, oh! Mediterranean Sea! / Naked, alone, without secrets, your sons await death. / Death will return them to you, pure at last, pure" (*YW,* 199). Equally, "The Hospital of the Poor Neighbourhood" (written in late 1934) in which Camus empathizes with the "fleshless bodies, reduced to bony lines" (*YW,* 213) of the Hôpital Mustapha in Algiers where his own condition is treated, voices his determination to defy the disease and to "colour [his] futur[e] with hope" (*YW,* 213). It is not a little surprising that Camus makes no clear connection in the latter text between the state of his health and his own social background. Indeed, in what is a rather odd turn of phrase, tuberculosis is described at one point in "The Hospital of the Poor Neighbourhood" as "a sickness for the rich" (*YW,* 213), rather than as a symptom of the poor sanitary conditions governing life in Camus's own "poor neighbourhood." Inasmuch as tuberculosis is attributed here to a social category beyond his own immediate experience, Camus's contraction of the disease does not seem to have occasioned a personal sense of injustice on the part of the young Albert himself. Rather, the illness is accepted with forbearance and is countered with what, in his preface to *Betwixt and Between,* Camus calls "[an] uncontrolled appetite for life" (*SEN,* 24), that is, an almost hedonistic embrace of reality which "raises in us the only truly virile love that this world holds: one that is generous and will die" (*SEN,* 90).

From our examination of the main (retrospective) writings on Camus's formative years in Algeria, two general conclusions may now be drawn. First, in relation to his initial attack of tuberculosis, there is no substantive (textual) evidence to suggest that Camus perceived that affliction in terms of a personal sense of injustice. Indeed, any profound feelings of anguish occasioned by the disease are significantly displaced in the relevant writings by a combination of stubborn hope and stoical optimism, sentiments predicated on what, in the 1936 essay "Love of Life," he was to call "a silent passion for what would perhaps escape me, a bitterness beneath a flame" (*SEN,* 60). Significantly, in the aforementioned "Manuscript Fragment for 'Bewteen Yes and No,'" any suffering experienced regarding the possibility of his own death is offset by a more profound sense of anguish in relation to the demise *of others* (*E,* 1215). As he notes in "The Wind at Djémila" (1937–38), "I say to myself: I am going to die, but this means nothing since I cannot manage to believe it and *can experience only other people's death*" (*SEN,* 78; my italics).[31]

On the other hand, there is some evidence to suggest that the young Camus does have a rudimentary sense of injustice about the social status of his own family or, at the very least, an awareness of inequalities existing within society and which work against his own family, resulting in the sense of shame he experiences and which he articulates in his private notebook. Indeed, the very first entry in the *Carnets* reveals that Camus's moral consciousness is raised by the nature of his own formative experience: "A certain number of years lived without money are enough to create a whole sensibility" (*CA1,* 1). However, I cannot agree with Jean Gassin when he highlights what he judges to be "the profound bitterness that Camus didn't stop nourishing about the poverty-stricken world where he was born."[32] Any sense of injustice which Camus did experience at the time in respect of his early years is compensated for in later writings and utterances on his childhood by focussing on the simple and natural pleasures which form an integral part of the natural world: what, in "The Desert," he calls "this loving understanding between the earth and the individual delivered from humanity"

(*SEN,* 97; translation amended). Correspondingly, Camus reconstructs in those retrospective writings dealing with his formative years a childhood experience where natural wonders offset the devastating consequences of social injustice. While private indignation induced by the nature of his own upbringing may, then, account to some extent for Camus's subsequent interest in justice as a moral problematic, the level of his sensitivity to the predicament of others still remains to be seen.

Sensitivity to Suffering as a Social Phenomenon in the *Youthful Writings*

From the outset of his intellectual development, Camus was eager to articulate in writing his perceptions of the world around him. Indeed, the very first entry in the *Carnets* (dating from May 1935) testifies to a desire to understand his own situation in the world by expressing it in words: "A work of art is a confession, and I must bear witness. When I see things clearly, I have only one thing to say. It is in this life of poverty, among these vain or humble people, that I have most certainly touched what I feel is the true meaning of life" (*CA1,* 1).[33]

While it is clear from these remarks that the young Camus perceives literature (in the broadest sense of the word) as a means by which to interpret his *own* reality, it remains to be seen whether the same principle may be applied to the circumstances *of other people.* To what extent is the Camus of this formative phase aware of, and sensitive to, the plight of *others*?[34] In his retrospective preface to *Betwixt and Between,* Camus draws attention to his "natural indifference" (*SEN,* 18) which, as Ray Davison has recently pointed out, "did not in any way predispose him to social engagement on behalf of others."[35] Yet how can that admission be squared with the self-imposed humanitarian mandate of Camus who, in correspondence with Jean Grenier dated August 21, 1935, expressed "such a strong desire to see reduced all the misfortune and bitterness which poisons humankind" (*Corr,* 23)?

A useful starting point for an investigation into this matter is an essay written in 1932 entitled "Jehan Rictus: The Poet of Poverty."[36] At first sight, this text—a critique of Rictus's *The Soliloquy of the Poor Man*—bears witness to the young Camus's perceptiveness in relation to the suffering of others, in that it deals with "the stumbling walk towards who knows where, with dragging feet, empty head, body stiff with cold and hunger" (*YW,* 124–25; translation amended) of an unnamed vagabond who is described as "helpless, hesitant [and] unhappy" (*YW,* 123).[37] Camus himself describes his commentary as "the sincere review of a sincere book" (*YW,* 125), a remark testifying to his underlying appreciation of Rictus's original poem. On closer inspection, however, it becomes apparent that Camus is not empathizing in his work with the vagabond as such; rather, he conjures up in his commentary a world of fantasy as a way of responding to, in the terminology of the text, the "humiliation," the "suffering" and the "pitiful condition" of the Poor Man (*PC,* 139; *YW,* 118). Substituting reverie for reality, illusion is thus considered a means by which to numb the pain of gruelling daily grind:

"this miserable creature, who finds only humiliation and suffering in his earthly life, seeks an outlet for his pitiful condition in dreams. More than any other, this man is happy only when he forgets he is a man. . . . He lives his dream. He forgets his fate, his condition, his hunger" (*YW,* 118, 120; translation amended).

It is interesting to note that the *volonté d'évasion* in evidence here—the propensity for romanticized escapism in the face of adversity—is also apparent in other of Camus's *Youthful Writings.* For instance, in "Intuitions," a series of writings from 1932 detailing some of his own anxieties, Camus is interested in creating "reveries . . . born of great lassitude" (*YW,* 156). And, in the "new worlds" (*YW,* 227) comprising "Melusina's Book," a fairy story from 1934 dedicated to his first wife Simone, Camus entirely embraces the imagination in an effort to offset reality: "It is time to speak of the fairies. In order to escape from the intrepid melancholy of expectation, it is time to create new worlds. Do not believe, though, that fairy tales lie. He who tells them lies—but as soon as it is told, the fairy miracle slowly floats up into the air and goes off to live its life, real, truer than the insolence of everyday. There is nothing left for the storyteller but the bitterness of having given and of having kept nothing. The bitterness or the fervent joy" (*YW,* 227).

Paul Viallaneix has usefully situated the idea of lyrical evasion in evidence in some of the writer's *Youthful Writings* in the context of Camus's formative views on art, a brief account of which is worthy of mention here, since it will provide an indication of his early response to suffering in society at large.[38] In "Essay on Music," a work from 1932 drawing on the aesthetic qualities of Schopenhauer and Nietzsche, Camus perceives art as "simply . . . an expression of the ideal" and "the creation of a Dream World attractive enough to conceal from us the world in which we live with all its horrors" (*YW,* 131). Similarly, in "Tragedy and Comedy," an early essay brought to light by Viallaneix, he considers art as stemming from the "need to flee from a too painful life" and a means by which to "bring forgetfulness" (*YW,* 21).[39] Camus shares the lyricism of his Greek ancestors in their response to reality: "Consequently, like the Greeks, who feel more than any other people the pain of their life and give themselves to dreams, abolishing all sense of the present, we ought, in order to forget the cruelty of this world—a cruelty we feel acutely because of our civilized sensibilities—to plunge ourselves into dream" (*YW,* 151–52).

These remarks from "Essay on Music" raise two interesting issues. First, the evasive response to what the writer perceives here as "the cruelty of this world"—a pivotal term to which I shall return presently—suggests that Camus's initial reaction to suffering as a social phenomenon is *not* to engage in the problem from a moral standpoint but, rather, to seek solace in lyrical rhetoric. This point is further borne out by Camus's excessive humility in responding to the social injustice portrayed in "Jehan Rictus": "I know that poverty sometimes spoils other people's happiness. But discomfort sometimes provokes acts of humanity, and hence may be desirable, pending something better" (*YW,* 117). Curiously apologetic in tone, Camus appeals to the realm of abstract imagery in his commentary on the destitution depicted in the original poem: "The homeless, the hungry, the vagabond, they, too, have hearts and souls—souls the more beautiful because they are swollen with longing" (*YW,* 118).

A second issue arising from the above citation from "Essay on Music" is, as I have intimated, what Camus actually means by "the cruelty of this world." Indeed, to understand this pivotal phrase is to grasp the nature of Camus's own sensitivity to suffering and so further elucidate the underlying principles of his moral sensibility from which his preoccupation with justice will be drawn. However, the expression "the cruelty of this world" in Camus's essay is saddled with ambivalence and my contention is that this lack of clarity is inextricably linked with his dual interest in the youthful (and, it may be said, other later) writings in both social *and* metaphysical concerns.[40] I want to argue that, at this early stage of Camus's intellectual development, the link between the social and the metaphysical domains is somewhat opaque, in the sense that he sometimes (con)fuses in his writings from this formative period the *ephemeral* nature of contingent adversity on the social scale with the *eternal* nature of *a priori* "unjust" features of human experience on the metaphysical scale. "Jehan Rictus" is a case in point here. Camus's commentary leaves us with a number of philosophical inconsistencies, inasmuch as the necessary distinction between social and metaphysical issues is, at best, ignored and, at worst, obscured by the writer:

> He has spoken the language of the Poor, . . . that which the Poor use to speak to each other about eternal human suffering, a language aristocratically coarse in which pain gives rise to astonishing discoveries. (*YW,* 117; translation amended)

> Sad, sordid, ragged and haughty, the Poor Man goes his way, scorning the impotent God. (*YW,* 123; translation amended)

> This great sad dream of naïve love is accompanied by another within him. His poverty, his anguish lead him to hope for better times. (*YW,* 121; translation amended)

In each of these extracts from "Jehan Rictus," there is an unexplained intersection in Camus's thinking between the social and metaphysical spheres of thought. Furthermore, in his account of Rictus's *Prayer,* a core component of the poem, Camus makes no attempt to disentangle from the original text the two strands of social suffering, on the one hand, and metaphysical suffering, on the other, the overall result of which is to leave the reader with an intellectual puzzle: "The song entitled *Prayer* is but one long appeal to the supreme hope. The Poor Man tells God the story of his lamentable life, a painful confession: it is springtime. The Poor Man, suffering from hunger and thirst, weeps also for love. And he asks God why his lot on this earth is the worst. It is the eternal lament of human beings" (*YW,* 123; translation amended).

There are two vexed issues here which require comment. First, it remains rather unclear whether, in posing the question "why his lot on this earth is the worst," the Poor Man is complaining about his own *social* status or whether, in contrast, his outburst is pitched against a *metaphysical* context. Clearly, if the former were the case, then the enigmatic phrase "it is the eternal lament of human beings" in Camus's text would be entirely inappropriate; if the latter were true, then the "lamentable life" described by Camus would embrace humankind in general even though, in the critique, he depicts the vagabond regretting "*his* lamentable life." Secondly, while we should recognize that complaining to God about the social injustice underpinning one's position does not in itself manifest a sense of metaphysical injustice, it does show that one has metaphysical beliefs (i.e. beliefs in God). Camus, of course, does not have such beliefs, which makes the fact that he should accept Rictus's account of the vagrant's *Prayer* as the eternal or universal one all the more intriguing. Presumably, neither Camus nor the underprivileged of his acquaintance necessarily prayed or complained about their predicament *to God.*[41]

Equally worthy of notice is the rather ambiguous character of the text when Camus actually introduces the concept of injustice into his commentary for the first time: "This miserable creature, who finds only humiliation and suffering in his earthly life, seeks an outlet for his pitiful condition in dreams. More than any other, this man is happy only when he forgets he is a man. But, alas! harsh reality too often sends his dreams scattering, and then he is faced with the injustice of his lot, with feelings of violent revolt, alas, all too justified" (*YW,* 118; translation amended).

It is interesting to note that Camus acknowledges here what he calls "the injustice of his lot" only after the avenue of escape, so to speak, has been sealed off; no reference is made to injustice until "harsh reality . . . sends his dreams scattering," that is, until reality dissipates the illusion created in the vagrant's mind. Moreover, it is still unclear whether Camus is using the key expression "the injustice of his lot" in connection with the vagabond's specific sense of inequity or, alternatively, in respect of the wider metaphysical condition.[42]

What appears to emerge from the above analysis is that in so far as Camus discharges his own perception of reality in the *Youthful Writings,* he adopts a *volonté d'évasion* and seeks solace from social adversity in lyrical rhetoric. In addition, there seems to be, at this formative stage of his intellectual development, some ambiguity as to what Camus actually means by ideas such as "suffering," "the cruelty of this world" and "a too painful life." It would be mistaken, however, to view these youthful writings solely in evasive terms since, as we shall now discover, Camus also uses some of these early essays to give added density and resonance to his own sensitivity to social difference, as discussed earlier.

The issue of social inequity is noticeable in "Jehan Rictus": "The Poor Man walks along, turning over his misery in his mind and ruminating on his distress. Growling within him are obscure desires and sombre feelings of revolt. What he is thinking about, the secret of the heart that beats beneath the sordid tatters, no one knows. *And yet what regrets, what aspirations are roused within him by the sight of other people's happiness!*" (*YW,* 116; translation amended; my italics).

Significantly, Camus notes here that the identity of the vagabond is inextricably bound up with the image the latter creates in his own mind of his more privileged peers. The "misery" and "distress" of the Poor Man contrast tellingly with the idea of "other people's happiness," toward which the wanderer directs "obscure desires" and "sombre feelings of revolt." In essence, then, Rictus's Poor Man only has an understanding of his *own* impoverishment (that is, the social injustice of which he is victim) once he becomes aware of a socially different *other.* The vagrant, who "*suffers* at the happiness of others" (*YW,* 121; my italics), sees his own shortcomings reflected in the prosperity of others. As Paul Henderickx rightly notes, this yields a polarity which has great resonance in relation to the concept of justice:

> Both as an aspiration and as an institution, justice cannot be understood without the idea of community, of society. . . . Indeed, talking of others amounts to talking of the relationship of a thinking individual with others, the latter only being able to exist mentally with regard to a conscious self. Justice therefore involves a link, a desire for equality between a thinking self and others, which . . . leads us to ask ourselves what sort of individual characteristics should be used to establish most productively this sense of a relationship, and also of a limit, between the rights of the individual and those of others.[43]

By portraying the effects of social inequality on the individual psyche in accordance with the view expressed here by Henderickx, Camus takes a significant step forward in "Jehan Rictus" in his perception of injustice as unwarranted social difference. In that essay, the suffering of the self is seen reflected in the prosperity of the other to yield an association of inappropriate relations. This is a state of affairs that, as we shall see in later chapters of this book, would be fundamental to Camus's concern for social and political justice. Indeed, it is worth anticipating a little here to note that the notion of *equivalent* and *appropriate* relationships will be instrumental to Camus's understanding of justice in the sociopolitical arena. In the wartime *Letters to a German Friend* (1945), for instance, he would pursue "*a just equilibrium* between sacrifice and a longing for happiness, between the spirit and the sword" (*RRD,* 19; translation amended) as a response to the moral nihilism of Nazism.[44] By the same token, in the polemical *The Rebel,* "la pensée de midi" (an attempt to formulate a philosophy of limits in the tradition of Greek Hellenism and embodied in the ancient goddess Nemesis) offers an antidote to revolutionary absolutism predicated on the Greek notion of *la mesure.*[45] In "The Moorish House," an essay dating from 1933, Camus reflects on his own propensity for romanticized escapism in the face of adversity and, in so doing, he sets in train a process of thought crucial to the issue of what constitutes appropriate relations between human beings: "By meditating . . . on suffering, ugliness and poverty, one can preserve within oneself a horror of all baseness and the pity one was afraid to show. . . . This is how, in the presence of my Algerian sky, I used to perceive the vanity of my anxieties and used to dream of unknown sufferings. From having wanted too much to escape from Reality, I learned that there is another, unrecognized evasion: forgetting the Dream in rapture over nature" (*YW,* 191; translation amended).

Inasmuch as he refers explicitly here to "unknown sufferings" (which I take to mean the suffering of others, as opposed to that experienced by the writer himself), these remarks amount to a realization on Camus's part concerning the issue of suffering as a social phenomenon. Significantly, in "The Moorish House," Camus identifies for the first time a specific group of others—the indigenous population of Algeria (*PC,* 216; *YW,* 190)—whose particular aspirations to justice would, as we shall see, preoccupy Camus throughout his lifetime. Furthermore, it is no coincidence that in a contemporaneous text entitled "Contradictions," the writer—with his own *volonté d'évasion* doubtless in mind—acknowledges clearly the issue of moral responsibility in the face of suffering and distress: "make no mistake: pain exists. *Impossible to evade*" (*YW,* 210; translation amended; my italics). As he had earlier recognized in "Jehan Rictus," avoiding the issue by seeking refuge in lyrical rhetoric offers only a temporary respite in the response to suffering, since sooner or later "harsh reality sends these dreams scattering" (*YW,* 118; translation amended). It is surely significant that in "The Moorish House," Camus points up the concept of revolt as he begins to awaken to the reality of suffering in the world around him: "on the threshold of this house, beneath the dome I had come back to, I saw the night drowning a delicate world and I forced myself to believe that youth was revolting within me, avid for the prostration it had wished to avoid and for the light of which it had been deprived" (*YW,* 189; translation amended).

While not in itself tantamount to the perception of injustice, Camus's sensitivity to "unknown sufferings" which is now beginning to emerge from the *Youthful Writings* is a significant reference point in the development of his morality. Or, put differently, Camus is now starting to make important observations about the society in which he lives as a basis for articulating a general sense of injustice which is inextricably bound up with fostering a concern for justice.

To conclude, while evidence is emerging to confirm the claim that Camus is now becoming increasingly sensitive to the suffering of *other* people—a necessary prelude to the perception of injustice—any personal insecurities harboured by the young man about the world, about *his* world, are compensated for in the relevant later writings by a hedonistic embrace of reality that rather diminishes the significance, in Camus's eyes, of the social injustice within his own family situation. Indeed, writing in the *Carnets* in 1946, he perceives the (social) injustice apparent in his own childhood as "natural" (*CA2,* 89), a curious turn of phrase which I take to mean "natural" in the sense of not worthy of being noted. As we have seen, Camus dissolves any personal sense of suffering induced by the nature of his formative years into the natural situation of Mediterranean Africa where "the sun and the sea cost nothing" (*SEN,* 18).

In view of the above, then, it seems reasonable to suggest that the nature of Camus's underlying engagement with justice, on the basis of which he develops his moral position, derives more from a sensitivity to suffering as a *social* phenomenon than from *personal* misgivings about his own circumstances. How such a sensitivity evolves into a lifelong preoccupation with justice will be illustrated and analyzed in the remaining chapters of this book.

2
Realization

I have such a strong desire to see reduced all the misfortune and bitterness which poisons humankind.

—*Correspondance Albert Camus / Jean Grenier*

FOLLOWING ITS COLONIZATION BY THE FRENCH IN 1830, ALGERIA had witnessed considerable economic development, coupled with administrative and financial autonomy. However, the resultant increase in European immigration into the province, leading to growing affluence for the settler community, would mean that the region's indigenous population was, within a short space of time, reduced from relative prosperity to economic, social, and cultural inferiority.[1] Indeed, although Algerian Moslems were classed as French, they were deemed "subjects" rather than "citizens" of the mother country and, as such, they were prevented from achieving parity with their European counterparts.[2] In addition, the division of Algerian territory created a two-tier system of municipal administration, with the Europeans very much in control.[3] In sum, the local Moslem population's rights to cultural distinctiveness and self-determination were slowly and systematically being undermined by the colonial authorities, masquerading as civilizing missionaries in Algeria. In the words of the once ardent assimilationist Ferhat Abbas who was to become increasingly sympathetic to the idea of Algerian autonomy, the colonial enterprise "denied that the Algerian people existed, . . . denied that its generals had conceived the plan to destroy us, . . . to seize hold of our land with the firm intention of creating a 'French province' where Arabs would have ceased being legally in their own country."[4]

Equally worthy of notice in connection with the contemporary debate about justice is the rising tide of fascism which, by the mid-1930s, was sweeping across much of mainland Europe. The reverberations of power politics were now starting to be felt in France, as well as permeating Algeria where, as Emmett Parker reminds us, "the clash between supporters of the Popular Front and the right-wing conservatives was especially violent."[5] A noteworthy manifestation of the menace posed by right-wing extremism locally was Augustin Rozis, an overt admirer of European fascism who, following a bitterly contested campaign, was elected to municipal office in Algiers in May 1935. Together with the general threat to civil liberties which fascism itself represented, Mayor Rozis's authoritarian rule brought despotism to the doorsteps of Algiers.

A Concern in Embryo

According to Herbert Lottman, the teenage Camus was already very acutely sensitive to the flagrant inequalities between, on the one hand, the Arabs, Kabyles, and Berbers constituting the local Moslem population of Algeria and, on the other hand, their European counterparts. Although drawing on only anecdotal evidence, the biographer observes how "[s]ometime during his lycée years," Camus joined a team of collaborators working on a local weekly called *Ikdam,* a publication founded in 1919 by Emir Khaled with a view to raising Moslem consciousness.[6] As Lottman elucidates, that journal championed what in its day was a revolutionary vision: "The paper's line was quite radical for that time, demanding equality of Moslem and French-European settlers, an end to special and discriminatory legislation for the indigenous majority, freedom of speech, of travel, the right to organize."[7] While very little is known about the nature of his interest in the initiative—none of the writer's other biographers even raise the matter for discussion—this youthful encounter, which Lottman goes on to spotlight as "Camus' first experience of Algerian Moslems and of their aspirations," is interesting in so far as it testifies to an early awareness on Camus's part of the discriminatory practices in evidence in Algeria's Moslem communities.[8] Later writings attest to his sensitivity to the racial distinctions in place in the province. For instance, in retrospective (1951) correspondence with Jean Grenier dealing with the issue of his childhood, Camus offers an interesting afterthought on the status of Algeria's Arabs *vis-à-vis* their (French) European counterparts: "I did not have an unhappy childhood, the real poverty where I lived was never really painful for me. . . . If it is true that I have since learned, at the *lycée* for example, that fortunes could be unequal, . . . social classes in Algeria are not as clear-cut as here [metropolitan France] (*the matter would have been different if I had been Arab*)" (*Corr,* 180; my italics). The issue of racial discrimination is also raised in *The First Man* when, notably, Camus records the absence of educational opportunities for most Arab children: "In this country of immigration, of quick fortunes and spectacular collapses, the boundaries between classes were less clear-cut than between races. If the children had been Arab, their feeling would have been more painful and bitter. Besides, although they had Arab classmates at school, there were few Arabs in the *lycée,* and they were always sons of wealthy notables" (*FM,* 158; translation amended).[9]

What these two extracts show is a later awareness on Camus's part of distinctions between individuals in Algeria drawn in line with racial differences: a clear discriminatory practice engendering socioeconomic persecution and political (i.e. colonial) exploitation. It should be stressed, however, that both of the preceding citations are retrospective in nature and, as such, they do not necessarily reflect the young Camus's sensitivity to the injustice of his indigenous counterparts. Indeed, as one of Camus's contemporaries, Jules Roy, observes, young French Algerians at the time were conditioned *not* to consider their Arab peers as their equals, so that any distinctions made between the two races were deemed wholly justified: "What I knew because it was repeated to me was that they [local Moslems] were of another race to me, a race inferior to mine. We had come to clear their land and bring them civilization."[10]

However, elsewhere, Roy vigorously acknowledges the instrumental role played by his friend in raising the profile of the *indigènes* and thus recalls how Camus "opened our eyes to everything. . . . He was the first to open our eyes, to show us that they were like any other people."[11] A reminiscing Jean Grenier likewise recollects that Camus was "one of the first to feel the injustice committed toward the Arabs," while Jean Guéhenno recalls the young Albert's moral mandate regarding the Algerian problem in general: "The first time that I saw him was in 1936 in Algiers . . . and already we spoke about the misery of his country, Algeria, and of the justice and freedom which were necessary."[12] Another contemporary, Louis Miquel, similarly attests to the young Camus's sensitivity to Arab poverty.[13] It is useful to set these various testimonies against the context of remarks reportedly made by Camus himself in conversation with Blanche Balain in December 1937 and quoted by Lottman: "In the Kasbah they sat at the Café Fromentin watching the passing scene while sipping mint tea. 'Look,' he [Camus] said of the Moslem crowd, 'how they are, how they go, so noble, indifferent.' He added: 'They are more civilized than we are.'"[14] A cultural intersection between Camus and the local Moslems? Perhaps.

While the preceding attestations record a clear awareness on the part of the young Camus of the plight of Algeria's *indigènes*—an observation confirming his sensitivity to the "unknown sufferings" highlighted in the previous chapter—these remarks do not in themselves tell us anything about the criteria on which he bases his response to their predicament. It is as though Camus feels instinctively drawn toward these victims of colonial oppression, without knowing, at this stage, what their oppression consists of exactly: his concern for the welfare of the *indigènes* springs perhaps more from personal than theoretical motives.[15] (This hypothesis will be verified later when Camus's *engagement* is in question.) This last point should not surprise us in the least, since a cogently argued response to the circumstances of the local population was far from uppermost on the Mediterranean agenda set by Camus and his like-minded friends: any sense of injustice regarding Algeria's indigenous population remains, for the moment at least, at an essentially humanitarian level. As Jules Roy reminisces, "at the time, we didn't care less about justice, and no one more so than me! No one had yet taught it to us. For all of us, our real homeland was the sun."[16]

Just as Camus's initial response to the victims of colonial oppression appears to be based on a deeply personal moral psychology, so his first overt political activity is grounded in essentially humanitarian sentiment. Instinctively left-wing in nature due to the proletarian values underpinning his origins, Camus was quick to condemn the flagrant disregard for both civil rights and principles of liberalism on which fascism thrives.[17] Indeed, as early as 1933, the young man's antifascist inclinations and "left-wing sensitivity" find concrete expression in his involvement in the Algerian wing of the Amsterdam-Pleyel movement, an organization established by the left-wing activists Henri Barbusse and Romain Rolland with a mandate for restoring peace to a fascist-threatened and warmongering world.[18] There has been a suggestion that Camus may have been more than a mere card-carrying member of that movement: in July 1935, Malraux—a writer much revered by Camus—was invited to give a lecture in Algiers by the *Comité de Vigilance des Intellectuels* and the *Comité de Coordination des Jeunes Antifascistes* (sister organizations of the Amsterdam-Pleyel association, established in Paris the year before).[19] Jacqueline Lévi-Valensi long ago indicated that Camus himself may have been responsible for reviewing Malraux's speech for *La Lutte sociale,* an Algiers-based newspaper of communist persuasion.[20] In the reviewer's report, attention is drawn to "fascism, killer of people and ideas" and the "grievously triumphant fascist authority in certain neighboring countries."[21] A telling indictment which, even if not penned by Camus himself (as now seems more likely the case), these remarks are indicative of his own intuitive condemnation of fascist intimidation that had originally induced him to support the Amsterdam-Pleyel initiative.[22] Indeed, one biographer reports that, on April 2, 1936, Camus was involved in a meeting highlighting the evils of the totalitarian mentality, reportedly remarking that "imperialism and fascism are the ultimate stages of capitalism."[23] Moreover, he is reported to have demanded "a little more justice, freedom for all, guaranteed work for everyone in better conditions, without fear of the future and above all world peace" as a testimony to Camus's emerging liberal humanist morality.[24] In the light of this evidence, one cannot agree with the charge made by Anne Durand that Camus remained "impassive and silent before the impending outburst of war-like Hitlerian fascism."[25] It should be remembered that Camus was still in Algeria at the time of Hitler's rise to power (in January 1933) and that, apart from the local wing of the Amsterdam-Pleyel organization, he actually had few public opportunities at the time to channel his instinctive outrage at fascist doctrine. Furthermore, although the influence of Hitler's national socialism was widely felt all over mainland Europe, Algeria's geographical situation meant that the immediate threat posed by the German Chancellor was not so great in the province as it was in other parts of the European continent.

From the above discussion, it can be deduced that Camus is not slow in situating his sensitivity to "unknown sufferings" within a sociopolitical context. Indeed, by the mid-1930s, Camus displays a rudimentary concern for the victims of, in broad terms, both social and political oppression: the former in relation to the ethnological divide in his own beloved Algeria (a discriminatory practice deriving from colonial injustice but which Camus does not yet appear to see as such); the latter regarding the wholesale denial of democratic ideals threatened by fascist coercion. It should be stressed, however, that such issues do not yet directly figure in Camus's (nonfictional) writings: those texts that are available from this period, such as the 1936 *Diplôme d'études supérieures* (admittedly, an academic essay, investigating the relationship between Greek and Christian thought in the philosophical writings of Plotinus and St. Augustine), the posthumously published *A Happy Death* and the essays comprising *Betwixt and Between* and *Nuptials* are all remarkably removed from political and/or social preoccupations and so will be disregarded here. In terms of monitoring Camus's concern for justice within the precise frame of the social and political domains, this general absence of relevant nonfictional writings from the time means that our analysis in the remainder of this chapter will need to take into account a wider range of material, incorporating Camus's formative experience of politics and theater, together with an assessment of other important biographical data.

L'Engagement

It has been widely acknowledged that Camus has little empathy with, or faith in, political ideology.[26] At one point, he would confide to the *Carnets* that he had become involved in politics "in spite of [him]self" (*CA2,* 140). Later, he proclaimed that "[his] pen has never been in the service of either a party or a state."[27] As he observed, "I am unsuited to politics since I am unable to wish for or accept my opponent's death" (*CA2,* 78). Camus is, then, a reluctant political animal and who, in the words of Jonathan King, "comes to politics very much on his own terms, whose political commitment is of the kind which seeks to transcend politics in the direction of moral and spiritual identity."[28] Put differently, Camus is interested in pursuing what, in the later *Letters to a German Friend,* he formulates as "the politics of honour" (*RRD,* 11): a political stance predicated on a sincere concern for the dignity and aspirations of human beings in society. These laudable sentiments lie at the heart of Camus's vision of justice in the political sphere and, in this respect, his political allegiance can be said to stem from a liberal humanist morality.

It is important to recognize that Camus is initially reluctant to sacrifice his own moral values on the altar of political responsibility. In private correspondence with Claude de Fréminville from April 1934, he writes: "To *join* would mean to force myself to hide my other beliefs. . . . I can't help it if everything pushes me toward silence and my own life, and away from whatever is social. If it's a question of action, then I act every day."[29] In the light of these remarks, Camus's subsequent decision to join the *Parti Communiste Français* (PCF) in the summer of 1935 testifies to a period of reflection on Camus's part regarding the motives for political action.[30] Indeed, Lottman holds that he "entered the political arena with sober determination, *after considerable deliberation,*" while Camus himself considers his allegiance as "an important turning point" in his political sensitivity.[31] To judge from observations made in his notebook dating from March 1936, Camus was, at the time of his adherence, already questioning whether the morally desirable end of a campaign of political commitment—the communists' desire to create an environment of social justice for the exploited and oppressed echelons of society while, at the same time, offering a clear alternative to the totalitarianism of *realpolitik*—justified the use of morally ambivalent means: "Grenier on Communism: 'The whole question comes down to this: should one, *for an ideal of justice,* accept stupid ideas?' One can reply 'yes,' this is a fine thing to do. Or 'no,' it is honest to refuse (*CA1,* 8; my italics).[32]

This is a significant citation for two reasons. First, it bears witness to the fact that Camus is now beginning to apply moral principles to his perceptions of "unknown sufferings" and, secondly, it sets in train a process of thinking on the means/end dichotomy that would culminate in 1951 with the publication of the polemical *The Rebel.*[33] Moreover, the prominence of the concept of justice in the young man's emerging moral stance is apparent from this early *Carnets* entry. Indeed, conversing years later with Carl Viggiani, Camus categorically states that it had been out of "the taste for *justice*" that he had become politically active in Algeria in the mid-1930s.[34]

Crucially, the PCF would offer Camus the means by which to begin to refine his instinctive concern for human welfare in both the political and socioeconomic fields. As an active division of Blum's Popular Front coalition, the party presented many young liberals like Camus with the opportunity to commit to the antifascist cause and thereby promote the movement away from a totalitarian regime toward a more fair and representative political system. In addition, as the standard-bearer of the working classes, the party aimed to empower the proletariat and so remove the potential for injustice in the form of socioeconomic exploitation among the lower social ranks. To this it should be added that the *Front populaire* generally, and the PCF in particular, represented a beacon of hope for Algerian Moslems, whose salvation from social impoverishment was now seen in the promised legislative programme of reforms.[35] In sum, a vehicle for the sociopolitical aspirations of the silent majority (i.e. the least prosperous members of society lacking the resources to voice their concerns for themselves), the PCF had a key role to play in realizing social and political justice. And, for Camus personally, the party was perceived as pivotal in his objective to "see reduced all the misfortune and bitterness which poisons humankind" (*Corr,* 23).

As Philip Thody reminds us, communism has always been perceived on the political left as revolutionary in essence, an image which doubtless appealed to the young Camus: "communism has always retained, even in its most tyrannical forms, a strong idealistic appeal: the creation of a just and egalitarian society, the use of science and industry in the service of mankind as a whole and not for the benefit of a privileged group, the end of the exploitation of man by man, the end of alienation, the humanization of human history."[36]

To these comments should be added the important point that Camus's adherence to the PCF coincided with what, in Algeria, amounted to a nationalist drive to draw more young Arab militants into the party rank and file.[37] To this end, the formation, in January 1936, of the *Parti Communiste Algérien* (PCA) was a small but significant development.[38] Hostile to the entrenched exploitation of (French) imperialism, the contemporary PCF was sympathetic to the cause of Arab nationalism and, in this respect, the party campaigned not only on an antifascist ticket, but also for anticolonialism. Indeed, what distinguished the PCF at the time from other left-wing political parties in France was the level of commitment it accorded its policy on anticolonialism. While the socialist *Section Française de l'Internationale Ouvrière* (SFIO), for instance, championed equality of opportunity for all Algerians, irrespective of race (and thus subscribed to a vision of sociopolitical justice based on an assimilationist perspective), the French Communist Party alone called for independence of the colonized nations. As *La Lutte Sociale* proclaimed in 1934, "only communism will liberate Algeria, nationally and socially."[39]

Now, according to Amar Ouzegane (the then secretary of the PCF in Algiers), Camus and his fellow *adhérents* were "in favor of the Arabization of the Party, in favor of not only its anti-fascist but also its anti-colonialist trend."[40] One must, however, treat with caution Ouzegane's view that the communist Camus belonged to the school of thought of those "who thought that the struggle for Algerian independence came before the struggle against fascism in Europe."[41] Indeed, given that he himself remained a strong advocate of Arab nationalism—after being one of the clandestine leaders of the later *Front de Libération Nationale* (FLN), he would go on to become a cabinet member of Ben Bella's first postcolonial government following the referendum on Algerian independence in July 1962—Ouzegane's remarks on the nature of Camus's militancy regarding Algeria almost certainly need refining.[42] There is doubtless a distinction to be drawn here between, on the one hand, Camus's "nontheoretical" approach to communism and, on the other hand, not being in favor of independence for Algeria. His initial response to manifestations of exploitation and oppression derives primarily from personal observation, so that his concern for social and political justice (now given concrete expression in his adherence to the PCF) stems more from a "person-to-person" acknowledgment of perceived injustice than from theoretical deliberations on the issue of (in)justice. As Jacqueline Lévi-Valensi observes in a recent programme broadcast on French radio, Camus's *engagement* is "more sentimental and more deep-rooted than intellectual and especially Marxist."[43] This claim is confirmed by Camus himself, when he clarifies that it was an empathy with human experience (as opposed to a clear understanding of Marxist philosophy) that underpinned his political commitment: "as a matter of fact, in the (faithful) experience that I will attempt, I will always refuse to put between life and human beings a volume of *Capital*" (*Corr,* 22).[44] An early "profession of faith," brought to light by André Abbou, similarly testifies to Camus's prioritizing of pragmatic reformism over political principle: "[We desire communism]. We do not believe in Hegel, we are not materialistic and do not serve the monstrous idol of Progress. We loathe all rationalism, we are Communists all the same. [That's impossible. No]. Because we do not wish to separate doctrine from life. And for me Communism is much more my cell comrade, worker or store-keeper than the third part of *Capital.* I prefer life to doctrine and it is always life which triumphs over doctrine."[45]

In view of the above remarks, it is interesting to cite one of Camus's communist contemporaries, Max-Pol Fouchet, who states that the idea of "justice" for these young militants was based not on political idealism, but on humanitarian pragmatism: "we were certain of the everlasting nature of the French authority. Our anticolonialism was not radical. We desired justice, the end of oppression, equality, but the idea of independence would have been premature for us. On the other hand, we could not bear the condition imposed on the Moslems, their exploitation, their destitution in hovels in the open country and shantytowns. That is why we entered politics without it being necessary for us to justify it with theory."[46] One might be inclined to think that the value of these comments lies alone in the fact that they further confirm the claim that what principally motivates Camus and his fellow *adhérents* is the pursuit of practical objectives rather than the faith in theoretical principles. It is indeed the case that Fouchet's testimony points up a proactive moral stance in keeping with Camus's own impulse to base his moral sensibility on empirical, not transcendent or abstract, considerations. Yet the above citation (assuming, of course, that it articulates Camus's own stance at the time) also marks a significant development in Camus's preoccupation with justice as an intellectual thematic, inasmuch as the highlighted "practical" stance is underpinned by theoretical deliberation. The fact of the matter is that concepts such as "oppression," "equality," and "exploitation" are all standard ingredients of ethical discourse and, as such, they carry a theoretical charge that is introduced into the young man's moral reasoning as he now begins to formulate his concern for justice. To put the point another way, it does not follow from the fact that what *provokes* an attitude is personal observation that that attitude does not involve some degree of theoretical deliberation; only, perhaps, that its *source* is not theoretical deliberation that is the case in Camus's preoccupation with justice. Rich in compassion and sensibility, Camus's understanding of sociopolitical justice embraces a moral standpoint whereby any theoretical aspects of his concern are in accordance with, impact on, but generally do not outweigh, practical objectives. As we shall see as the book progresses, this pragmatic approach to justice would necessarily be modified by the pressures of history or (personal) circumstance. However, with the notable exception of *The Rebel* where, as we will discover in chapter 7, the interplay of the "theoretical" and "practical" components of Camus's concern for justice noticeably changes emphasis, his underlying engagement with the concept is such that Camus pursues justice, not through an ideological prism, but "with the eyes of the body" and by means of "the physical sense" of the ideal (*E,* 1469). Highlighting in later correspondence what he calls his "inability to reason beyond a lived experience" (*E,* 1615), Camus would remain deeply sensitive to "those, whoever they are, who are humiliated or degraded" (*E,* 803). Such a moral stance stems from his conviction that "nothing is true which compels us to exclude" (*SEN,* 149) and, as we have already seen, is predicated on "such a strong desire to see reduced all the misfortune and bitterness which poisons humankind" (*Corr,* 23).

We shall return to the issue of Camus and colonialism in a later chapter.[47] For the moment, it is sufficient to observe that as a young man whose main duties in the PCF consisted, by his own admission, of "recruitment in Arab quarters," Camus's awareness was undoubtedly raised of the plight of local Algerians "whose conduct and honesty [he] admired," as he would later confide to Grenier (*Corr,* 180).[48] We should also mention as worthy of notice the fact that Camus's formative experience of theater in Algeria (of which more later) brought him into contact with many Moslems, some of whom actually went on to become future leaders following Algeria's independence from France in 1962.[49] In the light of this evidence, it seems reasonable to suggest that Camus was broadly supportive of the Arab cause (yet, crucially, he would not go so far as to support political independence for Algeria), an observation that can further be substantiated by an examination of the reasons behind the young man's departure from the PCF after just two years of commitment.

It is well known that as a result of the Franco-Soviet pact of May 1935, the official communist party line gradually moved away from anticolonialism toward antifascism. In Algeria, this change triggered a new wave of tension between the then-politically feeble PCA and the extremist *Étoile nord-africaine* (ENA).[50] The vital point here is that despite its humanitarian aspirations and objectives for political and socioeconomic reform in Algeria, the PCF, in following the revised party line, proved itself little more than a pawn of the Moscow Comintern, with very little scope to pursue campaigns beyond the party's remit.[51] Some fifteen years later, writing to Grenier, Camus recollects with emotion this shift in communist strategy: "A few who had escaped the pursuit came to ask me if I would let this scandal carry on without saying anything. That afternoon has remained engraved within me; I still remember how I was shaking while they were speaking to me; I was ashamed; I then did what was necessary" (*Corr,* 180).

These comments bear witness to the sense of injustice Camus perceives in respect of betrayed Arab militants following the volte-face of the PCF in Algeria. While many of his communist colleagues chose to toe the new line from Moscow, Camus himself could not turn his back on the Arab cause; to do so would have been to compromise the humanitarian principles underpinning his political commitment.[52] It appears that Camus was willing to risk the charge of sympathizing with right-wing extremists rather than betray the trust established between himself and his Arab colleagues.[53] And, judging from contemporary entries in the *Carnets,* Camus, confronted with the dilemma between personal ethics and political propaganda, was now further questioning the moral foundations of commitment itself. One such note from July 1937 ("the intellectual and commitment [fragment]" [*CA1,* 23]), indicates the start of a process of deliberation, the result of which was that Camus would never again pledge his support for a particular political party or organization. Rather, as he confides to Grenier, his objective henceforth was to "remain clear-sighted" (*Corr,* 23). Articulating in his notebook the discrepancy between human aspirations and political institutions, Camus's suspicion of political indoctrination is well-established by August 1937: "Every time I hear a political speech or I read those of our leaders, I am horrified at having, for years, heard nothing which sounded human. It is always the same words telling the same lies. And the fact that people accept this, that the people's anger has not destroyed these hollow clowns, strikes me as proof that people attribute no importance to the way they are governed; that they gamble—yes, gamble—with a whole part of their life and their so-called 'vital interests'" (*CA1,* 26–27; translation amended; cf. *CA1,* 44).

While these remarks doubtless confirm the young man's disillusionment with party politics, I cannot agree with Anne Durand when she claims that Camus's association with communism in the mid-1930s was "an unforgivable folly."[54] On the contrary, his two-year membership of the PCF enabled Camus to pitch his own sensitivity to "unknown sufferings" against a sociopolitical backdrop. As Emmett Parker has shown, comments made by Camus in his contemporary book reviews for *Alger républicain* suggest that he was able to draw certain conclusions on the subject of commitment, even if his own *engagement* was not a positive experience.[55] Surely, then, Jacqueline Lévi-Valensi is closer to the mark when she states that "adherence to the PC is, for Camus, neither an end in itself nor a radical point of departure, but a *stage* in his awareness and political action; an important stage, not only in itself, by the real, public or more secret activities which mark it and by the thoughts it occasions at the time within Camus, but also by the consequences it will have later in terms of his commitment and his choices concerning politics and human action."[56]

What ultimately emerges from Camus's formative experience of communism is, then, a picture of a young man with an intellectual honesty and humanitarian generosity. And, to judge from contemporary notes for the *Carnets* (*CA1,* 28, 34), Camus himself considered the "hinge" (*CA1,* 28; translation amended) of that experience as fundamental to his political realization, providing him as it does with an invaluable insight into the fragile relationship between politics and morality.

Théâtre Populaire

A further and important aspect of the period currently under consideration is Camus's formative experience of theater, an interest that, as has been well-documented, would later become a passion.[57]

It should be stressed from the outset that the theater lends itself very effectively to the communication of ideas and attitudes: appealing directly to the spectator's senses and powers of intellect, it can be said to be more spontaneous than other forms of literature. Theater is also bound up with the notion of *doing* something, as opposed to writing, which is essentially a *solitary* activity. Thus, while Camus's *Youthful Writings* may be defined by their qualities of contemplation, his early theater can be considered a springboard for action. In addition, inasmuch as it involves a social performance, theater brings people together, transcending divisions of race, class, and gender, and so it may be said that it is broadly "democratic" or "egalitarian" in nature, much in keeping with Camus's own liberalist mentality.

It will be recalled that the *Théâtre du Travail,* founded by Camus in 1935, was established under the auspices of the "Maison de la Culture," a communist-inspired initiative set up with a view to raising cultural and political awareness in the Maghreb nations.[58] As the movement's manifesto makes clear, the *Théâtre du Travail* set out to defend proletarian values by cultural means and so "demonstrate that art can sometimes manage to leave its ivory tower" to give credibility to the claim that "sense of beauty is inseparable from a certain sense of humanity."[59] A study of the list of productions staged by the troupe between January 1936 and May 1937 (when it would be disbanded) reveals the considerable extent to which Camus uses the stage to lend artistic expression to some of his own contemporary concerns, not least his emerging concern for social and political justice.[60] This is an important observation for two reasons. First, Camus now uses the theater to lend *public* expression to his private (moral) preoccupations: his aim, as he later explained to *Paris-Théâtre,* was to "carry out a theater of unrest, directly" (*TRN,* 1715) as a way of alerting people to issues of both local and international significance. Secondly, this use of drama as a vehicle for communicating to a wider audience some of his own concerns gives added density and resonance to the idea of Camus as a committed man of the theater. Once again, I find myself at odds with Anne Durand when she claims that "what especially impelled Camus toward the stage with a wild and calculated determination . . . is the desire to be *known.* A justifiable desire . . . with no less force, but a pressing and uncontrollable desire."[61] What Durand fails to point out is the fact that both the *Théâtre du Travail* and its successor the *Théâtre de l'Équipe* deliberately adopted policies of anonymity for their productions: in such circumstances, the assertion that Camus sought self-glorification through the theater is preposterous.

As an ensemble, the dramatizations of the *Théâtre du Travail* throw an interesting light on issues that we have already seen to play a key role in Camus's formative years. Producing a play like Gorki's *The Lower Depths,* for instance, with its poignant depiction of Moscow's squalor, enables Camus to discharge through the theater his own childhood experience of social injustice. Or, again, his adaptation of Aeschylus's *Prometheus Bound* provides him with the means by which to give intellectual depth to some of his more metaphysically-inspired ideas. And special mention must be made of Camus's own adaptation of Malraux's *An Age of Oppression* [*Le Temps du mépris*], a novel originally published in 1935 depicting a revolt among the European lower social classes against the tyranny of Nazism.[62] There is a close affinity between the latter work and Camus's proletarian values and antifascist convictions. (As has already been acknowledged, Malraux was greatly admired by the young Albert, who—judging from an entry for the *Carnets* from the time (*CA1,* 15)—was planning to write an essay on the author of *La Condition humaine* (1933). That projected essay was, however, later abandoned.) Although the interpretation is now lost, John Michalczyk has painstakingly pieced together fragments of Camus's adaptation and provides some interesting insights into the nature of the project in general:

> With Camus' adaptation of *Le Temps du mépris,* the Théâtre du Travail achieved an instant success attributable to several factors: first of all, the tense drama provided by Malraux's original work, filled with human emotion—surprise, anguish, camaraderie, and internal conflict; second, the inevitable identification of the public with Kassner [the communist revolutionary leader in the work]; third, the imaginative staging executed with slender means but with an abundance of creativity and dedication; and last, the political timeliness of the 1936 drama.[63]

Be that as it may, in the absence of the text itself, one must look to other means in order to gauge the significance of Camus's adaptation in relation to his emerging views on justice. An avenue worthy of investigation in this respect is the play's reception. In the contemporary Algiers-based press, the production attracted rapturous applause: billed as "the heroic expression of the proletariat," the adaptation was championed by *La Lutte sociale* as "a masterstroke" watched by "more than 1 500 people from every class."[64] *L'Écho d'Alger,* a newspaper of radical-socialist tendencies, likewise spotlighted "the success achieved . . . with a public belonging to all classes of society."[65] Charles Poncet, who himself attended the first performance of the play, recalls the momentous effect of the production "on this tense crowd which saw unfold on stage its own struggle against the degrading mindset of fascism" (*TRN,* 1690).[66]

It is clear from the above reviews that the play was able to transcend class boundaries in accordance with the notion of *théâtre populaire.* In addition, the tone of these various testimonies strongly suggests that Camus's defense of working-class values and contempt for totalitarian regimes—intuitive ideas, as we have seen, which are now given concrete expression in his adaptation—were well-received by contemporary critics. Given that he champions in the play proletarian values such as tolerance (as opposed to exclusion) and pragmatic reformism (as against abstract idealism), Camus identifies in his adaptation a particular socioeconomic category, the principles of which can be said to constitute the basis of his quest for justice in a *social* dimension. Similarly, inasmuch as he also expresses in the same production his disdain for regimes characterized by a concentration of power to a minority of individuals, Camus can be seen to use his adaptation not only to articulate what he perceives as *political* injustice—fascist intimidation—but also to promote the values on the basis of which political power may be deemed legitimate and just. Put simply, Camus's preexisting standard of justice on which a morally accountable political system depends rejects the tyranny of authoritarianism and embraces the standard of liberal democracy in which civil liberties are protected, the right to self-determination preserved and the importance of mutual respect and understanding promoted.

Further traces of Camus's defense of traditional democratic principles on which his understanding of sociopolitical justice will be based can be found in his (staged) response to the Spanish Civil War, a major historical landmark for people of Camus's generation, as he later acknowledged in *Combat:* "For the first time, people of my generation came face to face with injustice triumphing in history. At that time the blood of innocence flowed amidst a chatter of pharisees" (*RRD,* 58; translation amended). Camus's deep affection for Spain—his mother was of Spanish descent—has been well-documented, and the quest for a Spanish Republic, "one of the most just causes which could be encountered in a person's life" (*E,* 1792), remained, throughout his lifetime, one of the principal components of Camus's moral mandate.[67] While it is perhaps not a little surprising that we have no firsthand account by Camus on the actual outbreak of hostilities in Spain in July 1936, this does not mean to say that he was unaware of the magnitude of events at the time unfolding in his "second homeland" (*E,* 1814). Roger Quilliot notes that

> We must remember that Camus was born in 1913. . . . he wrote in collaboration *Revolt in Asturias* which actually dealt with Spain and latent forms of fascism. As for the rest, he did not dedicate any essays to this but, at 23 or 25 years of age, it is not extraordinary that he should have devoted so little attention to it.[68]

Notwithstanding these reservations, there is actually considerable evidence to suggest that Camus was not slow in taking a stand on events unfolding in Spain in the mid-1930s, thus confirming the democratic principles underlying his concern for justice. Indeed, while it is true that his precarious health prevented him from following in the footsteps, say, of Malraux—the author of *Man's Hope* (1937) joined the Spanish republican forces fighting fascism in the field—Camus is reported to have confided to Blanche Balain at the time of the outbreak of the civil war in Spain his private longing to sacrifice everything in the name of republicanism: "He [Camus] confessed that he would like to be in Spain, fighting with the Republicans. 'To possess everything, to accomplish everything, in an instant, and die!'"[69] Moreover, speaking in Algiers in February 1937, he would draw a clear distinction between, on the one hand, the cause of Spanish republicanism—what Camus calls "the truth which is being assassinated in Spain" (*E,* 1324)—and, on the other hand, what he condemns as "the lie which triumphed in Ethiopia" (*E,* 1324), a reference to the Ethiopian suppression in 1935 by Mussolini's fascist brigade in what amounted to a blatant breach of the League of Nations' call for international cooperation in the interests of global peace. We might also note in passing that in *The Plague,* Rambert comes to learn the true meaning of courage and dignity by having honored republican values during the Spanish Civil War as a further testimony to Camus's own sensitivity to the republican cause (*TRN,* 1351).

If, as the manifestation of "injustice triumphing in history" (*RRD,* 58), the war itself in Spain outraged Camus's sense of justice predicated on the vindication of political power through liberal democratic principles, then France's failure to lend assistance to her distressed republican neighbor was a veritable scandal.[70] We may anticipate a little here in order to note that, writing in 1939 for *Alger républicain* on what at that time he called "[the] unjust and bloody war" (*FC,* 2:608), Camus attacks with unprecedented perspicuity

France's policy of nonintervention in respect of the hostilities continuing to ravage Spain: "Some people do not . . . understand that what makes so many of us loyal to the Spanish Republicans is not vain political affinities but the irrepressible feeling that they have with them the Spanish people, this people so like their land with their ingrained nobility and their ardent love of life. . . . The methodical murder of the Spanish people continues. We can take pride in it: we have done all that was necessary to that end."[71]

Philippe Vanney has recently considered how the principle of nonintervention espoused by a given nation in a given situation has direct implications for the interests of the people that nation serves.[72] For Camus, a democratic nation like France consciously adopting a policy of nonintervention in a neighboring nation threatened by authoritarian rule compromises its own republican ideals and, in so doing, it implicitly accepts the legality of the alternative (fascist) regime. As he observes in a later speech, "one cannot be for nonintervention and want to prevent a party, whatever it may be, from triumphing in a country which is not yours" (*E,* 783). The fact of the matter is that noninterventionist theory can be implemented, and ultimately justified on moral grounds, only if the motives for nonengagement concur with the underlying principles of the particular nation-state advocating such policy. Such a state of affairs leads Camus in the same speech to affirm (with tongue firmly set in cheek) that "apart perhaps from Pontius Pilate, no one has ever really believed in nonintervention in foreign politics" (*E,* 784). If we transpose this thought on to the situation in Spain of the mid-1930s, then the moral ambivalence of France's approach toward her republican sister becomes clear. In Camus's eyes, one nation's perceived act of injustice—France's noninterventionist policy during the Spanish Civil War—is inextricably linked to the prolonged injustice of another nation—the substitution of dictatorship for democracy beyond the Pyrenees. For the young Algerian, it is the abiding memory of this "spectacle of an injustice which has never been rectified," as Camus puts it in his 1946 "Preface to *Free Spain*" (*E,* 1605), that drives his concern for justice in the Spanish dimension and underscores his concomitant polemics against Francoism.

The fact that in deference to his sense of justice, Camus was actively campaigning against the Spanish manifestation of fascism even before the cataclysm of July 1936 is evident from other plays in the *Théâtre du Travail* repertoire. The coauthored *Revolt in Asturias,* a play drawing on an uprising among militant Spanish workers in October 1934 headed by miners in the economically disadvantaged Asturias province, is a case in point here. Indeed, that play provides Camus with a further opportunity to refine his concern for justice in relation to *social conditions,* on the one hand, and *political systems,* on the other. As Walter Langlois highlights, the miners' insurrection was "the first major manifestation in Western Europe to have been provoked by the Fascist Right that was becoming an ever-increasing threat to human freedom and dignity everywhere on the continent."[73] For her part, Jacqueline Lévi-Valensi observes that *Revolt in Asturias* "bears testimony to the political acumen of Camus and his friends who had understood the full significance and stake of the events."[74] This last reading is borne out by Camus's own interpretation of the play as less a work of art and more a sociopolitical act in its portrayal of a historical quest to move away from the social oppressiveness and cultural devastation of a capitalist system toward a more humane and representative socialist stance: "After it was over he [Camus] would confide to a friend [Liliane Dulong née Choucroun] that [*Revolt in Asturias*] was not a good play, he would never have written anything like it alone, but for him it was less a work of art than an act."[75] While Camus may dispute the artistic merits of the play, his conviction that the insurrection on which the work is based was morally justified is beyond dispute since he is reported to have deemed the events in question "an example of human strength and greatness."[76]

Although a collective endeavor, *Revolt in Asturias* carries clear Camusian overtones. Indeed, Jeanne Sicard recalls that Camus was the group's "undisputed guide" (*TRN,* 1852) who assumed an instrumental role in the gestation of the play.[77] While a full account of the drama is beyond the scope of the present study, it is important to recognize that *Revolt* contains, in embryo, some of the issues later formulated by Camus in his intellectual preoccupation with justice as a moral problematic in the sociopolitical domain.[78] The bourgeois characters of The Pharmacist and The Grocer, totally indoctrinated by the disciplinary character of the fascist Falangists party ("All this riff-raff will soon be swept out. Orderliness . . . at last orderliness . . . at last discipline" [*TRN,* 408]); the honorable defiance of the left, epitomized by Pèpe, whose response to right-wing extremism interestingly anticipates the master-slave binary dialectic of *The Rebel* ("No! . . . it's been going on for too long. It had to end. Let me join them" [*TRN,* 409]); and Sanchez's blind quest for revolutionary power ("they must not tarnish our revolution" [*TRN,* 414])—all of these examples bear witness to Camus's intellectual investment in the play regarding issues threatening to undermine his liberal humanist instincts from which his vision of sociopolitical justice is derived.

One particular moral issue that is raised in *Revolt in Asturias* and that would go on to become a major concern for Camus in his understanding of political justice requires special mention. The murder of The Grocer by Sanchez in the play, an action which occasions The Pharmacist to ask the question "by what right do you kill? In a word, by what right" (*TRN,* 420), draws attention to the problem of whether political violence can be justified in the pursuit of a "just" revolutionary end. As we shall discover later, the quest for an ethical equilibrium in revolutionary protest, whereby the means remain consonant with the end of a given campaign, provides the fulcrum of Camus's postwar views on revolutionary justice, culminating in the publication of *The Rebel* in 1951. *The Just Assassins* (1950), too, explores the extent to which the use of violence within a political context can be justified on moral grounds. However, such preoccupations are conspicuously absent in *Revolt in Asturias,* where *all* means are deemed justified in the resolve to liberate the proletariat from social and political oppression. Indeed, Camus's later contempt for the Stalinist Stepan, whose quest for absolute justice finds expression in *The Just Assassins,* is not present in the case of Sanchez from the earlier play, even though both characters are equally merciless in their determination to realize their respective revolutionary dreams. What needs to be emphasized here is that in 1935, when *Revolt* was conceived, the problem of how to preserve morality in revolutionary action—the keystone of Camus's postwar ethics—is not an issue as far as the play itself is concerned. Only at the very end of the drama is there an implicit reference to the problem through the poignant words of the "Second Voice" (evidently that of Sanchez himself) highlighting the earlier uncompromising resolve to use human lives as political expedients: "In the strikes they said that I was the leader. . . . I really believed in my revolution, I really did. . . . *So many dead, so many dead*" (*TRN,* 436; my italics).

There is another aspect of *Revolt in Asturias* that is equally worthy of notice in relation to Camus's emerging views on justice. It will be recalled that, judged unsuitable by the local right-wing authorities in the run-up to the municipal elections of May 1936, the play was banned from being performed in public.[79] Such a prohibition is significant in that it brings fascist intimidation into Camus's personal experience for the first time. His contemporary correspondence bears testimony to the lengths to which he is prepared to go to remedy his private sense of injustice at not being allowed to articulate issues which, in his view, lie in the public interest: "Charming work for yours truly. Protest letters to newspapers in the polemical style. . . . Still to be organized are the printing of 2 000 pamphlets, 100 posters, a protest rally if possible, a sandwich-board man in town and cars with protest banners. I've already started."[80]

It is clear from the above that the outlawing of *Revolt in Asturias* raises Camus's awareness of basic human rights in a clear and direct manner. The ability to voice dissent is, of course, a fundamental component of the democratic right to freedom of expression and any unwarranted violation of that right amounts to an act of censorship. Accordingly, in an open letter to Rozis (the fascist mayor who was responsible for the ban) dated April 13, 1936, Camus highlights the issue of municipal misrule in his exposition of how local governmental procedure is hijacked by the mayor without apparent reason: "They [the members of the *Théâtre du Travail*] would not pretend to be surprised that the mayor refused an authorization already granted by the Prefect, . . . but the Prefecture's approval suggests that there is nothing subversive in the play."[81] As we shall see in the following chapter, such blatant breaches of fundamental rights and abuses of accustomed procedure are crucial factors in the crystallization of Camus's understanding of justice at *Alger républicain.*

In the course of an interview granted to *Paris-Théâtre* in 1958, Camus recalls his formative experience of theater in the following terms: "Frankly, I first of all wanted to carry out a theater of unrest, directly. Then, I understood that it was the wrong track. All things considered, I started where they want us to finish up today. But *An Age of Oppression* was an interesting experiment. And then, I liked that book" (*TRN,* 1715). I take the meaning of the pivotal phrase "the wrong track" to be what Camus perceives as the generic inadequacy of committed *theater,* as opposed to committed *literature,* which he would go on to reject later. As Jacqueline Lévi-Valensi observes, "it becomes clear that Camus does not confuse popular theater and political propaganda; his ambition is to make great theater popular and not to use theater as a place of indoctrination."[82] Significantly, none of Camus's own drama—with the exception of the collaborative *State of Siege* (1948)—would be committed in the style of the *Théâtre du Travail:* by the end of the 1930s, his days as a militant man of the theater were over.[83] From this, one can deduce that the aspiration of the *Théâtre du Travail* to provide a cultural outlet for the masses perhaps proved a little *too* successful for Camus personally. In other words, his original objective to use theater as a device by which to communicate some of his own contemporary preoccupations, not least his emerging views on social and political justice, is *ipso facto* displaced by an even more overwhelming passion: theater itself.

To conclude, it is clear that in Camus's formative experience of both politics and theater, he finds a means of articulating and refining his awareness of "unknown sufferings." In the absence of a relevant textual platform, the young man looks to communism and theater to voice his emerging concern for justice, which may now be formulated in terms of a growing sensitivity to both social conditions and political systems. The former has its origins in Camus's empathy with proletarian values inextricably bound up with his own social status and the latter derives from his intuitive liberal humanist morality. In both cases, his concern springs more from personal and humanitarian than from theoretical and ideological motives, so that his understanding of justice has as its point of focus the welfare and aspirations of human beings living in society. It is therefore reasonable to maintain that Camusian justice (in so far as one can use such a term) is essentially empirical in nature, drawn from a moral sensibility that is rich in compassion and generosity. This hypothesis will be further substantiated by the next key development in Camus's moral stance when, as journalist for *Alger républicain,* he consolidates his understanding of social and political justice by intervening on behalf of specific victims of persecution and oppression. This will form the subject matter of the next chapter.

3
Consolidating the Concern

> For too long and for too often injustice has triumphed and triumphs in this country. But its triumphs are due to the passivity of just people. It is time that these raise their voices and start serving their ideal with the same relentlessness that others bring to realizing their hatred.
>
> —Camus, *Fragments d'un combat, 1938–40*

"The honest newspaper of honest people"

Hitherto conditioned by imperial prejudice, the French Algerian press of Camus's era welcomed rather tentatively the founding, in October 1938, of *Alger républicain,* a newspaper with a mandate to serve as a mouthpiece for the province's indigenous population and lower social ranks.[1] Declaring itself "the disinterested friend of the oppressed" (*FC,* 1:46) and "the honest newspaper of honest people" (*FC,* 1:93), this new title sought to give a voice to those whose needs were not already being served by the contemporary press in the province.[2] While it never threatened to undermine either the right-wing *La Dépêche algérienne* or the radical-socialist *L'Écho d'Alger*—two newspapers sustaining the myth of the "civilizing mission" in Algeria—*Alger républicain* nevertheless exposed much of the internal inadequacy of what it called "the social conservatism which manages to keep our indigenous friends at a level of inferiority" (*FC,* 1:40). Conceived on a nonpartisan platform, the newspaper championed its free status and drew attention to the fact that its motives were derived from a liberal humanist morality.[3] As the very first issue put it on October 6, 1938, "for the first time, an absolutely independent press is going to support the cause of democracy in Algeria which is that of justice and peace" (*FC,* 1:40).

At the heart of *Alger républicain*'s quest to bring progressive politics to the *communes mixtes* and the Arab territories was a campaign to redress the balance of power between the "rulers" and the "ruled" in the province: to raise the profile of, by rendering justice to, those indigenous groups without the cushion of influence for protection. Thus, the newspaper committed itself to speaking out on behalf of those without the means to do so for themselves, proclaiming that "from Belcourt to Bab-el-Oued, we will listen to people and things with the same attention; we will question the most modest street and the most sordid district in order to get to know what constitutes their shame or their distress, we will put forward what would bring them back joy or health" (*FC,* 1:45). A focal point, then, for the "legitimate aspirations" (*FC,* 1:91) of the indigenous population, the newspaper fought to eradicate racial discrimination and thereby render to inhabitants of the Maghreb nations the constitutional rights on a par with those of "pure" French stock:

> For *Alger républicain,* there could not be two kinds of French person, but just one which includes equally the Parisian, native of Paris, the Marseillais, native of Marseilles and the Arab, native of Algeria. That is why we demand immediate social equality of all French people, whatever their origin, denomination or philosophy. That is why we demand the transportation of the native population of Algeria to political equality. That is why we demand, for the populations of North Africa, the benefit of social laws and aid and health measures which the inhabitants of Metropolitan France enjoy. (*FC,* 1:40)

It should be stressed that recognizing the equal worth, the equal rights and the equal respect to which all persons are entitled (until and unless, in the Aristotelian tradition, relevant differences dictate otherwise) underscores the standard of social justice. *Alger républicain* can usefully be deemed a vehicle for consolidating Camus's own intellectual preoccupation with the concept, where the principles of fairness and equality of worth between persons loom large. Indeed, his apprenticeship at *Alger républicain* and its short-lived successor *Le Soir républicain* (spanning the months October 1938 to January 1940) can be said to represent a natural progression from his interest in "the stage" to that of "the page." As Michel Maillard comments, "for Camus, journalism is one route and theater another. . . . And speaking of journalism, I was wondering whether a link could be established between the activity of Albert Camus the journalist and the activity of Camus as dramatist. It is another way of handling words in language which is perhaps more direct, without going through something which may systematically have the look of fiction."[4]

In the absence of a textual platform, Camus initially looks to the theater as a means by which to voice his formative views on social and political justice. Now, in his capacity as professional journalist, he is able to refine and articulate this moral sensibility further by engaging in matters of justice (social, political, and institutional) directly impacting on his Algerian situation.

Social Rightness and Common Human Decency

The moral concept of justice presupposes conflicts of interest. As John Rawls writes, "questions of justice arise when conflicting claims are made upon the design of a practice and where it is taken for granted that each person will insist, as far as possible, on what he considers his rights. It is typical of cases of justice to involve persons who are pressing on one another their claims, between which a fair balance or equilibrium must be found."[5] Defending the interests of minorities against the moral claims of majorities is fundamental to the ideal of "fair balance" and "equilibrium" sought after here by Rawls. Legal moralists such as Ronald Dworkin, who subscribes to a rights theory of justice, posit that the best means of achieving this is to start from the assumption that underscoring interpersonal morality is the right of each individual to equal consideration and respect. Rights violations, Dworkin insists, are affronts to human dignity: "the institution of rights rests on the conviction that the invasion of a relatively important right . . . is a grave injustice."[6] For Dworkin, justice involves the right to treatment as an equal, so that those owning the means of production "must not distribute goods or opportunities unequally on the grounds that some citizens are entitled to more because they are worthy of more concern."[7] Like justice itself, rights are matters of entitlement and not the property of the privileged few. Furthermore, by respecting the rights of each human being, one enhances human dignity.

Camus's approach to the standard of justice at *Alger républicain* can usefully be examined through the lens of human rights. As we shall see, his overall principle of social rightness is based on the realization of a code of basic human decency (a "minimum standard of justice"), in which the protection of fundamental human rights and civil liberties is not compromised by politico-ideological prejudice. As he insists at the end of his acclaimed inquiry into the social injustice prevalent in the Kabyle district of Algeria, "on any occasion, progress is made every time a political problem is replaced by a human problem" (*FC,* 1:335). Elsewhere, he likewise gives expression to his humanist morality when he submits that "a humane language is enough to prompt humane decisions" (*FC,* 2:368). The fact of the matter is that Camus's writings for *Alger républicain* primarily show, rather than argue, the reality of moral adversity undermining basic human rights. His pursuit of justice, grounded in a deep antipathy toward oppressive practices, now develops into a quest for social and political *reform* as a means by which to change the status quo of the underprivileged and the impoverished around him. In a later prefatory remark noted in the *Carnets,* Camus would highlight his "uncompromising reformism" (*CA2,* 139; translation amended), and it is noteworthy that this conviction first finds concrete expression in his *Alger républicain* journalism, a fact seized upon by Germaine Brée when she states that "justice is no abstract concept for Camus even at this time; it is a necessity born of his intense power of understanding the misery of others."[8]

Nowhere is Brée's claim more tellingly verified than in "Misery in Kabylia," the series of articles published in *Alger républicain* between June 5 and 15, 1939 (*FC,* 1:267–336). Admittedly, Camus's concern for social justice in those reports is more implicit than explicit in nature: the pieces are marked by a deeply personal tone and their portrayal of the Kabyle predicament is essentially pathetic and compassionate. Yet whatever the moral pitch of the survey, it is clear, as existing scholarship confirms, that "Misery in Kabylia" represents a significant milestone in Camus's general engagement with justice as a moral problematic. Jacqueline Lévi-Valensi deems the articles "the most remarkable set in Camus's contribution to *Alger républicain.*"[9] Emmett Parker sees traces of Jonathan Swift's *A Modest Proposal* (1729) in the pieces, while Roger Quilliot champions them as "remarkable already for their style, their restrained feeling and their humane sentiment."[10] Moreover, inasmuch as "Misery in Kabylia" is the only part of his *Alger républicain* journalism to be incorporated (with some modifications) into the 1958 *Actuelles III* [*Chroniques algériennes*] (*E,* 903–38), it is apparent that Camus himself attaches considerable importance to the series.

Overpopulated and in economic crisis, the Kabylia of Camus's era projected a desperate image to the outsider even by Algerian standards. When Camus visited the area in spring 1939, he witnessed at first-hand the social injustice underpinning the colonial enterprise. The expropriation of the Kabyle territory by French colonists had removed landownership from local producers, who subsequently faced bankruptcy because of the injustices of greedy capitalists. With high unemployment in the region, economic persecution was rife. Although in the interwar period high levels of emigration to France had helped to ease the problem of high population densities in the area, that avenue was eventually sealed off to the Kabyles in the mid-1930s because of the fragile state of the French economy.[11] The severe winter of 1938–39, yielding poor harvests for local produce (*FC,* 1:270n1), merely exacerbated the difficulties of "forgotten beings, deprived of all dignity and who were heading toward old age without knowing how to read or write, without being able to hope for legitimate rights."[12]

Unlike other investigations into the matter written from a colonial perspective—most notably, "Kabylia 39," published by Roger Frison-Roche in *La Dépêche algérienne* from June 8 to June 17, 1939—Camus does not baulk at exposing in "Misery in Kabylia" the plight of a people "living three centuries behind the times" (*FC,* 1:294).[13] In often graphic detail, he spotlights the "suffering" (*FC,* 1:280) and the "unbearable sights" (*FC,* 1:335) of "these long bitter days" (*FC,* 1:335), and describes destitution that "immediately brought tears to [his] eyes" (*FC,* 1:280) and that "followed [him] everywhere" (*FC,* 1:280). The social injustice in evidence in Kabylia is, for Camus, "vivid" (*FC,* 1:281) and "shocking" (*FC,* 1:286) and its effects pervade his consciousness: "the destitution here is neither an idea nor a topic for meditation. It is a matter of fact. It shouts out and drives to despair" (*FC,* 1:288). The potency of the crisis is given added poignancy as Camus sketches in the (Mediterranean) backdrop: "In one of the most attractive regions in the world, an entire people is starving and three quarters of its community are living off official charities" (*FC,* 1:279).

Appealing, then, to the reader's senses in his use of emotionally charged language to convey the social injustice prevalent in Kabylia—"it is not for a party that this is written," he insists, "but for human beings" (*FC,* 1:334)—Camus raises questions in "Misery in Kabylia" concerning the moral responsibility of the ruling colonists. However, any attack of colonialism as such remains largely implicit in the Kabyle series. As Parker notes, "in none of Camus's articles is his wish to avoid an ideological battle on political grounds more evident than in ['Misery in Kabylia']."[14] Be that as it may, there *are* moments in the reports when, confronted with the deliberate disregard for human rights by fellow human beings, Camus forces himself to relax his nonconfrontational stance toward the colonial authorities. What I specifically have in mind here is the report explicitly entitled "Insulting Salaries" (*FC,* 1:295–99). In that article, Camus highlights what he calls "the general contempt in which the colonist holds the unfortunate people of this country" (*FC,* 1:298), and he does not hide his indignation at the dehumanizing effects of economic exploitation by colonial profiteers: "I had been warned that the salaries were inadequate. I did not know that they were insulting. I had been told that the working day exceeded the legal limit. I did not know that it was not far from doubling it. . . . I do not wish to adopt an aggressive tone. But I am forced to say here that the system of work in Kabylia is a system of slavery. For I cannot see how else to describe a system where a laborer works between 10 and 12 hours for an average salary of between 6 and 10 francs" (*FC,* 1:295).[15]

Such explicit moments of criticism notwithstanding, Camus largely eschews the language of colonial condemnation in "Misery in Kabylia." One might be inclined to think that this general reluctance to expose and comment on the underlying causes of the crisis reveals astonishing short-sightedness on the part of the young journalist. However, while it is true that, as a *petit Blanc* Camus himself had vested interests in *not* exposing colonial injustices, it does not follow that his is a naïve response to the problems he portrays.[16] On the contrary, Camus's moral position in "Misery in Kabylia" is clear. He does not target his criticism at the colonial authorities ultimately responsible for the crisis since to do so would lose sight of the actual suffering in the region. In his quest for social justice on behalf of the Kabyles, Camus will, accordingly, once more point up the need for humanitarian pragmatism: "There is no more appalling sight than this destitution in the middle of one of the most beautiful countries in the world. What have we done for it? What have we done so that this country might get its face back? What have we done, all of us who write, speak or legislate and who, once back at home, forget other people's destitution? To say that we love this people is not enough. Love alone cannot do anything here and neither can charity nor speeches. What we must offer is bread, wheat, relief supplies and a helping hand. The rest is not important" (*FC,* 1:280–81).

A further noteworthy example of Camus's proactive moral stance at *Alger républicain* in the face of colonial injustice is provided by his investigation into the issue of state health entitlements for Algerian immigrant workers returning to the province, published in April 1939 (*FC,* 1:243–66). These workers lose their right to state health benefits upon returning to their families in Algeria, where medical provision is tellingly inadequate (*FC,* 1:304–8). For Camus, the plight of these laborers confirms "once more that a French subject is not necessarily treated as a French citizen" (*FC,*

1:246). In the eyes of the young reporter, who undertakes a series of interviews with various specialists in order to gauge public reaction to this "such clear injustice" (*FC,* 1:248), the immigrant workers are clear colonial casualties, "immediate victims of an imbalance which only interests institutions" (*FC,* 1:247). As Camus again stresses in concluding his survey (all the participants in which, with the exception of the local *Syndicat des Médecins,* favored the proposed reform to extend health entitlements to the Algerian *départements*), what is needed if justice is to be rendered to the immigrants is pragmatic reformism, not mere platitudes: "People will say that this requires a lot of time, the training of new doctors, funds and goodwill. But if time is needed, that is all the more reason to start without delay. The problem in essence is that an injustice exists. It will no longer be an injustice once we have done something to make it go away. But it remains what it is all the time we just regret it" (*FC,* 1:265).

In both "Misery in Kabylia" and the case of the Algerian immigrant workers, Camus demonstrates a clear social engagement on behalf of impoverished and persecuted categories within colonial society. Both the Kabyles and the immigrant workers are confronted with social injustice, in that the issue of identity is used as a differentiating device to engender discrimination, exploitation, and social misery. As we saw, the elimination of such arbitrary distinctions was uppermost on *Alger républicain*'s agenda. In the words of Kaddour Makaci, one of Camus's Moslem colleagues working on the newspaper, "the most elementary justice advocates that all Algerians, subjected to the same responsibilities and duties and all claiming to be representatives of the same nation, be treated equally. . . . Neither racial nor religious differences will be able to distort the beauty of the daily campaign which will be led by the valiant organ *Alger républicain* to bring people together and to ensure the achievement of democratic freedom."[17]

In keeping with this moral mandate, Camus posits a minimum standard of justice, subsuming racial and religious differences, by which to safeguard basic human rights in the face of moral adversity.[18] I say a "minimum standard of justice" because, as we have already seen in relation to both the social injustice in Kabylia and the predicament of the Algerian immigrant workers, Camus's primary concern is with actual human suffering (and with how best to alleviate this state of affairs) rather than with politico-ideological debates. In accordance with his conviction that progress is made when political problems are humanized, Camus prioritizes the issue of human betterment and appeals to common human decency to bring this about without the burden of ideological distraction. His understanding of sociopolitical justice can, accordingly, be formulated in terms of a self-styled revolutionary whose crusade it is to safeguard fundamental human rights irrespective of, and underlying, any other "contingent" considerations.

To support this claim, we might once more look to "Misery in Kabylia." Implicit in that series is the quest for a basic threshold of justice for the local population, which Camus undertakes in his view that persons reserve the right to what, writing later in *Le Soir républicain,* he would call "a life where people retain their chances of dignity" (*FC,* 2:736). This campaign to uphold a minimum standard of justice in the face of social impoverishment embraces a wide range of socioeconomic issues in the Kabyle series, such as the right to basic sustenance and shelter (a conviction born of the view that "ready-made ideas and prejudices become odious when they are applied to a world where people are dying of exposure and where children are reduced to the food of animals without having their instinct which would stop them from perishing" [*FC,* 1:294]); the right to fair wages and equality of opportunity at the work place ("Kabylia demands . . . policies which are perceptive and noble . . . and, for farmers, a return to dignity by work which is useful and justly paid" [*FC,* 1:327]); and the right to essential state entitlements like healthcare (thereby redressing the contemporary situation in which "on average, Kabylia has one doctor for 60 000 inhabitants" [*FC,* 1:305]) and the "instrument of emancipation" (*FC,* 1:309) of education ("The Kabyles demand . . . schools, as they demand bread" [*FC,* 1:314]). Clearly, such rights are supposedly inherent in the French nation—*le pays des droits de l'homme*—whose constitution assumes equality before the law of all persons irrespective of race, religion, or gender. Concluding the Kabyle inquiry, Camus does not mince his words when he appeals to the mother country not to allow paternalistic pride to impede her moral duty toward her colonized dependant: "I will not beat about the bush. It seems that, today, it is to behave as a bad French citizen to reveal the destitution of a French country. I have to say that it is difficult today to know how to be a good French citizen. So many different sorts of people today pride themselves on this title, and among them so many second-rate or self-interested people, that one might well be mistaken. But at least we can know what is a just person. And my disposition is that France could not be better represented and defended than by acts of justice" (*FC,* 1:334).

The preceding citation bears witness to Camus's refusal to let political considerations dictate moral obligations, and it is noteworthy that he now uses the ideal of justice as a crystallizing agent for recognizing moral responsibility. His reference here to the mother country's "acts of justice" raises two interesting issues which require comment. One is the relation between justice and charity/mercy and the other is the argument about what kind of economic system does most to reduce poverty. Let us now look at each of these questions in turn.

As we shall see in later chapters of this book, whether moral leniency serves the cause of justice is a vexed question for Camus. His polemic with François Mauriac at the time of the notorious *épuration* in France and his 1957 "Reflections on the Guillotine" are particularly noteworthy contributions to that important debate.[19] For Mauriac, as for Robert Garnier and John Milton, mercy is in the forefront of moral deliberation. Mauriac insists that "what is most revolting in the world is justice separated from charity."[20] In *The Jews* (1583), a work itself highlighting the issue of persecution, Garnier submits that "God always prefers clemency to justice," while in book 10 of *Paradise Lost* (1667), Milton writes: "Yet I shall temper so Justice with mercy."[21] Such sentiments underpin Camus's *chronique judiciaire,* as will be confirmed later. Yet in the context of such crises as that prevalent in Kabylia, to appeal to charity for an antidote to the social injustice at issue cannot suffice since, as Tanju Tuzun rightly observes, "to relieve human misery in this way actually undermines human dignity."[22] While immediate relief aid is unavoidable to alleviate the clear humanitarian crisis, such a moral strategy cannot be considered tantamount to justice since it leaves the underlying causes of the issue unresolved. Rather, it is a short-term solution to a long-term problem.

Camus's own poverty-stricken childhood gives him empathy for the victims of social injustice and the recourse to charity is acknowledged, albeit reluctantly: "I do not believe that charity is a pointless sentiment. But I do think that in some cases its results are and so what is needed instead are constructive policies for better living conditions" (*FC,* 1:291). In an article in which he bears witness to the distribution of "New Year couscous" to the local poverty-stricken people (*FC,* 1:240–42), Camus pays tribute to Mme Chapouton, "in her role as a woman"—an image drawing on the compassionate, healing properties of the female stereotype—dispensing "charity which is so indispensable and so helpful" (*FC,* 1:242). But his long-term moral strategy is clear: "we must recognize that the role of all of us ought to be to render this charity unnecessary" (*FC,* 1:242). As we will clarify later when his *chronique judiciaire* is under consideration, Camus's concern for sociopolitical justice at *Alger républicain* becomes more outspoken when he finds himself directly confronted with the human face of colonial injustice. Correspondingly, witnessing for himself the "remarkable and bitter sight" (*FC,* 1:241) of food distribution to the poor of Algiers, he once again momentarily relaxes his nonconfrontational stance toward the colonial authorities: "I have to say . . . that I have never seen a European population as destitute as this Arab population—and that really must be due to something" (*FC,* 1:242). Just as in "Misery in Kabylia" Camus portrays the human tragedy of a community where even the most basic of human rights is denied, so in his report on the "New Year couscous" he highlights the human misery resulting from the social injustice intrinsic to colonialism.

This last point is further verified when, in the Kabyle inquiry, Camus draws attention to the injustices inherent in grain distribution organized by the *caïdat,* a French-controlled but Algerian-run system of administration which "has only very distant links with democracy" (*FC,* 1:320). As he observes, the impartiality of the *caïdat* is consistently compromised by ulterior motives: "the choice of beneficiaries of the distributions is most often left to the arbitrary judgment of the chief or local advisers who are not necessarily independent" (*FC,* 1:291).[23] Thus, in Tizi-Ouzou, Camus relates how wheat was allegedly withheld from those Kabyles voting for the nationalist PPA while, elsewhere in Kabylia, the quality of grain actually distributed was so inferior that it was even rejected by the local livestock (*FC,* 1:291–92). To these manifestations of *caïdat* mismanagement it should be added that the so-called "charity sites," set up in certain *communes* with a view to alleviating social destitution through a system of paid labor, similarly betray a propensity for exploitation by local colonial administrators (*FC,* 1:292–93). The key point here is that by highlighting what he calls "this policy of adopting the worst possible line in order to attain one's own ends" (*FC,* 1:292), Camus takes a significant step forward in his understanding of the necessary principles of social justice. The reasons for this are twofold. First, his contact with the *caïdat* and other local officials raises his awareness of the issue of racial persecution perpetrated by a prejudicial system operating under the guise of a moral practice. Secondly, this behavior draws attention to the abuse of power and authority as such, a matter to which Camus remains sensitive in his concern for justice, as his exposition of local municipal misrule would further reveal.

This last point is borne out by Camus's treatment of Mayor Rozis in the pages of *Alger républicain.* A figurehead of the local authority and a man with an insatiable appetite for power and authority, Augustin Rozis embodies everything Camus's liberalist morality instinctively rejects.[24] Consisting of former military men whose extreme right-wing policies did little to curb the glaring inequities in the local social system, Rozis's regime campaigned rigorously against initiatives such as the Blum-Viollette Bill and the *Office du Blé*.[25] Moreover, the mayor himself violated his position as municipal leader by consistently beating his townspeople with the stick of civil persecution. Rozis, then, stands accused of perpetrating both social and political injustice, in that he not only blatantly breaches his own position of privilege to yield social destitution among the local community, but also puts his own interests before those in his political care. It will be recalled from chapter 2 that Rozis had also been responsible for the ban put on *Revolt in Asturias* in 1936, and so it seems reasonable to suggest that when, in autumn 1938, Camus once more crosses swords with the mayor (this time in *Alger républicain*), he injects an added dose of venon to his revelations concerning Rozis's conspiratorial empire.

Indeed, although Camus in *Alger républicain* was not alone in raising questions as to the accountability of the Rozis administration—*L'Écho d'Alger* and *La Lutte sociale,* notably, also raised questions to this effect (cf. *FC,* 1:149–52)—his own exposition of the corruption and abuse of municipal power manifested by "this ridiculous character who is becoming obnoxious" (*FC,* 1:171) is particularly striking and tenacious. The gratuitous dismissal by Rozis of the unionist Zittel in November 1938; the mayor's arbitrary decision in the following month to suspend over one hundred and fifty workers in a ruse to recoup lost monies (*FC,* 1:175–77; cf. *FC,* 1:161–64); his vindictive reprimand of a small group of employees "guilty, not of having been on strike on November 30, but of having had the intention to be on November 29" (*FC,* 1:171); his subsequent refusal "without any sign, not to say of the law, let alone justice" to reinstate the same workers even though a local council had found in favor of doing so (*FC,* 1:177); and his overt display of cruelty toward innocent victims (*FC,* 2:678–79)—all of these instances bear testimony to the flagrant disregard for civil rights by "the regrettable mayor of Algiers" (*FC,* 1:175) who "stifles the Republic under his kisses" (*FC,* 2:678).[26] Preserving Rozis's own interests at the expense of those of his constituents remains paramount and, in Camus's eyes, the mayor becomes "the little representative . . . of that divine justice which the Old Testament tells us is based on hatred and a mentality of vengeance" (*FC,* 2:682–83). And yet it is once again the human tragedy behind the mayor's "crepuscular justice" on which Camus focuses his attention.[27] His aim is not so much to "make Rozis give in" but to "defend the bread of our friends" (*FC*, 1:177) and thereby draw his readers' attention to "this elementary reasoning which means that seven dismissed employees makes seven starving families and a little more misery in a world in which M. Rozis's friends have already spread so much" (*FC*, 1:173; cf. *FC*, 1:179).

Just as Camus exposes the lack of moral accountability on the part of colonial administrators in "Misery in Kabylia," so he draws attention to the abuse of political power and authority in his revelations surrounding Rozis's municipal misrule. In both cases, it is with the *victims* of the injustices in question with which Camus remains primarily preoccupied. Calling, in the Kabyle inquiry, for a policy of relief aid conforming to the principles of fairness and disinterestedness, he is determined not to exacerbate existing injustice by sanctioning the use of morally unscrupulous methods: "For if there be charity, at least let it not be done on the cheap" (*FC*, 1:292). Yet whatever the immediate beneficial effects of charity, Camus makes it clear in the same article that "policies which would meet both the hunger and the dignity of the Kabyle people" would be needed in the longer term (*FC*, 1:292). Social justice, after all, requires not only the alleviation of destitution, but also, and more fundamentally, the implementation of appropriate socioeconomic legislation to curb poverty at the source. Economically, Kabylia is an impoverished region, with local industry depleted by the capitalist *gros colons;* politically, the Kabyles are a disfranchised people, removed from the rights of French citizenship so that they have no constitutional means by which to seek moral redress. For Camus, the crux of establishing long-term sociopolitical justice in Kabylia lies in the extent to which economic and political power are restored to the local community: "if anyone can improve the fate of the Kabyles, it is first of all the Kabyles themselves. . . . From now on, it is possible for the Kabyles to prove themselves in administrative matters" (*FC*, 1:320).

There is a clear link in Camus's reasoning between the reduction of poverty and the increase in local economic and political accountability. The measures he calls for in the Kabyle reports to alleviate destitution bear testimony to his faith in liberal democratic principles as a foundation stone for social harmony engendering, in turn, human prosperity. First of all, he demands appropriate and inclusive electoral representation to promote "at the heart of the Kabyle region a kind of little federative republic inspired by the principles of a really profound democracy" (*FC*, 1:323). Secondly, he appeals for legislation to reduce unemployment and encourage local industry, thus ensuring for Kabylia "an increase in economic value, the benefit of which would return to us some day" (*FC,* 1:327). Thirdly, he calls for the replacement of Kabylia's "palaces" by the building of "lots of schools which are sound and simple" to allow greater access to education and subsequent professional opportunities for local children (*FC,* 1:312). Finally, he would like to see the relaxing of immigration laws to encourage geographical mobility in the region (*FC,* 1:328). Certainly, Camus does not have a monopoly in demanding such action—local syndicalist movements had (in vain) long since campaigned for as much across the province.[28] However, what needs to be stressed here is that, in this proactive moral stance, Camus's concern for justice is now clearly developing into that of a *social reformer* as he engages in campaigns to change the status quo *on someone else's behalf.*

Justice on Trial

A further and important illustration of Camus's reformative justice on behalf of persecuted and oppressed social categories within colonial Algeria is provided by his *chronique judiciaire* at *Alger républicain.* A first point of interest regarding this aspect of his journalism, in which Camus engages with morally suspect legal procedure and matters pertaining to the institution of colonial justice, is that his concern for justice is rather more explicit here than in other areas of his apprenticeship. This significant change of emphasis can be explained due to the fact that, when entering the courtroom, Camus comes into direct contact with individuals mercilessly caught up in a morally dubious legal system. (It goes without saying that *The Outsider* provides a fictional representation of this experience.)[29] Whereas in "Misery in Kabylia," for example, Camus witnesses the effects of colonial injustice, the causes of which are "distilled" in the quest for reformative justice, his *chronique* is an altogether more focused moral platform on which to expose the infringements of civil rights, deliberately perpetrated by fellow human beings out of political self-interest. Or, as Denis Salas puts it, the colonial justice system in which Camus now finds himself embroiled is "neither more nor less than a machine which dispenses penalties according to the interests of a caste of colonists."[30] The young journalist is all the more outspoken when he sees for himself how the injustices inherent in the local institution of justice result in wanton suffering among the local community.

Particularly telling is the case of Michel Hodent (*FC,* 2:363–412). A local civil servant suspected by his superiors of anticolonialist sympathies, Hodent was arrested in August 1938 and imprisoned pending trial, which was called for early the following year. A victim of alleged administrative malpractice "that no pieces of evidence, apart from injustice and hatred, can substantiate" (*FC,* 2:372), this *petit bourgeois* quickly becomes an important symbol for Camus, representing as he does a human individual struggling to preserve his dignity and civil liberties in the face of a monolithic state apparatus in which, using Hodent's own words, "the rich *colons* have all the rights, they do whatever they like . . . it's always been like that and nobody cares."[31] One only has to glance at some of the headings and subheadings of Camus's three-month campaign on Hodent's behalf—"The Hodent Case or the Whims of Justice" (*FC,* 2:369); "Justice judges," "Justice goes back on its decision," "Justice considers itself" (*FC,* 2:369, 371, 372); "The Hodent Case or the duplication of abuses of power" (*FC,* 2:373); and "Will we let the scandal be sealed?" (*FC,* 2:379)—to appreciate the candid nature of the journalist's concern for justice in the Hodent case.[32] As he makes clear in an open letter to the governor general published in *Alger républicain* on January 10, 1939, "the case which we are today taking to heart . . . is crucial, because it is a complete injustice. It is urgent because it has not stopped being an injustice" (*FC,* 2:364–65).

Commenting on Camus's response to the Hodent affair, the editors of *Fragments d'un combat* remark that "justice takes on a mythical and sacred value for the writer" (*FC,* 2:537). Indeed, in Camus's eyes, the figure of Hodent embodies the cause of Justice itself, with its supposedly disinterested honesty and unimpeachable integrity. Correspondingly, for Camus, Hodent's trial comes to represent an acid test of moral accountability in local judicial practice: "If justice has got it wrong, it must recognize that. . . . It is not the appearance of justice which needs rescuing, but justice itself. And as paradoxical as it might seem, it can be a good thing for justice that judges may sometimes get confused" (*FC,* 2:379–80). Significantly, in his demands for "complete justice" (*FC,* 2:378) and "total justice" (*FC,* 2:381) by which to rectify the "profound injustice" (*FC,* 2:376) of the Hodent case, Camus anticipates the campaign for what, writing in *Combat* at the time of the purge in France, he would envisage as a perfect criminal justice system (although, in the case of the purge, as we shall see in chapter 6, he would also have to grapple with the morally complex issue of historical responsibility.)

Totally supporting the cause of civil rights in his defence of Hodent and recognizing that "all the signs of injustice, contradiction, shortcoming and eagerness to punish are brought together in this case" (*FC,* 2:367), Camus is at pains to draw attention to the injustices inherent in the local institution of justice.[33] Yet, in thus highlighting the internal deficiencies of the judicial process, Camus does not level criticism at the governing authorities as such. As Salas rightly observes, "in spite of everything, a certain trust toward this colonial justice system remains. No trace of what we might call a defense of disagreement shows through these articles. At no moment does Camus question the legitimacy of the courts. In these articles, we find no denunciation of class justice which would have made him an enemy of the people."[34] Rather, in keeping with both his proactive moral stance and his reluctance to engage in political vendettas, he appeals to reason as he tries to convince the ruling colonists that a miscarriage of justice has occurred in the Hodent case. Demanding the acquittal of "an innocent man, . . . defiled in all his human feelings" (*FC,* 2:376), Camus focuses, then, on the human indignity at issue, *not* on the underlying political scandal, so that the trial is represented as a matter of conscience: "we will see, then, if the scandal will be sealed or if there are people to be found in this country to give meaning to the words justice and humanity" (*FC,* 2:380; cf. *FC,* 2:396). Certainly, Camus makes the point (for it is doubtless his own belief) that "no human form of justice can compensate for the humiliation inflicted on an innocent person" (*FC,* 2:373) but, in announcing the news of Hodent's eventual exoneration, he remains optimistic in his conviction that rectitude will ultimately prevail: "He is today regaining, in the eyes of the world, a dignity which he had never lost. That is nothing in relation to what has been taken away from him. But there comes a time always when injustice is forgotten" (*FC,* 2:411).

If the Hodent case raises Camus's awareness of the social injustice of the local judicial process, then that of the so-called "Auribeau Arsonists" (*FC,* 2:511–23) confirms for him the conspiratorial nature of a colonial authority masquerading as an ethical system. The case involves a group of Algerian agricultural laborers implicated by their governors in a crime of arson after having exercised their democratic right to protest against unfair wage thresholds. Camus severely reprimands as "monstrous" (*FC,* 2:517) and "odious" (*FC,* 2:521) the "verdict, the cruelty of which is without precedent" (*FC,* 2:514) from "a trial begun without any evidence" (*FC,* 2:513) and resulting in the workers in question being condemned to a combined total of sixty years' forced labor. Once again, it is the human tragedy behind this "intolerable and deeply appalling case" (*FC,* 2:513) that Camus spotlights: "Before the case, the families of these men knew destitution; they now know hunger" (*FC,* 2:521). In his conviction that he "can give no more significant a conclusion to [his] protest than by drawing a picture of the families that the accused have left behind them" (*FC,* 2:521), Camus goes on to list the degrading effects of the court's decision on the families of those indicted (*FC,* 2:520). Moreover, such degradation is compounded by the fact that it stems from a state of affairs which was *already* counter to the principle of a minimum standard of justice at the work place: "And, to tell the truth, this punishes them for having earned 4 francs a day for years and for one day having dared to say that this wage was not suitable for human dignity" (*FC,* 2:513). Adding insult to injury, the judgment passed on the alleged arsonists amounts, then, to a flagrant breach of justice which Camus finds intolerable: "faced with this denial of justice, we see wretched people who, for a lifetime, have worked for insulting salaries and who are sent to the penal colony without scruples. If ever an injustice was glaring, and a judgment appalling, it is very much those" (*FC,* 2:520).

It is even more apparent in the affair of the so-called "Auribeau Arsonists" than in that of Michel Hodent preceding it that the accusations brought against the workers spring from *political* motives, a fact not overlooked by Camus in his coverage of the workers' appeal.[35] The alleged act of arson, so the "official" argument runs, was the work of a band of men "who wanted to take their revenge on their class enemies, the colonists" (*FC,* 2:515), following the outbreak of a domestic strike over wage levels. However, revised rates of pay had already been negotiated for those workers by the time of the supposed incident and so the claim that the laborers acted out of revenge is a curious one indeed. Rather, it seems more likely—and this is certainly Camus's reading of the events—that the accusation was contrived by the colonial authorities as a way of repressing what was, in effect, a demonstration of fundamental civil rights, as the workers demanded the economic power to which they were democratically entitled. The mechanics of the case are conveniently expressed in the subheading of Camus's opening article: "The story of a crime, or how a crime is devised for the needs of a charge" (*FC,* 2:512). Indeed, in comparison with the Hodent incident, in his reports on the "Auribeau Arsonists," Camus is much more unashamed to deal with the political dimension of colonial injustice, exposing as he does the retributivist mentality behind "*a politically-charged accusation,* where innocent people have become arsonists" (*FC,* 2:513; my italics). Condemning the prevarications of the allegations made against the accused as "the most certain sign of injustice and lying" (*FC,* 2:513), he does not hesitate to bring to light the corruption of a case in which political vengeance is substituted for dispassionate judgment: "what do likelihood, truth or justice matter here? It was about punishing. And that duty has been accomplished with all due recklessness" (*FC,* 2:520).

We need to pause for a moment at this point in order to consider a key development that is now emerging from Camus's understanding of justice at an institutional level: the *appropriateness* of sanction. As *The First Man* would later testify, punishment can either be "just" or "unjust," depending on its relation with the original misconduct. Jacques Cormery finds himself on the receiving end of both varieties. On the one hand, M. Bernard's reprimand of his pupil by means of the much-feared yet universally respected "sugar cane" "was accepted without bitterness, . . . because the teacher was absolutely fair" (*FM,* 118); yet, on the other hand, the "slap, with full force" (*FM,* 132; translation amended), later inflicted on Cormery by the curate, is deemed both unfair and demeaning and, as such, inherently unjust. Such punishment as that of the alleged fire-raisers of Auribeau is likewise morally unacceptable, in that it is clearly disproportionate to the crimes allegedly committed (*FC,* 2:515).

As in other areas of his *Alger républicain* journalism where Camus seeks to safeguard fundamental human rights through the implementation of a minimum standard of justice, his moral stance in relation to the local institution of justice is marked by the need not to allow the rush to judgment and punishment to transgress a basic moral threshold or "limit." Illuminating in this light is an article originally published on the front page of *Alger républicain* on December 1, 1938, entitled (and the phraseology is worth noting) "These men wiped from humanity" (*FC,* 2:358–63). Aboard the convict ship *Le Martinière* with its "distinctive and unusual merchandise" (*FC,* 2:358), Camus witnesses at first-hand the inhumane treatment of the (mainly Arab) captives facing embarkation in the name of colonial justice. Reporting the spectacle for his *Alger républicain* readership, Camus points up the degrading effects of the convicted prisoners now deprived of their humanity. He highlights, for instance, the "smell of solitude and despair" and the "feeling of neglect" emanating from the vessel's "shameful and pitiful cargo" (*FC,* 2:359, 362), and he draws attention to "the muffled and raucous sound rising on and off from the depths of the hold, like inhuman breathing" (*FC,* 2:359). The sight of such degradation, which Camus would apparently never forget, overwhelms the young journalist's humanist instincts, so much so that when one of the captives actually attempts to communicate, he finds himself paralyzed by his conscience and momentarily desensitized: "I leave. I know that there are other holds, other hands on the bars, other expressionless eyes. But that is enough. On leaving, one of the men asks me in Arabic for a cigarette. I know that the rules are against this. But what a pathetic response to someone just asking for a sign of support and a human gesture. I did not respond (*FC,* 2:361).[36]

Commenting on this article, André Abbou highlights how the young journalist "trembles in front of the need for fraternity of these men."[37] It is surely significant that as he watches the vessel preparing to cast off, Camus once again makes reference to the Arab who had asked him for the cigarette, as if castigating himself for his earlier inability to offer such a humane gesture to one so much in need (*FC,* 2:362). In a perceptive reading, Christine Margerrison argues that Camus's insecurity in evidence here is deflected on to the inquisitive "elegant ladies" (*FC,* 2:362) which he singles out for reprimand, "for, with these ladies, curiosity must not take away a feeling that it is embarrassing to have to remind them of and which is called decency" (*FC,* 2:362).[38] The representation of colonial power is perhaps unwittingly evoked here by Camus with the image of the "elegant ladies" casting a metaphorical judgment over Arab inferiors. For Margerrison, this female stereotype in Camus's report performs a healing role and "functions as a safety-valve through which he can safely vent his own emotions."[39] Margerrison perhaps places too much emphasis here on what is, after all, a passing comment in Camus's article, the main emphasis of which is to draw attention to the plight of the prisoners whose insuperable torment is offensive to the notion of a minimum standard of justice, an *injustice* to which the young reporter is very acutely sensitive: "It is not a question of pity here, but of something completely different. There is no more despicable sight than to see people reduced to an inhuman state" (*FC,* 2:362).[40] Whatever the crimes of those incarcerated aboard *Le Martinière*—and Camus is careful not to pass judgment on the prisoners, such sentencing having supposedly already been administered (*FC,* 2:362)—the justice meted out to the Arab captives is construed as a brutal instrument of reprimand with little, if any, moral accountability. And, as Camus's concession "I am not very proud to be here" (*FC,* 2:360) reminds us, what is at issue here is the whole question of colonial justice to which Camus himself, as a French Algerian, is inescapably tied.

Further confirmation, if it were needed, that colonial justice in Algeria transgresses basic human rights and degrades human dignity in its rush to judgment is provided by Camus's exposition of the systematic corruption brought to bear in the judicial *modus operandi* of the "Auribeau Arsonists" case. That the sentence passed on the workers is done so "in the name of the French people" (*FC,* 2:521)—a phrase recycled in *The Outsider* (*TRN,* 1201; *TO,* 107)—once again highlights the fact that what Camus is actually dealing with here is the contentious issue of institutionalized justice in colonial Algeria. As we have already seen in relation to the Hodent case, in this system dispassionate judgment is compromised by politico-ideological prejudice. Just as Hodent becomes a victim of morally flawed legal processes, so the alleged arsonists are prevented from exercising their right to be treated fairly in the eyes of the law due to the partisanship of the local judicial apparatus. Camus is adamant that the workers' appeal should be heard "in the context of a more real sense of justice" provided by an independent court of law (*FC,* 2:522), and he pulls no punches in exposing the "outrageous methods" (*FC,* 2:516) used for incriminating purposes.[41] As he chillingly observes at one point, "water, electricity and whips do not secure half-confessions, but full confessions" (*FC,* 2:519). News of the failure of the appeal, which Camus greets as "a sealed injustice" (*FC,* 2:523), only incites him to "restore justice" (*FC,* 2:519). To this end, Camus calls for judicial reform which he now formulates explicitly for the first time: "it would be pointless to put human stupidity in the dock and to defend a lost cause. It is more urgent to think about reforming threatened freedoms and lives that are doomed to destitution. We should not be content in stopping there. And after so many protests, all in vain, we still have a case to win: that of reform" (*FC,* 2:523).

An important observation to be made in relation to Camus's *chronique judiciaire* generally, representing as it does a crucial link in the chain of his preoccupation with justice at *Alger républicain,* is the emerging significance there of the relationship between justice and freedom. As we shall see later, this issue would go on to underpin Camus's postwar morality, but in each case he contends at *Alger républicain,* there is an unresolved tension between the two concepts. We recall that in *The Outsider,* Meursault comes to recognize that the suppression of one's individual freedom can be upheld as a way of apportioning justice (*TRN,* 1181; *TO,* 80). However, this idea needs to be qualified by the point that to remove one's freedom without at the same time securing justice makes a mockery of both ideas. As Camus later insists with regard to revolutionary protest, freedom can only be morally justified when it guarantees justice (and vice versa); to pursue one without the other (and, in the context of criminal law, to deny freedom without the guarantor of justice) almost invariably results in sacrificing ethics for the sake of ideology. The fact of the matter is that, in the cases of Michel Hodent and the alleged arsonists of Auribeau (and, albeit less overtly, in the report aboard *Le Martinière*), the right to personal freedom is removed for what are morally dubious motives. Yet these motives claim to uphold the institution of justice in Algeria. In his *chronique,* Camus exposes the blatant disregard for civil liberties that transpires in the name of justice. In so doing, he draws attention to the discrepancy between, on the one hand, the respect for basic human rights and, on the other hand, the system regulating interpersonal morality in the province. Although, as Parker rightly notes, Camus is now becoming aware of the need to delimit the notions of justice and freedom in the interests of social happiness, the young journalist is not yet in a position to formulate the necessary criteria on the basis of which an appropriate equilibrium between the two conflicting ideals can be developed.[42] Indeed, it is interesting to note that in his campaigns against human rights violations at *Alger républicain,* Camus gives precedence to the standard of justice in his view that "freedom is only a part of justice and demanding justice means demanding it entirely" (*FC,* 2:369). The need to *reconcile* the two notions as a blueprint for interpersonal morality only becomes a real issue for Camus when his concern for justice is confronted with the complex forces of history.

In his response to the human experience of colonialism at *Alger républicain,* Camus consolidates his concern for sociopolitical justice by taking issue with human rights violations. Appealing to common human decency in the quest for a basic threshold of justice by which to safeguard human dignity, regardless of racial or religious differences, he thereby provides a possible way out of moral adversity. And, as Abbou notes, "the number of deceptions that the writer decided to denounce demonstrates how much importance he attached to issues of justice and how much energy he knew how to find in order to face up to them, without caring for his health and his safety."[43] The human indignity Camus witnesses in his professional capacity ignites his quest for justice at *Alger républicain* and bears testimony to his undeniable commitment to human solidarity. Accordingly, the idea of justice as guardian of rights now comes strongly to the fore in his moral sensibility. Safeguarding this position leads Camus into the role of social reformer where he maintains his priority of putting practical objectives before theoretical deliberations, much in keeping with the view that "progress is made every time a political problem is replaced by a human problem" (*FC,* 1:335).

All of this raises an interesting issue regarding the wider picture of the writer at this time, for there is a curious discrepancy between the Camus of *Alger républicain* and the Camus of imaginative writings such as *A Happy Death,* a project in which he was also engaged while working for the newspaper. In the words of Philip Thody, "it is one of the paradoxes of Camus's early career that the man who, to judge by his first literary essays, was completely uninterested in social and political matters and apparently unable to believe in moral values, was also intensely preoccupied with justice."[44] It is as though, campaigning for justice at *Alger républicain,* Camus is instinctively drawn toward a scale of moral values, although such values are not yet supported by any theoretical or philosophical rationales. As the editors of *Fragments d'un combat* put it, Camus's moral stance at *Alger républicain* is bound up with "thinking determined by concrete issues, based on common sense and the passionate desire for justice" (*FC,* 2:227). However, the true nature of Camus's preoccupation with justice in respect of Algeria does not become entirely clear until it is situated against the contemporary sociopolitical backdrop of the province. In order to assess fully the resonance of his views on justice in the Algerian dimension, we now need to turn our attention to Camus's attitude toward the political structures of colonialism.

4
The Challenge of Colonialism

> I have a long-standing relationship with Algeria which will probably never end and which prevents me from being completely clear-sighted toward it.
>
> —Camus, *Essais*

CAMUS'S PREOCCUPATION WITH SOCIOPOLITICAL JUSTICE WHILE working for *Alger républicain* has so far been studied principally in terms of his recognition of, and responses to, the human experience of perceived injustice in colonial society. As we have seen, Camus consolidates his intuitive moral sensibilities by formulating a minimum standard of justice, whereby civil liberties and the basic right to human dignity can be acknowledged and safeguarded in the face of adversity. We now need to turn our attention to his views on justice in relation to the political structures of colonialism, with particular reference to Algeria.

In order to appreciate the essence of his conception of justice in connection with Algeria, an understanding of the dilemma facing Camus with regard to colonialism must be established. As we have already seen, the young Camus was broadly sympathetic to the Arab cause, campaigning as a communist in the mid-1930s not only on an antifascist platform, but also for anticolonialism. Indeed, according to Amar Ouzegane in a testimony part of which was cited earlier, Camus at that time gave precedence to the latter crusade: "Before joining the Communist Party, Camus was close to the cause of Algerian nationalism. . . . And, to be more precise, it is through conversations with Camus that I discovered . . . that he really was an activist, a truly sincere activist, and that he had understood the nationalist problem. . . . I considered him to be like the Communists and Arabized Europeans who had accepted and become identified with Arabs and Algerians and who thought that the struggle for Algerian independence came before the struggle against fascism in Europe."[1]

Be that as it may, it is important to recognize that in contrast to that of, say, Sartre, Camus's "anticolonialism" was actually far from clear-cut, since to sever all ties with the mother country was, in his view, tantamount to inflicting injustice on to the majority of (French Algerian) settlers (including his own family) who, "poor and without hatred, have never exploited nor oppressed anyone" (*E,* 897).[2] As such, they are deemed to have the historical right to reside in the province.[3] Equally, however, Camus was well aware of the social injustice of the colonial system in respect of Algeria's Moslem majority and he remained acutely sensitive to the oppression of the province's indigenous population. In this last respect, to borrow the phraseology of Susan Tarrow, Camus represented "a constant thorn in the flesh of the colonial administrators" in Algeria.[4]

In effect, then, as he matures to the role of crusading journalist, Camus, "a European in an Arab world,"[5] finds himself caught in a double bind: on the one hand, he endeavors to render justice to the local population of Algeria by campaigning to eradicate discriminatory practices from the province; yet, on the other hand, he is conscious that the preservation of his own identity as a French Algerian (and, as such, a representative of the colonial system his liberal instincts require him to dismantle) depends on the continuation of the status quo. Thus "torn between loyalty to his community of origin and his sympathy for some of the demands made by the Arab nationalists," Camus's developing concern for sociopolitical justice now has to contend with a set of historical circumstances from which he cannot fully detach himself.[6]

Colonial Anxiety and Journalistic Conventionality

Belonging to the family of "professional journalists" (*E,* 1565), Camus subscribed to what, writing in *Combat* on November 22, 1944, he would call the "duty to think and to be scrupulous which must be that of all journalists" (*E,* 268). Accordingly, in a series of articles written around the time of the Liberation of Paris, originally published in *Combat* and subsequently incorporated into the first of the three collections of *Actuelles* (1950) under the banner of "critical journalism" (*E,* 261–68), Camus stages a campaign for "a clear and virile press, with respectable language" (*E,* 264).[7] This, he hoped, would result in the demise of "appeals to this feather-brained shopgirl sensitivity" (*E,* 265) which had characterized so much of the press in France during the inter-war years.[8]

As "the honest newspaper of honest people" (*FC,* 1:93), *Alger républicain* was itself partisan to the cause of a genuinely informative press. Announcing the arrival of the new title on January 29, 1938, *La Lutte sociale* had proclaimed that "*Alger républicain* . . . will set out to provide its readers with true and complete news, drawn from the best sources, with a resolute concern for honesty and objectivity" (*FC,* 1:91). In addition, it promised that the newspaper would fight vigorously "against biased or incorrect news which at the moment represents the most effective measure of those opponents of democratic thinking and social progress" (*FC,* 1:91). This appeal to professional standards in deference to democratic responsibility finds concrete expression in Camus's own contributions to *Alger républicain,* although the issue of journalistic etiquette here is intricately bound up with the ambivalence surrounding the paradox of Camus as a *petit Blanc* writing for what was effectively an anticolonialist newspaper in Algeria.

Speaking with Nicola Chiaromonte in 1948, Camus explained how his initial interest in journalism had stemmed from an inner need to channel into the public domain some of his own instinctive reactions to perceived injustice. In keeping with his pragmatic realism, these reactions lacked a conceptual focus at the time: "I was a journalist because, when I got up in the morning and read the paper, there were pieces of news in it that made me mad. I wanted to express my anger as clearly as possible, but I was unable to do much more than that. I certainly didn't have a theory, much less a comprehensive ideology. I didn't want to go beyond the limits of what I was sure of."[9] Given its independent status, *Alger républicain* enabled Camus to "express [his] anger" in a relatively unrestricted context, a point singled out by the apprentice himself in contemporary correspondence with Jean Grenier: "I am doing some journalism (at *Alger républicain*)—dogs run over and reports—some literary articles as well. You know better than I do how much this job is deceptive. But I am nevertheless finding something in it: an impression of freedom—I am not constrained and everything I am doing seems to me to be full of life" (*Corr,* 33).

Yet in apparent accordance with the newspaper's "resolute concern for honesty and objectivity" highlighted above (*FC,* 1:91), the Camus of *Alger républicain* actually imposes on himself a number of restraints and regulatory standards bound up with his own ideal of journalism, "one of the finest [professions] I know," he later concedes to *Caliban,* "because it forces you to think about you yourself" (*E,* 1565).[10]

Evidence of this journalistic etiquette, an issue curiously overlooked by commentators, is particularly to the fore in "Misery in

Kabylia." As we saw in the previous chapter, in that series of articles Camus refrains from apportioning blame for the injustices he so vividly portrays, ostensibly on the ground of professional protocol: "My role is . . . not to look for illusory people who are responsible. I find no taste in the job of accuser. And even if I felt inclined to be so, many things would stop me" (*FC,* 1:334). Elsewhere in the series, phrases such as "I am attacking no one here" (*FC,* 1:280); "I would not like to adopt an aggressive tone" (*FC,* 1:295); and "I am going to present, without adding any comments" (*FC,* 1:295) likewise demonstrate a Camus who is concerned not to be *too* judgmental as he seeks to "put right the injustice" (*FC,* 1:334) of the region. As he states in one of a series of articles reporting a mysterious gas explosion in Algiers in December 1938—articles attesting, incidentally, to Camus's considerable talent as *fait-diversier* (*FC,* 1:185–208)—"our duty as informant is not to take responsibilities into account" (*FC,* 1:201).

On the one hand, by thus attributing an element of professional decorum to his own experience of journalism, Camus is responding to the potential charge of compromising his sense of duty toward his readership (i.e. that of providing dispassionate reporting of matters of public interest) in the heat of a given moment. Indeed, such self-regulation on Camus's part bears testimony to the high regard he holds for, and the intellectual commitment he invests in, this new-found profession. On the other hand, it can reasonably be argued that his self-imposed nonjudgmental stance adopted at *Alger républicain* conceals the apprehension behind what, at the end of his Kabyle inquiry, Camus calls "[the] anxious conquerors that we are" (*FC,* 1:336). It is no coincidence that this last expression would figure in an article written by Camus and published in *Combat* on May 23, 1945 (*CAC,* 530) as part of a wider series of reports on the ongoing Algerian problem. There, following on from his 1939 appeal to the colonizing Europeans in Algeria to "try to win forgiveness for this fervor and need for power" (*FC,* 1:336) responsible for the continuing persecution of the *indigènes,* Camus looks to "the wisdom . . . offered by the Arab civilization" (*CAC,* 530) as a means by which to "clarify a situation blurred by blindness and prejudice" (*CAC,* 530).

David Walker has demonstrated how the issue of colonial anxiety here is intricately linked to the whole question of what he calls "the tragedy of Europe grappling with its demons."[12] Susan Tarrow, supported by Bernard-Henri Lévy, shares the opinion that "Misery in Kabylia" exposes Europe's downside when she states that the survey stands as "a lasting indictment of colonialism and racist oppression."[13] Yet while I cannot disagree with the view that the concessions Camus makes to colonial malaise distinguish his Kabyle reports from other contemporary investigations written from the perspective of the mother country, as we have already seen, the series does not amount to a denunciation of the colonial system as such.[14] The fact of the matter is that, in "Misery in Kabylia," the link between *describing* the social injustice endured by the *indigènes* and *accounting for* its causes—colonialism's exploitation of dependence—remains rather opaque.[15] Or, to put the point another way, Camus's standard of sustained objectivity at *Alger républicain* becomes the mechanism by which to divert attention away from the contentious issue of colonial injustice.

Further support for this last claim is provided by Camus's coverage of the sheikh El Okbi's trial in June 1939 (*FC,* 2:413–510). An influential member of the *Association des Ulemas,* El Okbi's denunciation of Franco-Arab assimilation embroiled him in a complex case of murder, racism, and politics devised by the colonial administration in Algeria.[16] Interestingly, Camus's account of the affair is marked throughout by a strange, detached attitude, a stance which conveniently diminishes the need to expose the key point at issue of an authority overtly putting political self-interest before dispassionate legal processes.[17] During "the sequence of debates" ["le film des débats"] of the El Okbi proceedings (a phrase frequently used by *Alger républicain*'s *chroniqueur,* which, in the original French, evokes the theatricality of the case in general), Camus remains impassive and aloof. He feels unable to penetrate the character of the El Okbi enigma, as the following extract from correspondence with Grenier confirms: "The El Okbi case was fascinating. For the most part, the sheikh's friends and enemies acted on political motives. But he himself effortlessly remained *above it all.* It would indeed be desirable to 'know him.' But I think the matter impossible. On two or three occasions, El Okbi showed me a certain affinity. But even in these expressions, where ordinarily I had the best chance of *meeting* him, he behaved in a manner which was unfamiliar to me" (*Corr,* 35).

While I do not propose to dwell on the matter unnecessarily here, two observations are worthy of mention in respect of the El Okbi case.[18] The first is that Camus would base parts of the infamous courtroom drama in *The Outsider* on his exposé of the sheikh's trial (*FC,* 2:546; cf. *Corr,* 212).[19] The second is the rather curious point that Camus himself later insisted on the presence of El Okbi when, in January 1956, the then journalist from *L'Express* delivered his well-intentioned yet ultimately unrealizable "Appeal for a Civilian

Truce in Algeria."[20] This last observation testifies to the fact that there *was* a certain affinity between the two men later, if not at the time of the El Okbi trial itself. Be that as it may, what needs to be stressed here for present purposes is that Camus's objective stance in this and other aspects of his *Alger républicain* journalism can be interpreted as a kind of subterfuge by which to conceal the tension between his own (culturally privileged) identity as "a French Algerian writer" and his deep-rooted sensitivity to the victims of colonial injustice.[21]

Camus's concluding remarks to his Kabyle inquiry are also noteworthy in respect of this propensity to subvert the injustice intrinsic to colonial rule: "if the colonial conquest could ever find a justification, it is in so far as it helps the conquered people to keep their distinctive character. And if we have a duty in this country, it is to allow one of the proudest and most humane populations in this world to remain faithful to itself and its destiny" (*FC,* 1:335–36). By appealing to the principle of racial tolerance in an attempt to assuage (his) colonial fears, Camus draws here on moral rhetoric to produce a response which is curiously incommensurate with the nature of the crisis in Kabylia *as portrayed in the survey itself.*[22] Indeed, it is not a little surprising that, at the end of his inquiry, Camus employs the language of abstract ideals ("keep their distinctive character"; "remain faithful to itself and its destiny") when, earlier in the series, he had been at pains to emphasize that "ready-made ideas . . . become odious when they are applied to a world where people are dying of exposure and where children are reduced to the food of animals without having their instinct which would stop them from perishing" (*FC,* 1:294).[23] In pointing up the potential for creative interpersonal relations in Algeria, an idea explicitly expressed in the above quotation, Camus once again is able to redirect attention away from the reality of colonial oppression toward the prospect of colonial harmony in the province. His plea for a justice predicated on racial tolerance thus offsets the injustice of Algeria's colonial exploitation.[24]

What, then, is clearly emerging from our analysis so far in this chapter is the picture of a young man who, caught on the horns of a dilemma, seeks refuge in the standard of objective and nonjudgmental journalism in his response to the injustices inherent in colonialism.[25] Allied to the notion of French sovereignty in Algeria and thereby to the myth of *Algérie française,* Camus could not expose colonial injustices in categorical terms without compromising his own position as *pied-noir.* To understand the complexities—moral and political—of this position, the whole question of Camus's assimilationist pronouncements on the Algerian problem must now be addressed.

Camus and "The Assimilationist Dream"

Chapter 2 above dealt with the nature of Camus's political commitment in the mid-1930s. As we saw, although the young *adhérent* was broadly sympathetic to Arab nationalism, his personal loyalty toward Arab militants was not converted into lending his public support to a policy of political independence for Algeria. Indeed, while the general lack of relevant writings from this period makes the precise nature of his attitude at the time toward Algeria a difficult matter to pin down, a contemporary text that *is* available clearly reveals Camus publicly endorsing *not* separatism, but assimilation for his homeland.[26]

The text in question is the manifesto of 1937 in which Camus endorses the Blum-Viollette Bill (*FC,* 1:143–44), a plan proposing to grant to some 20 000–30 000 indigenous Algerians—the professionally educated minority most likely to instigate a nationalist insurrection in the province—full French citizenship and voting rights without, in return, having to renounce their Islamic identity.[27] Although welcomed by liberal nationalists such as Ferhat Abbas, these proposals were rigorously rejected by extremists like Messali Hadj, who viewed them as "a new instrument of colonialism aimed at dividing the Algerian people, by the usual French method of separating the élite from the masses."[28]

Perceived as "a great hope among the Arab communities" (*E,* 951), the Blum-Viollette project was greeted by Camus as "a stage in the full parliamentary emancipation of Moslems" (*E,* 1328). For him, the measures constituted "a bare minimum in the work of civilization and humanity which must be that of the new France" (*E,* 1329).[29] Deemed "the first step . . . toward the politics of assimilation" (*E,* 951), the Bill was thus seen as the first stage in rendering sociopolitical justice to "a people weakened by unprecedented destitution and bullied by emergency legislation and inhuman laws" (*E,* 1328). The cornerstone of this campaign was the implementation of a democratically accountable means of changing the status quo for Algeria's Moslem communities: "the only means of restoring to the Moslem masses their dignity is to allow them to express themselves" (*E,* 1328). As Camus later insisted in *Combat,* thus exercising one's democratic right to participate in the political process was key to eradicating discrimination from the province: "If the

Arab people wished to vote, it is because they knew that they could secure in this way, by means of the free exercise of democracy, the removal of injustices which poison the political climate of Algeria. . . . it would get rid of everything which keeps them in an inferior situation" (*E,* 952).

It is evident from the preceding comments that Camus's understanding of sociopolitical justice for Algeria is predicated on a Franco-Arab assimilationist perspective. Moreover, in adopting this position, he accepts the perceived moral integrity of the mother country in accordance with the tenets of France's "civilizing mission" (cf. *E,* 950–51). As Alec Hargreaves remarks, Camus makes the presupposition that "the road to justice in Algeria lay in the assimilation of the Muslims into the cultural and political life of the French, which seemed to offer the prospect of equality for all."[30] For Camus, then, assimilation is the means by which to create a culture of reconciliation in his homeland, whereby the injustice of entrenched racial intolerance may ultimately be eradicated. However, such an objective could only be realized if racial stereotypes were mutually rejected, as Camus confirms in a later message, the text of which has only recently been unearthed.[31] Correspondingly, writing in *Alger républicain* on June 11, 1939, he lays claim to a just French government, recognizing the equal worth of citizens regardless of racial background in his quest for Franco-Arab fraternity: "if we really want assimilation, and for this such dignified [indigenous] people to be French, we must not begin by distinguishing them from the French. . . . And my feeling is that it is only then that mutual acquaintance will start. I say 'will start' since, it has to be said, it has not yet been done and because of that can be understood the mistakes of our policies. Yet all that is needed is to hold one's hand out sincerely. But our task is to bring down the walls which divide us." (*FC,* 1:314).[32]

These remarks testify to the importance Camus accredits the principles of tolerance and mutual understanding—principles written into the French Constitution—in his pursuit of sociopolitical justice for Algeria. Yet the campaign for what, elsewhere, he calls France's "policies of friendship and protection with the Algerians" (*E,* 1530) also betrays a certain naïvety on Camus's part, as Hargreaves astutely observes.[33] The fact of the matter is that the assimilationist solution to the Algerian problem is *de facto* based on the assumption that the province's privileged settler community would agree to indulge its colonized subordinates—an unlikely event given what, in "Misery in Kabylia," Camus himself perceives as "the general contempt in which the colonist holds the unfortunate people of this country" (*FC,* 1:298).[34] Indeed, was it not Camus who, writing in *Combat* on October 13, 1944, remarked that "what is called there [Algeria], rightly or wrongly, the colonist mentality has always rebelled against all innovation, even that called for by the most basic justice" (*E,* 1530)? Two examples may be offered in support of this last statement. First, the engineering of elections in Algeria—most notably in 1944 and 1948—prevented Algeria's indigenous Moslems from achieving fair electoral representation even though, as Camus points out, "France's declared aim in North Africa was to open up progressively French citizenship to all Arabs" (*E,* 950–51). With the 1948 suffrage specifically in mind, he would note in *Actuelles III* a decade later that "the faked elections . . . both illustrated the lie and utterly discouraged the Arab people. Until that date the Arabs all wanted to be French. After that date a large part of them no longer wanted to be" (*RRD,* 103).[35] A second manifestation of what, writing in the opening issue of *Méditerranée-Afrique du Nord* in June 1939, Camus calls "the game of antidemocratic forces" (*FC,* 2:528), the artisans of which are "the mayors and colonists of Algeria who have opposed all reform of the indigenous people's status" (*FC,* 2:528), is the Blum-Viollette project itself which was to fall victim to a colonial backlash in early 1938.[36] Once again, the pursuit of a justice for Algeria, based on the principles of fairness and democratic accountability, remained unable to transcend the self-interest of the exploitative *gros colons* who, Camus is reported to have maintained, "wanted that the only law be theirs."[37]

Despite the swing toward self-determination in Algerian popular opinion, Camus continued (at least in public) to pledge his support to the politics of assimilation.[38] He perceived the rise in nationalist sentiment in Algeria as little more than a protest against the mother country's failure to abolish discrimination in the province by means of politico-economic reform. He could conceive of justice for Algeria only with reference to France's so-called "higher purpose." Thus, in *Alger républicain* on August 18, 1939, he avers that "the only means of checking Algerian nationalism is to eliminate the injustice from which it springs" (*FC,* 2:531). This, he maintained, would involve examining the demands of Algeria's indigenous Moslems "in a spirit of generosity and justice" (*FC,* 2:531)—a further reference to the perceived moral probity of the mother country.[39] In a similar vein, insisting that "in Algerian politics, it is true that a promise that is not kept wreaks more havoc than a flat refusal" (*FC,* 2:527), he interprets Hadj's 1949 electoral successes not as a statement of nationalism proper but as a protest vote over the failure of the Blum-Viollette Bill (*FC,* 2:526–29).[40] As an article, signed "Antar" and attributed to Camus by the editors of *Fragments d'un combat,* lamented on April 24, "by voting as they have done, Moslem electors have aimed to express their dissatisfaction and deep disillusion" (*FC,* 2:589). Later, in *Combat,* he would alert his metropolitan French readership to the disenchantment of "this people [who] seem to have lost faith in democracy, a caricature of which has been presented to them" (*E,* 952). Camus does not disguise the need of the mother country to recognize her own responsibility in the matter: "I read in a morning newspaper that 80% of Arabs wanted to become French citizens. On the contrary, I will sum up the present state of Algerian politics by saying that they really used to want this, but that they no longer do so. When people have lived for a long time on a hope, a hope which has been denied, they turn away from it and lose all desire. That is what has happened with the indigenous Algerians, and we are primarily responsible" (*E,* 950).

Yet if Camus thus professed to understand the reasons behind the Arab nationalist mentality in the province, the precondition of his reply to the "Algerian problem" remained the continuation of French occupancy in the province. For him, the European settler population was, in the words of Emmett Parker, "simply one of the given factors; to remove a part of the population, either Moslem or European, was no solution."[41] Respecting the Arab right to self-determination and the historical demands of the *pieds-noirs* are not mutually exclusive ideals for Camus, a position later clarified in the "Avant-Propos" to *Actuelles III:* "I believe in a policy of reparation in Algeria rather than in a policy of expiation. . . . there will be no future that does not do justice at one and the same time to the two communities of Algeria" (*RRD,* 87).

Based, then, on the principle of racial equality, Camus's vision of sociopolitical justice for Algeria is an *inclusive* moral concept, or what Denis Salas calls "this common measure between people brought together by the common good."[42] However, as Alec Hargreaves rightly observes, "if Camus's commitment to the idea of assimilation was the product of an unusually well-intentioned disposition, by comparison with most pieds-noirs, it also reveals his underlying inability to genuinely think beyond the mental horizons of his French background. Assimilation assumed that French civilization provided the ideal cultural model to which non-Europeans should aspire; its implementation necessitated French political control. The moral validity of French colonization was thus assumed to be self-evident, and the need to continue French rule was equally beyond question."[43]

There is a cultural arrogance here on Camus's part which Hargreaves is justified in highlighting. Undercutting his comment in the 1956 "Appeal for a Civilian Truce in Algeria" that he never distinguished Algerians along racial lines (*E,* 998; *RRD,* 101), Camus's faith in the *Union française* clearly classifies him as what both Raymond Aron and Albert Memmi independently refer to as "a good-willed colonizer."[44] Camus does, in fact, remain alienated from Algeria's Moslem communities by a cultural divide that he makes no concerted effort to bridge, a fact prompting Hargreaves to suggest that he was "far more narrowly attached than he liked to think to the pied-noir community in which he had been born and brought up."[45] Indeed, neither did Camus speak any Arabic nor did he have any specific understanding of Moslem cultural traditions. "No one is more closely attached to his Algerian province than I," he would later note, "and yet I have no trouble feeling a part of French tradition" (*RRD,* 172).[46] From this, it seems reasonable to deduce that, unable to penetrate the Moslem consciousness, Camus's campaign for social and political justice on behalf of Algeria's indigenous population was, in essence, that of a cultural outsider. As the Algerian writer Mouloud Feraoun puts it in correspondence with Camus dating from 1957, "I still regret with all of my heart that you do not know us sufficiently and that we have no one to understand us, to make ourselves understood and to help us to get to know ourselves."[47]

This absence of a cultural intersection between Camus and Algeria's Moslem communities occasions Azzedine Haddour, justifiably, to level against the writer the charge of moral impropriety, in that while claiming to help the *indigènes,* Camus himself is deemed to retain a safe distance from the realities of colonial life in the province.[48] His paternalistic attitude toward Algeria prevents Camus, Haddour contends, from addressing the fundamental inequalities inscribed in colonialism: "Camus's univocalised views about justice cannot surmount the injustice of the Algerian colonial situation and of a people held in conquest by the French."[49]

Justice and the "Second Conquest" of Algeria

In the light of Haddour's remarks, it will be useful to cast a critical eye over Camus's articles on the Algerian problem, written for the metropolitan French readership of *Combat* in order to "reduce a little the incredible ignorance of metropolitan France as far as North Africa is concerned" (*E,* 941). The result of a three-week fact-finding mission in Algeria, these reports were published in *Combat* between May 13 and June 15, 1945 and (with some modifications) would also be incorporated into the 1958 *Actuelles III* (*E,* 939–59). For present purposes, the significance of these texts is twofold. First, they confirm Camus's inability to purge himself of his colonial fetters in responding to the ongoing crisis in his homeland. Secondly, they testify to the significance, in relation to Algeria, of the standard of justice, an ideal which in Camus's eyes now takes on a legendary character by virtue of its relationship with the *grande nation française.*

It is perhaps important to stress that very little had actually changed in Algeria in socioeconomic terms by the end of the Second World War and that this unfortunate state of affairs proved instrumental in propelling the nationalist impetus across the province. If anything, as Camus explains in his opening article to the 1945 series, matters had grown even worse by the close of the hostilities: "The Algeria of 1945 is plunged into an economic and political crisis that it has always known, but which had never reached this degree of intensity. In this admirable country that a spring without equal at the moment covers with its flowers and its light, people are starving and demanding justice. This is suffering which cannot leave us cold, for we have known it" (*E,* 943).

The parallels between the *Combat* reports and those of the earlier "Misery in Kabylia" cycle need not delay us here; suffice it to say that the Ariadne's thread of Camus's position in both instances was politico-economic reform based on assimilationist principles.[50] Also, in 1945 as in 1939, the issue of moral responsibility is strongly evident since "when millions of people are starving, it becomes everyone's business" (*E,* 947). In the short term, the Camus of *Combat* appeals for "large-scale policies of importation . . . pursued . . . with the utmost vigor" (*E,* 947) to curb the immediate crisis. In the longer term, acknowledging that after having implemented such policy "there will still be everything to do" (*E,* 950), he highlights the need for France to "finally devise policies" (*E,* 950) by which to replace the injustice of "Algerian politics distorted by prejudice and ignorance" (*E,* 950). France, in Camus's view, must now choose "if it considered Algeria to be a conquered land whose subjects, deprived of all rights and rewarded with some extra duties, must live in our absolute dependence, or if it grants a fairly universal value to its democratic principles so that it may extend them to those populations for which it is responsible" (*E,* 951).

It is interesting to note that in "Misery in Kabylia," Camus had appealed directly to France for the financial support necessary to make good the democratic reforms for which he calls: "I know that, for all that, funds are necessary. . . . I quite understand when people tell me 'there is no reason why it should be the colony and the colonists who pay.' And I quite agree with them. Let us not count on this effort from the colonists as we are not sure that they want it. But if it is claimed that metropolitan France should give this help, then we agree two times over. For, by the same token, it is being proven that a system of government which distinguishes between Algeria and France brings France nothing but unhappiness. And the day when interests will be merged, we can be sure that hearts and minds will not be far behind" (*FC,* 1: 332–33).[51]

Targeted as they were at a metropolitan French readership, Camus's 1945 *Combat* articles on the Algerian crisis were more likely to affect the colonial conscience than the "distant" Kabyle reports of 1939. As such, they added a heightened sense of urgency to the moral responsibility of the mother country in respect of her Algerian protectorate. And yet, whatever the moral pitch of the survey, it is clear from an examination of the language used in the 1945 series that Camus's proposed solution to the problem remains that of a *petit colon:* "If we wish to save North Africa, we must show the world at large our resolve to make France known through its best laws and its most just people. . . . Let us really convince ourselves that in North Africa as elsewhere nothing that is French will be safeguarded without safeguarding justice. . . . It is the infinite force of justice, and that alone, which must help us to reconquer Algeria and its inhabitants" (*E,* 959).

These remarks confirm two important factors in respect of Camus's response to the growing crisis in Algeria. First, the fact that, in his view, "it is *the infinite force of justice, and that alone,* which must help us to reconquer Algeria," and that "in North Africa as elsewhere nothing that is French will be safeguarded *without safeguarding justice,*" bears testimony to the significance of justice as a moral concept in Camus's thinking here. Indeed, bound up with the notion of French sovereignty, the standard of justice now takes on something of a mythical quality as he appeals to what Paul Siblot and Jean-Louis Planche call "an ideal image of France" by which to resolve the contradiction of the mother country's colonial domination masquerading as a civilizing mission. The issues in question would be conveniently expressed in an interview granted by Camus to *Servir* on December 20, 1945: "If, in the years to come, France does not think up important Arab policies, it will have no future. . . . Let France truly establish democracy in Arab countries and it will have not only North Africa with it, but also all those Arab countries which traditionally trail behind other powers. True democracy is a new idea in Arab countries. For us, it will be worth one hundred armies and a thousand oil wells" (*E,* 1428).[53]

A second observation arising from the aforementioned quotation from *Combat* is that the aim to "*save* North Africa" and "*reconquer* Algeria and its inhabitants" verifies Camus's inability to break free from the mindset of a "goodwilled colonizer" in his response to the Algerian problem generally. Indeed, would he not insist from the outset of his 1945 survey that "the French have to *conquer* Algeria *a second time*" (*E,* 943; my italics), and that this "second conquest" (*E,* 943) amounts to "the last chance France has to safeguard its future in North Africa" (*CAC,* 529)? Viewed from this perspective, his call for "policies of friendship and protection with the Algerians" (*E,* 1530) becomes a mere euphemism for continued colonial dependency. Camus's appeal for a renovation of French colonial policy that, he anticipates, would "go to the heart of the matter, that is to say to the political and economic conditions which today render all just solutions impossible" (*CAC,* 576) cannot transcend his own colonial malaise.[54] This claim can be further substantiated with reference to his outlook on the French imperial vision on a more general level: "We will only find true support in our colonies once we have convinced them that their interests are ours and that we do not have two policies: one that would give justice to the people of France and another that would sanction with respect to the Empire" (*E,* 1530).

The point here is transparent. In line with his conviction that "before the world, France's face will be that of its justice" (*CAC,* 467), Camus posits that it is the moral integrity of the mother country (rather than the might of her armed forces) that will secure the future well-being of the colonized states. However, the idea that France's civilizing mission could thus embrace deeply entrenched political prejudices in the colonies smacks of idealism, as Lev Braun rightly acknowledges: "The spreading of French culture in overseas territories was regarded by Sartre and his friends as an imperialistic enterprise. Camus, in all simplicity, regarded it as sharing a common heritage. French culture, in his view, was humanistic before being French."[55]

The pioneering and polemical work of Conor Cruise O'Brien bears out the somewhat naïve approach Camus adopts toward France's civilizing mission to which Braun refers here.[56] Taking Camus to task for allegedly distorting colonial reality in much of his fiction by providing almost no trace therein of an indigenous identity, O'Brien asserts that the author of *The Outsider* "reveals himself as incapable of thinking in any other categories than those of a Frenchman."[57] Referring to an inaugural speech (*E,* 1321–27) delivered in honor of the Algiers-based *Maison de la Culture* in February 1937 in which Camus champions "the image of a lively, multicolored and down-to-earth civilization, transforming doctrines to its image" (*E,* 1325), O'Brien insists that such a vision of Mediterranean collectivism, supposedly transcending racial tension, stems from an essentially French model of culture: "It is quite clear, though never explicitly stated, that his Mediterranean culture is a European one and in Algeria a French one, and that the Arabs who have a part in this culture will have become French Arabs."[58] Subconsciously dominated by a colonial mentality, Camus's imaginative works provide, O'Brien goes on to argue, a vision of the colonial problem from a French metropolitan standpoint. This is a thesis that has also been cogently advanced by Henri Kréa who, with the 1942 masterpiece specifically in mind, suggests that the murder scene in *The Outsider* amounts to a vivid reconstruction of the French assimilationist dream: "When Meursault . . . shoots at 'the Arab,' he magically kills a racial entity which he is afraid of breaking up. This action . . . is the subconscious realization of the obscure and puerile dream of the little white man that Camus never stopped being."[59]

While O'Brien is justified in pointing up Camus's rather romanticized view of colonialism as more a matter of mutual cooperation than political subjugation, one cannot agree with his proclamation that "when a brilliantly intelligent and well-educated man, who has lived all his life surrounded by an Arabic-speaking population, affirms the existence of a form of unity, . . . it is not excessive to speak of hallucination."[60] This remark fails to do justice to Camus's genuine love for his Algerian homeland and underestimates his concern, apparent throughout his lifetime, for the welfare of Algeria's indigenous Moslems.[61] As Mouloud Gaïd testifies, Camus stands as "a passionate defender of social justice" and an individual who "always took the side of the oppressed, and we were the oppressed."[62] And, subscribing to similar beliefs, the late and distinguished Algerian novelist Mohammed Dib recently went so far as to classify Camus "an Algerian writer."[63]

Returning to Camus's configuration of justice predicated on the perceived moral probity of the mother country, a further manifestation of the vulnerable nature of that idea comes in the form of the now notorious nationalist insurrections in Algeria of May 1945.[64]

Marking as they did the failure of assimilation and the start of a new and crucial chapter in the history of Arab nationalism, that would soon spread to other corners of the French Empire, the events of May 1945 betrayed serious moral shortcomings in the mother country's so-called "civilizing mission."[65] Prefiguring the cataclysm of November 1954, the uprisings and subsequent massacres at Sétif, Guelma, and Bône exposed categorically the political self-interest underpinning colonial justice. In such circumstances, the notion of a Franco-Arab *rapprochement* cannot convince since, to use Ferhat Abbas's terminology, "the truth is that between colonized and colonizer, the use of force has ended by setting up an impenetrable barrier. The dialog has become a dialog of the deaf."[66]

Now, it is clear from his contemporary commentaries on the issue that Camus recognized the political repercussions of the 1945 riots and repressions.[67] According to Siblot and Planche, the position he adopted *vis-à-vis* the events constituted "the most clear-sighted and progressive in the French press."[68] Indeed, the "irrational prejudice of racial superiority" (*E,* 590n) at the heart of the matter would even merit a mention in the later *The Rebel.* Writing in the immediate aftermath of the events, he once more appealed to France to counter by moral means the climate of racial animosity in Algeria "in order to avoid an irreparable future" (*CAC,* 531): "This fervor, these wild desires for power and expansion will only ever be excused if we offset them by a scrupulous willingness for justice and an iron dedication" (*CAC,* 530). Thus stemming the tide of racial prejudice was, in Camus's view, critical if France's claim to rectitude was to prevail: "Everything that we can do for *French* and humane truth, we have to do it against hatred" (*E,* 959; my italics).[69] His subsequent ultimatum to the readership of *Combat* would be telling in its prophecy: "At the end of this investigation, I only ask the French people who today know what hatred is: 'Do you seriously want to be hated by millions of people, as you have hated thousands of other people? If yes, let North Africa get on with it. If not, receive these people beside you and make them your equals by the appropriate means' (*CAC,* 532).[70]

Colonialism posed Camus with an insoluble problem. His underlying engagement with social and political justice, by which he sought to "see reduced all the misfortune and bitterness which poisons humankind" (*Corr,* 23), was frustrated, in the face of the colonial power structure, by a set of historical circumstances in which he himself was implicated. While he remained highly sensitive to the abuses of the colonial system and waxed eloquent about individual violations of civil rights, he would not—he *could* not—condemn colonialism as such without compromising his own status as a French Algerian. How far Camus's inability to break free of the colonial and imperialist basic assumptions about cultures like Algeria is based on reasons of self-interest is, however, a moot point. They may simply be assumptions that—for whatever reason—he never questions (or *barely* questions). Indeed, when he expresses fears about his own family, in one sense this can be construed as self-interest and in another sense as the opposite of *self*-interest. Whatever the truth of the matter, it is clear that, unlike Sartre, Camus was apparently never able to think beyond a certain framework, and that framework is associated with a certain "colonialist" mentality. One is, then, rather inclined to agree with Bertand Jakobiak when he expresses the view that Camus remains "a colonizer opposed to certain injustices undoubtedly, but in reality allied to a system that he does not wish to challenge."[71]

With the political processes of colonialism, historical circumstances impact on Camus's moral thinking for the first time. Henceforth, he would have to contend with an increasingly complex international situation which would throw his concern for justice into sharp relief. Indeed, how the forces of history now begin in earnest to impinge on, and come into conflict with, his general preoccupation with justice in the sociopolitical domain comes into sharp focus with regard to what was now happening on the world stage. From the relative isolation of Algeria, Camus was about to be precipitated into the chasm and confusion of global war. How he is forced to adapt his humanist understanding of justice in relation to this completely different set of circumstances will be the subject matter of the next chapter.

5
War

> I began the war of 1939 as a pacifist and I ended it as a Resistance fighter. This inconsistency, for this is what it is, made me more moderate.
>
> —Camus, *Essais*

Justice and the Forces of History

With the prospect of war looming large on the horizon, Camus's preoccupation with justice was about to be immersed in an entirely different set of circumstances to that experienced previously. In Algeria, his various campaigns for social and political justice had been pitched at an essentially *localized* level.[1] His moral stance hitherto had been predicated on purely humanitarian principles and on the assumption that adhering to a basic code of ethics such as that in force in Camus's own locality and endorsed by him—most notably in "Summer in Algiers" (*E,* 72; *SEN,* 86)—was adequate against everyday adversity. As Philip Thody notes, Camus's "complimentary description of the general morality which prevailed among the working classes of Algeria gives the impression that he himself found it sufficient to most of the problems which confronted him in ordinary life."[2] War, however, is not the stuff of "ordinary life" but an "extreme situation" laden with moral complexity, and an understanding of justice based on a rudimentary "highway code" (*SEN,* 86) can no longer be seen as a satisfactory instrument for dealing with it. This fact notwithstanding, as we shall discover, there is a general sense of continuity in Camus's thinking as he confronts the new international situation and the new moral challenges this creates. His view of sociopolitical justice before the war is entirely compatible with that during the war, but changing historical circumstances would now require an extending and reworking of that view in a vastly different (war) context. This precipitation from the relative isolation of Algeria to the throes of a European conflict and its concomitant moral dilemmas would be an unsettling experience for Camus who, once more to cite Thody, was now to be "taken from the world in which social justice could very well find its place by the side of pagan hedonism, and plunged into one where philosophers created injustice and abstract ideologies justified mass-murders and deportations."[3] His response to the cataclysm of war marks, then, an important milestone in Camus's general engagement with justice as a moral problematic, as the forces of history (manifested through the collective experience of war) now impinge in earnest on his moral sensibility.

The Propensity to Despair

Not surprisingly perhaps, Camus was depressed at the prospect of war, noting in *Le Soir républicain* on November 16, 1939, that it represented "the destruction or degradation of all human wealth and values" (*FC,* 2:643). Hitherto responding to perceived injustices primarily as a humanitarian pragmatist, he could come up with little by way of a considered response to events in the period prior to the cataclysm of September 1939.[4] As he admits to Jean Grenier in correspondence dated February 2 of that year, "I understand less and less both domestic and foreign politics. I have a feeling that all this will end in ruin without our even being able to raise our hands" (*Corr,* 34). Later, as Hitler prepared to invade Poland, he concedes to Francine Faure his sense of despair, remarking that "failing a miracle, everything will collapse."[5] Moreover, following the actual outbreak of hostilities, this despondency at the turn of events would find telling expression in the *Carnets:* "They have all betrayed us, those who preached resistance and those who talked of peace. . . . And never before has the individual stood so alone before the lie-making machine" (*CA1,* 78).

Privately, then, the prospect of war frustrates Camus's innate sense of sociopolitical justice in which the safeguard of human dignity is paramount. As he explains to Grenier, he could not accept what he labeled "the show of hatred" without "much heartbreak" (*Corr,* 39, 38). Be that as it may, in his contemporary journalism, Camus maintains a public persona of optimism *vis-à-vis* the "absurd event" (*CA1,* 77), with the notable exception of an editorial published in *Le Soir républicain* on September 17, 1939, bluntly entitled "The War" (*FC,* 2:630–31): "Never before perhaps have left-wing activists known so many reasons to despair. Many hopes and many beliefs have collapsed at the same time as this war. And among all the contradictions in which the world bustles about, forced to lucidity, we are then led to deny everything."[6] These remarks provide potent public expression of Camus's private despondency. As he also notes, "so much effort for peace, so many hopes placed on people, so many years of struggle have ended up in this collapse and this new carnage!" (*FC,* 2:631). With "a sense and taste of inevitability" (*FC,* 2:631), Camus confronts "this mortal hour" (*FC,* 2:631) with a demoralized psychology, such is the enormity of events now overtaking him. He was, to borrow the phraseology of Emmett Parker, "depressed by the complete collapse of all efforts to avert the conflict" and felt betrayed by "the resigned acceptance of its inevitability" by politicians and ordinary people alike.[7]

It is surely significant that "The War" is the only editorial from the time where Camus's private despair permeates his public persona. From this, one could justifiably assume that, in deference to his own journalistic standards identified earlier, Camus consciously maintains a public position of hopefulness at odds with his private inclination toward hope*less*ness. However, basing his remarks on an examination of the writer's notebooks from the time, Steve Robson is right to point out that Camus would seek to rise above this state of despondency, since "to despair was to enjoy a private privilege that he could not allow himself" in the continuing quest for peace.[8] Purging himself of his private propensity to despair was thus imperative if Camus was to assume the public role of moral arbiter and thereby "testify against the intolerable."[9]

How he undergoes this process of personal purging and so moves forward in terms of his concern for justice in the face of international crisis can be illustrated with reference to two of Camus's contemporary writings. First, the unpublished and, as Parker perceptively observes, self-directed "Letter to a man in despair," drafted in the *Carnets* in November 1939 (*C1,* 178–82; *CA1,* 83–85), provides Camus with a virtual arena in which to confront his despair.[10] This imaginary letter—the first in a sequence of such texts—amounts to an experiment in self-conviction on Camus's part, as he seeks to overcome his earlier despondency arising from a situation in which "never before have we been so completely handed over to destruction" (*CA1,* 83).[11]

The language of the "Letter" testifies to what Camus perceives as the ultimate victory of lucidity over despair: "despair is a feeling, and not a permanent condition. You cannot stay on in despair. And feelings must give way to a clear view of things" (*CA1,* 83).[12] Refusing the moral abyss of war is dependent on the individual's capacity to rise above adversity and so find a solution to the crisis through reasonable means—an ability denied those involved in the First World War, Camus contends: "when you really think about it, the men who went off to war in 1914 had more reasons to despair, since they understood things less clearly than we do" (*CA1,* 84). What is stressed in the "Letter" is the idea that war is by no means inevitable if the "certain zone of influence" (*CA1,* 85) available to all is used to champion the cause of the alternative (i.e. peaceful) solution. Fatalism is thus outlawed, replaced instead with a lucid and stubborn attitude in the face of suffering and distress. Camus doubtless has himself in mind when, concluding the letter, he remarks that "war is made as much with the enthusiasm of those who want it as with the despair of those who reject it with all their soul" (*CA1,* 85), a reminder of the earlier concession that war is made with, among other things, "the despair of those who don't want to fight" (*CA1,* 82).

A second text worthy of notice in his attempt to rid himself of his tendency to despair is *The Myth of Sisyphus,* the "philosophical" essay on which Camus was working at the time.[13] Relatively few critics commenting on that text have made direct reference to the link between *The Myth* and Camus's *personal* purging of his despair.[14] In essence an imaginative, lyrical and nonliteral project, *The Myth* amounts to a disclaimer of the propensity to despair, an emotional state which, as well as being projected on to a world conditioned by the absurd, also extends into the realm of Camus's own "intellectual malady" and, specifically, his own despair at the onset of war.[15] As he would elucidate in a 1955 preface to the English translation of the work, "written . . . in 1940, amidst the French and European disaster, this book declares that even within the limits of nihilism it is possible to find the means to proceed beyond nihilism" (*MS,* 7). In terms of the argument formulated in *The Myth* itself, *even if* the world is unjust, the most appropriate and philosophically consistent means of responding to this state of affairs is *not* by the evasive course of self-annihilation (mental or physical), which Camus dismisses as "an escape" (*MS,* 38) denying the truth of the absurd predicament, but by the lucid route of revolt.[16] This last concept, for Camus, represents "a constant confrontation between the human individual and his/her own obscurity" (*MS,* 53; translation amended), which accords "life its value" (*MS,* 54) and "restores its majesty to that life" (*MS,* 54).[17] It is a means by which one can consciously confront one's torment since, Camus contends, "living is keeping the absurd alive" (*MS,* 53), a phrase which brings to mind the earlier comment from *Betwixt and Between* that "there is no love of life without despair of life" (*SEN,* 60).[18] Hence the frustration of an inevitable and brutal destiny is transformed in *The Myth* into a determination to live life in total lucidity without recourse to evasion: "By the mere activity of consciousness I transform into a rule of life what was an invitation to death—and I refuse suicide" (*MS,* 62). The paradox of the absurd becomes, then, the basis for positive action in Camus's eyes by which to promote a sense of human greatness: "There is but one useful action, that of remaking people and the earth. I shall never remake people. But one must do 'as if'. For the path of struggle leads me to the flesh. Even humiliated, the flesh is my only certainty. I can only live on it. The creature is my native land. This is why I have chosen this absurd and ineffectual effort. This is why I am on the side of the struggle. . . . Greatness has changed camp. It lies in protest and the blind-alley sacrifice" (*MS,* 81–82; translation amended).

These remarks highlight human potential within the confines of the absurd predicament. As Henry Amer puts it, "this treatise which begins with a description of a desert ends with a promise of paradise. A purely earthly and human paradise."[19] Rejecting suicide and the temptation of transcendent ideas as a solution to the absurd predicament, Camus refuses to acquiesce in the absurd and thereby maintains his consciousness in the face of moral uncertainty. Furthermore, by thus pointing up the empirical foundation for maintaining the absurd and its incommensurability with an abstract justification for collective values, Camus provides himself with a mental framework in which to situate a prophylactic against war. Here, as elsewhere, Camus substitutes pragmatism for abstraction as the touchstone for action.

A remark made by Camus in the original manuscript of *The Myth,* but which would not be retained in its definitive version, conveniently makes the point on which I want to lay stress with regard to both the "Letter to a man in despair" and *The Myth of Sisyphus:* "It is in the direction of one's illness that the patient finds the cure" (*E,* 1430). By discharging the (i.e. *his*) propensity to despair on to a fictional encounter (in the "Letter") or on to the world at large (in *The Myth*) in an effort to "know whether I can live with what I know and with that alone" (*MS,* 42), Camus reemerges from his earlier despondent state with renewed vigor and lucidity in keeping with his vision of "the absurd man" as "he who is not apart from time" (*MS,* 69). In the words of John Cruickshank, "the myth of Sisyphus means for Camus that the most appalling truths can lose their power over us once we have resolutely recognized and accepted them."[20]

In essence, then, what in the present reading of these texts Camus is doing in the "Letter to a man in despair" and *The Myth of Sisyphus* is to engage in an experiment of "writing the self better," an idea instrumental to autobiographical discourse and which, as we shall see later, can also be applied to *The Rebel.*[21] That such a process ultimately proves successful is confirmed by a contemporary editorial published in *Le Soir républicain* on November 6, 1939, where Camus could write: "The people of goodwill that we are at least wish not to despair and to maintain values that will prevent a collective suicide" (*FC,* 2:723). Admittedly, the precise meaning of the phrase "values that will prevent a collective suicide" remains rather obscure; how, after all, can "values" prevent a "collective suicide" (i.e. war)?[22] But the rallying quality to these remarks is beyond dispute. Indeed, in another essay written during this period, Camus is now clearly upbeat, claiming that "one thing alone can kill the spirit and that is despair which leads to all sorts of submissions" (*FC,* 2:739).[23] At the same time, notes in the *Carnets* from the period attest to his awaking to the reality of international conflict: "There is nothing less excusable than war, and the appeal to national hatreds. But once war has come, it is both cowardly and useless to try to stand on one side under the pretext that one is not responsible. Ivory towers are down" (*CA1,* 80).[24] This psychological shift away from despair toward lucidity reflects, then, Camus's response to the prospect and actuality of war. Against this background, it is now time to move on to examine his views on sociopolitical justice in the new international situation.

"Waging war by peaceful means"

Clamence, in *The Fall,* "used to wage war by peaceful means" (*TF,* 63), a phrase reflecting the irony at the heart of that work's "penitent judge." In keeping with what the editors of *Fragments d'un combat* call Camus's "militant pacifism" (*FC,* 2:615), this same expression may reasonably be attributed to the writer's own initial approach to the onset of war, in that once he has rid himself of the propensity to despair, Camus seeks to maintain a moral momentum even (or especially) in the most immoral of circumstances, as his coauthored and unpublished "Profession of Faith" attests:

> Today, when all parties have failed and when politics has degraded everything, all people have left is the awareness of their solitude and their faith in human and individual values. We cannot make people be just

amidst universal madness. . . . But we can at least force no one to be unjust. Aware of what we are doing, we will reject injustice for as long as we can and we will support the individual against the partisans of anonymous hatred" (*FC,* 2:729).[25]

As is evident from his contemporary pieces for *Le Soir républicain,* what Camus finds repugnant in the Hitlerian incarnation of fascism is the blatant breach of liberalist principles such as tolerance and mutual understanding by "a regime in which human dignity counts for nothing and where freedom becomes a mockery" (*FC,* 2:722).[26] Repudiating "censorship on the mind" (*FC,* 2:749) and "dictatorship, especially on thought" (*FC,* 2:750), he perceives Hitlerism as intrinsically unjust, politically, dissolving as it does in its "will to power" (*FC,* 2:655) the interests of the individual into those of the nation-state: "Authority in Germany puts the national mission which it holds before all concern for freedom, justice, benefit for the people and even simply truth. . . . Under such a regime, there are no citizens, only subjects, whose intelligence and will are molded or stifled" (*FC,* 2:747, 748).[27] As Camus puts it in the heavily-censored "Letter to a young Englishman on the state of mind of the French nation," the desperate nationalism posited by Nazism—a matter given critical attention in the celebrated *Letters to a German Friend*—poses a question targeted at the very heart of sociopolitical justice, "that of domestic freedom" (*FC,* 2:760). It is in this context that the rallying cry, published under the aegis of the newspaper's "War Highlights" on December 17, 1939, should be read.[28] Elsewhere, championing the cause of "human truth, that which shrinks back before suffering and aspires to joy" (*FC,* 2:723), Camus gives voice to the capacity of the human individual to rise above the moral nihilism of the "hitlerian doctrine," that he considers "one of the most abominable forms of *evil* in political thought and in political life" (*FC,* 2:635). Inasmuch as it violates the international code of conduct by championing power at the expense of reason and truth, Hitler's *realpolitik* poses not only a severe political threat, but a moral one too.[29] Struggling, as the aforementioned "Profession of Faith" put it, "against the systematic use of hatred and oppression" (*FC,* 2:727), Camus seeks to preserve the ethical principles fundamental to the progress of humankind.

Analyzing Camus's early wartime journalism through a moral lens, whatever the rallying qualities of his articles, one of the problems he faces in his initial response to the hostilities lies with his difficulty in understanding what is happening, so overwhelmed is he by the changing nature of the international context in which his concern for justice is now operating. Indeed, the way in which Camus writes about these events (for instance, when he calls Nazism "one of the most abominable forms of *evil*" or, again, when he highlights the need to "maintain values that will prevent a collective suicide") is such that he tends to substitute moral rhetoric for political analysis, a contention further borne out by his later description of fascist coercion as "the poison which impregnated Hitlerism."[30] This tendency to bypass political analysis in his use of moralizing language in his early journalistic pieces on the war perhaps explains why, writing in *Le Soir républicain* on November 6, 1939, Camus is reduced to the simplistic and undefined dichotomy of justice (peace) and injustice (war): "Obstinacy in injustice can only be defeated by obstinacy in justice" (*FC,* 2:721). A demand made *in the name of justice,* Camus's appeal for a "'lasting and strong' peace" (*FC,* 2:721) is how he seeks to maintain a moral momentum in the face of the cataclysm: "And we demand that this clearly defined peace, overwhelmingly approved by the French people, be put forward without any let-up, even in the middle of fighting, every day if necessary" (*FC,* 2:721). Camus is here using the standard of justice as a means by which to resist what, in the *Carnets,* he calls "the reign of beasts" (*CA1,* 79) and "the hatred and violence that you can already feel rising up in people" (*CA1,* 79): "We continue to believe that the system of aggressions has spread because it has not been set against that of justice" (*FC,* 2:650). In *Le Soir républicain* on November 11, 1939, Camus catalogs the salient features of his vision of (political) justice, that are now threatened by the "aggressive dictators" (*FC,* 2:643): "Respect for democracy, individual freedom, dignity and welfare, within the armed nation, military apparatus and hostilities. The will to spare the population as much as possible from the absurdities and horrors of the military and aggressive system, to give people back their homes, the warmth and work of peace, the opportunities and joys of an open, independent and fraternal humanity" (*FC,* 2:638).

In his initial response to the war, then, Camus links the concept of political justice with the pursuit of a solution to the crisis in which bloodshed can be spared and human values promoted. This vision derives from his conviction that "you can change everything, you can stop the war and even maintain peace, if you want to do so intensely and for a long time" (*CA1,* 80).[31] This last statement provides another example of Camus's tendency to draw on abstract ideas in his response to the political reality. Once more, he takes refuge in a moralizing language to shield him from engaging in the moral complexities raised by the war. The fact of the matter is that the Camus of *Le Soir républicain* rejects the use of violence in the name of justice and perceives peace as the only solution available. The quest for justice and the quest for peace are, for Camus, "anxious sisters who could not live without one another" (*FC,* 2:743). In a variant of this last formulation published in *Alger républicain* on August 28, 1939, he had stated that "democracy and peace are like two anxious sisters. We must not separate their destinies" (*FC,* 2:695). The interchange here of justice and democracy confirms Camus's liberalist morality in the face of political authoritarianism.

The dialectical relationship of justice and peace pursued by Camus in *Le Soir républicain* calls for two further comments. The first is that in his overriding quest for peace in respect of the particular threat posed by Hitler's Germany, Camus can perhaps be charged with ignoring related injustices elsewhere. Indeed, given his general empathy with the victims of perceived injustice, it is not a little surprising that, upon the outbreak of the conflict, he makes no concerted effort to campaign on behalf of those in either Poland or Czechoslovakia or, indeed, the Jews themselves, all of whom were facing persecution by the fascist war machine. Was it that Camus felt that by securing peace, such injustices would naturally be redressed? Perhaps. The second point is that for all his "*desire for peace*" (*FC,* 2:638), Camus remains committed to the (democratic) values underscoring his understanding of political justice; to compromise such values would, in his view, be "shameful and dangerous, contrary to the principles of freedom and justice and peace" (*FC,* 2:645).[32] Rather, stemming from his conviction that "peace cannot function without justice" (*FC,* 2:743), Camus's objective is to secure what he labels "lasting, full and real peace, 'true peace' as we call it" (*FC,* 2:643). This quest is pursued in accordance with, but not to the detriment of, democratic responsibility—hence Camus's remark on the eve of the outbreak of hostilities in Europe that "we are arming ourselves in order to defend democracy" (*FC,* 2:694). The key point here is that, whatever his hopes for peace, the young *Soir républicain* reporter is *not* a pacifist in the true sense of the word. As he had remarked in *Alger républicain* as early as March 14, 1939, "we do not have *the right* to be passive when we are defending justice and the law."[33] Later, in conversation with Nicola Chiaromonte, he likewise observes that "the greatest political achievement I can conceive of today would be that we succeed in letting the younger generation grow up in peace. *And may I insist that I am not a pacifist.*"[34]

Camus's commitment to the cause of peace based on and immersed in justice in the face of the nascent political crisis in Europe finds further concrete expression in his appeal for an immediate truce—a means, that is, by which to "speak the language of understanding and not that of cannons" (*FC,* 2:648).[35] Camus hoped that such a truce would form the basis on which to instill a justice of international tolerance (*FC,* 2:650). For months following the outbreak of hostilities, he waxed lyrical about the prospects of an international brotherhood, "made by peoples' freedom and mutual aid on the basis of their ethical and legal equality, their mutual tolerance and understanding and their great human compassion" (*FC,* 2:651). What Camus is advocating here is a new social order, regulated by and for human beings. Or, as he puts it in *Le Soir républicain* on December 15, 1939, a "Society of People" in which individual freedom coexists with social justice (*FC,* 2:648–49).[36] (Such an idea was clearly beyond the reach of the contemporary League of Nations, and Camus does not shy away from exposing the internal inadequacy of that supposedly powerful organization [*FC,* 2:649]).[37] Confronted with the extremity of war, Camus is now beginning to formulate a blueprint for an international code of conduct, founded on the principles of equality and fairness across nations and which, in the postwar "Neither Victims nor Executioners," he would elaborate further by championing the politics of collective enterprise in the pursuit of a justice of international democracy.[38]

Be that as it may, Camus's hope of finding a rational solution to the escalating crisis in Europe smacks of idealism in a context increasingly conditioned by belligerency. In accordance with his resolve to "start by looking for what is valid in every human being" (*CA1,* 80; translation amended), Camus had written in *Alger républicain* on August 28, 1939 that "peace is a rational thing [that] can only rise up in reason" (*FC,* 2:695). Yet how was one able to muster sufficient strength of spirit to believe in the power of reason when the apparently *irrational* forces of fascism were currently undermining such beliefs across Europe? Moreover, could the use of violence be morally justified in responding to these forces? As the *drôle de guerre* in France made way for the Nazi *Blitzkrieg,* liberal humanist thinkers like Camus were soon forced to grapple with such contentious questions. Already, while still in Algeria, Camus himself had not been afraid to advocate the use of force if the call for peace failed to convince (*FC,* 2:644). But the crystallization of this mentality would come into effect only when Camus had left his Algerian homeland and experienced for himself the reality of war. Only when in France, himself in the midst of the crisis, would he recognize the need to reflect on, and ultimately to endorse the use of, *a priori* unjust means in the pursuit of a just end.

JUSTICE AND MORAL NIHILISM

"Living means not being resigned," Camus remarks in "Summer in Algiers" (1937–38) (*SEN,* 90). This stoical attitude is given potent expression in *The Myth of Sisyphus* where, faced with an absurd universe and in the aim to "live *without appeal*" (*MS,* 53), the writer explores whether the human individual can transcend the status quo and so create his/her own *raison d'être.* Or, as Camus later puts it in *Combat,* "it is a question of knowing . . . whether people, without the help of the eternal or rationalist thought, can themselves create their own values" (*E,* 312).[39] It is, then, in the issue of how to define value in an absurd universe that Camus is primarily interested in *The Myth* and *not* the Absurd as such. As he points out in a review of Sartre's *Nausea [La Nausée* (1938)] published in *Alger républicain* on October 20, 1938, "establishing the absurdity of life cannot be an end, but only a beginning. It is a truth from which all the great minds have started. It is not a discovery which interests, but the consequences and rules of action that are drawn from it."[40]

It is with his concept of revolt that Camus hopes to respond to the moral nihilism of the "absurd sensitivity" (*MS,* 10). I shall not revisit that territory here, since it has been so well covered by others.[41] Suffice it to say, in his response to the "confrontation between the human need and the unreasonable silence of the world" (*MS,* 32), Camus advocates the ethic of revolt that, he holds, arises from "the mere activity of consciousness" (*MS,* 62) to restore a sense of grandeur to a world devoid of meaning (*E,* 139; *MS,* 54).[42]

There is little need to elaborate on this point. Camus who, from the outset of his intellectual inquiry, maintained that "the world is beautiful, and outside it there is no salvation" (*MS,* 100), posits that the only way of living within an absurd universe is to transform the inhumanity of the world into one where the human being forms the focal point. Camus's introductory remarks to the chapter entitled "Absurd Freedom" in *The Myth of Sisyphus* conveniently sum up the matter: "I don't know whether this world has a meaning that transcends it. But I know that I do not know that meaning and that it is impossible for me just now to know it. What can a meaning outside my condition mean to me? I can understand only in human terms. What I touch, what resists me—that is what I understand" (*MS,* 51).

The repetitive use here of the first person subject pronoun is indicative of the "solitary" nature of the book in general. Indeed, Philip Thody is quite right to judge *The Myth of Sisyphus* (along with, one might add, *The Outsider*) as "the high-water mark of his [Camus's] meditation on man *as an individual.*"[43] Yet, to judge from contemporary entries in the *Carnets,* while still working on *The Myth,* Camus was also beginning to think in terms of a *collective* ethos—hence the connotation of the word "Idiotic" at the end of the following note from March 1940: "More and more, when faced with the world of people, the only reaction is one of individualism. Human beings are an end unto themselves. Everything one tries to do for the common good ends in failure. Even if one likes to try it from time to time, decency demands that one does so with the required amount of scorn. Withdraw into oneself completely, and play one's own game (Idiotic)" (*CA1,* 96; translation amended).[44]

In keeping with these remarks, mention may usefully be made here of Camus's (albeit not yet clearly defined) empathy with those volunteering for the French Army upon the outbreak of hostilities in Europe: "I enlisted on September 3, not because I 'joined up', but . . . because I felt solidarity with all the poor souls who were leaving without really knowing why" (*Corr,* 38). I am rather inclined to agree with Laurent Martin when he submits that Camus "enlisted above all in order to support the people who were mobilized. He did not enlist in order to wage war against Nazism."[45] As such, although one must of course await the publication of *The Plague* for Camus to champion the cause of human solidarity in the face of adversity, there is evidence to suggest that the writer was not unaware of such an ethic, nor of the value of collective revolt, even before his participation in the French Resistance.[46]

Indeed, in view of the above, one can argue that the defeat of France in June 1940 merely consolidates what was in any case a psychological movement on Camus's part toward human solidarity. Specifically, the French collapse raises Camus's awareness of the notion of nationhood. In conversation with Carl Viggiani, he remarks that "we must struggle to avoid war with our nation. When it is here, we must support our nation."[47] It is surely significant that he should identify with the French nation at a moment when its republican values are most threatened by fascist oppression. According to Charles Poncet, "he who had felt Algerian during all his youth told me as having felt French the day of the Germans' entry in Paris."[48] Camus himself, moreover, indicates as much when, in a marginal note for *The First Man,* he writes: "discovery of the Fatherland in 1940" (*FM,* 162n).[49]

Camus's experience of the absurd and his discovery of human solidarity and the ethic of (collective) revolt are germane to his moral reflections once he is himself in the midst of war.[50] By the time of the debarkation of Allied forces in North Africa in November 1942, he would be landlocked in France, separated from his family and beloved Algeria. The extent to which he was traumatized by this series of events should not be underestimated and some illustrations of Camus's contemporary frame of mind are worthy of mention here. Visiting him in his rural retreat of Le Panelier in 1943, Blanche Balain reports that she found her friend "changed by the hardships of the Occupation" and "a more anguished man than the self-confident Camus of the Équipe rehearsals."[51] His notebooks and private correspondence from the time bear out such testimony: "A life of silence and despair that the whole of France endures while waiting for something to happen" (*CA2,* 16); "I am starting to get fed up with overcast skies and tracks covered with snow. I have never thought so much about light and heat. It really is exile" (*Corr,* 86; and cf. *Corres,* 119–21).[52] These ideas would be given dramatic expression in *The Misunderstanding* (1944), as Camus readily acknowledges (*TRN,* 1793). *The Plague,* too, reflects Camus's wartime psychology, with the themes of separation and landlocked claustrophobia at the heart of that book.[53]

It is clear from the above remarks that France's humiliating defeat, coupled with the subsequent establishment of Pétain's Vichy administration, had a demoralizing effect on Camus. The fall of France alerted him to the seemingly defenseless nature of French republican ideals—ideals on which he had predicated his quest for sociopolitical justice in the early stages of the hostilities—in the face of Nazi *realpolitik.* In a sense, his own alienation from those he loved was reflected in France's contemporary moral vacuum. While the absence of textual evidence from the time makes Camus's precise attitude toward Vichy a difficult matter to pin down, Roger Quilliot makes the point that "he reacted vigorously against the spirit of resignation that Vichy maintained; in it he saw a form of stagnancy, of nihilism and evidence that our civilization needed to be reformed" (*E,* 1462). And he goes on to acknowledge that: "A Resistance fighter could not record his or her feelings in writing. The silence of the *Carnets* is hardly surprising; we would find the contrary suspicious" (*E,* 1462). However, McCarthy surely has a point when he questions why, given what we can reasonably assume to be his anti-Vichy convictions, Camus did not make more of the "ample opportunity" he apparently had to join the French Resistance in 1941.[54] As it is, he would not contribute to the movement until late 1943/early 1944, at which point he joined forces with the clandestine "Combat" organization where, according to Jacqueline Bernard, he played "a decisive role at a time when every meeting and every initiative entailed serious risks."[55] Whatever the truth of this, Camus himself maintained that his own activities in the French Resistance paled into insignificance when compared with those who, like René Leynaud, made the ultimate sacrifice for the cause (*E,* 297–98, 1472–79; *RRD,* 31–38).[56] A significant feature of the Resistance for present purposes is that it poses the problem of the use of *a priori* unjust means (human sacrifice) in the pursuit of a just end (political transformation), a problem with which Camus would now be forced to grapple. To see how his understanding of sociopolitical justice evolves to accommodate this problem, an analysis will now be made of his wartime writings, that attempt to formulate a moral rationale by which to justify the use of violence in the face of Nazi terror.

As we have seen, Camus entered the war rejecting killing in the name of his idea(l) of political justice. However, as a member of the French Resistance, he would now seek a moral justification for precisely the same idea. A turning point in Camus's moral sensibility, the writer's participation in the Resistance alerts him to what Emmett Parker calls "the seeming contradiction . . . of having to justify the taking of human lives in the name of a justice founded on the inviolability of human life."[57] Yet the *Combat* journalist does not question the moral accountability of the Resistance movement as such, and there is doubtless substance in Jonathan King's claim that "rather than always seeing the Resistance for what it was, Camus in a sense projected onto it his own cherished ideas and ideals."[58] Indeed, its own manifest moral and political ambiguities notwithstanding, the Resistance is perceived by Camus as a model of a social order in which individual liberty could coexist with a justice of collective responsibility and where a climate of trust and mutual respect between people transcends the class divide.[59] As he puts it in *Combat* on September 1, 1944, "it really is a new order that is being established. An order where the human face appears in a broad light" (*E,* 1523–24).[60]

Championing the Resistance as "a privileged moment in the long struggle . . . for human freedom" (*E,* 1752) and supported by men and women "mad about freedom and justice" (*E,* 1543), Camus vindicates the Resistance with a clear conscience: "The Resistance fighter bore a grudge against Germany for having responded through crime to their dreams of peace and at the same time made it profit from the memory of these dreams. Yes, if ever there were a sound struggle, it really was that one which was entered into after having shown that it was not wanted" (*E,* 1488). Subsequently, in an unsigned article published in *Combat clandestin* in March 1944 and which can plausibly be attributed to Camus, what is called for is "total resistance" (*CAC,* 124–25) and, more specifically, "acts of sabotage, strikes, demonstrations organized with the whole of France" (*CAC,* 125) which the writer deems "the only ways of responding to this war" (*CAC,* 125).[61] Such a proactive (military) strategy stands in stark contrast to the desire for peace which had underpinned Camus's understanding of justice at the outset of the hostilities. Indeed, it is significant that, in accordance with a contemporary *Carnets* entry highlighting that "duty lies in doing what we know is right and good" (*CA2,* 55), he now interprets *this* course of action as the only morally acceptable one. Obliged to act "in the choice between shame and action" (*E,* 1523), Camus responds without hesistation. When later pressed by Emmanuel Vigerie about the reasons behind his alliance with the French Resistance, he could only explain that his sense of justice and dedication to duty had left him no choice (*E,* 356).[62] Writing to his wife of his act of adherence, he thus notes: "I thought a lot about it and did it in all clear-sightedness because it was my duty."[63]

Forced, then, by changing historical circumstances to modify his response to the war from one of "pacifism" to one of "Resistance," Camus comes to recognize that the quest for justice in the political arena and the use of violence can no longer be regarded as mutually exclusive propositions. Or, to put the point another way, amid the extreme situation of war, abstention is at best expedient and at worst morally indefensible.[64] Camus's criticism in *Combat* on September 17, 1944, of the German people "who refuse to speak out in their own defense" (*CAC,* 196) in the face of Hitler's authoritarianism bears out this logic. However, in his contention that "Camus's decision to join the Resistance seems to have come with the realization that when the forces unleashed by the nihilists inflict widespread death, the only answer is to kill in return," Parker raises a question fundamental to Camus's wartime ethics: what, in a later interview, he calls "the temptation of hatred" (*RRD,* 172), an issue which we must now bring into sharper focus.[65]

It is no coincidence that just as Camus is forced to enter the historical process, so his preoccupation with justice as an intellectual problematic gathers momentum. Noting in his *Carnets* the "attraction which certain minds feel for justice and for the absurdity of its workings" (*CA2,* 2; translation amended), Camus now attempts to theorize his own "attraction" in terms of a moral response to the nihilism of his time, to the "destruction of souls" (*E,* 259) inherent in Nazism. In a context conditioned by intolerance where the rights of the individual are systematically denied in the will to power, Camus voices a determination to preserve what he calls "human greatness" (*RRD,* 30; translation amended). This laudable quest is reminiscent of the philosophy of the "absurd man" from *The Myth of Sisyphus* and is expressed in terms of the human individual's resolve to be "stronger than his or her condition" (*RRD,* 30; translation amended). "And if this condition is unjust," Camus clarifies, "there is just one way of overcoming it, which is to be just oneself" (*RRD,* 30; translation amended).

It is in the *Letters to a German Friend* that Camus attempts to formulate a moral response to authoritarianism and thereby provides a moral justification for the Resistance movement.[66] In a 1945 preface, he describes the *Letters* as a "document emerging from the struggle against violence" (*RRD,* 3), written in order to "throw some light on the blind battle we were then waging and thereby to make our battle more effective" (*RRD,* 3). Camus points up the difference between, on the one hand, the nihilistic passion of Nazism whereby the end necessarily justifies the means and, on the other hand, the mentality of "'we free Europeans'" (*RRD,* 3) for whom the end must remain consonant with the means: "There are means that cannot be excused. And I should like to be able to love my country and still love justice. . . . I want to keep it alive by keeping justice alive" (*RRD,* 5).[67] It is curious that while, in the preface, Camus identifies his terms of reference with the phrase "I am contrasting two attitudes, not two nations" (*RRD,* 3), his attack in the letters themselves is not targeted at "a *Nazi* friend" but, rather, at "a *German* friend." Moreover, there appears to be some inconsistency in these "topical writings" (*RRD,* 3) between Camus's condemnation of his German friend and his association, in the preface, with what he calls "we free Europeans" which, strictly speaking, should include Camus's "German friend"—even though it is clear that this *German* is actually a *Nazi*.[68] I am not suggesting here that Camus is to be charged with ideological uncertainty in his understanding of the contemporary political situation in Europe; rather, my point is that while he is now clearly thinking in terms of national identity, there appears to be some unresolved questions in Camus's reasoning as to the principles determining nationhood. Interestingly enough, although the Vichy regime was an elected constitution and recognized as the legitimate French government by many outside observers—most notably the United States—Camus himself could not accept the legitimacy of the Vichy administration. This mindset suggests that his notion of nationhood rejects the idea of citizenship. Indeed, Camus's position here is not unlike that of De Gaulle himself who called for resistance to Nazism in the name of *la grandeur française,* an idea given concrete expression in *Combat*'s opening "Appeal": "Our best arm is our Faith. . . . Our arm is also the Truth. . . . We shall fight against the anaesthesia of the French people."[69]

A significant feature of the *Letters* is that, driven by "the inspiration of intelligence" (*RRD,* 18), Camus now explicitly uses the principle of *justice* to uphold standards of morality in the face of political tyranny. This is in keeping with his formulations of the concept in *Combat* where, on November 22, 1944, he posits that "justice is at the same time an idea and a warming of the soul. Let us learn how to handle it in its human aspect, without transforming it into this terrible abstract passion which has mutilated so many people" (*E,* 268). Earlier, he had stated that "justice is a matter of judging people by themselves and not by their names or their ideas" (*CAC,* 183) as further testimony to Camus's refusal to allow his morality to be compromised by political indoctrination. What, in essence, Camus is doing here is rehearsing one of his core concerns of the later *The Rebel*—how an ethical equilibrium may be preserved and safeguarded in revolutionary protest—and bases his reasoning on the understanding that the end must not necessarily dictate the means of a given campaign: "We know just how quickly means are taken for ends; we do not desire any old justice. . . . It is about serving human dignity by means which remain dignified in the middle of a history which is not" (*E,* 279).

However, it must be stressed at this point that Camus and his German friend are not totally dissimilar in their outlook. Indeed, starting from the same premise that the world is absurd (*E,* 239–40; *RRD,* 20–21), they are now fighting "for fine distinctions" (*RRD,* 8) against a backdrop, Camus explains to his German friend, of "the constant temptation to emulate you" (*RRD,* 6).[70] He makes clear (and the phraseology is worth noting) that were it not for "a detour that safeguarded justice" (*RRD,* 7), he could very well have followed his erstwhile friend's desperate nationalism, indicative as it is of the contemporary influence of German philosophies of despair.[71] What ultimately separates them is the notion of "a higher love" (*RRD,* 9), reminiscent of Chéréa's desire "to live, and to be happy" (*CP,* 47) in *Caligula* and formulated in the *Letters* in terms of the extent to which moral behavior is deemed worth preserving amid morally contentious circumstances.

To draw once more on *The Myth of Sisyphus,* even if in theory (metaphysically) "nothing is forbidden" (*MS,* 65) in a world in which there are no preconceived values by which to govern behavior, in practice "everything is not permitted" (*MS,* 65; author's gloss). Camus is highlighting here the dangers of philosophical absolutism. Qualifying Karamazov's equivalence ethic, he proceeds from an attitude of "excess" to one of "moderation" in his quest for an antidote to moral nihilism (*E,* 149; *MS,* 65). This reasoning is borne out by the *Letters:* on the one hand, the German friend's pretensions of nihilism amount to a collusion with the absurd (*E,* 240; *RRD,* 21); on the other hand, Camus's affirmation of a moral identity offsets the moral abyss left in the wake of the absurd (*E,* 240; *RRD,* 21; cf. *E,* 228; *RRD,* 11). The dispute is conveniently expressed in a key sequence from the fourth letter which owes much to Nietzschean thought: "Where lay the difference? Simply that you readily accepted despair and I never yielded to it. Simply that you saw the injustice of our condition to the point of being willing to add to it, whereas it seemed to me that human beings had to exalt justice in order to fight against eternal injustice, create happiness in order to protest against the universe of unhappiness. . . . In short, you chose injustice and sided with the gods. . . . I, on the contrary, chose justice in order to remain faithful to the world" (*RRD,* 21; translation amended).

This passage formulates Camus's faith in justice as a concrete moral standard in the face of his German friend's moral nihilism. Steeped in reality, Camus's vision of justice (unlike that of his German friend) is an attainable moral proposition with the human individual as the principal point of reference. Like Caligula, who assumes "the foolish, unintelligible face of a professional god" (*CP,* 41) in his resolve to "follow where logic leads . . . until the consummation" (*CP,* 45), the German friend represents a social system where power is paramount and the human individual a political expedient.[72] Camus refuses to yield to such political extremism and, in his determination to uphold his standard of justice, he is prepared to accept the uncertainty of "disorder" rather than risking the immorality of "injustice" (*E,* 227; *RRD,* 10).

To the "blind anger" (*RRD,* 14) underpinning his German friend's "politics of reality" (*RRD,* 11), Camus opposes, then, "a fierce love of justice" (*RRD,* 21) in which human integrity is sovereign: "I continue to believe that this world has no ultimate meaning.

But I know that something in it has meaning and that is human beings, because they are the only creatures to insist on having one" (*RRD,* 21; translation amended).[73] Whereas the monolithic state mentality of the German friend denies the right of the human individual to self-determination—"you . . . are fighting against everything in human beings that does not belong to the mother country" (*RRD,* 11; translation amended)—Camus himself points up what, elsewhere, he calls "human greatness" (*RRD,* 30; translation amended) and "human salvation" (*E,* 279). As "the man of injustice" (*RRD,* 22), the German neighbor stands accused of sacrificing honor on the altar of political ideology ("you scorned knowledge and spoke only of strength" [*RRD,* 18]), while Camus himself represents those "defenders of the spirit" (*RRD,* 14) who, imbued with justice, are able to rise above moral adversity and thereby resist the temptation to "yield to hatred" (*E,* 1488).[74] This "gamble on the human," to borrow the phraseology of Paul Ginestier, finds striking expression at the end of the *Letters* when, spotlighting his former friend's imminent "just defeat" (*RRD,* 24), Camus rejects the lure of hatred in a paean to human probity: "This is why, at the end of this combat, from the heart of this city that has come to resemble hell, despite all the tortures inflicted on our people, despite our disfigured dead and our villages peopled with orphans, I can tell you that at the very moment when we are going to destroy you without pity, we still feel no hatred for you. And even if tomorrow, like so many others, we had to die, we should still be without hatred. . . . we want to destroy you in your power without mutilating you in your soul" (*RRD,* 23).[75]

"That justice exists is the leitmotiv of the letters," notes Germaine Brée.[76] As Camus himself makes clear, the vision of justice portrayed in *Letters to a German Friend* is no abstract ideal; rather, it is a concept steeped in emotional conviction. Moreover, Camus is under no illusions as to the human cost of sustaining such a vision, noting in *Combat* that "once more, justice must be bought with people's blood" (*RRD,* 27; translation amended) and that "sacrifice goes hand in hand with justice" (*CAC,* 390). Justice, Camus insists, is no glorious trophy of war—"seeing beloved friends and relatives killed is not a schooling in generosity," he later explains. "The temptation of hatred had to be overcome. And I did so. This is an experience that counts" (*RRD,* 172)—but a value born of "morning executions and evening death throes" (*CAC,* 186) and one embracing the trials and tribulations of "frenzy, waiting and terror" (*CAC,* 186). Camus's contemporary correspondence with Jean Grenier is equally revealing in this matter, highlighting as it does his discovery of the true meaning of nationhood via the spectacle of selfless sacrifice (*Corr,* 88). And, as he emphasizes in the opening letter to his sometime German companion, it is not in spite of, but because of such sacrifice that justice will ultimately prevail:

> we shall be victorious thanks to . . . that suffering which, in all its injustice, taught us a lesson. . . . It taught us that, contrary to what we sometimes used to think, the spirit is of no avail against the sword, but that the spirit together with the sword will always win the day over the sword alone. . . . We had first to see people die and to run the risk of dying ourselves. We had to see a French workman walking towards the guillotine at dawn down the prison corridors. . . . Finally, to possess ourselves of the spirit, we had to endure torture of our flesh. . . . But we have our certainties, our justifications, our justice; your defeat is inevitable (*RRD,* 7–8).[77]

It should be clear by now that the moral concept of justice is a principle largely unrivaled in Camus's wartime ethics, as expressed in his contemporary nonfictional writings. What he pursues in the *Letters to a German Friend* is "a *just equilibrium* between sacrifice and a longing for happiness, between the sword and the spirit" (*RRD,* 19; translation amended; my italics). In response to the moral nihilism of the German friend, he seeks to "exalt *justice* in order to fight against eternal injustice" (*RRD,* 21; my italics).[78] And, in keeping with his humanist instincts, he chooses justice "in order to remain faithful to the world" (*RRD,* 21). Justice, then, for Camus is a beacon of moral endeavor in the midst of moral nihilism, and it is no coincidence that references to the concept appear frequently in the writer's private notebooks throughout this period. A first note, "*On justice*" (*CA2,* 56), appears in the *Carnets* in November 1943 and is associated with Camus's indictment of Christianity as "a doctrine of injustice" (*CA2,* 56). References relating to the projected "Novel on Justice" (*CA2,* 64) also appear frequently until mid-1945 (cf. *C2,* 127–28, 128, 130; *CA2,* 64–65, 65, 66), but these eventually fade away until almost a decade later, when Camus begins in earnest his preparations for *The First Man.*

Moreover, in *Combat,* justice is championed as "a superior principle" in the name of which social order must be established: "there is no order without equilibrium and agreement. For social order, this is an equilibrium between the government and the governed. And this agreement must be made in the name of a superior principle. This principle, for us, is justice. There is no order without justice. . . . It is not order which strengthens justice, but justice which lends certainty to order" (*E,* 276).

Elsewhere, in remarks which anticipate *The Rebel,* he points up the significance of the concept in terms of revolutionary activity: "A thousand guns pointed at a man will not stop him from believing within himself in the justice of a cause. And if he dies, other just people shall say 'no' until force grows weary. Killing the just person is therefore not enough, it is necessary to kill his or her spirit for the example of a just person renouncing human dignity to dishearten all just people together and justice itself" (*E,* 259).

And, as the Second World War finally comes to an end, in an editorial which Norman Stokle attributes to Camus, the writer spotlights the standard of justice as a principle underpinning social struggle: "Today more than ever, we know that there is only one effective force in this world, which is that of justice. So let us be happy in the justice of our cause, as we have been unhappy for it. Without doubt, nothing will ever be able to compensate for the death and the misfortune of people. But if there is something that can make up for this world of iniquities, it is our struggle toward justice."[79]

The advent of the Second World War marks a watershed in Camus's general preoccupation with social and political justice. Prior to the onset of the hostilities, Camus simply had had neither the occasion nor the incentive to consider how his own ("Algerian") code of morality would work out in times of a collective disaster like the war proved to be. The questions he had addressed concerning the ideal of "justice" during his formative years were different in kind from those that, with the outbreak of hostilities, he now had to address. As we saw, what drives Camus's concern for justice in the first phase of his moral sensitivity is a personal and pragmatic psychology whereby social reformism takes precedence over politico-ideological idealism. Subsequently, with the arrival of war, this proclivity to base his concern for justice on empirical rather than abstract considerations is for the first time frustrated by external forces and historical circumstances which require Camus to rework his views to reflect the new international state of affairs. What is so distinctive of Camus is the fact that he attempts to use the concept of justice as one of the main threads through *both* types of situation. This may or may not have been an intellectually sensible thing to do, but it *is* what Camus chooses to do, and some of the difficulties he experiences in trying to adapt his thinking to the wartime environment necessarily derive from this fact.

In essence, then, while the notion of justice has one distinct set of meanings before the war and a quite different set of meanings during the war, Camus attempts to link the two groups of phenomena and to hang on to the same label for both. As his wartime writings testify, he is now struggling for some understanding of the term that can embrace both his new priorities (how best to uphold standards of morality in morally ambiguous circumstances) and his old ones (safeguarding the fundamental human right to dignity). As we have seen, from the first Camus has a strong feeling that people should be fairly treated. Throughout, he tends not to theorize this concern, preferring instead to take "action" (which includes the writing of campaigning articles) in the name of fair treatment and justice as he sees it. In this way, his early experiences of politics, theater and journalism bear witness to a man engaged in a "person-to-person" response to perceived injustice deriving from a highly compassionate and proactive moral psychology. However, both emotionally and intellectually, the war situation overwhelms Camus and this mindset of a humanitarian pragmatist *en situation.* His first attempt to maintain his concern for sociopolitical justice in the new situation—"militant pacifism" (*FC,* 2:615)—ultimately proves unsustainable, such is the nature of events now overtaking him on the international scale. Admirably and rightly by our standards, he moves to a position of "Resistance" for what are, deep down, the same reasons and the same concerns, but the fact is that he remains rather ambivalent at theorizing what is actually happening. There is, after all, doubtless some substance in the claim that whatever its merits as a rallying cry in the midst of moral crisis, *Letters to a German Friend* is a work written "more from the heart than for the mind."[80] By the same token, Camus's *Combat* editorials have also been charged with tending to deal with emotion at the expense of reason.[81]

Recalling the suffering of the war years in *Combat* at the time of Paris's liberation from Nazi tyranny, Camus remarks that "one cannot always live on murders and violence. Happiness and proper affection will have their time" (*RRD,* 30). And he stresses that the hardship of life under the German Occupation could now serve as a springboard for a national renovation: "These years have not been in vain. The French who entered them with the simple reaction of an honor which had been humiliated leave those years with a higher knowledge which from now on makes them put above everything intelligence, courage and the truth of the human heart" (*CAC,* 142).

Like many of his intellectual contemporaries, Camus hoped that the moral and political standards arising in France from its resistance to the Nazi aggressor could be preserved and safeguarded in the postwar period. Like others, he would join the *Comité National des Écrivains* (CNE), the main objective of which was to prepare people of all political persuasions for the envisaged renaissance of France following the end of the war. *Combat*'s masthead "From Resistance to Revolution" (selected by Camus himself) encapsulated the collective aspirations for moral and political renewal in the postwar period.

Yet the end of the Second World War would not mark the end of Camus's moral dilemmas now impacting on his concern for sociopolitical justice; indeed, it intensified them. As he notes in *Combat* in response to the bombing of Hiroshima and Nagasaki in August 1945, "the mechanical civilization has just reached its last degree of savagery. We are going to have to choose, in the not too distant future, between collective suicide or the intelligent use of scientific achievements" (*E,* 291).[82] The moral challenges of proceeding from "Resistance" to "Revolution," set against the backdrop of such shifting historical circumstances, will form the focus of the next chapter.

6
From Resistance to Revolution

> The postwar period has begun. . . . We are not yet in justice, but we have at least come out of a despicable world where injustice was queen.
>
> —Camus, *Camus à "Combat"*

Toward a Dialogic Code of Ethics

Morally speaking, the response to Hitlerism had been abundantly clear. Faced with the threat of nihilism, the use of military means was both a necessary and morally defensible course of action. As Grand puts it in *The Plague,* "why, *that's* not difficult! Plague is here and we've got to make a stand, that's obvious. Ah, I only wish everything were as simple!" (*TP,* 112). In the postwar period, however, the criteria by which to judge moral behavior were by no means so clear-cut, since the complexities of this new era required an entirely different conceptual apparatus to that in force during the war.[1] Speaking to an audience at Columbia University in March 1946, Camus would sound a cautious note in his exposition of the postwar scenario: "It is too easy . . . simply to accuse Hitler, and to say that the snake having been crushed, the poison is gone. For we know perfectly well that the poison is not gone, that we all bear it in our very hearts, as can be seen from the residue of anger present in the way nations, parties and individuals continue to regard one another."[2]

Writing in *Combat* on October 6, 1944, Camus is at pains to point out the need to remain morally vigilant in victory: "We do not wish for a justice without victory. But we have dedicated four years to know that a victory which spurns justice would just be scornful" (*CAC,* 237; cf. *CAC,* 359–62). As the editorial confirming Paris's Liberation had put it, "the struggle continues" (*E,* 1520–21). Camus has no doubts about the principles underpinning France's new constitution as he envisages it. Writing on August 24, he states that "the Paris that is fighting tonight intends to command tomorrow. Not for power, but for justice; not for politics, but for ethics; not for the domination of France, but for her grandeur" (*RRD,* 28). He waxes eloquent about the need not to allow France's postwar administration to put political self-interest before moral responsibility: "the political revolution cannot take place without an ethical revolution which underpins it and which gives it its true importance" (*E,* 1529; cf. *E,* 1545). As he notes in *Combat* on September 4, "we are determined to do away with politics and replace it with ethics. It's what we call a revolution" (*CAC,* 171).[3] Just as Saint-Just had sought to revolutionize France by bringing an end to the impositions of the *ancien régime,* so Camus now seeks similar objectives for France in the postwar period.[4] Correspondingly, in his pursuit of "justice for tomorrow" (*RRD,* 27), Camus demands that the "forces of surrender and injustice" (*RRD,* 27) of the defunct Third Republic and defeatist Vichy regime be replaced by a new order in which "the forces of money, corridor maneuvring and personal ambitions" (*E,* 1525) make way for a culture in which individual freedom coexisting with social justice could prosper: "it is for all of us a question of reconciling justice with freedom. That life may be free for each individual and just for everyone is the objective that we have to pursue" (*E,* 271). To the partisanship of the old regime, Camus responds with a new political mandate: "this old order . . . was not democracy, but its caricature. We still have to create true democracy" (*E,* 1525).[5]

A first point of interest about Camus's postwar moral vision is related to the significance he now accredits the aim to reconcile justice and freedom. Admittedly, in pledging his allegiance to the Resistance movement during the German Occupation, Camus had supported the struggle against Nazi tyranny in the name of these ideals: for Camus, the Resistance represented "a force of renovation that conceived the idea of a *just* France, at the same time as creating a *free* France" (*E,* 1542; my italics). It is, however, only in his deliberations on the factors relating to postwar France that Camus *formulates explicitly* the goal to bring justice and freedom together as a basis on which to create a morally viable system of government. In *Combat* on October 1, 1944, he thus defines his terms of reference: "We will call . . . justice a social state in which each individual receives all his or her opportunities at the outset, and where the majority of a country is not kept in a shameful condition by a minority of privileged people. And we will call freedom a political climate in which human beings are respected for what they are as for what they say" (*E,* 1527–28).

This sequence from *Combat* is significant in that it represents the first (and, as far as I have been able to ascertain, only) categorical statement of what Camus actually means by justice as a social ideal, together with an equally clear explanation of his understanding of freedom.[6] Two immediate observations present themselves in relation to Camus's remarks. One is that his vision of social justice here is clearly based on liberal democratic principles, whereby each human individual reserves the right to treatment as an equal and the standard of fairness to all citizens is actively promoted. The other is that freedom, as articulated here by Camus, is inextricably linked with social justice, in that the rights to freedom of expression and freedom of conscience can only be exercised in a context where the members of a given community have mutual regard for one another as free and equal moral persons.

The ideal of justice is often formulated in terms of a social organization regulating the mutual relations of human beings. Or, put differently, justice can be conceived of as "social happiness," whereby individual freedom is guaranteed by a social order. Pierre-Henri Simon long ago submitted that "in essence, it is through the notion of happiness that we need to pass in order to understand what Camus calls justice. What is just is a human order where *everyone* would be happy together."[7] While it may well be the case that human happiness underscores Camusian justice—"what would justice be like without the possibility of happiness . . . ?" (*E,* 299), the *Combat* reporter inquires on December 22, 1944—Simon's remarks underestimate the moral complexities of realizing "social happiness." Indeed, would not the English philosopher and jurist Jeremy Bentham, whose empiricism recognized the impossibility of bringing about the individual happiness of each member of society, famously define justice in terms of "the greatest happiness of the greatest number"?[8] Posing to himself the question "does absolute justice equal absolute happiness?" (*CA2,* 62), Camus is likewise suspicious of positing absolutes of morality. After all, just as a situation in which personal freedom inhibits social interaction compromises the well-being of all, so a system of social justice that fails to respect individual freedom cannot provide a context in which human happiness can flourish. As "moral absolutes"—as moral values existing without qualification—justice and freedom are, then, contradictory and irreconcilable concepts. *The Rebel* would demonstrate this in detail, as we shall see in the following chapter, but Camus is already aware of the problems at issue when, in *Combat* on September 8, 1944, he states that "freedom for each individual is also the freedom of the banker or the ambitious person: that's injustice restored. Justice for everyone is submission of personality to the common good. So how can we speak of absolute freedom?" (*E,* 271).[9]

It should be clear from the above remarks that Camus is now moving away from his earlier moral standpoint where, notwithstanding his personal preoccupation with the issue of how best to preserve civil liberties in the sociopolitical process, justice (as opposed to freedom) was the highlighted moral concept, toward a dialogic code of ethics.[10] Justice and freedom are now sought *together* and each, Camus insists in his call for the "necessary reconciliation" (*E,* 1528) and "superior balance" (*E,* 271) between the two ideals, must be seen to qualify the other.[11] Put simply, to be morally accountable, justice, as Camus now formulates the concept, must serve as a guarantor for human freedom and freedom must not compromise the realization of social happiness intrinsic to justice. In political terms, Camus holds, this strategy translates as the objective to "impose justice on the economic programme and guarantee freedom on the political programme," thereby creating what he calls "a collectivist economy and a liberal politics" (*E,* 1528). The reference here to a *collectivist* economy may seem a rather odd concept for Camus to support, given his intellectual distrust of those regimes requiring the sacrifice of individual autonomy in the name of abstract ideals. As he explains to his *Combat* readership on November 24, 1944, "social justice can very well come about without an ingenious philosophy. It requires some revelations of common sense and those simple things that are perceptiveness, energy and disinterestedness" (*E,* 281). However, as he also makes clear, it is in the "firm and strict balance" (*E,* 1528) between the justice of an economy in which the means of production are owned by society at large and the freedom of a liberal political system, constitutionally guaranteed by the creation of "a true people's democracy" (*E,* 1528), that human happiness best prospers.[12]

Jean Grenier's *Essay on the Spirit of Orthodoxy* [*Essai sur l'esprit d'orthodoxie*] (1938) doubtless influences Camus's postwar moral vision in which justice *and* freedom form the points of reference: "It is not because the free-market economy has gone bankrupt that a totalitarian regime is necessary. Destitution does not find its solution in tyranny. Justice must not become the enemy of freedom. It is better to build socialism based on people rather than on the State, through membership rather than through coercion."[13] Inasmuch as it portrays the political and economic principle that the means of production should be owned and controlled by members of society as a whole rather than by a privileged minority, socialism, as highlighted here by Grenier, is the ideal vehicle for the postwar popular democracy envisaged by Camus as he seeks to preserve an ethical balance between justice and freedom. Indeed, Camus himself looks to the "great idea" (*E,* 1537) of socialism which, in his view, represents "one of the great opportunities for the France of tomorrow" (*E,* 1537). However, again following Grenier, Camus distinguishes the socialism of the Resistance movement, which had struggled for "the resolute, chaotic but unremitting improvement of the human condition" (*E,* 282) from the prewar Socialist party in France which "used love of humanity as an excuse to get out of serving people" (*E,* 281).[14] As he insists in *Combat* on November 23, 1944, "socialism is not a fashion, it is a commitment" (*E,* 1541). Significantly, Camus looks to the traditional working-class principles of pragmatic reformism and mutual tolerance for the inspiration necessary to incite the new France: "Indeed, we believe that all politics that parts with the working class is futile and that France will tomorrow be what its working class will be" (*E,* 1528; cf. *E,* 1545). Thus, what he demands for the post-Liberation period is "a true people's *and workers'* democracy" (*CAC,* 143). From the moment that the "socialist hope" (*E,* 1579) becomes imbued with messianic overtones, the quest for an equilibrium between justice and freedom is invariably compromised, as will be confirmed later.[15]

A further and important feature of Camus's reasoning in relation to postwar France is the need to "save intelligence" (*RRD,* 45)—intelligence which "is backed by courage" (*RRD,* 46) and which "for four years paid whatever was necessary to have the right to respect" (*RRD,* 46). In accordance with *Combat*'s motto to proceed "from Resistance to Revolution," Camus judges it only natural that those who had risked everything for their nation during the war years now exercise the right to play an instrumental role in the "new France" (*E,* 256; *RRD,* 27), insisting that "our world has no need for half-hearted souls" (*E,* 284). The spirit of national unity underpinning the years of austerity now needed to be retained in postwar France (*E,* 1556). Moreover, there is a heightened sense of urgency in Camus's thinking when, writing in *Combat* on November 29, 1944, he states that "it is at once that we must eat and it is at once that the world must be just. For France as for Europe, the tragedy is that we have to lead at the same time a war and a revolution" (*CAC,* 361). Yet the task of following what, on October 20, he envisages as "this just path where the force of revolutions forms an alliance with the lights of justice" (*E,* 1532) was a difficult proposition given the myriad of moral complexities of the time. Chief among these was the purge, which, as well as exposing the contemporary internal inadequacies in the French institutional base, would also have a profound effect on Camus's own understanding of justice as a moral concept.

The Purge and the Moral Ambiguity of Justice

In institutionalized terms, moral reciprocity—"doing to others as one would have them do to oneself and giving an equal return for benefits received"—is often formulated as retaliative justice.[16] Mill, notably, sought to reconcile such a notion with his utilitarian beliefs, the argument being that the instinctive desire to retaliate may be rendered a principle of justice by limiting it to those instances where a grievance threatens the integrity of society as a whole and where retaliative justice can serve as a useful deterrent.[17] Meritorian theorists of justice (i.e. those advocating "Justice as Desert") also posit that individual human beings must be held accountable for their actions. Punishments and rewards, codified in institutional laws and practices, should therefore be distributed in accordance with socially undesirable (i.e. "bad") and socially desirable (i.e. "good") behavior.[18] Indeed, justice requires that, other things being equal, people ought to get (or be given) what they deserve—hence the notion of a "just desert"—and so the *appropriateness* of a reward or a penalty is indispensable to a morally accountable penal system and criminal justice policy. The institution of justice, then, presupposes a disinterested and objective base from which to administer the "distribution of desert": prejudicial predispositions make the apportionment of justice null and void. And, inasmuch as any convictions resulting from judicial procedure are supposedly found in the interests of society at large, institutionalized justice is inextricably bound up with social welfare. In the words of Sadurski, "what counts is conscientious effort which has socially beneficial effects."[19]

In the light of these preceding comments, it is not difficult to see why the purge was such a crucial issue in the reconstruction of postwar France. It was also, however, a morally contentious problem which would henceforth profoundly affect Camus's intellectual preoccupation with justice.[20] The purging of collaborators who, as an unsigned editorial from *Combat clandestin* puts it, "consciously or not, through cowardice or weakness, out of treachery or spinelessness, played Germany's game" (*CAC,* 127), was deemed by the vast majority a necessary basis for the new France.[21] In this respect, Camus is not alone in his condemnation of those politicians labeled as "men of treachery and injustice" (*E,* 1536) who had been primarily responsible for the nation's wartime shame.[22] It was on the *grands responsables* that Camus himself would principally focus in his quest for justice. With the insurrection and eventual liberation of Paris taking place around him, Camus singles out, in a *Combat* editorial significantly entitled "Time for Justice," Pétain and his former premier Laval, "these men who imposed rationing on us for everything except shame" (*CAC,* 145) who could, he states, now expect from France "neither forgetfulness nor leniency" (*CAC,* 146).[23] As the writer makes clear in the same article, justice demands that those whose "dirty hands" were red with the blood of innocent victims be brought to account before their maneuvres were allowed to pollute postwar politics in France: "justice demands that those who killed and those who allowed murder be equally responsible before the victim, even if those who wrapped themselves up in murder today speak of double standards and realism. For this language is one which we despise the most" (*CAC,* 146; and cf. *CAC,* 212–14).

In accordance with his objective to reconcile justice and freedom as a basis for future prosperity, Camus highlights the need for the eradication of France's enemies to be undertaken in the name of a swift and disinterested justice in order to ratify the liberation from Nazi tyranny. As we saw in the preceding chapter, it was in the name of justice that the wartime Camus had offered a moral response to totalitarianism; now, in the immediate aftermath of the hostilities, that response needed to be reinforced by the law. As he insists in *Combat* on November 29, 1944, "freedom is never wanted without by the same token demanding justice. And for these four years when freedom was the only bread of starving people, their thirst for justice increased accordingly" (*CAC,* 361). However, as has been well-documented, the necessary impartial apparatus of justice to which mention was made earlier remained conspicuously absent from the now notorious purge prosecutions. This state of affairs is perhaps unwittingly recorded by Clamence in *The Fall* when he submits that "the keenest of human torments is to be judged without law" (*TF,* 86).[24]

As Tony Judt observes, around 75 percent of the judges presiding over the purge trials in France had themselves collaborated with the Vichy administration, "the very institutional marsh they were supposed to be draining."[25] The lack of a rule of law by which to administer the purge would mean that the apportionment of objective and dispassionate justice was, at best, arbitrary. Not only, then, was justice not being done, but it was also seen not being done. As the partner of an American diplomat at the time attests, "the purge trials preoccupied us all . . . and the incoherence with which justice was meted out did much to cause the *crise morale,* or crisis of conscience among the French."[26] Increasingly, the purge degenerated into trials of private retribution since, in the words of Guillaume Hanoteau, "each had his or her own pet hate to which he or she personally bore a grudge."[27] François Mauriac who, like Camus, accepted the moral principle of the purge and who could even justify execution in his *a posteriori* conviction that "the French people who handed over to the enemy other French people must be executed by firing squad . . . the blood of those shot does not shout vengeance but justice," demanded disinterested judges and impartial law courts as means by which to mete out justice.[28] Anything less than a "precise and swift justice," as he puts it in *Le Figaro* as early as September 4, 1944, would affront French judicial procedure.[29] As Mauriac later maintained, "there is no worse politics in a democracy than that which doesn't care about justice."[30]

A curious feature of Camus's own reasoning on the issue is that during the first phase of the purge (in the months surrounding the Liberation), he appears to "play down" the institutional inadequacies of the purge process by perceiving justice more as a moral ideal than as an institutionalized principle: "It is the fiction of legality that Vichy has created which forces us to substitute *moral justice* for *justice of the law* and which makes a case for those who ought to remain silent for always" (*CAC,* 302; my italics). In that same article, with Pétain specifically in mind, he demands "the most merciless and the most determined of justices" (*CAC,* 303) *not* in the name of a codified judicial practice, but as a means by which to avenge "the voices of torture and shame" (*CAC,* 303). Earlier, he had pointed up the principle of "the law of hearts" (*CAC,* 211) over that of "the written law" (*CAC,* 211). Only when it becomes evident that the purge had failed in France would Camus highlight the inadequacies of its institutional foundation: "The issue, for justice to have been swift, was to make it clear. . . . It was a question of creating the law we needed, of putting it into words that were clear and beyond reproach" (*E,* 1548, 1549). The use here of the past tense points up Camus's retrospective standpoint on events.

The nineteenth century playwright Henry Becque insists that "with age, we realize that vengeance is still the surest form of justice," a view which Camus also seems to share in his initial association of justice and retributivism, couched in the uncompromising language of "impossible pardons" (*E,* 1534) and "necessary sacrifices" (*E,* 1535).[31] The fact of the matter is that Camus's conception of justice in relation to the purge—incompatible, it should be stressed, with his vision of the principle for the new France—is *absolutist* in nature.[32] Moreover, mercy has no place in such a configuration, as Camus makes clear in his public polemic with Mauriac: "the issue of justice consists in stifling mercy" (*E,* 1535). This last remark brings to mind Camus's personal maxim from his preface to *Betwixt and Between:* "We must put our principles into great things, mercy is enough for small ones" (*SEN,* 20). Just as the Camus of *Alger républicain* had rejected charity in the interests of social and political justice, so now he deems it a moral duty of France to punish her enemies and a moral evasion to pardon them.[33] As he puts it in a further response to his moral adversary, "every time that with regard to the purge, I have spoken of justice, Mr Mauriac has spoken of charity. . . . I would just like to say to him that I see two roads to death for our country. . . . These two roads are those of hatred and forgiveness" (*E,* 285, 286). Thus, writing in *Combat clandestin* in May 1944 of the cold-blooded murder of eighty-six innocent French civilians, he would state that "it is not a question of knowing whether these crimes will be forgiven, it is a question of knowing whether they will be paid for" (*CAC,* 131). Later, writing against the backdrop of Paris's Liberation, he likewise posits a retaliative justice by which to amend France's wartime horror: "Who would dare to speak here of forgiveness? . . . It is not hatred that will speak tomorrow, but justice itself, based on memory" (*E,* 259).

It is worth pausing on the issue of Camus's polemic with Mauriac, since that controversy raises questions as to the moral accountability of Camus's position *vis-à-vis* the purge. Furthermore, the consequences of this crisis of conscience would be considerable in terms of Camus's subsequent engagement with the moral concept of justice. The dispute, which confronts Camus in *Combat* with Mauriac in *Le Figaro,* reached its peak between October 1944 and January 1945.[34] Divided, as Mauriac himself later maintained, by "this insurmountable distance that separates one who is arriving from one who is moving away," he and Camus embody two diametrically opposed attitudes toward the purge.[35] On the one hand, Mauriac (a committed Catholic) judges the purge an increasingly arbitrary affair and demands that justice be tempered with mercy in the name of Christian charity; on the other hand, Camus (a nonbeliever) justifies the purge on political (i.e. as a necessary means by which to rid France of her traitors) and moral (i.e. by virtue of the "eye for an eye" reasoning) grounds. To put the point another way, to the "divine justice" advocated by Mauriac, whereby judgment is deferred to God, Camus counters "people's justice" (*E,* 1536), "human justice with its terrible imperfections" (*E,* 1536) and "a swift justice, marked by time" (*E,* 1537). In his view, this temporal vision of justice could alone bring France's traitors to account, there being no God to administer justice beyond the realm of human experience.[36] To the "injustice" of Christianity, Camus thus opposes "this deeply moving human creation which is called justice" (*E,* 1597).[37] While Mauriac equates justice with mercy, Camus upholds a ruthless and implacable vision of justice requiring the sacrifice of the self but which at the same time, in Denis Salas's words, remains "capable of rebuilding a community beyond the injuries of history."[38]

Indeed, even prior to the purge proper, Camus had been prepared to sacrifice his own moral standards (i.e. his belief in the sacrosanctity of human life) in the interests of his perception of justice, as his response to the case of Pierre Pucheu, a conspirator and collaborator executed in Algiers in March 1944, confirms.[39] In an article of somewhat uncertain attribution, but which may have been written by Camus, Pucheu's demise is expressed without emotion: "Pucheu condemned to death, shot for conspiring with the enemy. One feeling dominates: justice is dispensed to France."[40] A month later, in a piece that can be attributed with certainty, Camus insists that the execution of Pucheu had left him "without hatred and without compassion" (*E,* 1468). There is no sign here of the "wave of revolt" (*E,* 356) which Camus later recalls having experienced upon reading of Gabriel Péri's execution. Notwithstanding his "loathing for the justice of men on duty" (*E,* 1468), Camus deems it just that a man who, amid the bureaucracy of the Vichy regime, had approved legislation ultimately resulting in the deaths of French innocents but who had "lacked imagination" to understand this, should now surrender his own right to life (*E,* 1468–69). Similar psychology informs his attitude in anticipation of executions in Paris: "We well know that the day when the first death sentence is announced in Paris, we will find it revolting. But then we will have to think of so many other death sentences which have hit true people, of dear faces returned to the earth and of hands which we used to like to shake. When we are tempted to prefer to the black chores of justice the generous sacrifices of the war, we need the recollection of the dead and of the unbearable memory of those among us whom torture has made traitors" (*E,* 1533–34; cf. *E,* 1536).

Unusually for Camus, what this passage clearly shows is that in his aim to rid France of her enemies and traitors, he is prepared to justify the sacrifice of human life in the name of what is in effect an as yet unrealized ideal of justice (the precise principles of the postwar constitution, in the interests of which the purge was supposedly administered, being subject to negotiation.) In marked contrast to his thesis advanced in *The Rebel,* and in spite of his reasoning on the *dialogue* between justice and freedom envisaged for the new France, Camus here supports the view that the end justifies the means, i.e. that the human individual can be deemed justifiably expendable in certain (extreme) circumstances. The moral accountability of this position is predicated on the point that the "end" is indeed pure: that—in relation to the purge—those principally responsible for France's years of Occupation were being brought to account in the eyes of the law; and that—with regard to the projected "new France"—the Resistance's fight for justice and freedom would be vindicated by the postwar political agenda. However, it has to be said that, in both cases, what was going to happen would render such an argument morally invalid: after all, those chiefly to blame for France's humiliation were escaping justice, while lesser offenders were being ruthlessly reprimanded; and the nascent Fourth Republic would soon assume an uncanny resemblance to the conniving political attitudes prevalent in the Third, confirming that *plus ça change, plus c'est la même chose.* Camus himself may have sensed that the writing was indeed on the wall when, in *Combat* on October 18, 1944, he states that "the purge is necessary. . . . It is not a question of purging many, it is a question of purging well. But what is a good purge? It is a purge which aims to respect the general principle of justice, without sacrificing anything as far as people are concerned" (*CAC,* 264).

These remarks raise (Camus's) awareness of the disproportionate sentences passed in the purge resulting in a travesty of justice. Clearly, the *Combat* reporter is concerned here with the inappropriate way in which justice is being meted out: "In the case in point, what is the general principle of justice? It is all about proportion. It is ridiculous to sacrifice such and such a head clerk who continued to live in the habit of obedience without, on the other hand, touching those chiefly responsible" (*CAC,* 264). Yet, despite these internal inadequacies, Camus would continue to uphold publicly his belief in "human justice *with its terrible imperfections*" (*E,* 1536; my italics), the alternative being finally to acknowledge the failure of the purge and the moral consequences of that failure both for himself and his nation. Only at the beginning of the following year, by which time the *justice manquée* of the purge was becoming increasingly apparent, does Camus acknowledge that "it is now very likely too late for justice to be done" (*E,* 1548), before proceeding to point up the consequences of such a moral miscarriage for the new France: "A country which makes a mess of its purge prepares itself ready to make a mess of its renovation. Nations have the face of their justice. Ours ought to have something else to show to the world than this disorderly face" (*E,* 1550). Writing in *Combat* the following day under the pseudonym of "Suétone," Camus's own disillusionment with justice as a result of the purge's failure to deliver comes unequivocally to the fore: "Justice is a large machine which is used for punishing and rectifying errors as far as possible. It is a little like a slot machine. You put in a token and all the machinery sets off. It is noisy and creaky and in a great din something falls out: a head, a handful of years in prison. You never know. Sometimes, nothing comes out. The small bond bearers are paid off short of what was put in. We cannot say that there is someone responsible for it. It is a machine. We don't even know who made it. And in this great country, no mechanic can be found capable of improving it."[41]

Further confirmation that Camus is now growing increasingly disillusioned with the idea that a morally accountable vision of justice could be upheld by the purge is provided by his response to the case of Robert Brasillach. It will be recalled that Brasillach, a prolific writer who, during the war, had edited the fascist *Je suis partout,* was, in January 1945, found guilty of collaboration. Furthermore, despite appeals for clemency (notably from Mauriac), he was duly executed at Fresnes on February 6.[42] To sign Mauriac's petition in support of Brasillach was a vexed question for Camus. On the one hand, to support clemency was to admit that he had been wrong to demand that human lives be sacrificed in the name of justice; on the other hand, to reject clemency was to pay lip service to a criminal justice system clearly now determined by prejudice and private malice. Writing to Marcel Aymé in correspondence dated January 27, 1945, Camus—who would in the end support the call for mercy—explained that he had acted out of personal morality:[43]

> I have always detested the death sentence and I have been of the opinion that, as an individual at least, I could not be involved in it, even through abstention. . . . And this is a scruple which I imagine will really make Brasillach's friends laugh. It isn't for him that I am adding my signature to yours. . . . Even if I had been tempted to take an interest in it, the memory of two or three of my friends mutilated or killed by Brasillach's friends while his diary encouraged them would prevent me from doing so. . . . It isn't by chance that my signature is going to be found among

yours, while that of Brasillach was never made on behalf of [Georges] Politzer or Jacques Decour [resisters murdered by the German militia].[44]

Equally worthy of notice is a lecture entitled "A Defense of Intelligence," delivered by Camus less than two months after penning the above remarks (*E,* 313–16; *RRD,* 44–46). In that speech, in which he records the residue of hatred in France following the defeat of Nazism, Camus highlights the persisting desire in many of his fellow countrymen to exact revenge: "The executioners' hatred engendered the victims' hatred. And once the executioners had gone, the French were left with their hatred only partially spent. They still look at one another with a residue of anger" (*RRD,* 45). It was imperative, he insists, that such base sentiments be eliminated and replaced by a morality of tolerance if the victory over Nazism was ultimately to be vindicated: "the most difficult battle to be won against the enemy in the future must be fought within ourselves, with an exceptional effort that will transform our appetite for hatred into a desire for justice" (*RRD,* 45).[45] The very same sentiment underscores a disturbing article, published some two years later in *Combat,* following the aggressive reprisals by the French in Madagascar in March 1947: "the fact is there, as clear and hideous as the truth: in these cases, we are doing what we criticized the Germans for doing" (*E,* 322).[46] As Camus goes on to insist in that same article, "it is justice which France ought to represent" (*E,* 322).

It is clear that the failure of the purge would have a profound effect on Camus's own intellectual engagement with the ideal of justice. One is reminded here of the following maxim from La Bruyère's *Characters* [*Caractères*] (1688): "A guilty person who is punished is an example for the rabble; an innocent person who is sentenced is the business of all honest people."[47] Camus would now relinquish his membership of the CNE—an important symbol of his disillusioned frame of mind—and, in the postwar period, he would be intensely preoccupied—one might say *haunted*—by the issue of (legalized) murder, and with the question of whether violence can be morally justified as a political instrument in revolutionary protest.[48]

Moreover, it is no coincidence that following the failure of the purge, Camus writes in the *Carnets* that freedom must be allowed to prevail over justice, "for even if *we do not achieve* justice, liberty still keeps the power to protest against injustice and preserves communication" (*CA2,* 69). What the experience of the purge confirms is that justice is conditioned by history; the modifications of Camus's own understanding of the concept when faced with the collective situation of war had already indicated as much. Although, in the same notebook entry, he acknowledges that freedom "should *at the same time* demand justice, as has been said" (*CA2,* 69), it is significant, as Jeanyves Guérin rightly observes, that freedom would now be spotlighted in Camus's moral thinking.[49] As he puts it in the course of an interview granted to the *"Diario" de Sao-Paulo* on August 6, 1949, "I believe that the most serious issue today is that of freedom. Anyone who understands all its reach knows very well that it is the indispensable condition for all human progress and peace" (*E,* 1697–98). Just like his fictional creation Tarrou in *The Plague,* Camus had now "lost [his] peace" (*TP,* 206); it would be a considerable time before he could come to terms with his sense of "anguish" so strikingly recorded in the *Carnets:* "Anguish at having increased injustice in the belief that I was serving justice. At least knowledge that this happened and then discover this greater anguish: acknowledge that total justice does not exist. To acknowledge, after the most terrible revolt, that one is nothing, is real suffering" (*CA2,* 129).

This passage from the *Carnets* in mid-1948 is significant for two reasons. First, it attests to Camus's own crisis of conscience in finally recognizing the impossibility of establishing an ideal human system of justice, which is what he hoped the purge would be. As he states in an open address dated December 5, 1946, on behalf of Lucien Rebatet, "for a long time I believed that this country could not do without justice. But . . . justice since the Liberation has turned out so difficult that we must now feel that all human justice has its limits and that this country, in the end, might also need mercy" (*E,* 1887). These remarks are also in the spirit of Camus's confession at the Latour Maubourg monastery in Paris, where he openly states that he had been mistaken to oppose Mauriac in the public polemic over the purge (*E,* 371–72; *RRD,* 49–50).[50] As he concedes to the *Carnets* in a note relating to the purge and reminiscent of his earlier view of pacifism, "justice cannot accompany violence" (*CA2,* 89).

Secondly, Camus's private admission that "total justice does not exist," an idea given public expression in *Combat* on May 7, 1947, with the assertion that "absolute justice is impossible, as are impossible eternal hatred or eternal love" (*E,* 324; cf. *C2,* 200; *CA2,* 103), indicates that, in his eyes, human prosperity is best served by a *plurality* of moral values.[51] As Camus reportedly confides to Jean Grenier, the task, now, was to "look for moderate values in the absence of absolute values to which we could finally be connected" and thereby "achieve an agreement between people in the face of disaster."[52] Camus's objective to forge a strategy whereby justice and freedom could be reconciled (an aim clearly impossible if each were pursued as moral absolutes) is perfectly consistent with this idea. Why, then, did he idealize justice in his response to the purge and so jeopardize the much sought after dialogic code of ethics between justice and freedom? To this I would respond by stating that so urgent and powerful was the issue of the purge in emotional terms that it forces Camus temporarily to suspend the pursuit of any notion of equilibrium between the two ideals: the purge was essentially an *extreme* moment to which the idea of an ethical *balance* inevitably succumbed. One can almost hear Clamence's disclosure here that "the very word 'justice' gave me strange fits of rage" (*TF,* 67). It remains to be seen whether the lessons learned as a result of the purge would now enable Camus to rise above his evident disillusionment and thereby respond to the problems and complexities of a world "governed by forces both blind and deaf" (*E,* 331).

Justice and "comfortable violence"

In *State of Siege,* Camus states that "there is no justice, but there are limits" (*TRN,* 299; cf. *C2,* 236; *CA2,* 122), a remark which conveniently expresses his principal moral standpoint in the wake of the failed purge in France. In that play which, notably, Camus deems of all his works to resemble him the most (*TRN,* 1732), the issue is raised of so-called "comfortable violence" (*E,* 356; cf. *C2,* 214; *CA2,* 111). In "Witness of Freedom" (1948), he defines this idea in terms of organized state terror, whereby "the executioners have taken up their duties in ministerial seats. They have just replaced the axe by the ink stamp" (*E,* 401).[53] Similar preoccupations underscore a series of lectures delivered by Camus during his stay in the United States and Canada between March and June 1946. As he ironically remarks in one speech, "one is no longer right because one has justice on one's side, one is right because one is successful. And the more one is successful, the more one is right. It is almost the justification of murder" (*E,* 1620). And, in another, he raises his audience's attention of the fact that "the death or torture of a human being can, in our world, be examined with a feeling of indifference, with friendly or experimental interest, or without response."[54] An early title for *The Plague—Terror*—continues the same preoccupation.[55] *The Just Assassins,* too, points up the issue of murder as a political instrument, while *The Rebel* would concern itself with the implications of an "era of premeditation and perfect crimes" (*TR,* 11).[56] Haunted, then, by his own recent condonation of capital punishment at the time of the purge, Camus now becomes deeply preoccupied with the issue of whether murder could ever be justified on moral grounds. Thus, in a sense, his postwar moral position becomes associated with the idea of "self-defense," as Camus transposes his own preoccupation with the problem on to institutional and ideological responses to the same issue. In April 1946, he articulates in the *Carnets* what, confiding to Grenier, he calls his "fixation with murder" in the following terms: "Revolt. Beginning: 'The only really serious moral problem is killing. The rest comes afterwards. But what must be discovered is whether I can kill this person in front of me, or allow this person to be killed; and what must be realized is that I know nothing until I know if I can kill'" (*CA2,* 88).[57]

With an ironic reference back to *The Myth of Sisyphus,* these remarks also anticipate *The Rebel,* the preparation of which was now in full effect. Indeed, much of Camus's published writing in the postwar period—most notably, "Remark on Revolt" (1945); "Neither Victims nor Executioners" (1946); "The Fastidious Assassins" (1948); and the two plays already mentioned—feed directly into the "Essay on Revolt," but even before this, he projects his concerns regarding the moral justification of violence on to Tarrou in *The Plague,* who "lived a life riddled with contradictions" (*TP,* 237).[58] Like Camus, Tarrou is haunted by the issue of capital punishment (*TRN,* 1422–23; *TP,* 203–4) and, in his resolve no longer to "propagate the microbe," condemns *all* forms of violence: "So that is why I resolved to have no truck with anything which, directly or indirectly, for good reasons or for bad, brings death to anyone, or justifies others' putting a person to death" (*TP,* 207; translation amended).[59]

It should be stressed, however, that Camus himself does not share Tarrou's *absolute* rejection of violence (a Utopian vision explaining why Tarrou would eventually succumb to the plague) in his aim to maintain standards of morality in revolutionary justice. The fact of the matter is that violence is often used as a means to an end and, as Camus's wartime *Letters to a German Friend* testifies, this course of action can be morally justified where moral criteria are attached to the means as well as to the ends of the revolutionary campaign. As he states in his polemic with *Libération*'s Emmanuel Vigerie, a prominent figure in the French Resistance and recent communist convert who takes issue with the anti-Soviet stance adopted in "Neither Victims nor Executioners," what Camus is now struggling against is the violence embroiled in political fanaticism: "I believe that violence is inevitable, the years of Occupation taught me as much. To be honest, there were, at that time, acts of terrible violence which gave me no problem. So I shall not say that we must put an end to all violence, which would be desirable but actually utopian. I just say that we must refuse all legitimatization of violence, whether this legitimatization comes from absolute reasons of State or from a totalitarian philosophy. Violence is at the same time inevitable and unjustifiable" (*E,* 355; cf. *E,* 334).

Violence and revolution are not simple synonyms for Camus: in responding to the moral challenge of the relationship between the two ideas, he seeks to formulate the principles for the vindication of political power intrinsic to his vision of political justice. Maintaining a moral impetus in any violent insurrection is, for Camus, the touchstone of the pursuit of revolutionary justice, and all "legitimatization of violence" is seen to hijack this impetus by sacrificing moral accountability on the altar of politico-ideological extremism. Correspondingly, in "Neither Victims nor Executioners," where, with communism's Soviet manifestation specifically in mind, he highlights, in "the century of fear" (*E,* 331), "the quite particular fear of murderous ideologies" (*E,* 332) and "a world in which killing is legitimized and where human life is deemed futile" (*E,* 333).[60] At first sight, it is tempting to interpret this anti-Soviet stance as being inconsistent with *Combat*'s support during the Resistance years for the proposition that "'anticommunism is the start of dictatorship'" (*E,* 272).[61] However, amid postwar revelations that Stalinism and Hitlerism were essentially two sides of the same totalitarian coin, Camus does not hesitate to condemn both as equally unjust regimes. Indeed, to take what Camus himself deems "a good example of legitimized violence: the concentration camps and the use of political prisoners as a labor force" (*E,* 365), unlike many French left-wing intellectuals who, sensing the threat of Stalinist totalitarianism, could only offer what Harold Wardman calls "considered criticism" of the Soviet forced labor system, Camus does not shirk condemning the Gulag in his conviction that "there is no reason in the world, historical or other, progressive or reactionary, which could make me accept the fact of concentration camps" (*E,* 365).[62] (Lottman suggests that Camus's "Title for the future: System [1,500 pages]" (*CA2,* 99) would have focused on the issue of concentration camps.)[63] For Camus, justice and tyranny are mutually exclusive: he cannot condone the use of human suffering as a political expedient since, as he later puts it during the controversy surrounding the publication of *The Rebel,* "to liberate people from all restrictions in order to then practically cage them up in historical necessity in fact comes back to taking away first of all their reasons for fighting so as to in the end throw them into any sort of party, provided that this has no rules other than efficiency. So it is about passing, according to the law of nihilism, from extreme liberty to extreme necessity; it is nothing other than devoting oneself to manufacturing slaves" (*E,* 770).

Camus's rejection of Stalinist totalitarianism is made, then, on political *and* moral grounds. In his view, political justice cannot embrace the principle that the end justifies the means where moral accountability crumbles in the face of ideological prejudice; to accept such philosophy was to condone civil persecution in the name of political absolutism. As he remarks in a manuscript note for "Neither Victims nor Executioners" reminding us of Camus's earlier response to the purge in France, "for my part, I have learned in these two years that I will put no truth above the life of a person. . . . I have thought about my inability to have a person shot whether it be in the name of a truth or an illusion of a truth" (*E,* 1512; cf. *E,* 350). Diego, in *State of Siege,* is equally dismissive of political idealism in his conviction that "no person has enough virtue to be able to be granted absolute power" (*TRN,* 291; cf. *E,* 1783). Rejecting the messianic pretensions of Marxism, Camus makes his own position clear in his first response to Vigerie: "justice is no longer at issue. What is at issue is a prodigious myth of the deification of human beings, of domination, of unification of the universe by the sole power of human reason. . . . What weight do justice, the life of some generations and human suffering carry next to this excessive mysticism?" (*E,* 361). To endorse Stalin's supposed socialist state would be to accept the legality of authoritarian socialism—what Camus calls "the socialism of concentration camps" (*E,* 386, 1590)—and thereby reject morality (formulated in terms of the aim to reconcile justice and freedom in an ethical equilibrium) in favor of political ideology (*E,* 382, 387). The promise of justice tomorrow cannot justify the practice of injustice today since, as Camus emphasizes in a later interview, "none of the evils which totalitarianism (defined to start with by the single party and the suppression of all opposition) claims to remedy is worse than totalitarianism itself" (*E,* 1764).[64] For Camus, failing to apply moral criteria to the *means,* as well as to the end, of the quest for revolutionary justice renders the process morally invalid.

A further illustration of what, according to Camus, is the moral indefensibility of the principle that the end justifies the means is provided by *The Just Assassins,* a play based on historical reality

(*TRN,* 1733, 1834, 1846–51).[65] In that work Stepan, who "doesn't love life, but justice which is something higher than life" (*CP,* 130; translation amended), embodies the Stalinist conviction that all means are justified in the quest for justice (here, the restoration of social justice which had collapsed under Czarist Russia): "Nothing that can serve our cause should be ruled out" (*CP,* 141). With no respect for human life, and incapable of expressing human emotions like love—his experience of torture drains such sentiments (*TRN,* 356; *CP,* 154)—Stepan is the totalitarian incarnate.[66] His disciplined outlook ("We must have discipline," he tells Annenkov [*CP,* 124]) requires the sacrifice of moral considerations for the sake of revolutionary justice.[67] By contrast, Kaliayev, who "joined the revolution *because* [he loves] life" (*CP,* 130), and who fights tyranny in the name of humanist ideals ("I love beauty and happiness. That's why I hate tyranny!" [*CP,* 131; translation amended]), cannot justify the killing of innocents "for the sake of some unknown distant city" (*CP,* 143; translation amended), that is, in the name of an abstraction of justice: "I refuse to add to the living injustice around me for the sake of a dead justice" (*CP,* 143; translation amended). As Dora insists in the key moral exchange from act 2, "even destruction has a right and a wrong way, and there *are* limits" (*CP,* 142), a remark provoking Stepan's violent diatribe to the contrary (*TRN,* 338; *CP,* 142).

For a Justice of International Tolerance

Further support for the claim that, in the postwar period, Camus eschews political absolutism and the vision of a political system to which human rights are sacrificed is provided by his formulations of a politically "modest" moral vision for the world stage. Two of the core concerns that now impinge on Camus's preoccupation with sociopolitical justice—the problem of how best to reconcile the contradictory ideals of justice and freedom and the pursuit of a "moderate course of treatment" (*E,* 319) in the absence of moral absolutes—now come together in his response to the new situation emerging from the years of war. Indeed, the aftermath of the hostilities consolidates and develops the international dimension of Camus's concern for sociopolitical justice inasmuch as national boundaries are now being surpassed by the changing historical circumstances. As Camus notes in "Neither Victims nor Executioners," "one doesn't cure plague with the means applied to head colds. A crisis which splits the whole world must be settled on the universal scale" (*E,* 347). Similarly, in his "Remarks on International Politics" (1945), he appeals to France to contribute to the cause of global security or suffer the consequences (*E,* 1572–76).[68] Instinctively opposed to political fanaticism in his conviction that "there is nothing more dignified than refusing reasons of State set up as an absolute" (*E,* 1838), Camus now proceeds on the basis of what he calls "moderate political thinking, that is to say free from all messianism, and released from nostalgia for an earthly paradise" (*E,* 335). Against the backdrop of the *univers concentrationnaire,* he now begins in earnest to conceptualize "another Utopia, more moderate and less exorbitant" (*E,* 338) and a "relative Utopia which leaves an opportunity for action and people at the same time" (*E,* 341). The key point here is that as he seeks to uphold moral standards in the new world situation, Camus once more draws on the principle of liberal democracy, "the social and political exercise of moderation" (*E,* 1580), by which to instill, on the international scale, the much sought after dialogue between justice and freedom which proved unrealizable for postwar France: "The democrat, after all, is one who accepts that an opponent can be right, who therefore allows him or her to express him/herself and who agrees to think about his or her arguments" (*E,* 320).

Now, given Camus's generally ambiguous attitude toward Europe, it is perhaps somewhat surprising that he should look to that continent as a model for realizing his envisaged "new world order": "I want, like everyone, freedom and social justice and I believe that, if these contradictory notions can meet in a more flexible compromise, it is in Europe that it will be achieved" (*E,* 1586).[69] These remarks from the December 7, 1948, issue of *Franc-Tireur* recall an earlier conviction in *Combat* that "world peace depends in large measure on the swiftness with which *the European mentality* will find the reconciliation between justice and freedom" (*CAC,* 578). Geographically situated between the two "superpowers," Europe represents, for Camus, "a perpetual temptation toward imperialism" (*E,* 1573). Establishing a *juste milieu* between the *politique des blocs* is deemed necessary in the interests of international tolerance. In terms highly reminiscent of his attitude upon the outbreak of hostilities in Europe in September 1939, Camus lays stress on the idea that to resign oneself to the tragic inevitability of a new war between East and West is henceforth to compromise the quest for justice by which international politics will be determined: "We are speaking to the people of Europe and the world in order to suggest to them a common action and in order to ask them to recognize with us that war can and must be avoided, not because it is more important to live in peace than in justice, which would be the language of servitude and capitulation, but because from now on it will be impossible to believe in the light of justice if we stop for a single moment to . . . fight in peace" (*E,* 1579).

To understand Camus's vision here of "common action" with a view to averting a new global conflict, we need once more to turn our attention to "Neither Victims nor Executioners," the series of articles offering an ethical balance between the opposing political ideologies of East and West but which, interestingly enough, as David Walker perceptively remarks, was conceived and composed *before* the principal events in central Europe (chiefly in 1947) precipitating the Cold War.[70] This last observation draws into question how central a commentary Camus's articles actually are on the crisis. Be that as it may, it is in "Neither Victims nor Executioners" that Camus formulates his quest for an international democracy, constitutionally validated by global elections, "where the law is above governments, this law being the expression of the will of everyone, represented by a legislative body" (*E,* 343).[71] Given that national governments are not always sufficiently representative of their people, Camus now pitches the envisaged new order in a worldwide context: "the new world order that we are looking for cannot only be national or even continental and especially neither western or eastern. It must be universal" (*E,* 342).[72] Predicated on the principle of equality and fairness across nations, such a vision of global solidarity produces, for Camus, a new climate of cooperation conducive to creating and redistributing wealth and so ensuring free trade across national boundaries. In essence, what Camus is doing here is formulating a blueprint for an international code of conduct ushering in a new era of promoting respect for human beings and their fundamental freedoms on the world stage. It should be emphasized, however, that in thus calling for a new social contract (*E,* 346), Camus is *not* giving voice to an ideological standpoint; rather, in his demands for "an international order *based on justice and dialogue*" (*E,* 347; my italics), he is primarily preoccupied with the issue of how best to realize the prosperity and aspirations of the international community at large: "it is clearly evident that it would not be a question of creating a new ideology. It would only be a question of seeking a way of life" (*E,* 348). Although the criticism can be leveled against Camus that his projected new order is hopelessly idealistic in nature, it is significant that "the first article" of the "code of international justice," that he envisages as a means by which to regulate the new social contract, is the worldwide abolition of capital punishment (*E,* 348; cf. *E,* 385). This is a crucial component of his view of social justice which, as will be further confirmed later, would also remain a personal obsession.[73]

Fundamental to the idea of a "code of international justice" is the issue of rights and, in one of its dimension, "Neither Victims nor Executioners" is tantamount to a Bill of Human Rights. This last claim can further be substantiated by reference to Camus's concern, throughout the turbulent period currently under consideration, for victims of intolerance and human rights violations and by his interventions, undertaken in the spirit of the 1946 articles and in the tradition of Voltairean *engagement,* on behalf of victims of international persecution. Indeed, his practical moral mandate in this regard can be said to elucidate the theoretical deliberations of the envisaged new world order formulated in "Neither Victims nor Executioners." This is in keeping with his determination to keep theoretical arguments in key with practical objectives while, at the same time, providing further insight into the climate of fear underscoring the *univers concentrationnaire.* Thus, partly documented in Camus's contemporary writings, his concern for sociopolitical justice on the international scale now also finds practical expression, a brief examination of which is worthy of mention here.

Even before the composition of "Neither Victims nor Executioners," Camus was campaigning tirelessly on behalf of one particular group of persecuted people on the world stage: Spanish republicans. As he states in *Combat* in January 1945, "we will be told that we speak of Spain with too much passion. Yes, we do speak about it with passion. But we speak about justice also with passion" (*CAC,* 437). Earlier, at a time when the threat posed by fascism in its Nazi manifestation was finally receding elsewhere in Europe, he highlights that with the continuing regime in Spain, the triumph over Hitlerism had been a pyrrhic victory: "We still think that our struggle is theirs and that we can be neither happy nor free as long as Spain is wounded and enslaved" (*CAC,* 231; cf. *CAC,* 174–76, 341–44 and 379–81). And he would not be afraid to speak out against the conspiracy of silence when, under Pétain's Vichy administration, countless Spanish republican exiles were handed over to Franco (*E,* 393; *RRD,* 59). Deposited at L'IMEC in France is an article, partially cited by Olivier Todd who dates the piece from 1947–48, that is worthy of extended quotation here inasmuch as it points up Camus's incapability of vindicating the democratic objective to reconcile justice and freedom on the international scale so long as Spain remains subject to fascist totalitarianism:[74]

> In 1944, we shared a great hope. . . . Since we had been in the same defeat, my idea was that we must be in the same victory. But, appar-

> ently, my idea was not reasonable. And we spoke in vain and there is no victory today for anyone since there is no justice for Spain. Justice is like democracy, it is total or it doesn't exist at all. Who will dare to tell me that I am free when the proudest of my friends are still in Spanish prisons? . . . Spanish comrades, we know now that the world is cowardly. You thought you were a model and you were only a stake. . . . A day will come perhaps when . . . the already dying civilization will wish to come back to spiritual concerns and find again an art of living. . . . That day, and for the first time in eight years, an enormous weight of shame and bitterness will be lifted and I could finally breath freely.[75]

Further evidence of Camus's conviction that victims of international intolerance need to be supported in the interests of establishing the international dialogic code of ethics between justice and freedom in the world at large can be found in his alternative course of intellectual commitment to that championed by Sartre, in October 1945, in the opening issue of *Les Temps modernes.*[76] Camus, who "like[s] people who take sides more than literatures that do" (*CA2,* 92; translation amended), and who later would liken the role of the intellectual to "a military service . . . involved in the galley of the time" (*E,* 1079), rejects Sartrean *engagement* on the ground of his refusal to subscribe to ideological principles as standards for action (*TRN,* 1746). Thus, while he gives only limited support to *intellectually* inspired movements seeking mediation between the mutually opposing ideologies of communism and capitalism—Sartre's *Rassemblement Démocratique Révolutionnaire* (RDR) is a case in point here—Camus lends considerable weight to organizations with a *practical* mandate for liberating enslaved communities from despotic political regimes.[77] The *Groupes de Liaison Internationale,* a Franco-American initiative set up to help victims of totalitarian practices worldwide, deserves special mention in this connection. Indeed, it appears that Camus played an instrumental role in establishing the French branch of that organization (reminiscent of the latter-day movements such as *Amnesty International, Médecins Sans Frontières,* and *The International Red Cross*). According to one contemporary member, the movement was known locally as "Camus's group," and it was Camus himself who wrote the movement's manifesto calling for "a solid international friendship" by which to "[give] to millions of solitary people clear and valid reasons to hope."[78] (There is a clear overlap here with the "code of international justice" demanded in "Neither Victims nor Executioners.") Even when saddled with political and ideological disputes—the *Groupes* were ultimately disbanded in mid-1950—Camus was keen not to see the organization collapse, thus testifying to his commitment, undertaken in the name of justice and freedom, to the struggle against tyranny in the international community.[79]

In sum, then, throughout the immediate postwar period and beyond, Camus campaigns vigorously for those on the world stage whose civil rights are being systematically eroded by a monolithic state mentality. His other countless interventions on behalf of political detainees, carried out in the spirit of his quest for reconciliation between the justice of a social order and the freedom of individual responsibility, have been well-documented by the writer's biographers. In his notorious "Response to Albert Camus" published in *Les Temps modernes* in August 1952, Sartre would pay eloquent tribute to the Camus of this period: "you were not far from being exemplary. For in you you summed up the struggles of the time, and you outstripped them by your eagerness to live them. You were *someone,* the most complex and richest of people, the last and the best to come from the heirs to Chateaubriand, and the painstaking defender of social causes."[80]

In the postwar period, changing historical circumstances and further moral dilemmas impacting on Camus's understanding of social and political justice force him to consolidate and develop his concern in order to accommodate the increasingly volatile international situation. The failure of the purge in France, an institution to which he had been prepared to sacrifice his own innate sense of justice based on humanist principles, confirms for Camus the impossibility of maintaining absolutes of morality within the historical process. His subsequent quest for a dialogic code of ethics, whereby the conflicting ideals of justice and freedom would come together in a social order guaranteeing individual autonomy, finds expression in the socialist-styled new France which Camus defends in *Combat* and which, once the *révolution manquée* in the *Hexagone* becomes apparent, he transposes on to the world stage where tyranny and totalitarianism threaten international security. In this dimension of his concern for sociopolitical justice, Camus offers an alternative vision to the *politique des blocs,* whereby the political absolutism of the *univers concentrationnaire* makes way for the dialogue of a moral relativism by which to realize a code of international justice based on the democratic principles of tolerance and mutual understanding.

A significant element of Camus's general consideration of justice throughout the postwar phase is the intellectual weight he now lends to the issue of how (political) violence can be morally justified in revolutionary action. As we have seen, this issue impacts on Camus at personal, national and institutional levels and provides a further and telling example of how he is forced to adapt his understanding of sociopolitical justice in the context of radically changing historical circumstances. Indeed, his own misguided idealism in response to the purge now forces the issue on to Camus who, henceforth, would never cease investigating how far violence can be justified in the pursuit of justice. Nowhere is this better illustrated than in the polemical *The Rebel,* published on October 18, 1951, at a moment when the Cold War was in full bloom and its associated political controversies were at their zenith. How the moral resonances and complexities of that controversial book further shape Camus's understanding of justice will form the subject of the next chapter.

7
The Rebel or "an attempt to understand the time I live in"

> In our darkest nihilism I have sought only reasons to go beyond it. Not, I would add, through virtue, nor by a rare elevation of the soul, but by an instinctive fidelity to a light in which I was born, and in which for thousands of years people have learned to welcome life even in suffering.
>
> —Camus, *Selected Essays and Notebooks*

IN AN EARLY REVIEW OF *THE REBEL* PUBLISHED IN *COMBAT,* ONE OF CAmus's former colleagues inauspiciously wrote of the work that "it is a book the impact of which is going to be huge."[1] Indeed, revered by some and reviled by others, the book is a telling piece of Cold War polemic. On the one hand, it has been welcomed as "a major book," "the most brilliant analysis ever made of modern nihilism" and "the key book of modern historico-political theory."[2] On the other hand, it has been dismissed as "a labored study," "a failed great book," and "not merely his [Camus's] worst book but one that did him great harm."[3]

Inasmuch as he invests quite considerable time and effort in the project, *The Rebel* ranks as a significant book for Camus personally, a claim further verified by the writer's own perceptions of his work such as "among my books, . . . the one that I am most fond of" and "my most important book" (*E,* 1629).[4] In essence, the book marks the culmination of a process of protracted reflection occasioned by the moral complexities both during and following the Second World War. The merest glance at Camus's nonfictional writings dating from the postwar period shows that he was intellectually engaged with the fundamental ideas articulated in *The Rebel* well before its actual publication in October 1951. "Remark on Revolt" (*E,* 1682–97), written in 1943–44 and published in *L'Existence* in 1945, is the first version of the opening chapter of the later work, while "Murder and the Absurd," published in 1949, attempts to show a sense of continuity and progression between *The Myth of Sisyphus* and the later "Essay."[5] Polemical pieces on surrealism and Nietzsche, as well as "The Fastidious Assassins" (*TRN,* 1827–33), were all published separately prior to their incorporation into *The Rebel.*[6] In addition, "Neither Victims nor Executioners" (*E,* 329–52) (1946) and "Prometheus in Hell" (*E,* 839–44; *SEN,* 128–31) (1946) rehearse debates consolidated in the "Essay on Revolt," while "Helen's Exile" (*E,* 851–57; *SEN,* 136–40) (1948) looks forward to the antidote to revolutionary nihilism provided by "la pensée de midi." In sum, far from representing a new phase in Camus's moral sensibility, *The Rebel* unites in one work a whole series of reflections and ideas that had engrossed him for much of the preceding decade.[7] Moreover, given that in his essay Camus attempts to formulate an "ethical justification of justice" in relation to revolutionary protest, the work represents a crucial link in the chain of his intellectual engagement with this crucial concept.

Indeed, unlike, say, the *Letters to a German Friend* (where, as we saw in chapter 5, the ideal of justice is formulated in response to the moral dilemmas provoked by the particular historical event of the Second World War), *The Rebel* takes the form of a general treatise ("it is the demonstration of a philosophical thesis, in fact," notes Lionel Dubois) seeking to diagnose an ethical response to univocal quests for justice which, infected with revolutionary nihilism, engender injustice and tyranny.[8] As Raymond Gay-Crosier puts it, "the main issue of [*The Rebel*] can be summarized in a single question: what is justice?"[9] It can thus be maintained that the interplay of the "theoretical" and "practical" components of Camus's concern for sociopolitical justice noticeably changes emphasis in the 1951 "Essay." While in earlier campaigns—most notably, "Misery in Kabylia" and the *chronique judiciaire* for *Alger républicain*—any theoretical aspects of Camus's views on (social and political) justice are in key with, impact on, but—crucially—do not take precedence over practical objectives, in *The Rebel* by contrast, *theoretical* deliberation precedes *practical* purpose.[10] At first sight, it is tempting to interpret this apparent change of direction on Camus's part as being inconsistent with his self-avowed distrust of philosophical "systems" (*E,* 1427). However, while it is indeed the case that in *The Rebel* Camus is, conceptually speaking, breaking new ground in his attempt to theorize his understanding of revolutionary justice, he makes clear that the body of arguments advanced in the book deals with, and is predicated on, practical (and, as we shall see later, his own personal) experience.[11] Before an analysis can be attempted of the moral and political emphases at issue here, it is necessary to flesh out Camus's views of revolution and revolt on which the whole work hinges.

The Ethics of Revolt

It was noted in an earlier chapter that in *The Myth of Sisyphus,* Camus uses his concept of revolt as a response to the moral nihilism of the "absurd sensitivity" (*MS,* 10). Building on this earlier reasoning, now molded by the historical situation of War and Resistance, he meditates in *The Rebel* on the problem of whether, in a world devoid of transcendent meaning, it is possible to define a human form of revolt as a protest against injustice and tyranny, without falling into the moral abyss of revolutionary nihilism. In other words, in a universe where God is dead and where there is no higher law to determine moral behavior, Camus now explores whether alternative human values can be created by which to uphold standards of justice and freedom within the historically volatile context of revolutionary idea(l)s. Thus, from the quest for happiness in a world conditioned by the Absurd (*The Myth of Sisyphus*), Camus goes on to pursue the quest for an ethical justification of justice in a world where moral absolutism prevails (*The Rebel*). From Sisyphus, then, proceeds Prometheus, who (legend has it) defied the established order of things because of his desire to bring justice to humanity and so becomes, for the Camus of *The Rebel,* the paradigm of authentic revolt.[12] To clarify this more precisely, we must pin down what Camus means by revolt and its role in relation to revolution.

Camus first formulates his idea of revolt as an ethical attitude in the 1945 "Remark."[13] Interestingly, the master-slave binary dialectic of the first chapter of *The Rebel,* providing the basis for the detailed analysis of revolt in the three substantive sections of the study, is not yet in place in this original essay.[14] There, Camus draws on the functionary's sense of injustice *vis-à-vis* his employer—a mindset doubtless reminiscent of Nazi bureaucracy during the years of the Vichy administration—to illustrate his philosophical focus (cf. *E,* 1618–19). The change of accent between the 1945 "Remark" and the 1951 "Essay" reflects Camus's increasing familiarization with Hegelian and—more intriguingly—Nietzschean interpretations of the master/slave duality.[15] By taking the side of the master, Nietzsche destroys the equilibrium between affirmation and negation fundamental to Camusian revolt (see below) and, in so doing, he threatens to undermine Camus's entire ethical system. As Maurice Weyembergh has observed, Camus does not dwell in *The Rebel* on Nietzsche's master/slave typology, since to do so would have entailed a far more rigorous consideration of Nietzschean immoralism than Camus—in deference to his own thesis—was apparently prepared to make.[16] (It is perhaps worth recalling here that Camus's thinking generally is deeply influenced by Nietzsche.) Rather, it is Hegel who, in the words of Philip Thody, emerges as "the real villain of [*The Rebel*]" and whose dialectics provide Camus with a conceptual model within which to situate his own moral philosophy of revolt.[17]

What, then, is the thrust of Camus's moral philosophy? Revolt, as he formulates it, is an instinctive reaction or "first truth" (*E,* 1694) and "arises from the spectacle of the irrational in the face of an unjust and incomprehensible condition" (*TR,* 16; translation amended).[18] Recognizing the existence of a "boundary" (*E,* 1682) beyond which he deems it morally reprehensible for his superior to pass, the rebel acknowledges his own rights in relation to his oppressor. His act of revolt thus embraces attitudes of both negation and affirmation, "refusal and consent," and Camus writes of the necessity of maintaining the "perpetual state of tension" (*TR,* 27) between these two polarities if revolt is to retain its ethical impetus.[19] The "no" of the rebel, who refuses to allow the degradation of his person, is, then, also a "yes," since in revolting against his unacceptable condition, the rebel reestablishes his own status in the world while also rediscovering values intrinsic to human beings. It follows that Camusian revolt is not a selfish proposition. The rebel stages his act of revolt "in defense of a dignity common to everyone" (*E,* 1685–86), thus reinforcing human integrity and precipitating human solidarity: "At the same time as repulsion toward the intruder, there is in all revolt a whole and instantaneous support of the individual for a certain part of human experience" (*E,* 1682). Camus draws on a Cartesian-type argument (or inference) to demonstrate the link between the solitary act of revolt and the ethic of human solidarity (*E,* 432; *TR,* 28), and he uses this logic to forge the existence of a human nature: "The analysis of revolt leads us to the suspicion that, contrary to the postulates of contemporary thought, a human nature does exist, as the Greeks believed. Why revolt if there is nothing worth preserving in oneself? The slave asserts himself for the sake of everyone in the world" (*TR,* 22; translation amended). It is, however, not clear from Camus's argument whether one can actually posit a link between the ethic of revolt and the existence of a human nature, since both in the "Remark" and *The Rebel* (*E,* 1687, 429; *TR,* 25), he describes revolt as primarily a *western* idea. Whatever the truth of this, it is clear that because Camus sees revolt to be undertaken in the name of universal values like justice (formulated in terms of equality of worth between persons) and freedom (from oppression, persecution and tyranny) to which humanity aspires, it has the potential of providing a philosophy on the basis of which the idea of a human nature may be developed. Be that as it may, it has to be said that Camus's argument here is open to very serious objections: while, on his own terms, "revolt" provides him with a moral basis on which to build, one cannot claim that he has actually solved anything philosophically with his argument; the question of "universalizability" in ethics is, it has to be said, still hotly disputed. As such, there is a much clearer distinction to be made than Camus allows for between what happens at the individual level of revolt and anything that involves cooperation or collaboration between two individuals or more.[20]

One further point needs to be made on this issue. Inasmuch as a quest for justice drives the rebel to revolt—Camus holds that what primarily motivates the rebel is the will "to serve justice so as not to add to the injustice of the human condition" (*TR,* 249)—it is permissible to infer that he now deems justice an innate idea in all human beings. This hypothesis that Camus perceives justice as a or the fundamental universal value is further substantiated by his reference to Chamfort which he makes, first, in 1944 (*E,* 1101) and subsequently in *The Rebel* itself: "'One must be just before being generous, as one must have bread before having cake'" (*TR,* 75). Justice for Chamfort, as for Camus, is indispensable to interpersonal morality although, for the author of *The Rebel*—as we shall further confirm later—it can only be realized as a relative idea, qualified by freedom.

Whatever the ethical potential of the concept, as an idea in itself the ethic of revolt is limited in scope and it is only through the process of revolution that Camus considers that it can be given concrete expression. As early as September 19, 1944, writing in *Combat,* he had drawn the necessary distinction between the two notions: "Revolution is not revolt. What carried the Resistance for four years was revolt. That is to say the whole, stubborn and at first almost blind refusal of an order wishing to bring people to their knees. Revolt is first of all about the heart" (*E,* 1526). Revolution, as Camus formulates it, immerses the "spontaneous impulse" (*E,* 1526) of revolt into "concerted action" (*E,* 1526), thereby lending actual form to the rebel's realization and so plunging the act of revolt into the processes of history. As Camus goes on to acknowledge in the "Remark," "the word revolution . . . is a movement which comes full circle, which passes from one government to another after a complete translation. . . . The movement of revolt, on the other hand, and in its origins, comes to a sudden halt. It is only an expression. Revolution starts from the clear idea. Exactly, it is the transition of the idea into historical experience, while revolt on the other hand is the movement which leads from individual experience to the idea" (*E,* 1689).[21]

The thrust of Camus's argument in *The Rebel* is that for revolutionary protest to be vindicated, a dialectic of revolt and revolution must be established, so that the revolutionary quest for justice and freedom does not compromise the ethical imperatives of the two ideals.[22] What the body of arguments advanced in Camus's thesis amounts to is an illustration of these ideas by contrast, that is, a justification of these ideas by illustrations of contrary processes (an approach which, incidentally, the writer also adopts in *The Myth of Sisyphus*). There are two fundamental reasons why Camus uses this method. One is that using cult figures such as Sade, Saint-Just, Lautréamont, and Rimbaud, as well as fashionable ideas like Marxism, doubtless adds to the persuasive power of his general argument as he draws on people and concepts then in vogue to make his own thesis more popular and, perhaps, more accessible for his readers. The other is that such an approach would almost inevitably increase sales of the book and so it can be considered a good tactical move on Camus's part in his objective to convince as wide a readership as possible of the validity of his argument—and which succeeded in so far as *The Rebel,* apparently to the author's surprise, had sold 75,000 copies by the time Camus read the typescript of Philip Thody's first book on him in the summer of 1956.[23] Yet how successful is this approach in terms of Camus's attempt to formulate a moral justification of justice? Is it possible, through an account of *révolution manquée,* to discover how revolutionary justice can actually be vindicated? In order to answer these questions, the whole issue of the twin ideals of justice and freedom in relation to revolutionary activity, as analyzed by Camus in *The Rebel,* must now be examined.

JUSTICE, FREEDOM, AND REVOLUTIONARY NIHILISM

The history of modern revolution as Camus assesses it in *The Rebel* is one where justice and freedom are deemed antagonistic ideals. This state of affairs recalls his own quest for reconciliation between the two principles throughout the postwar period and beyond: "These two demands are already to be found in the principle of the movement of revolt, and are to be found again in the first impetus of revolution. The history of revolutions demonstrates, however, that they almost always conflict as though their mutual demands were irreconcilable. Absolute freedom is the right of the strongest to dominate. Therefore it prolongs conflicts which benefit injustice. Absolute justice is achieved by the suppression of all contradiction: therefore it destroys freedom. The revolution to achieve justice, through freedom, ends by aligning them against one another" (*TR,* 251–52; translation amended). Confirming Camus's earlier claim that human prosperity is best served by a plurality of values, these remarks reveal that as absolutes of morality, justice, and freedom are contradictory and irreconcilable concepts. Once revolution accepts the suspension of freedom, then terror pervades it and injustice ensues. Similarly, once justice is suspended, enslavement prevails. In both cases, by applying ethical criteria solely to the *end* of the campaign, moral integrity is sacrificed on the altar of revolutionary ideology: "When revolution aims at absolute justice or absolute freedom, it doubtless leads to the assertion of a total rationalism or determinism which contradicts the very nature of the assertion of revolt" (*E,* 1692). Let us bring into sharper focus the dangers of moral absolutism that this remark raises.

The origin of the modern pursuit of justice, manifested in the historical revolutions of notably France and Russia, is, according to Camus, metaphysical in nature.[24] Just as the slave revolts because he can no longer tolerate the treatment inflicted on him by his master, so the metaphysical rebel, "frustrated by the universe" (*TR,* 29), rejects God, the Great Architect of human suffering and death, in the name of justice: "He confronts the injustice at large in the world with his own principles of justice. Thus all he originally wants is to resolve this contradiction and establish a common reign of justice, if he can, or of injustice if he is driven to the end of his tether" (*TR,* 29–30; translation amended). For Camus, the archetypal metaphysical rebel is Dostoevsky's Ivan Karamazov (*E,* 465–71; *TR,* 50–56). In his revolt against the injustice of human mortality (which finds its most poignant expression in the death of innocent children, an injustice to which Camus himself is very acutely sensitive), Karamazov denies God in the name of a higher ideal of justice: "Ivan will no longer have recourse to this mysterious God, but to a higher principle, namely justice. He launches the essential undertaking of revolt, which is that of replacing the reign of grace by the reign of justice" (*TR,* 50; translation amended).[26] Yet, whatever his altruistic motives for action—based on the idea of compassion for his fellow beings, Ivan's vision of justice embraces the plight of all people facing the same prospect of death (*E,* 466–67; *TR,* 51)—Karamazov's revolt collapses into nihilism since he cannot conceive of justice beyond the realm of the divine. With the concept of ethical constraint removed from the world, all actions are necessarily of equivalent value and, as such, equally justified according to *a priori* logic: "if there is no virtue, there is no law: 'Everything is permitted'" (*TR,* 52; translation amended). Devoid of all moral parameters, "justice" and "injustice" become indistinguishable, so that Ivan can no longer posit a human vision of justice in opposition to the injustices perceived as inherent in the divine order. To the question "can one live and hold one's ground in a permanent state of revolt?" (*TR,* 53; translation amended), Ivan responds with logical absolutism. His "everything is permitted" represents a crucial factor in the legitimization of murder and so is seen, in Camus's eyes, as pivotal to the history of twentieth-century nihilism: "With this 'everything is permitted' the history of contemporary nihilism really begins. . . . Ivan rebels against a murderous God; but from the moment that he begins to consider the reasons for his revolt, he deduces the law of murder. . . . Long reflection on our condition as people sentenced to death only leads to the justification of crime" (*TR,* 52, 53; translation amended).[27]

If, in Camus's reading, Dostoevsky illustrates how an uncompromising pursuit of *justice* can lead to injustice and tyranny when the ethical principles of the ideal are jettisoned in favor of moral absolutism, Nietzsche demonstrates how similar consequences can arise from revolutionary action where *freedom* is rendered a moral absolute (*E,* 475–89; *TR,* 57–71).[28] In effect, the German philosopher begins where the Russian writer ends in that Nietzsche advocates that it *is* possible to live in a state removed from all transcendent values: "With him," Camus notes of Nietzsche, "nihilism becomes conscious for the first time" (*TR,* 57). In a world where God is dead, the human being is total freedom and must create his or her own values. Nietzsche proposes to replace all value judgments "by absolute assent, a complete and exalted allegiance to this world. Thus, from absolute despair will spring infinite joy, from blind servitude freedom without obligation. . . . Total acceptance of total necessity is his paradoxical definition of freedom" (*TR,* 63–64). Inasmuch as his *amor fati* amounts to an affirmation of all things past, present and future (conveniently summed up as "fate"), Nietzsche effectively deifies destiny and reestablishes the world as god that human beings, by manifesting their freedom, can recreate in whatever image they choose: "To say yes to the world, to reproduce it, is simultaneously to recreate the world and oneself, to become the great artist, the creator. . . . Divinity without immortality defines the extent of the creator's freedom" (*TR,* 65). The "superior type of humanity" (*TR,* 69) which, in Camus's reading, ultimately results from Nietzsche's consenting "Yes" once again provides fertile ground for political nihilism, the most telling historical example of which is, of course, the spurious justification of German National Socialism.

It can thus be seen that both Dostoevsky's Ivan Karamazov and Nietzsche's absolute affirmation demonstrate Camus's principal prognosis in *The Rebel:* when pursued without qualification, as absolute ideals, justice and freedom both forfeit their ethical meaning and so degenerate into moral nihilism. By dissolving the "yes/no" equilibrium of Camusian revolt, justice and freedom, when polluted by nihilistic logic, destroy the potential for interpersonal morality and ultimately lead to intolerance and terror.[29] In Hegelian terminology, "the slave starts by begging for justice and ends by wanting to wear a crown" (*TR,* 31). To see how this crisis develops in Camus's moral and political philosophy, an analysis will now be made of his assessment of historical revolt, which, "more that of Cain's children than Prometheus's disciples" (*E,* 443), has fallen into nihilism.

In the second substantive section of his study, "Historical Rebellion," Camus spotlights the events of the French Revolution as the moment when the principles of metaphysical revolt first find expression in the historical process (*E,* 521–40; *TR,* 82–102).[30] More than a revolt against the impositions of the *ancien régime,* the French revolutionaries of 1789 attacked in the name of absolute human justice in what is commonly yet somewhat confusingly understood to be the legacy of Jean-Jacques Rousseau's *Social Contract* [*Contrat social*] (1762) the principle of divine right and the legitimacy of the monarchical constitution in which the human Kingdom of Justice was secondary to the divine Kingdom of Grace (*E,* 522; *TR,* 83).[31] Destroying as it does the principle of divine right, the execution of Louis XVI on January 21, 1793, provides, in Camus's reading, a symbolic thrust for all subsequent revolutions, where the quest for justice, predicated on human reason, effectively becomes the new deity. The legacy of the French Revolution—the legitimization of murder as a means of political change (cf. *E,* 518; cf. *TR,* 79)—thus has great resonance in the history of political nihilism and totalitarianism as Camus sees it: "The regicides . . . are succeeded by the deicides of the twentieth century, who wish to take the logic of revolt all the way and wish to make the earth a kingdom where human beings are God. The reign of history begins and, identifying themselves only with their history, human beings . . . will henceforth devote themselves to the nihilistic revolutions of the twentieth century" (*TR,* 102; translation amended).

Camus's reading of the French Revolution requires comment, since as a republican himself (i.e. for the politics of equality and against the politics of privilege), he displays a surprising sympathy for the myth of divine monarchy and its embodiment in the king whose merciful nature in relation to social justice particularly attracts the writer's attention: "The king, in one of his aspects, is the divine emissary in charge of human affairs and therefore of the administration of justice. Like God himself, he is the last recourse of the victims of misery and injustice. In principle, the people can appeal to the king for help against their oppressors. 'If the king only knew, if the Czar only knew . . .' was the frequently expressed sentiment of the French and Russian people during periods of great distress. It is true in France, at least, that, when it did know, the monarchy often tried to defend the lower classes against the oppressions of the aristocracy and the bourgeoisie" (*TR,* 83). As long as the divine incarnate was perceived as a savior gracefully dispensing justice to the socially impoverished, the idea that justice could be established without the king, a principle on the basis of which the French Revolution was staged, is preposterous. Just as Ivan Karamazov cannot believe in a morality removed from the realm of God, so the subjects of the *ancien régime* define their code of justice (social, political, and constitutional) in relation to divine monarchy and misericord. Only when the revolutionaries, whose thirst for a justice built on *human* values makes them yearn for equality, dispelled the myth of divine monarchy, does justice emerge as a principle in its own right. This principle, no longer subordinate, lies in direct opposition to the Divine Kingdom: "Justice has this in common with grace and this alone, that it wants to be total and to rule absolutely. From the moment that they conflict, they fight to the death" (*TR,* 84). Faced with the choice between absolute justice and absolute grace, Camus—with two centuries of historical evidence to guide him—opts for the latter since, in the words of Susan Dunn, "arbitrary grace appeared less threatening than the Revolution's desacralized principle of rational and merciless justice."[32]

This last remark raises an interesting issue. By once more highlighting the dilemma between (human) justice and (divine) mercy in his account of the French Revolution, Camus in effect makes a retrospective link to his own response to the morally contentious issue of the purge in France, as discussed in the preceding chapter.

I shall return later to Camus's own claim that *The Rebel* is, in a sense, "a confidence" (*E,* 743), but two points in this connection must be mentioned immediately in the light of the above. One is that by offering a retake, as it were, of his earlier confrontation with Mauriac over the issue of the purge, Camus—who now chooses mercy over revolutionary justice—confirms his earlier error of judgment in having deemed human individuals political expedients.[33] The other is that such an interpretation indicates a therapeutic motive for the writing of *The Rebel,* a book which, as we have already acknowledged, Camus himself considers "an attempt to understand the time [he] live[s] in" (*TR,* 11). In this reading, the "Essay on Revolt" becomes less a universal testimony and more a personal avowal: a means by which Camus attempts to purge himself of his own earlier disillusionment at the time of France's *révolution manquée* (an account of which, incidentally, is conspicuously absent from *The Rebel* itself).[34]

Returning to the conflict between justice and grace immortalized by the French Revolution, if the nineteenth century still offered a hope that the two ideals could be reconciled, then twentieth-century historicism, for Camus, heralds the overthrow of both: "How to live without grace—that is the question that dominates the nineteenth century. 'By justice,' answered all those who did not want to accept absolute nihilism. To the people who despaired of the Kingdom of Heaven, they promised the kingdom of human beings. . . . The question of the twentieth century . . . and which tortures the contemporary world has gradually been specified: how to live without grace and without justice?" (*TR,* 191, 192; translation amended)

It is to Hegel (*E,* 541–55; *TR,* 103–17) and his successors that one must turn if the implications of these remarks are to be fully grasped.[35] Applying many of the ideas of the French revolutionaries while at the same time attempting to eliminate the causes of their eventual failure, the author of *Phenomenology of Spirit* seeks to apply the revolutionaries' abstract justice to the concrete experience of history. History (*Geschichte*) is a fundamental concept for Hegel, who considers "world history" as essentially the development of human freedom, an idea which will only be fully realized with the end of history. In Hegel's philosophical system, meaning and significance are derived from the course taken by human history, the final outcome of which is an ideal "rational" state in which individual and collective interests lie in complete harmony.[36] In Camus's somewhat dubious reading of Hegel, moral values are rendered redundant in the present and are reborn "in the future of the world" (*TR,* 103), so that the realization of principles such as justice and freedom can only be achieved at the end of history. Admittedly, Hegel is resigned to the reality of evil and suffering *within* history, deeming it a necessary link in the chain leading toward the goal of reason.[37] However, contrary to what Camus argues, it does not necessarily follow from this that issues of morality are deferred until the future. Hegel's view of history is, after all, empirical and, far from undermining principles of citizenship, his view of the "rational State" is dependent on the individual freely consenting to the moral codes of the collective.

Be that as it may, Camus's understanding of Hegel is such that in political terms, morality is deemed subservient to efficacy, a view borne out by his readings of the Marxist, Leninist, and Stalinist manifestations of Soviet communism (*E,* 593–647; *TR,* 156–211). Following the model of Hegel's historical determinism, human lives are considered expendable in the cause of "just" political ends, which are seen to constitute the onward flow of history. Hegel's view of justice, as Camus understands it, thus destroys provisional morality in the quest for historical achievement: "Hegel probably permits the forgiveness of sins at the end of history. However, until then, every human activity is sinful" (*TR,* 113; translation amended). Such a vision provides Camus with a philosophical rationale for the modern will to power ("to kill or conquer" [*TR,* 109]) and so paves the way for terrorism in what he refers to as both its "rational" and "irrational" totalitarian forms. However, once again, Camus's reading here is open to criticism, not least since Hegel's idea of the state does not preclude, but is itself preordained by, the will of its individuals. Far from representing the state as the enemy of the people, Hegel is preoccupied with how best to establish a social set-up in which the interests of the collective *and* of the individual are in harmony. The idea that by positing the absolute moral authority of the state, Hegel defends totalitarianism is actually a distortion of his notion of a rational state, a distortion to which Camus himself remains very acutely sensitive in his general reading of Hegel.

Camus goes on to suggest that the early results of Hegel's philosophical idealism first find expression in the actions of young Russian nihilists who, repelled by the injustice prevalent in their own country, sought to change their situation by engaging in revolutionary justice through acts of terrorism, often leading to their own deaths. He spotlights "three of the possessed"—Pisarev, Bakunin, and Netchaev (*E,* 560–70; *TR,* 122–33)—whom he considers exemplifications of Hegelian reasoning since, together, these nihilists apply the "to kill or conquer" principle to the revolutionary arena.

At the same time, they develop the range of destruction to include their own sacrifice.[38] Terroristic messianism and the creation of martyrs are seen to prolong the cycle of political murder and repression, while the prospect of justice "for the sake of some unknown distant city" (*CP,* 143) justifies, according to Camus's reading of Hegelian logic, the use of human lives as political expedients.

We need to pause for a moment at this point, however. For while in keeping with the method to illustrate his ideas by contrast, Camus uses the examples of Russian revolutionaries such as Pisarev, Bakunin, and Netchaev to show how historical revolt jettisons its ethical origin and falls into revolutionary nihilism when the end is seen to justify the means, his interpretation of one particular band of Russian revolutionaries, "The Fastidious Assassins," momentarily breaks this cycle (*E,* 571–79; *TR,* 133–42). Indeed, the revolutionaries of 1905, whose terroristic acts are given dramatic expression in *The Just Assassins,* offer a counterblast to the other manifestations of revolutionary nihilism analyzed in *The Rebel* where "revolt cuts itself off from its roots and abstains from any concrete morality" (*TR,* 101; translation amended). As such, it will be useful to give special consideration to Camus's assessment of "these exceptional souls" (*TRN,* 1834), since his interpretation will tell us much as to the principles on the basis of which he will formulate his moral justification of justice.

For "The Fastidious Assassins," as for Camus himself, violence is "necessary" and "inexcusable" (*E,* 575; *TR,* 138). On the one hand, it is deemed necessary for the terrorists to kill "in order to build a world where there will be no more killing at all" (*CP,* 131; translation amended); on the other hand, murder is deemed morally reprehensible and the instrument of "revolting executioners" (*E,* 721). In his account of these terrorists, Camus points up the opposing components of their revolutionary quest, claiming that "tortured by contradictions" (*TR,* 135) (like Tarrou in *The Plague*), they have "lived out the rebel destiny in its most contradictory form" (*TR,* 138). Unlike many of the other examples Camus draws on in *The Rebel* to illustrate his thesis by contrast, the Russian revolutionaries of 1905 keep intact the "yes/no" equilibrium of authentic revolt. They exhibit a profound respect for human life without denying the necessity of revolutionary justice. Drawn to terrorism "through a personal obligation as much as through their political system" (*TRN,* 1827), this band of revolutionaries for whom Camus expresses "respect and admiration" (*TRN,* 1834) refuses to justify the means of their revolutionary campaign by the end they ultimately pursue. Only by ensuring that the means remain consonant with the end—the counter to Camus's reading of Hegelian logic, where the end is seen to justify the means—do they justify their cause. As Kaliayev puts it in *The Just Assassins,* "to die for our ideal—it's the only way to prove myself worthy of it, . . . it's the only justification" (*CP,* 132). Murder is thus vindicated by selfless sacrifice: "A life is paid for by another life, and from these two sacrifices springs the promise of a value" (*TR,* 138).[39] In "The Fastidious Assassins" ["Les Meurtriers délicats"], the first version of this section of *The Rebel* originally published in *La Table ronde* in January 1948, this "value" is defined in more precise terms as one "which must serve the progress of justice" (*TRN,* 1832), thus reinforcing the point that justice is not only perceived as the end for which the Russian revolutionaries stage their campaign, but also as a moral concept attributable to the means by which the end is to be obtained.

Interestingly, the "meaning" of "The Fastidious Assassins" is already alluded to in the opening pages of *The Rebel:* "If an individual actually consents to die, and, when the occasion arises, accepts death as a consequence of his rebellion, (s)he demonstrates that (s)he is willing to sacrifice him/herself for the sake of a common good which is considered more important than his/her own destiny. If (s)he prefers the risk of death to a denial of the rights (s)he defends, it is because the latter are considered more important than (s)he is. (S)he acts, therefore, in the name of certain values which are still indeterminate but which are felt are common to him/herself and to all people" (*TR,* 21; translation amended). In the spirit of these remarks, by applying moral criteria to the *means* as well as to the end of their revolutionary campaign, the Russian revolutionaries of 1905 ensure that political action remains relative to moral values, and it is this ethical framework that provokes their dilemma and sense of "torture." It is surely significant that the idea of justice brought about through a "redemptive" death, which is essentially the lesson Camus draws from Kaliayev's example, is evident in some of his other (imaginative) writings. In *A Happy Death,* for instance, upon murdering Zagreus, Mersault contracts the "feverish shiver" (*HD,* 9; translation amended, 103; cf. *CA1,* 47) to which he ultimately succumbs, so that a life given atones for a life taken away. Jean Sarocchi, recognizing a similar trait in *The Outsider,* goes on to deem Kaliayev in *The Just Assassins* "a Meursault recycled in terrorism."[40] One might add that Lucius's readiness to yield his right to life to save the emperor in *Caligula* (*TRN,* 92; *CP,* 55), and Diego's consent to sacrifice his life in exchange for that of Victoria in *State of Siege* (*TRN,* 287), also demonstrate Camus's particular sensibility in relation to this issue.

However, whatever Camus's personal curiosity, it is clear that as an idea in itself, "redemptive justice" is devoid of practical import and, as such, one must question why he attaches so much importance to an idea which, as Fred Willhoite and John Cruickshank rightly observe, appears inconsistent with his earlier reflections on the value of human life as expressed in *The Myth of Sisyphus.*[41] This disparity notwithstanding, I cannot agree with Jean-Jacques Brochier's assessment that Camus's affection for Kaliayev is merely a Utopian gesture: "a life for a life . . . is offset by the idealism of the noble soul."[42] Such a view underestimates the considerable deliberation Camus privately undergoes before endorsing Kaliayev's example. Indeed, to judge from the *Carnets,* Camus initially offers a partial disclaimer of Kaliayev's act of redemptive justice: "A life is paid for by a life. The reasoning is fallacious but worthy of respect? (A life that is taken away is not the equivalent of a life that is given)" (*CA2,* 102). This hesitation—due, perhaps, to the nature of his earlier reasoning in *The Myth*—shows how Camus's own scruples regarding the inviolable nature of human life inform his interpretation of revolutionary justice. At that stage (mid-1947, the date of the aforementioned *Carnets* entry), he does not deem an equivalence between a life deliberately taken and a life deliberately given; only later, as his research for *The Rebel* intensifies, does Camus introduce the notion of *limit* by which to render Kaliayev's example morally defensible: "The final stage of the argument of revolt: agree to kill oneself so as not to become an accomplice of murder in general" (*CA2,* 134; cf. *CA2,* 151).

Indeed, it is on the idea of *limit* that one must focus if the significance of "The Fastidious Assassins" is to be fully understood. The fact of the matter is that in the example of the Russian revolutionaries of 1905—reminiscent of what, elsewhere, he calls "innocent murderers"—Camus discovers how standards of morality can be maintained in revolutionary action.[43] The point is conveniently made in a 1955 prefatory remark to *The Just Assassins:* "I only wanted to show that action itself had limits. Only that which recognizes these limits and which, if it is necessary to cross them, at least accepts death, is good and just action" (*TRN,* 1733). Earlier (1950), drawing a distinction between "dead justice" and "living justice," Camus asserts the ethical imperative not to allow revolutionary apocalypticism to dictate moral obligations, since "justice dies the moment that it becomes comfortable, the moment that it stops being a burning sensation and a strain in itself" (*E,* 721). Anticipating "la pensée de midi," Camus formulates here a moral justification for his sense of justice.

One further point should be made on the issue of "redemptive justice." I have already had cause to indicate that as well as a general commentary on his era, *The Rebel* can also be read in terms of personal testimony. This claim is further substantiated by Camus's special consideration of the Russian revolutionaries of 1905, in that it is possible to infer that he discovers in the example of these fastidious terrorists a moral justification for the French Resistance movement. The members of the Resistance, like "The Fastidious Assassins," triumphed over nihilism by being prepared to risk, and sacrifice, their own lives in the revolutionary quest for justice and freedom. Camus doubtless has the Russian terrorists in mind when, in "Defense of *The Rebel*," he observes that "at the end of the experiences and thoughts that I have consigned to *The Rebel,* I can say . . . with firmness that, if today it were necessary to relive what we lived through during the 1940s, I would at the same time know against whom and why I am fighting" (*E,* 1714).

Before returning in our next section to the idea of *limit* as a response to revolutionary nihilism as fostered by "la pensée de midi," mention must be made of what is undoubtedly the most controversial aspect of Camus's work. Whatever the specific significance of "The Fastidious Assassins" in the body of arguments advanced in *The Rebel,* the moral imperatives of these revolutionaries appear to be subsumed within a different, broader, perspective of historical revolt which Camus provides as he moves away from considering individual acts of terrorism toward an examination of what he refers to as state terrorism (*E,* 583–653; *TR,* 146–218).[44] Here, the quest for justice becomes inextricably bound up with the pursuit and preservation of political power and authority. In this section of his study, Camus spotlights what he calls "the growing omnipotence of the State" and "the strange and terrifying growth of the modern State" (*E,* 583; *TR,* 146) which he deems the result of modern revolutionary ideology: "1789 brings Napoleon; 1848 Napoleon III; 1917 Stalin; the Italian disturbances of the twenties, Mussolini; the Weimar Republic, Hitler" (*TR,* 146; translation amended). The product of nineteenth-century nihilism, the "irrational terror" of Mussolini and Hitler provides Camus with an unstable projection of Hegel's degenerate passion to dominate: "They were the first to construct a State on the concept that everything was meaningless and that history was only written in terms of the chances of force" (*TR,* 147; translation amended). Yet he insists that fascist ideology does not merit the title of revolution as it lacks "the ambition of universality" (*TR,* 146). Rather, it is Marxism that Camus deems the most comprehensive historical expression of revolutionary dogma since Hegel and, as such, it is seen by him as the most significant threat to traditional democratic values upholding the sociopolitical standards of justice and freedom.

However, just as Camus's reading of Hegel in *The Rebel* is open to serious criticism, so his analysis of Marxism is, at best, contentious.[45] In essence, Camus applauds the social criticism made by Marxism but rejects its utopianism. In other words, while he has no dispute with the Marxist campaign to revolutionize social strata and thereby quash the injustices of the capitalist system, he has no truck with Marxist messianism which, Camus insists, "reintroduced crime and punishment into the unchristian world, but only in relation to history. Marxism in one of its aspects is a doctrine of culpability on the part of human beings and innocence on history's" (*TR,* 207; translation amended). Notes for the *Carnets* (*C2,* 164, 240; *CA2,* 83, 123) likewise draw attention to the link Camus forges between notions of Christian and Marxist Revelation, while in his "First Response" to Emmanuel d'Astier in June 1948, he makes his antiMarxist position clear: "Despairing of immediate justice, Marxists claiming to be orthodox have chosen to dominate the world in the name of a future justice. In a certain sense, they are no longer on this earth despite appearances. They are in logic" (*E,* 362).

In 1957, Camus would insist: "if I have been a Communist, I have never been a Marxist."[46] Indeed, whatever its other characteristics, *The Rebel* is essentially a criticism of Marxism as a threat to traditional democratic values upholding justice and freedom. Formulated in terms of the perfect (i.e. "classless") society, that can only be achieved at the end of history when Communism reaches its maturity, Marxist justice is rejected by Camus as totalitarian paternalism. Repudiating God, Marx puts his faith in humanity's ability to make good absolute justice in the future. However, while thus anticipating the realization of a perfect morality as the end of his revolutionary dream, Marx is charged by Camus of not applying moral criteria to the means by which to bring about this perfect morality: "The end of history is not an exemplary or a perfectionist value: it is an arbitrary and terroristic principle" (*TR,* 191). Indeed, for Camus, whatever hastens the attainment of the Marxist prophecy is deemed justified: "The golden age, postponed until the end of history and coincident, to add to its attractions, with an apocalypse, therefore justifies everything. . . . Utopia replaces God by the future. Then it proceeds to identify the future with ethics; the only values are those which serve this particular future" (*TR,* 175, 176).

From such political expediency, offending as it does provisional morality, it is a short step to the justification of murder in Camus's eyes, a state of affairs leading him to bracket Marxism and fascism as similar ideologies of State terror.[47]

Inasmuch as he thus perceives it as an instrument of state totalitarianism, Camus's critique of Marxism is not dissimilar to that developed by Karl Popper in *The Open Society and its Enemies* (1945), a book with which he was familiar and whose influence on *The Rebel* as a whole should not be underestimated. Indeed, Maurice Weyembergh has provided a useful account of the points of convergence between Camus's rejection of *historisme*—the deification of the historical process—and Popper's critique of *historicism*—"[the most powerful of] those social philosophies which are responsible for the widespread prejudice against the possibilities of democratic reform."[48] Yet such views are in fact a distortion of the Marxist perspective which, contrary to Camus's claims, does *not* deny democratic ideals. Indeed, in his criticism of Hegel's "Civil Society," Marx himself states his belief in democracy: "Just as religion does not create man, but man creates religion, so the constitution does not create the people but the people the constitution."[49] He would also never approve the use of revolutionary terror.[50] Yet in his general distrust of ideological doctrines, Camus remains acutely critical of Marxist historical determinism, where the quest for justice is deemed subservient to expendiency in that it is seen to allow the sacrifice of human integrity underpinning interpersonal morality.

Camus's critical reading of Marxist messianism in *The Rebel,* in part, accounts for the hostile reception of the work by contemporary left-wing, pro-Marxist critics, spearheaded by Sartre and Jeanson in *Les Temps modernes,* whose polemics with Camus fueled what was an already fierce intellectual debate on the ethics of revolutionary communism.[51] Central to this debate were the revelations surrounding Stalin's forced labor camps where, in Communism's Soviet manifestation, human suffering and the suppression of individual freedom were consciously being institutionalized as a means to an end. Although he had (somewhat belatedly, it has to be said) himself denounced the existence of these camps in *Les Temps modernes,* Sartre's support for Communism as the only credible ideology to help the victims of capitalist oppression was now becoming increasingly discernible. Evidence of his *rapprochement* with the PCF in particular is provided by "The Communists and Peace," [*Les Communistes et la paix*] an (unfinished) essay which one commentator deems "the most unambiguous expression of Sartre's support for the Communist Party," that appeared in *Les Temps modernes* in three parts between 1952 and 1954.[52] Although himself never joining the PCF and becoming a "contemporary" Marxist, Sartre was by this stage a self-avowed fellow-traveler who perceived (French) Communism as the perfect vehicle for realizing social justice.[53] While, in *The Rebel,* Camus resists historical determinism in the name of human morality, Sartre deems history fundamental to the concept of "situation" and thus indispensable to the manifestation of human freedom on which the quest for social justice depends: "we live in history like fish in water, we have an acute awareness of our historical responsibility."[54] Accordingly, in his now infamous "Response to Albert Camus," Sartre accuses his adversary of austere moralism, denying historical reality and lying in stark contradiction with his own embrace of history during the war years from which Camus is seen to emerge as "the admirable union of a person, an action and a work."[55] For Sartre, embracing the historical process is fundamental to achieving social justice, since "in order to deserve the right to influence people who are struggling, one must first of all take part in their struggle, one must first of all accept many things if one wants to try to change some of them."[56] It is in this context, and in contradistinction to the thesis advanced in *The Rebel,* that one should read the first volume of Sartre's *Critique of Dialectical Reason* [*Critique de la raison dialectique*], which explores the idea of Marxism as an ideology of salvation by applying existentialist subjectivity to the Marxist ideal of historical materialism.[57] While for Camus, then, the quest for sociopolitical justice is almost invariably obscured by the ideal of historical fulfillment, Sartre considers the two necessarily and inextricably tied.

It is clear from the above analysis that *The Rebel* is a work of considerable intellectual investment on Camus's part and that its arguments are of universal significance (not to say controversial). However, as well as this "stand on current affairs" (*E,* 729), the book can also usefully be read as a *personal* testimony of Camus's misguided idealism, that, as we discovered in the preceding chapter, temporarily clouded his concern for justice at the time of the notorious purge trials in France. Camus himself justifies such a reading of *The Rebel* when, in an interview granted to *La Gazette des Lettres* in February 1952, he remarks of his intentions in the work that "I just wanted to recount an experience, mine, which I also know is that of many others. In certain respects, this book is a confidence, the only kind of confidence at least of which I am capable" (*E,* 743). Elsewhere, as has already been noted, he emphasizes the significance he personally accords the work (*E,* 1629) while, in correspondence with Philip Thody, he concedes that he had "been associated with all the thoughts of which he speaks" in the book and that "at one time or another of his life," he had "felt attraction or solidarity for every one of them."[58] And, in correspondence with Mamaine Koestler dated November 23, 1951, he writes with regard to *The Rebel,* "without appearing to, I have confessed in it."[59]

It seems reasonable to deduce from all this that in one of its dimensions, *The Rebel* is a very personal piece of writing: a testing ground for ideas or, as Camus himself puts it in the original French, "une épreuve."[60] My contention is that Camus uses the book, in part, as a means by which to purge himself of his own sense of "anguish at having increased injustice in the belief that [he was] serving justice" (*CA2,* 129), instigated by his earlier condonation of capital punishment as a means to an end in postwar France. The following extract from one of Camus's "Letters on Revolt," as collected in *Actuelles II* in 1953, can be offered in support of this claim: "If *The Rebel* . . . judges anyone, then it is firstly its author. All those for whom the questions raised in this book are not just rhetorical have understood that I was analyzing a contradiction which to begin with had been mine. The thoughts of which I speak fed me and I wanted them to continue by ridding them of what, in them, prevented them in my mind from progressing. . . . The only passion which drives *The Rebel* is precisely that of revival" (*E,* 753).[61]

These comments bear witness to the personal motives for writing *The Rebel,* thus further confirming the private significance of the book for Camus. The intellectual disillusionment that Camus experiences in the face of the *justice manquée* of the purge in France, an issue that is fundamental to the "therapeutic" reading of the 1951 "Essay," was highlighted in chapter 6 but is conveniently recalled here.[62] Camus's disenchantment *vis-à-vis* the failure of the purge translates into a sense of personal "anguish," that he records in the *Carnets* (*C2,* 250; *CA2,* 129). His support in favor of fascists such as Brasillach and Rebatet attests to Camus's recognition of the impossibility of establishing a perfect human system of justice, even though, in his initial responses to the purge, this is precisely what he had championed in *Combat.* Indeed, just as many of the figures and ideas he draws on in *The Rebel* are seen to justify the suspension of provisional morality in the pursuit of a "just" end somewhere in the future, so Camus, in his quest for justice to prevail in postwar France, had initially supported the view that the end justifies the means, i.e. that the human individual can justifiably be deemed expendable in certain circumstances. What the whole experience of the purge confirms is that justice is conditioned by history—not in a Hegelian sense, but in that absolutes of morality are incompatible with historical circumstances. Camus makes clear his mistaken moral idealism in his temporary belief to the contrary in a public address in December 1946: "for a long time I believed that this country could not do without justice. But . . . justice since the Liberation has turned out so difficult that we must now feel that all human justice has its limits and that this country, in the end, might also need mercy" (*E,* 1887).

Viewed from the particular perspective of Camus's own crisis of conscience at the time of the *justice manquée* of the purge in France, *The Rebel* can usefully be considered a means by which the writer attempts to purge himself of his earlier "Saint-Just" idealism. Yet whatever the personal motifs of *The Rebel,* it is clear that the book is not *presented* as personal testimony. Indeed, as we have seen, the work takes the form of a treatise in its quest for an antidote to revolutionary nihilism. Having demonstrated how Camus illustrates his ideas by contrast, it is now time to return to Raymond Gay-Crosier's fundamental question on which the work pivots: "what is justice?"[63]

A Moral Justification of Justice

There is, it seems, a distinct lack of continuity between the final section of *The Rebel,* "Thought at the Meridian" ["La Pensée de Midi"], which purports to provide a moral response to revolutionary nihilism in the tradition of Greek Hellenism, and the preceding analyses of revolt which has morally imploded. In the words of John Cruickshank, "near the end, the book begins to fall apart. Despite Camus' eloquence and ingenuity it is difficult to find a genuine link between the criticisms he has made and the conclusions he draws. The final pages strike one as an unsuccessful attempt to turn a fundamentally negative argument into a positive one. . . . After 350 pages of admirably clear and direct prose Camus allows himself a series of lyrical flights."[64] However, as Raymond Gay-Crosier observes, "to say that *la pensée de midi* has only a feeble rhetorical or poetic value is not to recognize that the generating power of an idea is not measured by its immediate realization but by the number and the quality of its germinations"[65] It is fair to say that *in itself* "la pensée de midi" is a nebulous philosophy which offers a response incommensurate with the actual crises portrayed in the rest of the book; yet, as a moral philosophy on the basis of which it is possible to establish standards of justice and freedom in political struggle, it provides a rationale worthy of consideration.

"The demand for justice ends in injustice if it is not primarily based on an ethical justification of justice" (*TR,* 177). For Camus, the meaning of this pivotal phrase from *The Rebel* owes its intellectual authority and justification, in part, to classical Greek philosophy.[66] Camus's indebtedness to the Ancient Greeks has been well-documented and I do not propose to dwell on the issue here; suffice it to say, sensing within him "a Greek heart" (*E,* 380), Camus looks to Greek thought for inspiration in the modern quest for moral understanding (see, for instance, *C1,* 99–101; *CA1,* 44–45).[67] His self-avowed affinity with pre-Socratic Greek thinking (*E,* 1615), the essence of which is that the human quest for unity is modeled on and achieved through the contemplation of the perfect order of the cosmos, is germane to "la pensée de midi" where, in his quest for a moral justification of justice, Camus draws inspiration from Mediterranean "beauty."[68] Just as the pre-Socratics perceived Nature as the source of moral reason, so Camus, who "does not have enough faith in reason to subscribe to a belief in progress, or to any philosophy of History" (*SEN,* 125), looks to the earth for the "truth" of moral meaning (*C2,* 174; *CA2,* 89; cf. *E,* 595; *TR,* 158). Or, as Denis Salas puts it, "in the sense of a harmony between human beings and nature, justice becomes synonymous with beauty and happiness."[69] The idea formulated in "la pensée de midi" in contradistinction to Hegelian historicism that "real generosity towards the future lies in giving all to the present" (*TR,* 268) recalls Camus's earlier paeans to his "loyalty to the Earth" to be found, for instance, in "Summer in Algiers" and the epigraph to *The Myth of Sisyphus* (from Pindar's *Pythian*).[70]

"Remaining loyal to the earth" is an idea fundamental to Camus's ethical justification of justice which, as he makes clear in "Defense of *The Rebel,*" takes reality as its point of reference, since "if justice is only an instinct, then injustice is also justified as an instinct" (*E,* 1703). For Camus, who "can understand only in human terms" (*MS,* 51), and who posits that "the world is beautiful, and outside it there is no salvation" (*SEN,* 100), the acid test determining the moral accountability of the quest for justice is its capacity to uphold moral values in reality, as opposed to its conceptualization as a moral cog in the machine of the future. Thus resisting Hegelian historicism, Camus will not neglect injustices in the *present* on behalf of the (predicted) *future:* "In this noon of thought, the rebel thus disclaims divinity in order to share in the struggles and destiny of everyone. We shall choose Ithaca, the faithful land, frugal and audacious thought, lucid action, the generosity of those who understand. In the light, the earth remains our first and our last love. Our brothers are breathing beneath the same sky as us; justice is a living thing. Now is born that strange joy which helps us to live and die, and which we shall never again renounce to a later time" (*TR,* 280; translation amended).[71]

Contra the Hegelian ideal of a perfect morality or "absolute justice" to be realized at the end of history, Camus's understanding of justice, as formulated in "la pensée de midi," is such that it can only be vindicated by virtue of its potential to maintain moral parameters *within* the historical process. It follows that Camus's "ethical" vision of justice which ultimately emerges from *The Rebel* is as a *relative* concept, qualified by other values—most notably, freedom—to yield a moral philosophy in keeping with that of authentic revolt: "Revolt . . . only aspires to the relative and can only promise an assured dignity coupled with relative justice. It supposes a limit at which the community of human beings is established" (*TR,* 254; translation amended). As we saw in the preceding chapter, the idea of reconciling justice and freedom was one of the leitmotivs of Camus's postwar morality. The fact that, in *The Rebel,* he sets great store by the need to bring together these two contradictory concepts in the interests of human prosperity bears witness to the continuity and progression in his thinking. Born of a relative moral psychology, justice and freedom, in Camus's reading, must be pursued *together* if they are ultimately to rescue politics from moral degeneration: "The revolution of the twentieth century has arbitrarily separated, for over-ambitious ends of conquest, two inseparable ideas. Absolute freedom mocks at justice. Absolute justice denies freedom. To be fruitful, the two ideas must find their limits in one another" (*TR,* 255).[72]

This leads us to two further ideas from Ancient Greek civilization to which Camus appeals in "la pensée de midi" for an intellectual justification of his moral position: *limit* and *moderation.* Erecting absolutes of human reason (the cornerstone of what Camus calls "European pride" [*TR,* 16]) is a practice anathema to the classical Greek mentality where, as he observes, "the only crime is excess" (*E,* 440). In the words of Gay-Crosier, "he uses Greek thought as a model because it is entirely based on dialog and not on monolog."[73] As Camus earlier acknowledges in "Helen's Exile," "Greek thought always took its stand upon the idea of limit. It carried nothing to extremes, neither religion nor reason, because it denied nothing, neither religion nor reason" (*SEN,* 136).[74] In contrast to the rebels of Europe, "daughter of excess" (*SEN,* 136), the Greek rebel is seen by Camus *not* to violate fundamental moral imperatives in the here and now and so maintains the duality necessary for authentic revolt: "the yes counterbalances the no" (*E,* 439). To the uncompromising vision of the European mind-set, Greek thought responds, then, by positing an idea of justice which "supposes a limit" (*SEN,* 136; translation amended). Here, we discover another component in Camus's formulation of an ethical justification of justice: an inviolable limit conditioning what actions can be morally justified between human beings, undertaken in the name of principles such as justice and freedom. As he concedes, "if . . . revolt could found a philosophy it would be a philosophy of limits" (*TR,* 253; translation amended). Such a notion highlights the potential of interpersonal morality, a point seized upon by Camus when he writes: "If I renounce the project of making human identity respected, I abdicate in favour of oppression, I renounce revolt and fall back on an attitude of nihilistic consent" (*TR,* 250).[75] Nihilistic logic, which "rejects the idea of any limit" (*TR,* 246), perverts the original pursuit of justice and, as we have seen, comes to justify the practice of injustice. Unlike Camus, whose "relative justice" (*TR,* 254) requires that one has *proximate* ends which reflect human capability, Hegel's view of justice noticeably jettisons the principle of equivalence by pursuing an infinite ideal (History) which is disproportionate to the status of (finite) human beings. Correspondingly, while Hegelian idealism posits that the end necessarily justifies the means, for Camus, it is the *means* which, in accordance with the notion of *limit,* determine and ultimately vindicate the revolutionary end: "When the end is absolute, historically speaking, and when it is believed certain of realization, it is possible to go so far as to sacrifice others. When it is not, only oneself can be sacrificed, in the hazards of a struggle for the common dignity. Does the end justify the means? That is possible. But what will justify the end? To that question, which historic thought leaves pending, revolt replies: the means" (*TR,* 256; translation amended).

The significance Camus here accords the idea of "equivalent and appropriate relations" in the means/end dichotomy is further confirmed by his intellectual preoccupation with the concept of *moderation* [*la mesure*] which, like that of *limit,* is fundamental to his formulation of an ethical justification of justice. As Thomas Warren has established, Camus's understanding of *la mesure* derives from the classical Greek notion of *sophrosyne* or "some appropriate equivalent."[76] Significantly, the ideas of "extremes" and "equilibria" loom large in Camus's thinking generally; a recent conference explored some of the various formulations of this important duality.[77] As was noted earlier, works spanning Camus's lifetime demonstrate his predilection for the juxtaposition of opposites, while the notion of "equivalence" pervades much of his writing.[78] Bruce Ward, supported by Hazel Barnes, draws attention to the significance of Heraclitus's tension of opposites in Camus's understanding of *la mesure* which he formulates as "pure tension" (*TR,* 264) between mutually opposing forces.[79] In terms of the means/end bisection, this tension ensures a moral equilibrium between, on the one hand, the need to preserve provisional morality and, on the other hand, the demands of revolutionary justice. Camus uses Heraclitus to demonstrate how a balance may be maintained between "Being" and "Becoming," that is, between Nature and History:

> it cannot be said that existence takes place only on the level of essence. Where could one perceive essence except on the level of existence and evolution? But nor can it be said that being is only existence. Something that is always in the process of development could not exist—there must be a beginning. Being can only prove itself in development and development is nothing without being. The world is . . . both movement and stability. The historical dialectic, for example, is not in continuous pursuit of an unknown value. It revolves around the limit which is its prime value. Heraclitus, the inventor of the constant change of things, nevertheless set a limit to this perpetual process. This limit was symbolized by Nemesis, the goddess of moderation and the implacable enemy of excess. (*TR,* 259–60; translation amended)

What the preceding citation confirms is that to be "loyal to the Earth" is not in itself sufficient to bring about the much sought after ethical justification of justice. As Ward rightly observes, "the Greeks do not finally provide the great image Camus needs," since "they gave too great a share to beauty and not enough to man's responsibility for ameliorating his situation."[80] As Camus himself acknowledges in what is a rare criticism of Ancient Greek civilization, "in Greece, there were free men because there were slaves" (*CA1,* 112; cf. *CA1,* 118–19).[81] Rather, so that it meets the challenges posed by the historical process, the Hellenic vision on which Camus bases his Mediterranean philosophy needs to learn from, while itself providing an inspiration for, the modern (western) quest for justice, thus further verifying the significance for Camus of the notion of equivalence in moral determination. Camus makes his position clear in "Defense of *The Rebel*": "I did not—a futile venture—set the Mediterranean against Europe, but maintained that the latter had quite proved that it could not do without the former. Neither Faust without Helen nor Helen without Faust, that is what I believe" (*E,* 1711). The Heraclitean model provides Camus with an intellectual stimulus for his understanding of *la mesure,* born of and sustained by a contradictory duality: "Moderation. They consider it to be the resolution of the contradiction. It can be nothing other than the assertion of the contradiction and the heroic decision to keep to it and live by it" (*C3,* 31; cf. *C3,* 209).

What is equally worthy of notice in relation to the aforementioned extended quotation is the significance Camus now accredits Nemesis, the Greek goddess whose own characteristic of "moderation" is such that justice—formulated in terms of "moral desert"—is seen as a (Mediterranean) corrective to the (European) psychology of "excess": "Our Europe . . . in its madness pushes back the eternal limits, and at once dark Furies swoop down upon it to destroy. Nemesis is watching, goddess of moderation, not of vengeance. All those who go beyond the limit are by her pitilessly chastised" (*SEN,* 136; translation amended). One should not underestimate the role of Nemesis in Camus's moral reasoning—the first reference to the Greek goddess in the *Carnets* dates back to 1947 (*C2,* 198; *CA2,* 102)—since, as he insists in "La Pensée de Midi," "a process of thought which wanted to take into account the contemporary contradictions of revolt should seek its inspiration from this goddess" (*TR,* 260; translation amended). Indeed, at the time of his death, Camus was preparing a long essay on Nemesis which, it seems, was anticipated to provide a more explicit formulation of the ideas expressed in "La Pensée de Midi."[82] Had he lived, Camus might well have proceeded to create an animated interpretation of the mysterious Greek goddess (that, to judge from the *Carnets,* was, along with *The First Man,* set to be the centerpiece of the "third stage" of his *œuvre* based on the ideal of love [*C3,* 187]) and thereby respond to the claims of his critics that the author of *The Rebel* was intellectually suspect and inclined to seek solace from historical responsibility in lyrical rhetoric.[83] This remains a speculation, however, and Camus was killed before any such project could be realized. Yet, as was the case with the groundwork for *The Rebel,* the frequency of entries in the *Carnets* referring to Nemesis clearly suggests that a work of considerable significance was in the making. A series of notes under the heading "*For Nemesis*" dating from just weeks before his death illustrates Camus's indebtedness to Heraclitus as he prepared the essay:

> Black horse, white horse, a single human hand controls both rages. At breakneck speed, the journey is great. Truth lies, frankness conceals. Hide in the light.
> The world fills you and you are empty: fullness.
> Small noise of the foam on the morning beach; it fills the world as much as din and glory do. Both come from silence.
> The person who refuses chooses him/herself, the person who covets prefers him/herself. Neither ask nor refuse. Accept in order to renounce.
> The flames of ice crown the days; sleep in the motionless fire.
> (*C3,* 276)

Whatever the nature of the planned work on Nemesis, it is clear that *The Rebel,* a project in which Camus invests great time and intellectual energy, is itself distinctive in the corpus of writings in which he articulates his concern for justice. Not only in that work does Camus seek to "understand the time [he] live[s] in" (*TR,* 11), but he also hopes to *transform his time.* As he notes in the "Avant-Propos" to *Actuelles II,* "it isn't enough to criticize our time, we also need to try and give it a shape and a future" (*E,* 714). However, the proof of the pudding is in the eating, and one of the most sustained (and, it has to be said, justified) criticisms of *The Rebel* stems from the fact that while Camus's diagnosis is clear, his prognosis in pragmatic, political terms remains obscure. This "puzzle" with which the reader of *The Rebel* is left raises the rather awkward question as to Camus's overall intention in his work. After all, unduly theoretical in its approach, the book falls noticeably short of advocating a concrete proposal by which to implement his long-labored *pensée solaire.* It is true that at the end of *The Rebel,* Camus champions the cause of "revolutionary syndicalism" as a means by which to protest against injustice without falling into the abyss of moral nihilism (*E,* 700–701; *TR,* 262). However, as Ian Birchall observes in an insight worthy of extended quotation,

> the problem with this is that it is quite unclear what Camus is talking about. If what he means by *syndicalisme révolutionnaire* is the doctrine and practice of the pre-1914 CGT, then the claim is, to say the least, implausible. Revolutionary syndicalism in this sense died in 1914, and even before then had had a significant influence only in certain countries. . . . The French word *syndicalisme* can, however, translate as both "syndicalism" and "trade unionism." And it is certainly at least possible to argue that trade unionism . . . played a significant role in raising working-class living standards. But if that is what Camus meant, then why slide in the word "révolutionnaire"? . . . It is hard to avoid the conclusion that what he is presenting is an argument in defense of

reformism—but slipping in a covert signal to his leftist friends to assure them that he is really on their side.[84]

Birchall is justified in pointing up the ambiguity of Camus's proposed solution to the problems he portrays in *The Rebel,* a solution that is, at best, rather vague and, at worst, hopelessly unrealistic. There is, in any case, something inherently unsatisfactory in Camus's perfunctory exposition of what is essentially a pre-Marxist socialist stance—there is a passing reference to this effect in respect of Scandinavian social democracy (*E,* 701n; cf. *E,* 1528)—in a work consisting for the most part of lengthy critiques presenting the perceived shortcomings of other approaches, of which revolutionary communism is the most telling example. One must look beyond the pages of *The Rebel* for elucidations of Camus's political vision. Thus, publicly endorsing the contemporary British Labour Party, that Camus praises as a "kind of socialism without ideology," he lays claim to a political program predicated on a belief in trade unionism, that both supports social reformism and safeguards justice and freedom but which—crucially—eschews Marxist pretensions on historical determinism.[85] Significantly, Camus hoped that a new French republican alliance led by Pierre Mendès-France could learn from the Labour Party's vision of reformist politics to yield a *travaillisme français.*[86] That Camus looks to traditional socialist beliefs to give substance to his moral philosophy emerging from *The Rebel* is further confirmed by his keynote speech delivered at the Bourse du Travail at Saint-Étienne on May 10, 1953 (*E,* 792–99; *RRD,* 65–71). In that speech, in which he examines his philosophy of revolt through the prism of social justice, Camus submits that it is possible to reconcile the demands of economic justice ("to be liberated . . . from . . . hunger" [*RRD,* 70]) and the quest for political justice ("to be liberated . . . from . . . masters" [*RRD,* 70]). The principles of liberal constitutional democracy, ensuring as they do the moral equilibrium between social happiness and individual autonomy, are deemed the most efficient means of sustaining economic prosperity. The success of such a system, Camus insists, is dependent on the extent to which freedom and justice are conceived of as interdependent principles and pursued together: "Choosing freedom is not, as we are told, choosing against justice. On the other hand, freedom is chosen today in relation to those who are everywhere suffering and fighting, and this is the only freedom that counts. It is chosen at the same time as justice and, to tell the truth, henceforth we cannot choose one without the other" (*RRD,* 69).[87] In short, the politics of authentic revolt are best formulated in terms of a socialist-styled reformism, upholding the moral duty of justice to eliminate social destitution through an equitable distribution of societal resources but that, in so doing, does not compromise the open communication that underscores human freedom. Camusian justice—in so far as one can reason in such terminology—thus rejects the prospect of absolute distributive justice and embraces the politics of pluralist democracy with its potential of interpersonal morality regulated by constitutional powers.

However plausible such a political vision may seem, and whatever the historical vindication of his moral position, the fact remains that the hostile reception of *The Rebel,* while ensuring the book's *succès de scandale,* would, in the words of Germaine Brée, leave Camus in "a splendid political isolation."[88] The deep psychological impact of his quarrel with Sartre and Jeanson, that would find striking resonances in the "calculated confession" (*TRN,* 2015) behind *The Fall,* instills into Camus sentiments of self-doubt and disillusionment with regard to what he maintained to be "his most important book."[89] The following extract from private correspondence with his wife, dated September 5, 1952, will be sufficient to demonstrate Camus's crisis of confidence in the wake of the controversy surrounding the publication of the book: "I am really paying dearly for this unfortunate book. Today I am full of doubts about it—and about me who resembles it so."[90] And, as if to confirm his personal crisis, the specter of civil war in his Algerian homeland, "country of both excess and moderation" (*CA1,* 68), was about to cast a long shadow over his whole attitude toward social and political justice. This last, crucial phase of Camus's preoccupation will form the subject matter of the final chapter.

8
Crisis and Reappraisal

> the long demand for justice exhausts the love which nevertheless gave it birth. In the clamour in which we live love is impossible and justice not enough. This is why Europe hates the daylight and can do nothing but confront one injustice with another. But I rediscovered at Tipasa that, in order to prevent justice from shrivelling up, from becoming a magnificent orange containing only a dry and bitter pulp, we had to keep a freshness and a source of joy intact within ourselves, loving the daylight which injustice leaves unscathed, and returning to the fray with this re-conquered light.
>
> —Camus, *Selected Essays and Notebooks*

BOTH PERSONALLY AND PROFESSIONALLY, THE 1950S WOULD PROVE A difficult decade for Camus. Not only, as we have seen, would the controversy surrounding the publication of *The Rebel* leave an indelible mark, but also the pressures of history would increasingly impact on his concern for social and political justice throughout this troubled period.[1] In the words of Carl Viggiani, "the last decade of Camus' life began in dread and in a dream prophecy of what his last few seconds must have been."[2] Whereas *The Rebel* represents the *theoretical* culmination of Camus's preoccupation with justice as an intellectual thematic, Camus's topical writings throughout the remainder of his life once more testify, as we shall see in this final chapter, to his commitment to react to events in *empirical* fashion.

"The War of the Left" and Social Reformism

Camus's lifelong concern for sociopolitical justice as analyzed in this book finds natural expression on the political left which traditionally "has always been in conflict with injustice, obscurantism and oppression" (*E,* 1720; cf. *EX,* 35).[3] Yet in full bloom of the Cold War, the conflict between the communist and noncommunist left in France—what Camus refers to as "the war of the left" (*EX,* 31)—would now threaten to destroy that historical accolade, a prospect which Camus himself takes seriously: "I was born in a family, the left, where I will die, but whose decline it is difficult for me not to see" (*E,* 1753). Yet remaining loyal to his left-wing sensitivity in his conviction that "if, after all, the truth seemed to me to be on the right, that's where I would be" (*E,* 754; cf. *C3,* 273), Camus refuses to follow the doctrines of Marxist ideologs. His polemics with Jean-Marie Domenach (*E,* 1750–58) and *France-Observateur* (*E,* 1758–62) are useful reminders of the contemporary debate surrounding the issue of independence on the political left in France. We may also point out in passing that both *The Fall* and "The Renegade" (one of the stories in *Exile and the Kingdom*) were, in one of their dimensions, intended as a depiction of what, in Camus's eyes, was the nihilistic abstraction underpinning "the new Left."[4] Confirmation that, for Camus, the "communist paradise" was entrenched in socialist authoritarianism is further provided by his polemic with Sartre over *The Rebel* which, as we saw in chapter 7, sealed the rift between the former's rejection of politico-ideological monolog and the latter's pro-Marxist moral stance. With one notable exception—the Algerian crisis, a crucial matter in the story of Camus's concern for social and political justice to which I will return in the next section—Camus's topical writings throughout the remainder of his life would (as he sees it) continue to be nonideological in character. Thus, his understanding of justice, tempered with freedom, is such that it safeguards human prosperity and guarantees human rights without itself being compromised by (totalitarian) *idées fixes.*

Correspondingly, to the pressures of history and circumstance that manifest themselves throughout this period, Camus by and large responds with moral transparency. While Sartre, notably, chose to speak out against Soviet military strategy in Eastern Europe only upon the violent suppression of the nationalist rebellion in Budapest in October 1956, Camus's anticommunism comes strongly to the fore in his condemnation of Soviet force used to crush the nationalist insurrections initiated by workers in East Berlin (1953) (*E,* 1771–75), Poland (1956) (*E,* 1775–78), as well as Hungary (*E,* 1778–89).[5] In each instance, what drives Camus is the certitude underscoring his vision of political justice that "there is no possible evolution in a totalitarian society. Terror does not evolve, except for the worst" (*E,* 1783). In supporting the anticommunist cause in the Eastern bloc, Camus once more demonstrates his conviction that justice devoid of freedom is morally bankrupt. The fight for political freedom from the yoke of Soviet communism is deemed a necessary and justified course of action to uphold the cause of justice in Eastern Europe. There is, though, an inconsistency between this position (and, one might add, Camus's continued support for the Israelis [*E,* 1859; *E,* 1907] and the Spanish republicans struggling against Francoism) and his refusal to support the campaign for political independence in his homeland by which to render justice to the indigenous race of Algerians (cf. *E,* 1878–79).[6] While in the case of Eastern Europe, Camus perceives nationalist insurgency as the instrument of the freedom fighter by which to secure justice in the face of authoritarian rule, the FLN's insurrection in Algeria in the face of colonial subjugation is considered the action of the terrorist and is condemned accordingly.

Just as Camus defends democratic values threatened by the absolutist mentality of the Soviet presence in Eastern Europe, so he refuses to allow political ideology to dictate moral action in response to civil rights violations. The plight of the French sailor Henri Martin is a case in point here. Condemned to five years' incarceration for having exercised his right to freedom of expression in campaigning against French military action in Indo-China, Martin's cause was taken up by many French left-wing intellectuals, including Camus (*E,* 775–80). However, contrary to the communist-inspired protest on behalf of the imprisoned sailor to which Sartre and others subscribed, Camus pledged his support in *Franc-Tireur,* an erstwhile organ of the French Resistance and latterly a journal of right-wing persuasion.[7] The fact of the matter is that, in deference to his sense of justice unpolluted by historico-political idealism, Camus refuses to join forces with the campaign to free Martin staged by those prepared to condone what he deems "the socialism of the concentration camp" underpinning the Soviet bloc: "from now on it is jeopardizing the values of freedom, among other values, to defend them next to the *Temps modernes* and those who agree with it" (*E,* 777).[8] As he would later confirm in *L'Express,* while the intellectual has a duty and a commitment to defend freedom whenever it is threatened by adversity, to secure someone (some people) freedom without at the same time safeguarding justice would be a mockery (*EX,* 61).[9] In his response to the Martin affair, Camus rejects the language of political ideology and embraces that of moral empiricism with a view to transcending the dogmatic divide.

Further support for this last claim is provided by Camus's "uncompromising reformism," (*CA2,* 139; translation amended) that he once more brings to bear in relation to France's own volatile political situation at the time following the collapse of successive constitutions in Paris.[10] Upon his return to professional journalism in May 1955 when he joined the team at *L'Express,* Camus publishes an article, unique in his journalistic writings, explaining why he will support a republican alliance led by the Radical leader Pierre Mendès-France in the forthcoming French legislative elections:[11] "I am unable to vote for the right, its blind and paralytic people, for they are against all true justice. Nor am I able to vote for the Communists, their friends and servants, for they are against all freedom. From the right to the left, the mentality of injustice and tyranny have become wedded together while fighting to sclerose the political and moral life of France. Only a French Labor brand of socialism that at the same time, and in practice, will serve justice and freedom will give the country a chance of survival" (*EX,* 146).[12] Further confirming Camus's aversion to extremism on both the right and left in contemporary French politics, these remarks are consistent with the "syndicalist solution" advocated at the end of *The Rebel.*[13] (And, as we shall confirm presently, there is a structural parallel between Camus's support here of societal reform, as opposed to ideological politics, and his appeal for a civilian truce, rather than "taking sides," in his response to the Algerian War.) Just as Camus's anticommunism, once more in evidence here, rejects the political vision in which democratic freedoms are sacrificed in the pursuit of historical justice, so his anticapitalist stance, also formulated in the aforementioned quotation, dismisses the idea of a liberal bourgeois democracy based on class privilege, where injustice in the form of exploitation of the working class prevails. For Camus, thus refusing the extremes of both communism and capitalism, socialist-styled reformism is key to averting political and economic crisis in France: "Everything that risks extending the status quo increases the chances of this defeat. . . . Between the opposition to social change sanctioned by the financially privileged and the refusal of reforms on the pretext that they compromise revolutionary possibilities, there is a place for a policy of immediate reform" (*EX,* 144, 145).

It is worthy of note that underlying this quest for societal reform as a means by which to reconcile justice and freedom in a rejuvenated social order guaranteeing civil liberties is the demand for what Camus calls "the reintegration of the working class with all its rights through the abolition of the salaried class" (*EX,* 109). Camus, "supporting the common man and woman" (*RRD,* 170; translation amended) and who sets great store by traditional working-class principles such as tolerance and pragmatic reformism—principles from which he hoped (French) society at large could benefit—never claimed himself to be the spokesman of the proletariat (or, indeed, that of any other social group [cf. *E,* 1925]).[14] Yet it is clear from his writings on the matter in *L'Express*—most notably the articles of November 25 and December 13, 1955 (*EX,* 108–10, 125–27)—that as long as capitalist society continued to justify the exploitation of the working class, plans for social reformism by which to realize "true justice" in France would, in Camus's view, be null and void. Camus was essentially for the politics of social inclusion; what he once called "socialist hope" (*E,* 1579) remained, in his eyes, the most realistic and the most socially advantageous means by which to reconcile the quest for social justice and the protection of individual freedom. Positing a political system based on class privilege is completely alien to this mentality. To adapt a remark he would later make in defense of his anti-Marxist convictions, if Camus had once been a communist, he had never been, nor would he ever be, a capitalist.[15]

Dialog of the Deaf: Camus's Algerian Monolog

What emerges from the above discussion is the picture of a Camus who, in keeping with his earlier moral stance, once more rejects the monolog of political absolutism in favor of the dialog of moral relativism. Confronted with moments of historical crisis, Camus predicates his response on the democratic principle of social inclusion and he has no truck with the politics of exclusion. There is, however, one remaining historical turning point that, more than any other, would threaten to destroy Camus's moral transparency in this respect. Heralded in November 1954 by the FLN's insurrection against colonial domination and the subsequent French repression, the "dirty war" in Algeria was, in the words of Alec Hargreaves, "by far the bloodiest and most traumatic episode in French decolonization."[16] Resulting in the murder of an estimated one million Algerian Moslems and as many expulsions among the European settler community following the recognition of Algeria's sovereign state in July 1962, the "war without a name" stands as a divisive issue in contemporary Algerian history. Following the nationalist successes in Morocco, Madagascar and Tunisia and the telling French defeat at Dien Bien Phu in May 1954, paving the way for independence in Indo-China, the future of the *Union française* was at the time hotly contested within the French intelligentsia, as the issue of the mother country's hold over Algeria—the jewel in the colonial crown—increasingly came to dominate the domestic political agenda.[17] As in many other areas of contemporary French policy, polarizing views in respect of the Algerian crisis served to consolidate further what was already deeply entrenched political extremism. The PCF's anti-imperial slogan, "Algeria is Algeria," on the one hand, confronted the right-wing reconquest motif of "Algeria is France," on the other.

Now, unlike many other contemporary French left-wing commentators on the issue, Camus could not afford the luxury of critical distance in his response to the Algerian drama, tantamount to "a personal tragedy" (*RRD,* 96).[18] For Camus, "programmatically committed to resist" but whose anticolonialism, as we saw in chapter 4, is a matter laden with ambivalence, the Algerian War caused insuperable torment.[19] A vocabulary of discomfiture accompanies his utterances on the issue: he experiences "suffering from Algeria as others suffer from their lungs" (*RRD,* 91) and feels "torn" (*E,* 1844) and "really anguished" at the unfolding scale of events that "poisons his days."[20] Personal conflicts of loyalty over his "land of the soul" (*SEN,* 89) meant that Camus's hopes of seeing realized "the Algeria of justice, where French and Arabs will go into partnership freely" (*EX,* 159) posed emotional as well as political problems, since he always considered himself both French *and* Algerian.[21] Denis Charbit goes to the heart of the matter when he asks, "where is the greatest injustice? In the case of one million people displaced or in that of nine million Arabs oppressed?"[22] On the one hand, to advocate the vision of justice as the unconditional right of the indigenous majority to political self-determination—a view held, most notably, by supporters of *Les Temps modernes,* that had been championing the cause of Algerian independence ever since the end of the Second World War—was, for Camus, to inflict injustice on to the minority *pied-noir* population (including his own family) that claimed the historical right to residence in *L'Algérie française.* Both in his journalism for *L'Express* and his "Avant-Propos" to *Actuelles III,* Camus is at pains to correct the misconception of the European settler community as "a million of colonists with whip and cigar, and in a Cadillac" (*RRD,* 86–87) in the hope of reforming deeply entrenched beliefs. In a similar vein, *The First Man,* Camus's unfinished autobiographical novel in which he examines *L'Algérie française* through the optic of his own ancestral heritage, has been memorably described by Edward Hughes as "a passionate, seductive and obdurate celebration of the French Algerians."[23] On the other hand, to accept that justice requires the prolongation of the French presence at all costs was to deny the indigenous Algerians their democratic right to self-determination and, what is more, to condone more than a century of systematic oppression and persecution in the province. Justice and the continuation of colonial rule in Algeria are mutually exclusive ideas for the FLN activist.

To these political problems exposed by Camus's consideration of the Algerian War must be added the ethical questions posed by the conflict itself. One such issue is whether, in order to redress the original brutalities intrinsic to the colonization of the province, resulting in racial division and political injustice, it is justified for the indigenous race of Algerians to embark on a revolutionary quest, the end of which would inevitably mean the expulsion of the French Algerians from their territory. For Camus, whose "forced amnesia" in relation to the original injustices of the French colonizing enterprise comes particularly to the fore in his unfinished autobiographical project, the idea of victims of persecution turning persecutors (*PH,* 178; *FM,* 149–50; and cf. *E,* 717–19) cannot convince since "there are other ways of re-establihing the necessary justice than by substituting one injustice for another" (*RRD,* 90; translation amended).[24]

A further ethical issue occasioned by the crisis to which reference should be made surrounds the asymmetrical nature of the hostilities. This fact makes the task of determining whether or not the conflict constitutes a "just war" all the more difficult to discern. While the FLN consisted of a comparatively small group of committed militants, the French Army was a major military force, so that in sheer numerical terms the war was waged on a clearly inequitable basis. According to Ferhat Abbas, "France knew perfectly well that it was waging an unjust war on the Algerian people. But, for the majority of French people, this war became 'just' from the moment that the means to make it so were assembled. The notion of justice remains subordinate to that of power. Since, for 130 years, the strongest law in Algeria has been the 'Law', why should it not remain so? This is how the colonialists reason. For them, being strong is all that is needed in order to be right."[25] Although Abbas is right to point up the morally ambiguous nature of justice for the French *colonisateurs,* it should of course be remembered that both of the warring factions in Algeria waged a dirty war, and that both justified the service of unjust means in the pursuit of what was perceived as a just end. Thus, while the FLN used naked violence as a political instrument, the French Army used torture to extract information from political prisoners threatening to undermine the claims pertaining to France's sovereignty in Algeria.[26] How far violence can be morally justified in the quest for justice is, as we have seen in earlier chapters of this book, a moot point.

Writing with the benefit of hindsight, Jeanyves Guérin holds that "the Algerian War saw the triumph not of pure justice, but of a lesser injustice over a worse injustice."[27] Ongoing internal unrest in the FLN following the second Evian peace talks in March 1962 gives the lie to the notion that "justice" and "injustice" in the arena of the Algerian Civil War are clear-cut concerns.[28] Yet Camus himself can be charged with simplifying the questions at issue when—in his conviction that "unity is first of all a harmony of differences" (*RRD,* 173)—he naïvely yet no doubt sincerely holds to the view that justice with regard to Algeria is an inclusive moral concept that, subsuming racial differences and transcending racial antagonisms, can only be realized if it embraces a *seuil de tolérance* between the different factions "condemned to live together" (*RRD,* 91): "I believe in a policy of reparation in Algeria rather than in a policy of expiation. . . . And there will be no future that does not do justice at one and the same time to the two communities of Algeria" (*RRD,* 87). The point is even more forcefully articulated in a manuscript note (not retained in the definitive version) for the "Avant-Propos" to Camus's "essays in negotiation": "justice is not the systematic and indeterminate exalting of one of the parties implicated. It is equity distributed to both parties. . . . We ought more than ever not to forget these requirements and to try to dispense justice to all the people of Algeria, whether they be Arab or French" (*E,* 1851).[29] And, to fellow *pied-noir* Jean Daniel, he would similarly insist that "the two peoples of Algeria have an equal right to justice, an equal right to retain their homeland," adding that he personally would campaign "for the establishment of both moral and political conditions that, one day, will allow dialog."[30] As he makes clear in his very first article for *L'Express* dealing with the Algerian problem (published on July 9, 1955), no solution to the crisis could be achieved so long as a climate of extremes remained: "In politics, killing or running away are two forms of resignation, and two ways of abandoning the future" (*EX,* 40).

Be that as it may, despite insisting on feeling "a solidarity with everyone, French or Arab, who is suffering today in the misfortune of [his] country" (*RRD,* 173), and despite his repeated calls for dialog and for each of the warring factions to reflect on "the adversary's reasons"—a phrase which occurs frequently in his various writings on the Algerian problem (*EX,* 79–82; *EX,* 83; *E,* 893; *RRD,* 82; *E,* 994; *RRD,* 97)—with a view to finding a political solution to the crisis by rational means, Camus himself remains incapable of dealing with the Algerian crisis in terms other than those of monolog, i.e. by means of an imposed French metropolitan solution.

A number of points can be made to support this claim. First of all, there is the practical problem of implementing reformative justice in the province since, as we discovered in chapter 4, any such policies assume—unrealistically—the willingness of Algeria's *colonisateurs* to make concessions to its *colonisés.* It will also be recalled from chapter 3 that Camus opposed the attempts of the Daladier administration in 1938–39 to redress the grave economic and political situation following the collapse of Blum's Popular Front coalition in France by means of a series of authoritative decree laws.[31] Yet, in the mid-1950s, faced with the stark choice of either an *Algérie française* or an *Algérie algérienne,* Camus himself effectively advocates an imposed French series of measures as the only means of overcoming *pied-noir* opposition to politico-economic reform in Algeria. Thus, the "great" and "resounding restoration" by which Algeria's indigenous race of Moslems would be granted justice is, for Camus, to be realized "by France entirely and not with the blood of the French Algerians" (*EX,* 75).

In addition, we must mention as worthy of notice that whatever his broad support for "the Arab cause"—manifested most notably by the *adhérent*'s pro-Moslem position for which he was expelled from the PCF in the mid-1930s—at no time does Camus publicly perceive as intrinsically just the right of Algeria to political independence, even though it had been on arguably similar premises as those of the Algerian nationalist insurgents that he had justified the French Resistance movement in the face of the Nazi threat. Confiding in Roger Quilliot in 1958, Camus explains that in the event of independence being granted to Algeria, he would leave France without hesitation.[32] Moreover, *even if* the cause for independence were just—and, by mid-1958, before Camus finally descends into silence, he appears in private at least to concede that it is—it remains unacceptable to him because it would entail social division in his homeland, an idea alien to a man whose self-avowed role in Algeria "has never been and never will be to divide, but rather to use whatever means [he] ha[s] to unite" (*RRD,* 173).[33]

Publicly, Camus does not differentiate between the "justifiable violence" of the Resistance and the "unjustifiable murder" of the FLN, although there is evidence to suggest that *privately* he acknowledges the inconsistency between, on the one hand, his support of the French Resistance and, on the other hand, his refusal to support the Algerian Resistance. Herbert Lottman cites a telling confession which Camus reportedly makes to Suzanne Agnely: "It's true that I wasn't shocked by resistance to the Nazis, because I was French and my country was occupied. I should accept the Algerian resistance, too, but I'm French."[34] At the very least, this remark indicates that Camus's understanding of sociopolitical justice in relation to the Algerian crisis remains unable to surpass his own sense of nationalism, a position once more in evidence in comments made during a conversation with Robert Mallet in December 1958: "I do not love Algeria like a serviceman or a colonist. But can I love it any differently than as a Frenchman? What too many Arabs do not understand is that I love it like a Frenchman who loves Arabs and who wants them to be at home in Algeria, without himself feeling a foreigner there."[35]

The fact of the matter is that in his deliberations on the Algerian War, Camus precludes the idea that political change from the (colonial) status quo is a precondition of justice in his homeland. His *idée fixe* is such that he simply cannot conceive of a future for the province beyond the structures of *L'Algérie française.*[36] He summarily dismisses the notion of an Arab-dominated independent Algerian state as an abstract idea with no historical justification: "However well-disposed one may be towards the Arab demands, one has to admit that, as far as Algeria is concerned, national independence is a conception springing wholly from emotion. There has never yet been an Algerian nation. The Jews, the Turks, the Greeks, the Italians, the Berbers would have just as much right to claim the direction of that putative nation. At present the Arabs do not alone make up all of Algeria. The size and seniority of the French settlement, in particular, are enough to create a problem that cannot be compared to anything in history" (*RRD,* 104).

Camus goes on to deem the quest for independence in Algeria a manifestation of Arab imperialism led by Nasser (*E,* 1013; *RRD,* 105), a view entirely predicated on the point that Algeria's indigenous population lack the will and autonomy to aspire to human betterment on the basis of their own cultural heritage. As Alec Hargreaves points out, such a mentality distorts the Islamic dimension of the Arab cause to suit the needs of the *petit colon* that Camus remains.[37] Certainly, writing in the mid-1950s at a time when assimilation was clearly no longer a viable option in Algeria, Camus readily acknowledges that "the colonial regime has had its day" (*EX,* 48) and that "the injustice from which the Arab population has suffered is linked to colonialism itself, to its history and its administration" (*RRD,* 104). Yet if he supports in principle the process of decolonization, whereby the right of indigenous cultures to determine their own future through democratic means is restored, Camus retains in practice the political structures of colonialism. Take, for instance, the rather vague notion of a "Franco-Arab association" that he views as an attempt to humanize the colonial experience in the province:

> *If colonization could ever find a justification, it would be in so far as it helps the conquered people to keep their distinctive character.* It would then be not colonization, but association, whether progressive or not, of two peoples where one brings its technology and the other its human richness. The Franco-Arab association must take into consideration the tradition, language, culture, in a word the Arab personality, while colonization has up until now become confused with the depersonalization of the colonized people. The French and Arab community must therefore be established on dialog between people. (*EX,* 48–49)

It is no coincidence that Camus here recycles phraseology originally used in "Misery in Kabylia" (*FC,* 1:335–36) where, we recall, he had responded to the injustices of social impoverishment and political disfranchisement with a reformative justice based on broadly assimilationist principles. Although by the 1950s the "assimilationist dream" is no longer realizable, to judge from Camus's repeated calls for a "Franco-Arab community" (*EX,* 39), a "Franco-Arab association" (*EX,* 48) and a "free association between French and Arabs" (*EX,* 170), he cannot purge himself of the idea of colonial dependency in Algeria.[38] Indeed, even his final pronoucements on the issue in *Actuelles III,* where Camus supports the idea of a federal solution in the style of the Lauriol Plan, cannot break him free from the French imperial trajectory by which the crisis is conditioned.[39] As Michèle and Claude Duchet submit, "having, here and there, put his finger on the absurdity of the colonial system that provokes situations such that they can only be resolved by its radical negation, he moves back horrified."[40] From this, it seems reasonable to deduce that with assimilation now entirely out of the question, but unwilling to accept the only credible alternative of an *Algérie algérienne,* Camus has no choice but to retreat into moral rhetoric evidenced by the aforementioned quotation and by well-intentioned yet ultimately implausible initiatives such as the "Appeal for a Civilian Truce in Algeria" (*E,* 989–99; *RRD,* 95–102) in an attempt to offer an alternative way forward in his own inability to find a solution to the Algerian War proper.

Indeed, it is important to recognize that in the "Appeal," an attempt to "humanize the war" delivered at Le Cercle du Progrès in

Algiers on January 22, 1956, Camus noticeably changes dimension in his response to the Algerian drama.[41] This movement reflects his growing sense of hopelessness at the turn of historical events.[42] Hitherto, writing in *L'Express,* he had sought a political solution to the crisis by which to reconcile the indigenous and nonindigenous communities of Algeria in a spirit of mutual understanding, tolerance, and respect. (We may note in passing that Camus's "Letter to an Algerian Militant," addressed to Aziz Kessous in October 1955 and republished in *Actuelles III* in 1958 [*E,* 961–66; *RRD,* 91–94] provides a microcosm of the intercommunal justice sought by the journalist in *L'Express*). Appealing in turn in his capacity as *interlocuteur valable* to the French metropolitan (*EX,* 72–75), French Algerian (*EX,* 76–78) and militant Arab (*EX,* 79–82) communities, Camus implored each of these parties to understand "the adversary's reasons" in his quest for "a new Algerian politics" (*EX,* 50). He looked to rational discourse as the most profitable means by which to secure an equitable outcome: "the idea of a round table where representatives of all tendencies, from the circles of colonization to the Arab nationalists, will meet cold seems to me still viable" (*EX,* 70). In his "Appeal" by contrast, billed as "a group of purely humanitarian measures" (*E,* 1003) and "a purely humanitarian appeal" (*RRD,* 95) that "has nothing to do with politics" (*RRD,* 95), Camus, still refusing to "take sides" in accordance with his liberal views, is preoccupied with the welfare of a specific category of people embroiled in the crisis ("the civilians"). Thus, as events increasingly illustrate the unlikelihood of a diplomatic solution to the drama, and as the pressures of history, now being exerted on him at both a personal and public level as the Algerian War intensifies, become increasingly intolerable, Camus offers an alternative *social* response to what is a fundamentally *political* problem.[43] While this is perhaps a naïve and unrealistic and certainly inadequate initiative to adopt in scale to the problem at issue, it is entirely consistent with Camus's narrowing down of political problems to moral ones, first formulated in "Misery in Kabylia" (*FC,* 1:335) as a means by which to bring about reformative justice. And, as we shall presently discover, a similar focus on specific moral problems (as opposed to vast political issues) characterizes Camus's pronouncements on matters of social justice throughout the remainder of his life once the failure of his hopes concerning Algeria becomes apparent.

A further point of interest concerning Camus's "civilian truce" appeal is that he uses that speech to give concrete expression to the concept of *limit* which, as we saw in the preceding chapter, underscores "la pensée de midi" from *The Rebel.* Indeed, there is a clear parallel to be drawn between "The Fastidious Assassins"—the band of Russian revolutionaries analyzed in the "Essay on Revolt" who refuse to allow political idealism to rule over moral responsibility—and the demand in the "Appeal" for innocent civilians not to be used as political expedients. As Camus puts it in *L'Express* on October 28, 1955, when the notion of a "civilian truce" is still in embryo, "when the oppressed seize arms in the name of justice, they take a step on the land of injustice. But they can move forward, more or less, and if such is the law of history, it is in any case the law of the mind that, without stopping to demand justice for the oppressed, they may not approve of it in its injustice beyond certain limits. Precisely, massacres of civilians . . . go beyond these limits and everyone must recognize this clearly. On this question, I have a proposition to make which concerns the future and which I will speak about soon" (*EX,* 80). These remarks, germane to the "Appeal," raise an interesting issue in relation to what we have already noted as Camus's "new" idea(l) of "true justice." In his final article for *L'Express* ("Thanks to Mozart," published on February 2, 1956), Camus makes the point that respect for the individual is needed *as well as* justice (or, perhaps, that "true" justice includes respect for the individual): "at the same time as justice and peace, respect is needed for what is sovereign in every single life. Although today we do not stop talking about justice, above the slave camps, and peace, in the middle of the factories of death, this respect, without which all justice is terror and all peace resignation, has disappeared from our political conscience. Contemporary tyrannies hate Mozart and what he represents, even if they pretend to honor him" (*EX,* 176).[44]

The idea that "there are means that cannot be excused" (*RRD,* 5), that the struggle for justice and freedom is morally impaired once it accepts the sacrifice of the means (respect for human life) to the end (quest for political change) is borne out by the "Appeal," where Camus highlights that "no cause justifies the death of the innocent" (*RRD,* 97), a remark clearly reminiscent of the moral philosophy underpinning *The Just Assassins.*[45] This leads us to Camus's oft-cited comment in response to an Algerian student who, at a press conference in Stockholm in December 1957, reportedly accused the Nobel Laureate of approving the French repressions in the province by failing to support the FLN: "I believe in justice, but I will defend my mother before justice" (*E,* 1882). Much has been written about this curious statement, that, contrary to popular belief, was actually *not* a spontaneous proclamation on Camus's part during the Nobel Honors; he had earlier expressed similar sentiments to both Jean Amrouche (*C3,* 238) and Emmanuel Roblès (*E,* 1843). For many commentators, Camus's statement amounts to a Freudian slip revealing that, if necessary, he would side with the *pieds-noirs* rather than support the cause of justice for Algeria's *indigènes.*[46]

Jean Sarocchi's is perhaps the most incisive interpretation of Camus's justice/mother declaration: "This rash retort does not mean that one must prefer the bond of blood to justice, justice itself is under threat. There is no justice which sets little value on filial sentiment, no justice if all loyalty is lost."[47] It is not a matter of choosing one's mother *over* justice, but of loving justice as much as one loves one's own mother—and threatening neither. (The idea that justice is impossible without a certain form of love is fundamental to an understanding of *The Just Assassins.*) While Camus tacitly concedes in his statement that justice is on the side of the indigenous Algerians, he is adamant that any such justice remains morally indefensible as long as it is dependent on arbitrary acts of terrorism that may result in civilian casualties and fatalities.[48] Correspondingly, in choosing his mother over and above the cause of justice, Camus gives expression to the idea that human life is more precious than *all* abstract notions of justice. His priority (to draw on earlier phraseology from *Combat*) is to champion justice "in its human aspect, without transforming it into this terrible abstract passion which has mutilated so many people" (*E,* 268). Returning, in the 1958 "Avant-Propos" to *Actuelles III,* to the mother/justice declaration that he deems to have been "commented upon most strangely" (*RRD,* 82), Camus maintains the view—but, interestingly enough, now substituting the brother for the mother as he does so—that he has no truck with those for whom abstract moral principles mean more than the preservation of human values: "anyone [who] still thinks heroically that one's brother must die rather than one's principles, I shall go no farther than to admire them from a distance. I am not of their stamp" (*RRD,* 82; translation amended).

Returning to the "Appeal," the failure of that initiative, representing as it does the collapse of the liberal response to the Algerian War on which Camus had pinned his hopes of an intercommunal justice of peaceful coexistence, exposes the internal inadequacies of his attempt to reconcile, in a dialog of justice and freedom, what are actually irreconcilable differences in Algeria.[49] The historical shift away from assimilation toward Arab separatism in the course of the previous decade bears witness to the fact that the indigenous population's democratic right to justice and freedom could *not* coexist with the continuation of French rule whose premises undermine Algerian autonomy.[50] To this it should be added that the failing of the "civilian truce" initiative, a measure to which Camus had "sacrificed everything," marks the beginning of his infamous silence over Algeria that, using Michael Walzer's phraseology, stands "eloquent in its hopelessness."[51] Judging from Camus's contemporary correspondence, an air of desperation now descends upon the French Algerian who, on February 26, 1956, admits to André Rosfelder that "at the moment, there is within me someone who is dying of shame. If I could see a possible course of action, even the most insane, I would attempt it. . . . But we are hurtling down toward the abyss, we are there already. . . . I am shattered, to tell you the truth."[52] Unable to offer any other way out of this impasse, Camus's silence translates into a crushing inability to articulate a position in relation to the crisis. Certainly, he would momentarily break his silence when, in May 1958, he published (to almost complete critical indifference) *Actuelles III,* but his public display of optimism in that book is clearly at odds with what Camus privately accepts as the truth. This division between the public and private Camus is tellingly recorded in his letter to Jean Grenier dated August 4, 1958: "Like you I believe that it is no doubt too late for Algeria. I haven't said so in my book because *lo peor no es siempre seguro*—because we have to give fate a chance—and because one doesn't write to say that everything is done for. In that case, one stays silent. I am getting ready to do so" (*Corr,* 222; cf. *C3,* 251).

Surely Steve Robson is right when, of the writer's public/private dichotomy over Algeria, he submits: "Perhaps Camus's battle against fatalism in the public arena was a projection of an internal combat, an effort to convince himself as much as to convince his readers."[53] Significantly, this is not the first time that Camus uses the medium of writing to confront, with a view to overcoming, his private inclination to despair in the face of moments of (historical) crisis impacting on his concern for social and political justice. In chapter 5, we saw how he uses the self-directed "Letter to a man in despair" and the principles of *The Myth of Sisyphus* as a means by which to purge himself of his despondency upon the outbreak of hostilities in Europe in September 1939, while, in the preceding chapter, I suggested a reading of *The Rebel* as a response to Camus's misguided idealism at the time of the purge in France. It is interesting to speculate how far the unfinished *The First Man,* with its clear focus on the settler mentality in French Algeria but which, as Edward Hughes observes, "simultaneously, and more radically,

. . . nudges towards an awareness of a local culture, as fleeting traces of an African identity begin to emerge," might have similarly gone on to afford Camus an opportunity to confront his own Algerian crisis by providing, perhaps, a coda to his understanding of sociopolitical justice with regard to Algeria.[54]

As it is, the status of *The First Man* as it has been given to us precludes conclusive interpretations of the text and, in any case, a full account of that unfinished autobiographical novel falls beyond the remit of the present study. Yet the quest for origins (personal and tribal) that is inherent in the project's very title—Camus had at one point thought of calling his book *Adam*—merits consideration, since, as we shall now see, what characterizes Camus's pronouncements on justice following the failure of his Algerian campaign is a return to the "person-to-person" response to perceived injustice from which his whole concern for justice originates.[55]

"Pilgrimage to the Source"

Even before his psychological anguish occasioned by the Algerian débâcle, Camus was beginning to revert to aspects of the "years of happiness" (*C3,* 100) from his Algerian youth to offset his increasing sense of "giddiness faced with the future" (*E,* 1627).[56] Research for his "book on Algeria since 1914" was also now well under way.[57] Equally, other writings such as "Return to Tipasa" (1953), where Camus rediscovers "ancient beauty . . . which . . . had saved [him] from despair" (*SEN,* 152), and preparations for the later retrospective preface to *Betwixt and Between* (1958), where he undertakes to "take his bearings, draw closer to his own centre, and then try to stay there" (*SEN,* 26), also bear testimony to his "pilgrimage to the source."[58] To this corpus should be added *The Fall* and *Exile and the Kingdom*—works arguably more personal in nature than, say, *The Outsider* or *The Plague*—neither of which, interestingly, figure in Camus's originally planned *œuvre* (cf. *C2,* 201; *CA2,* 103–04).[59] This last observation suggests that just as *The First Man* is an unashamedly personal project, so those later works are cast from a more liberated psychology than that determining the earlier writings. As Jean Sarocchi notes, "until [*The First Man*] Camus applied a strict control on his prose; with [*The First Man*] he releases it and lets himself go."[60] As early as 1949, Camus himself had highlighted the need to personalize his *œuvre* (*C2,* 267; *CA2,* 137) that "for some years," he conceded in 1953, "has not liberated but enslaved me" (*C3,* 76). Correspondingly, in his final works, where personal preoccupations and a general return to origins are the principal leitmotivs, Camus appears to be writing primarily for his own benefit and for therapeutic reasons, in keeping with the "stages of a recovery" recorded in the *Carnets:*

> Stages of a recovery.
> Let the will sleep. Enough of "you have to".
> Completely depoliticize the mind to make more human.
> . . . .
> Cut out the chewed over morality of abstract justice.
> Stay near to the reality of beings and things. As often as possible, come back to personal happiness.
> . . . .
> Recover energy—at the center.
>
> (*C3,* 220, 221)

These jottings noted in the *Carnets* in early 1958 attest to Camus's decision generally to narrow down the nature of his concerns—including, most notably, his whole attitude toward justice—in the quest for moral and personal renewal. The 1957 "Reflections on the Guillotine," providing a further and important illustration of how, in the face of difficulties impacting on his current situation, Camus returns to aspects of his past personae for guidance and support, is a work cast from the mold of this shifting psychological focus.[61] A text drawing on a lifetime's obsession with capital punishment whose personal significance for Camus should not be underestimated, "Reflections" surely ranks among Camus's most intuitive of writings, highlighting as it does a private passion within his moral sensibility.[62] Contrary to Camus's only other obviously "conceptual" work on justice—*The Rebel,* an attempt to "understand his time" in which practical objectives appear secondary to theoretical reasoning—"Reflections on the Guillotine" is essentially a reformative essay where cogent argument and practical campaign merge in a single, clear aim: the suppression of capital punishment as a social and codified practice within the French penal code. (The idea of Camus as social reformer is, we recall, already well to the fore in his capacity as professional journalist at *Alger républicain,* thus providing yet further confirmation of his tendency, now, to revert to aspects of his past in order to confront the future.) Few critics dispute the quality of Camus's text, both in the logic of its argument and the clarity of its style.[63] For Patrick Henry, "Reflections on the Guillotine" contains "both emotional and intellectual, instinctive and reflective opposition to the death penalty."[64] For his part, Fred Willhoite submits that Camus's essay is "one of the best of the innumerable writings on this much-disputed subject."[65] And Philippe Vanney considers the views formulated in Camus's essay to be "the most sophisticated statement of his ideas presented in a scattered way until that point."[66] It is possible to read the "Reflections" as a work set within the wider context of Camus's scaling down of his formulations of justice, a process in turn in tune with the personal preoccupations of the writer on a more general level throughout this period as he now pulls in his horns to focus on concrete social issues relating to specific human individuals following the collapse of his political hopes with regard to Algeria.[67]

A number of points may be made in support of the above. Particularly noteworthy is the clear transition Camus makes in "Reflections on the Guillotine" from his preoccupation with complex *political* issues pertaining to justice inherent in the Algerian crisis to the interest he now accords the *social* institution of capital punishment. To this it should be added that while in both *The Rebel* and his consideration of the Algerian War, Camus had been concerned with matters of justice relating to revolutionary *groups,* his focus in the "Reflections" is on a social and judicial practice relating to specific *individuals.* And, just as his appeal for a "civilian truce"—itself an illustration of a rethinking of priorities in the face of moral and political crisis—had concentrated on innocent civilians embroiled in the Algerian conflict, so "Reflections on the Guillotine" lays stress on specific categories of people perceived as being treated unjustly.[68] In both cases, it is with concrete moral objectives (rather than abstract moral ideals) that Camus is primarily concerned, in accordance with his decision to "cut out the chewed over morality of abstract justice" (*C3,* 221), highlighted earlier.

In addition to the above, we may also mention as worthy of notice that traces of the "scaling-down process" to which Camus's whole attitude toward justice is now subjected can be seen in the manner of his argument in "Reflections on the Guillotine." Indeed, in the work, huge moral pretensions are undermined in order to expose "the obscenity hidden under the verbal cloak" (*RRD,* 128) and the "revolting butchery" (*RRD,* 165) and the "outrage inflicted on the person and human body" (*RRD,* 165; translation amended) inherent in capital punishment's "primitive rite" (*RRD,* 128).[69] Thus, a series of claims as to the supposed moral accountability of capital punishment's "ultimate justice" (*RRD,* 127; translation amended) are considered and then rejected by Camus as "not only useless but definitely harmful" (*RRD,* 129).

The first argument he eliminates is that the death penalty's "exemplary value of the punishment" (*RRD,* 130) functions as a deterrent to others ("If society justifies the death penalty by the need to make example, it must justify itself by making the publicity necessary" [*RRD,* 135]); secondly, the idea that capital punishment operates as a judicial arm of the State ("This is an emotion, and a particularly violent one, not a principle. Retaliation is related to nature and instinct, not to law" [*RRD,* 142]); thirdly, the absolutist nature of a codified social practice which "usurps an exorbitant privilege by claiming to punish an always relative culpability by a definitive and irreparable punishment" (*RRD,* 150)[70] and which cannot accommodate the reality of judicial error ("If justice admits that it is frail, would it not be better for justice to be modest and to allow its judgments sufficient leeway to correct possible mistakes?" [*RRD,* 154; translation amended]); and, finally, the idea that such uncompromising justice assumes the impossibility of rehabilitation on the part of the offender (a state of affairs denying "this right to live, which allows a chance to make amends" [*RRD,* 157; translation amended] and which, in Camus's view, "is the natural right of every person, even the worst" [*RRD,* 157; translation amended]). In sum, dispelling the myth of capital punishment, Camus reveals the "vile death" (*RRD,* 165) underscoring the death penalty's "crude surgery practised under conditions that leave nothing edifying about it" (*RRD,* 134) and which "besmirches our society" (*RRD,* 129).

In his capacity as death penalty abolitionist, then, Camus once more gives concrete expression to his views on tolerance and his prioritizing of human beings before abstract moral principles. He bases his opposition on the conviction that the rights of the human individual outweigh the (dubious) moral assertions of the state: "Justice and expediency command the law to protect the individual against a State given over to the follies of sectarianism or of pride" (*RRD,* 161).[71] Indeed, he makes clear "in our principles and institutions, that the individual is above the State" (*RRD,* 162). Thus, his earlier retributivist morality, maintained at the time of the purge in France, is now completely inverted in the view that "if justice has any meaning in this world, . . . it cannot, by its very essence, divorce itself from compassion" (*RRD,* 154).[72] Significantly, this attitude marks a return to the Camus of prewar Algeria: to the young man who, witnessing the spectacle of the convicts caged aboard *Le Martinière,* had responded to the issue of inhumane punishment by emphasizing that "there is no more despicable sight than to see people reduced to an inhuman state" (*FC,* 2:362). (We may note in passing that Camus was now thinking of writing a short story based on his experience aboard that convict ship [*C3,* 148]). Just as the idea of a minimum standard of justice, which Camus brings to bear both in his report on *Le Martinière* and other aspects of his *Alger républicain* apprenticeship as discussed in chapter 3, seeks to safeguard the fundamental right to human dignity over and above morally suspect social and legal processes, so he insists in the "Reflections" that, in the event of capital punishment *not* being abolished, it should at least be sufficiently humane so as to allow the offender to die with dignity (*E,* 1064; *RRD,* 165).

Camus's "Reflections on the Guillotine" raises an interesting issue when viewed from the perspective of Kaliayev's "redemptive justice" analyzed in *The Rebel.* Indeed, in the case of the Russian terrorist, execution appears morally justified, while in the "Reflections" it clearly is not. Moreover, the argument maintained in the 1957 work that execution fails to compensate for the original murder ("supreme justice . . . is . . . no less repulsive than the crime, and this new murder, far from making amends for the harm done to the social body, adds a new blot to the first one" [*RRD,* 127; translation amended]) seems to be in conflict with Camus's view in "The Fastidious Assassins" that it does. These apparent inconsistencies suggest that the execution of a convicted murderer does not, in Camus's thinking, achieve the same ends as Kaliayev's redemptive death, by which not only justice is administered, but also a moral equilibrium maintained between a life taken and a life given. Indeed, in the "Reflections," Camus spotlights how such moral equilibrium is *not* respected in the institutionalized practice of capital punishment, where revenge invariably substitutes for justice. As such, the notion of a "redemptive death" no longer applies: "Let us admit that it is just and necessary to compensate for the murder of the victim by the death of the murderer. But beheading is not simply death. It is just as different, in essence, from the privation of life as a concentration camp is from prison. It is a murder, to be sure, and one that arithmetically pays for the murder committed. But it adds to death a rule, a public premeditation known to the future victim, an organization, in short, which is in itself a source of moral sufferings more terrible than death. Hence there is no equivalence" (*RRD,* 142–43).

It should be clear from the above that "Reflections on the Guillotine" provides Camus with a vehicle for reappraising his whole attitude toward matters of justice in the wake of the Algerian "collapse." No longer is he preoccupied with large-scale manifestations of sociopolitical justice, but with a specific codified practice relating to particular social categories. It is no coincidence that, confronted with crisis at both a personal and professional level, Camus now turns his attention to capital punishment—an issue that, as we have seen, concerns him greatly throughout his lifetime—as he reverts to aspects of his past in an attempt to readjust his views on justice in readiness, perhaps, for future moral campaigns. While the intellectual authority underpinning the "Reflections" is clear, how far Camus was ultimately successful in converting this into other areas of his moral sensibility is a matter for conjecture, for he would be killed before being able to write any other works relating to social and political justice. To judge from entries in the *Carnets* dating from the final months of his life, Camus's "stages of a recovery," recorded earlier, had not yet borne fruit since, in April 1959, he was still in the process of self-confrontation, seeking to "rebuild a truth—after having lived all [his] life in a kind of lie" (*C3,* 266). Two months later, moreover, he claims to have "abandoned the moral point of view" (*C3,* 268), a remark that recalls the psychology of the retrospective preface to *Betwixt and Between* where Camus the public man makes way for Camus the private individual:

> Like everyone I have tried, as best I could, to improve my nature by morality. This, alas, is what has cost me most dear. With energy, which is something I possess, we sometimes manage to act morally, but never to be moral. The person of passion who longs for goodness yields to injustice at the very moment when (s)he speaks of justice. Human beings sometimes seem to me to be a walking injustice: I am thinking of myself. If I now have the impression that I was wrong, or that I lied in what I sometimes wrote, it is because I do not know how to make my injustice honestly known. I have doubtless never said that I was a just man. I have merely happened to say that we should try to be just, and also that such an ambition involved great toil and misery. But is this distinction so important? And can the man who does not even manage to make justice prevail in his own life preach its virtues to other people? (*SEN,* 24; translation amended)

I have quoted the above passage at length because it shakes Camus's lifelong concern for sociopolitical justice to its very foundations. The sense of misjudgment underpinning Camus's comments ("the impression that I was wrong, or that I lied") provides further confirmation of a rethinking of his general consideration of justice as the pressures of history and personal circumstance become increasingly overpowering. Conceding that he had been mistaken to "improve [his] nature by morality"—a reference to his own tendency to sacrifice personal morality on the altar of moral abstraction, that is particularly to the fore in his response to the purge in France—Camus exposes his moral uncertainty as he contemplates campaigns from the past. And the final rhetorical question, "and can the man who does not even manage to make justice prevail in his own life preach its virtues to other people?" (cf. *C3,* 125), gives the lie to the deeply entrenched view of Camus as a moral guide.

Yet this process of self-confrontation is only part of the story of the retrospective preface, since as well as seeking to shed aspects of his past, Camus also looks forward to the future and, more specifically, to the long-planned project deriving from his "unique source" (*SEN,* 18; translation amended) (*Betwixt and Between*) with, at its core, "the admirable silence of a mother and the effort of a man *to rediscover a justice* or a love which matches this silence" (*SEN,* 26; my italics). Once more, Camus looks "back to the future" as he attempts to rediscover a moral identity lost in the tide of history. Clearly, what he has in mind is *The First Man,* the autobiographical quest for origins that Camus deems of considerable importance both personally and professionally.[73] As he makes clear to Catherine Sellers in correspondence dating from just days before his death, "as long as this monstrous book is not finished, there will be no peace for me."[74] Perhaps poised, then, on the verge of discovering a rejuvenated moral persona from which a renewed understanding of social and political justice may have derived, Camus was destined to be dispatched at a pivotal moment. How far his planned third "cycle" on Happiness and Love—of which *The First Man* was set to be the centerpiece—would have gone on to provide Camus with a vehicle for further reworking his formulations of justice, begun, as we have seen, in "Reflections on the Guillotine," one can but wonder.[75]

Conclusion

> I do not claim to be anyone exemplary and I am very far from all virtue (something shudders within me when you write that I am a man of justice. I am a man without justice and this weakness torments me, that's all).
>
> —Camus, *Essais*

THIS BOOK HAS SOUGHT TO ASSESS THE EMPHASES AND COMPLEXITIES of Albert Camus's lifelong preoccupation with justice within the sociopolitical sphere against a background of changing personal and historical circumstances. Building on existing scholarship, it has provided a chronological account of Camus's developing ideas on the concept, as expressed in his nonfiction, where the writer's personal concerns come directly to the fore.

Three main phases in Camus's consideration of justice emerge from our analysis. In the first, that of the writer's formative years in Algiers, played out against the paradoxical background of personal poverty and Mediterranean magnificence, what characterizes his initial moral sensibility is a "person-to-person" response to perceived injustice. While, in the later retrospective writings dealing with this early period, any sense of injustice which Camus feels about his own circumstances is more than compensated for by a feeling of oneness with the world and a union with nature, the young man's sensitivity to the suffering of others and, more specifically, to the issue of unwarranted social difference, begins to find concrete expression in some of his youthful writings. This realization with regard to "unknown sufferings" (*YW,* 191), fundamental to the pursuit of justice, is further stimulated by Camus's early experiences of politics and theater. In the absence of an appropriate textual platform at this time, both of these provide a useful vehicle for situating his emerging morality within a sociopolitical context relating to social conditions, on the one hand, and political systems, on the other. Throughout this first stage of his concern, Camus's remains a deeply personal and proactive psychology, so that his understanding of justice, rich in compassion and sensibility, is essentially empirical in nature, pragmatic reformism taking precedence over political idealism. This is in keeping with his view, formulated in the celebrated "Misery in Kabylia" which Camus undertakes to write for *Alger républicain* in 1939, that "on any occasion, progress is made every time a political problem is replaced by a human problem" (*FC,* 1:335).

The culmination of this first phase of his engagement with justice, Camus's *Alger républicain* apprenticeship affords him an opportunity to "bear witness" to human indignity in his local situation. This, in turn, ignites the young man's quest for justice on behalf of impoverished and disfranchised social categories. A self-styled revolutionary in his attempt to safeguard basic human rights in the face of adversity, Camus now assumes the role of reformer. But here his underlying engagement with justice—a determination not to allow the pursuit of practical objectives to be compromised by politico-ideological prejudices—becomes frustrated by a set of historical circumstances in which he is himself implicated, that is, the practice of French colonialism in Algeria.

The issue of how external forces impact on, and come into conflict with, Camus's concern for social and political justice is crucial to the second phase of his preoccupation. While his prewar view of justice is largely compatible with that during "those wartime years that marked for me the end of my youth" (*SEN,* 148), changing historical circumstances require a reworking of it in a completely different (war) context. Here, Camus is forced into thinking in more collective terms (although his "Algerian morality," of course, already had a strong, if different, collective dimension). This is necessarily bound up with the notion of nationhood, but his first attempt to maintain his concern for justice in the new situation ("pacifism") proves unsustainable. As he acknowledges in 1945, "complete pacifism seems to me to be badly thought out and from now on we know that there always comes a time when it is no longer tenable."[1] Moving to a position of "Resistance" for what are essentially the same reasons and the same concerns, he is compelled to grapple with the ethical problem of the use of violence as an instrument of revolutionary justice, an issue with which henceforth Camus would never feel at ease and which he would never cease investigating. The *Letters to a German Friend* and the concomitant *Combat* editorials provide a potent rallying cry as Camus seeks to maintain moral values in the face of Nazi nihilism.

Further moral dilemmas impinging on Camus's concern for sociopolitical justice continue to manifest themselves in the postwar period. The *justice manquée* of the French purge, an ideal to which he had been prepared to sacrifice his own innate sense of justice based on humanist principles, confirms, for Camus, the impossibility of maintaining absolutes of morality within the historical process. His subsequent quest for a dialogic code of ethics, whereby the conflicting standards of justice and freedom would be reconciled in a social order guaranteeing individual autonomy, underscores the socialist-styled revolution that Camus envisages for postwar France. Transposing this vision on to the international community, Camus provides an alternative scenario to the *politique des blocs,* whereby political absolutism makes way for a "moderate course of treatment" (*E,* 319) predicated on democratic principles, to be undertaken in a spirit of tolerance and mutual understanding.

The polemical *The Rebel* testifies to the consistency and continuity in Camus's thought throughout the postwar period, where his principal moral preoccupations remain the balance between justice and freedom and establishing a moral response to (revolutionary) nihilism. With his own misguided idealism at the time of the purge still very much in mind, Camus is deeply preoccupied during the postwar phase with the issue of murder and political violence, and *The Rebel*—"an attempt to understand the time I live in" (*TR,* 11)—can be read as both a universal *and* personal *mise au point* as he engages in debates demonstrating how, when pursued as unqualified ideals, justice and freedom forfeit their moral value in the revolutionary quest. As the "Essay on Revolt" starkly illustrates, violence can never be just where the legacy is murder and where nothing is actually achieved. Correspondingly, Camus's postwar vision of justice is such that it can only be vindicated when qualified by freedom (and vice versa); for it to be morally accountable, justice needs to be relative, with proximate ends pursued by means in accordance with the preservation of provisional morality, since "solitary justice [ends] in oppression" (*SEN,* 149). For Camus, revolutionary justice is a matter requiring equivalent and appropriate relations between "means" and "ends"; to justify the means by the end is to sacrifice morality on the altar of ideology.

The profound psychological effect made upon Camus by the hostile reception of *The Rebel,* a work in which he had invested great intellectual effort, ushers in the third and final main phase of his engagement with justice, where the pressures of history and personal circumstance increasingly lead to frustration and disillusionment in the writer's thought. The ongoing attempt to reconcile justice and freedom as a basis for human prosperity is now finally overwhelmed by the personal and political conflicts exposed by Camus's response to the Algerian War. Insurmountable difficulties with regard to the Algerian crisis force Camus, toward the end of his life, to undertake a rethinking of his whole attitude toward justice, with a possible view to reinvigorating his then-frustrated moral stance. Initiatives such as the 1956 "Appeal for a Civilian Truce in Algeria" and the 1957 "Reflections on the Guillotine" bear testimony to a "scaling-down process" in Camus's thought, as earlier lofty political pretensions concerning justice and freedom are now replaced by concrete social issues relating to specific categories of people whose plight is perceived as unjust. Interestingly, this "narrowing-down" is set against the backdrop of a more general return to origins, as Camus reverts to aspects of his past for guidance and support. In terms of his concern for justice, Camus's final utterances on the subject mark a return to the personal nature of his preoccupation characteristic of the writer's formative years in Algeria, so that there can be seen to be a cyclical aspect to his overall engagement with the concept. However, how far this "pilgrimage to the source" would have gone on to result in a rejuvenated moral psychology is necessarily a speculative question, given the tragedy of Camus's untimely death.

Highly reactive to perceived injustice in the sociopolitical domain, Camus's approach to the question of justice differs markedly from that of distinguished thinkers such as Plato, whose ideal of justice is formulated in terms of a theoretical model to which humanity should aspire. Camus's understanding of social and political justice is essentially that of a humanitarian pragmatist, whose underlying engagement with the concept assumes that theoretical deliberation may accompany, but must not be allowed to override, the pursuit of practical objectives. There is surely substance in Serge Doubrovsky's view that "it is precisely the 'lived in' rather than 'thought out' nature of the Camusian approach which gives it . . . its value."[2] Indeed, the furor surrounding the publication of *The Rebel,* a text where theoretical considerations take precedence over practical aims, demonstrates tellingly the pitfalls of the pragmatist momentarily taking on the persona of moral philosopher, a role that, elsewhere, Camus is at pains to reject (*E,* 1427). As he writes in *Combat* on November 24, 1944, "social justice can very well come about without an ingenious philosophy. It requires some revelations of common sense and those simple things that are perceptiveness, energy and disinterestedness" (*E,* 281). Certainly, changing historical circumstances, as charted in these pages and that impinge on

Camus's concern for justice, require a modification of this commonsense attitude. Accordingly, in his attempt to uphold standards of morality in the face of adversity, he does not shirk "dirtying his hands" as events dictate. And yet, throughout, whatever the pressures brought to bear by history and by the different phases of his own life, Camus maintains his humanitarian generosity and refuses to compromise his moral responsibility (cf. *E,* 251). Wherever possible, and in keeping with his "such . . . strong desire to see reduced all the misfortune and bitterness which poisons humankind" (*Corr,* 23), Camus eschews ideological debate and embraces moral empiricism in the interests of social accomplishment and the safeguard of "a dignity common to everyone" (*TR,* 24; translation amended) that is "always to be defended" (*TR,* 25; translation amended). His own poverty-stricken childhood gives Camus the right to feel "[at] one with the people who suffer" (*RRD,* 61; translation amended), since "poverty leaves those who have lived through it an intolerance that endures badly those speaking about a certain destitution other than in knowledge of the facts" (*E,* 1111). An intellectual with a social conscience, then, Camus offers a message of hope "for those who . . . cannot live: . . . the humiliated" (*TR,* 268), a position he would rationalize in his Nobel Prize Acceptance Speech: "We others, writers of the 20th Century, . . . must know . . . that our only justification, if there is one, is to speak, as far as we are able, for those who cannot do so" (*E,* 1092).

Deeply antipathetic to the politics of oppression in his conviction that "there is nothing more dignified than refusing reasons of State set up as an absolute" (*E,* 1838; cf. *E,* 1072; *RRD,* 196), Camus's view of sociopolitical justice implies tolerance and compassion ("I have need of others who have need of me and of each other," he insists [*TR,* 261]), based on a belief in the potential of human beings to establish meaningful interpersonal relations. "That is why the only society capable of evolution and liberalization and the only one that should keep both our active and critical liking is where the plurality of parties is established" (*E,* 1783). As *The Rebel* confirms, the absolute justice advanced by Marxist-Leninists is, in Camus's eyes, a formula for tyranny, while the "supreme justice" (*RRD,* 127) of capital punishment is deemed morally indefensible by virtue of the fact that, ultimately, "if justice has any meaning in this world, . . . it cannot, by its very essence, divorce itself from compassion" (*RRD,* 154). Thus, for it to be morally accountable, justice, as Camus finally comes to understand it, must remain a relative moral concept with, at its core, a respect for the human individual and an inviolable limit determining what actions between human beings can be morally justified.

In his general conviction that "there can be no justice without rights and there are no rights without free expression of these rights" (*E,* 387), Camus can be said to be closer to John Rawls than John Stuart Mill in his understanding of justice: the standard of fairness, rather than the idea of maximum aggregate benefit (which invariably leads to social discrimination and exclusion, ideas alien to the French Algerian writer) is a useful yardstick by which to measure the moral caliber of Camus's position. Indeed, "Camusian justice" is socially inclusive, since "nothing is true which compels us to exclude" (*SEN,* 149), and it is no coincidence that Camus himself—who, we recall, "was only ever happy and at peace when in a profession or doing a job carried out with other people [he] could like" (*C3,* 164)—spotlights "the experience of justice *through sport*" (*CA2,* 61), where team spirit promotes the value of collective endeavor based on equality of worth between the players as a model for interpersonal morality.[3] Politically, this ethos of shared experience and collective responsibility finds expression in Camus's support of decentralized government, whereby citizens become involved in the decision-making process, thus rendering politics "everyone's business" in the belief that "politics is made for people and not people for politics" (*E,* 1327). *Contra* the bureaucratic, autocratic state machinery of totalitarian justice, Camus would, accordingly, look to the politics of pluralist democracy, "the social and political exercise of moderation" (*E,* 1580), for a basis on which to develop a "civilization of dialogue" (*E,* 348) where a climate of cooperation, conducive to the reconciliation of social justice and individual freedom, could flourish. While readily acknowledging the imperfections of the idea (*E,* 319; cf. *E,* 1582), Camus defends the standard of liberal democracy in his belief that freedom of expression, which such a system allows, offers the best response to nihilism while, at the same time, ensuring the safeguard of human freedom, a concept fundamental to his moral stance.[4] "For even if *we do not achieve* justice, liberty still keeps the power to protest against injustice and preserves communication" (*CA2,* 69). Following the terrorist attacks of September 11, 2001, and the subsequent "War on Terror", these words today resonate with added poignancy.

In the words of Patrick McCarthy, "if one demands 'justice for Camus', . . . then one must first admit that he was a man sorely tried by an impossible age."[5] Today, in a world riddled by terror, Camus remains a beacon of moral optimism.[6] Indeed, there are more than a few parallels to be drawn between the moral and political challenges facing Camus during his own lifetime and those facing us at the dawn of the twenty-first century. Such ongoing relevance makes Camus's voice all the more compelling in current debates on the relationship between personal freedom, state interest and the exercise of power. Camus's legacy, then, remains strong. As Elie Wiesel observes, "despite the melancholy that some of his writings emit, we emerge from them fortified, not to say reassured."[7] In the last analysis, as "both a spokesman and a symptom of his times" (to use John Cruickshank's phraseology), Camus was a man whose passion for justice was modified by the turbulent processes of history: an often traumatic, sometimes frustrating, but—perhaps—ultimately rewarding experience since, in the *Carnets,* he would note that "it is in struggle that, in the end, I have always found my peace" (*C3,* 182).[8] If, as Joseph Joubert claims, "justice is truth in action," then Camus may reasonably be deemed the embodiment of the ideal.[9] He once conceded that "a single thing in the world seems to me to be greater than justice: it is if not truth itself, at least the effort toward truth."[10] This book is intended to record the stages and details of that momentous quest.

Notes

INTRODUCTION

1. Jules Romains, *Les Hommes de bonne volonté,* vol. 3, *Les Amours enfantines* (Paris: Flammarion, 1958), 15.

2. Plato, *The Republic of Plato,* trans. Allan Bloom (New York: Basic Books, 1968), especially bks. 2:357–67; 4:441–45; and 9:588–92.

3. Aristotle, *Nicomachean Ethics,* trans. Terence Irwin (Indianapolis, IN: Hackett, 1985), bk. 5.

4. Jeremy Bentham, *"A Fragment on Government" and "An Introduction to the Principles of Morals and Legislation,"* Blackwells Political Texts (Oxford: Blackwell, 1948). John Stuart Mill, *Utilitarianism, On Liberty and Considerations on Representative Government,* ed. H. B. Acton (London: Dent, 1972), especially chaps. 4 and 5 of *Utilitarianism.*

5. John Rawls, *A Theory of Justice* (Oxford: Oxford University Press, 1971).

6. "Des écrivains nous disent (Hommages à Camus)," *Le Figaro,* January 6, 1960, 4.

7. René Ménard, "Albert Camus devant un secret," *NRF* 8 (1960): 611.

8. Jean Grenier, *Albert Camus: Souvenirs* (Paris: Gallimard, 1968), 149.

9. Jacqueline Lévi-Valensi, "Regards sur l'homme, lecture de l'œuvre," *Europe* 77 (1999): 3.

10. Cf. Rieux's remark to Tarrou in *The Plague* (1947): "Heroism and sanctity don't really appeal to me, I imagine. What interests me is—being a man" (*TP,* 209). These sentiments would later be reiterated in, notably, the "Final interview of Albert Camus" (1959) (*E,* 1925).

11. Raymond Gay-Crosier, for instance, deems justice "a cardinal notion throughout Camus's entire work" (Raymond Gay-Crosier, *L'Envers d'un échec: étude sur le théâtre d'Albert Camus,* Bibliothèque des Lettres Modernes 10 [Paris: Lettres Modernes Minard, 1967], 214). Similarly, Paul Ginestier considers the concept as "one of the most important pivots" of Camus's thought (Paul Ginestier, *Pour connaître la pensée de Camus* [Paris: Bordas, 1964], 160), while Bernard East highlights Camus's "passion for justice", an ideal whose value for the writer is seen as "fundamental" (Bernard East, *Albert Camus, ou l'homme à la recherche d'une morale* [Paris: Cerf, 1984], 147).

12. Denis Salas, *Albert Camus: la juste révolte,* Collection le bien commun (Paris: Michalon, 2002), 9.

13. Grenier, *Albert Camus,* 71.

14. It is not unreasonable to suggest that the fiction and drama provide Camus with an outlet for what, in "The Enigma" (1950), he calls a writer's (his?) "nostalgias" and "temptations" (*SEN,* 144). After all, in his imaginative works, Camus is able to experiment with ideas and hypotheses in ways which ill befit, say, the journalistic editorial.

15. Farah Nayeri, "A Skeleton Rattles Its Bones," *Independent,* April 23, 1994, 26.

16. Camus's preoccupation with so-called "metaphysical justice" comes more strongly to the fore in his imaginative writings and, as such, need not delay us here.

17. Beaunier, André, ed., *Les Carnets de Joseph Joubert* (Paris: Gallimard, 1938), 1:144.

18. Aleida Joanna Gehrels, "The Concept of Justice in the Fiction of Albert Camus" (PhD diss., University of Arizona, 1969). Maxime Pierre Meto'o, "Les thèmes du bonheur et de la justice dans l'œuvre d'Albert Camus" (PhD diss., University of Western Ontario, 1982).

19. Tanju Tuzun, "Les positions sociales et politiques d'Albert Camus dans son œuvre" (PhD diss., University of Poitiers, 1968). Azzedine Haddour, "Camus: The Other as an Outsider in a Univocal Discourse" (PhD diss., University of Sussex, 1989); and cf. by the same writer, *Colonial Myths: History and Narrative* (Manchester, UK: Manchester University Press, 2000).

20. See Robert Roeming, *Camus: A Bibliography,* 15th ed. (Milwaukee: University of Wisconsin Computing Services Division, 2000); and Raymond Gay-Crosier's on-line bibliography at http://www.clas.ufl.edu/users/gaycros/Bibliog.htm.

21. Henry Bonnier, *Albert Camus ou la force d'être* (Lyons: Vitte, 1959). Georges Hourdin, *Camus le Juste,* Collection Tout le monde en parle (Paris: Cerf, 1962). Ginestier, *Pour connaître la pensée de Camus.*

22. Olivier Todd, *Albert Camus, une vie,* Biographies NRF Gallimard (Paris: Gallimard / Olivier Todd, 1996).

23. Pierre-Henri Simon, *Présence de Camus* (Paris: La Renaissance du Livre, 1962). Emmett Parker, *Albert Camus: The Artist in the Arena* (Madison: University of Wisconsin Press, 1965). East, *Camus.* Susan Tarrow, *Exile from the Kingdom: A Political Rereading of Albert Camus* (Tuscaloosa: University of Alabama Press, 1985). Jeanyves Guérin, *Albert Camus: portrait de l'artiste en citoyen* (Paris: Bourin, 1993).

24. Simon, *Présence de Camus,* 64. East, *Camus,* 147.

25. Gay-Crosier, *L'Envers d'un échec,* 214. André Abbou, "Combat pour la justice," in *AC5,* 36.

26. Paul F. Smets, *Albert Camus: ses engagements pour la justice et la justesse* (Brussels: Ceuterick, [1998]). See note 12 above.

27. Simone de Beauvoir, *La Force des choses,* Collection Folio (Paris: Gallimard, 1963), 1:277.

Chapter 1. Justice, Injustice, and the Search for Origins

1. Herbert R. Lottman, *Albert Camus: A Biography* (London: Weidenfeld and Nicolson, 1979), 615.

2. Actually, to judge from the *Carnets,* Camus was thinking of writing a novel about justice as early as late 1944, a time when he was deeply preoccupied with the morally contentious issue of the purge in France (*C2,* 127–28; *CA2,* 64–65); cf. *C2,* 216; *CA2,* 111. The personal nature of the projected "Novel on Justice" reflects Camus's private attempt to come to terms with the *justice manquée* of the purge: see below, chapter 6, 132–41. For a useful account of the genesis of *The First Man,* see Yosei Matsumoto, "*Le Premier Homme:* le processus d'élaboration," in *AC20,* 15–32.

3. See *C2,* 297–98; *CA2,* 153; and cf. Roger Quilliot's remarks from his commentary on the work in *E,* 1179–80.

4. Cf. L. Martin-Chauffier, ed., *François La Rochefoucauld: Œuvres complètes,* Bibliothèque de La Pléiade (Paris: Gallimard, 1964), 413: "love of justice is, for the majority of people, just the fear of suffering injustice."

5. For accounts of Camus's formative years in Belcourt, see Lottman, *Albert Camus,* 26–35; Patrick McCarthy, *Camus: A Critical Study of his Life and Work* (London: Hamish Hamilton, 1982), 10–44; and Todd, *Albert Camus,* 24–35. To these titles should be added the first two chapters of Alain Vircondelet's splendidly illustrated *Albert Camus: vérité et légendes* (Paris: Chêne-Hachette Livre, 1998), 12–44; and "Une Jeunesse algérienne," the first of three commemorative programmes on Camus, originally broadcast on French radio in 1980, in which Jules Roy retraces his friend's early years in Algeria and revisits Camus's erstwhile residence on the rue de Lyon (Jean Montalbetti, *Un homme, une ville: Albert Camus à Alger, par Jules Roy* [Cassettes Radio France, RF 300], 3 cassettes, 1 "Une Jeunesse algérienne.")

6. However, Camus's brother Lucien would later tell Herbert Lottman that, although poor, they were not paupers (Lottman, *Albert Camus,* 681 n16).

7. Morvan Lebesque, *Camus par lui-même,* Écrivains de toujours (Paris: Seuil, 1963), 16.

Carl A. Viggiani, "Notes pour le futur biographe d'Albert Camus," in *AC1,* 206. Cf. *PH,* 81; *FM,* 65, where mention is made of the fact that "she [his grandmother] more than anyone else had dominated Jacques's childhood." See also *PH,* 56, 84; *FM,* 42, 67 for examples of the grandmother's harsh discipline toward her grandson. In the words of Anthony Rizzuto, "her [the grandmother's] system of justice is founded on the presumption of guilt" (Anthony Rizzuto, *Camus: Love and Sexuality* [Gainesville: University Press of Florida, 1998], 124).

8. Claude Treil, *L'Indifférence dans l'œuvre d'Albert Camus* (Quebec: Cosmos, 1971), 33.

9. Viggiani, "Notes pour le futur biographe d'Albert Camus," 206.

10. Although a full analysis of *The First Man* falls beyond the remit of the present study, this tragically truncated work is worthy of mention here on the ground of its considerable autobiographical content. Annotating the manuscript for publication, Catherine Camus describes the draft left by her father as "a preliminary draft which is completely autobiographical and so much so that my mother thought that my father would not have published it in that state. I'm quite persuaded that he would not have published it as it stands" (Catherine Camus et al., "Albert Camus: *Le Premier Homme,*" *Bulletin d'Information de la Société des Études Camusiennes,* 33 [1994]: 15). The ambiguous nature of the text as we now have it means, of course, that any account of *The First Man* must necessarily remain inconclusive.

It is worthy of note that the infamous "Everything is good," uttered by the lucid Kirilov in Dostoevsky's *Devils* (trans. and ed., Michael R. Katz [Oxford: Oxford University Press, 1992], 250) and which Camus, in *The Myth of Sisyphus* (1942), would himself champion as "the recipe for the absurd victory" (*MS,* 109–10), is based on the belief that life brings both pleasure and pain and that each acts as a counterbalance of the other (cf. Ray Davison, *Camus: The Challenge of Dostoevsky* [Exeter: University of Exeter Press, 1997], 77). An interesting parallel may be drawn here with Montaigne—an author not unknown to Camus—who philosophized on the complementary nature of the extremes of pain and pleasure in human experience, the idea being that one cannot exist without the other. In his *Essais,* Montaigne would thus submit that

> we must learn to put up with that which we cannot avoid. Like the harmony of the world, our life is made up of contrary things and also of various tones—soft and harsh, high-pitched and flat, dull and deep. What would a musician say who only liked half of these? [S]he would have to know how to use and blend them together. It is the same for us with the good and bad things which are consubstantial with our life. We cannot be without this combination where the one set is no less necessary than the other. (Albert Thibaudet and Maurice Rat, eds., *Œuvres complètes de Montaigne,* Bibliothèque de La Pléiade [Paris: Gallimard, 1962], 3:1068).

One might add that "extremes" would go on to play an important role in Camus's own thinking, a claim that can be substantiated with reference to the titles of works spanning his lifetime: *Betwixt and Between* (1937) and *Exile and the Kingdom* (1957).

11. Lessons that would have a lasting effect on Camus are not exclusive to his lycée years, however. Mention may usefully be made here of the role, in *The First Man,* of Cormery's primary school teacher, M. Bernard (clearly styled on Camus's own *instituteur* Louis Germain, to whom the writer would dedicate his Acceptance Speech for the 1957 Nobel Prize for Literature) in the child's (moral) education. As Philippe Marlière rightly observes, "honesty, fraternity, equality, justice, tolerance, rationality, respect, politeness: these are some of the values M. Bernard teaches his pupils. . . . M. Bernard's example, as an adoptive father, provides a clear moral landmark for Camus's (Philippe Marlière, "Camus against the tide: Algeria and the intellectual doxa," in "Constructing Memories: Camus, Algeria and *Le Premier Homme,*" ed. Peter Dunwoodie and Edward J. Hughes, vol. 6 [1998] of *Stirling French Publications:* 50). In a similar vein, Nina Sjursen detects a sense of justice in "the child's games" (*PH,* 41–56; *FM,* 30–42) and the spectacle of the "donnades" (*PH,* 143–46; *FM,* 117–21) (Nina Sjursen, "Jeux, justice et amour dans *Le Premier Homme,*" *Narcisse* 16 [1996]: 53–65).

12. David Sprintzen, *Camus: A Critical Examination* (Philadelphia: Temple University Press, 1988), 25.

13. Lottman, *Albert Camus,* 67. However, this biographer also reports that Camus did receive visitors at either his brother's or uncle's residences and, once his finances permitted him to leave the family home, at his own abode (67).

14. Although Jacques and Pierre—"destined from the beginning to be friends," Camus explains (*FM,* 108)—do recognize their own distinct individuality, neither of the boys in *The First Man* views his social background with hostility (*PH,* 204; *FM,* 173–74). Indeed, despite the exotic appeal of Georges Didier, representing "what it was to be a middle-class French family" (*FM,* 162), Cormery remains more comfortable among people of his own ilk: "In this way, while Jacques might be intoxicated with the strange potions of bourgeois tradition, he remained devoted to the one who was most like him, and that was Pierre" (*FM,* 164; translation amended). Cf. Cormery's psychological alienation at the *colonie de vacances* (*PH,* 138; *FM,* 113–14) and his personal sense of loss following his success at the *lycée* entrance examination (*PH,* 163; *FM,* 137). For a useful assessment of how Cormery remains immune to bitterness concerning his humble origins, see Christian Morzewski, "*Le Premier Homme* ou l'anti-enfance d'un chef," *Roman 20–50* 27 (1999): 89–102.

15. As a matter of interest, in *The First Man,* Camus consciously chooses to "speak of those [he] loved. *And of that only*" (*FM,* 250; my italics), a remark implying that there is another, more cheerless, side to his childhood which, while evident, will remain untold. The camaraderie of natural amusements on the beach, where Jacques and his friends "reigned over life and over the sea" (*FM,* 41); the

magnificent surroundings of the *Maison des invalides,* where "to wander in this fragrant jungle, to crawl in it, to snuggle your face in the grass . . . was rapture" (*FM,* 185–86; translation amended); and the child Cormery's hunting excursions with his uncle Étienne, during which Jacques felt "the richest of children" (*FM,* 87)—these instances can indirectly be attributed to Camus's own childhood experience, as a means of compensating for "the cruel and demanding necessity" (*FM,* 96) conditioning the life of a child "who had grown up in the midst of a poverty as naked as death" (*FM,* 48; translation amended). As Edward Hughes perceptively remarks, *The First Man* "offers glimpses of Jacques Cormery keenly inhabiting a form of intermittent paradise. . . . In these privileged spaces, Jacques enjoys edenic, if transient pleasures" (Edward J. Hughes, *Albert Camus, "Le Premier Homme"/ "La Peste,"* Glasgow Introductory Guides to French Literature 33 [Glasgow: University of Glasgow French and German Publications, 1995], 17–18).

16. Curiously, Camus perceives the joy he derives from the Mediterranean clime in paradoxical terms: "There are many injustices in the world, but there is one that is never mentioned, that of climate. For a long time, without realizing it, I profited from that particular injustice" (*SEN,* 19). The use of landscape to express personal psychology is well to the fore in much of Camus's imaginative writing, not least the pivotal murder scene of *The Outsider* (*TRN,* 1167–68; *TO,* 62–64). It is also worth noting that among the many jobs undertaken by the young Camus was a stint at the Institut de Météorologie, where his intellectual interest in the weather doubtless originates (Lottman, *Albert Camus,* 163–65).

17. Germaine Brée, *Camus and Sartre: Crisis and Commitment* (London: Calder and Boyars, 1974), 65.

18. Quoted in a round-table discussion, "Le style camusien révélateur d'une morale," in *Albert Camus entre la misère et le soleil: Actes du Colloque international de Poitiers, 29–30–31 mai 1997,* ed. Lionel Dubois (Poitiers, France: Éditions du Pont-Neuf, 1997), 124.

19. Cf. Nelly Stéphane, "La Mer heureuse," *Europe* 77 (1999): 132–44.

20. Viggiani, "Notes pour le futur biographe d'Albert Camus," 209; cf. Lottman, *Albert Camus,* 42–46.

21. Jacques Delarue, *La Tuberculose,* Collection Que sais-je? 15 (Paris: PUF, 1972), 72, quoted in Pierre Petit, "Tuberculose et sensibilité chez Gide et Camus," *Bulletin des Amis d'André Gide* 9 (1981): 284.

22. According to Lottman, Camus later disclosed to both Jean Bloch-Michel and Max-Pol Fouchet his belief that tuberculosis was a "metaphysical" illness, inasmuch as "you can cure yourself if you want to" (Lottman, *Albert Camus,* 46, 685 n18; cf. *E,* 1217; *YW,* 213).

23. Especially in Camus's time, tuberculosis posed a severe threat to human life, a reality which is tellingly recorded in an early draft of "Between Yes and No": "He had always had the feeling that he could not die, not because of any [2 illegible words] feeling of immortality which philosophers speak about. It was a question of a natural death. Thinking about it, he judged impossible the fact that he might die. He had never dared to conclude. But he contented himself with noting one fact. At the most serious stage of his illness, the doctor implicitly gave up hope of saving him. He hadn't had a single doubt. Besides, the fear of death haunted him very much" (*E,* 1215). The third person narrative voice used in these remarks heightens the sense of alienation Camus experiences in the face of death. Cf. *C1,* 17–18; *CA1,* 2; and *PC,* 179, 192; *YW,* 156, 168.

24. When Charles Poncet advised him to stay in a sanitarium for the sake of his health, Camus reportedly declined on the ground that "he could not live in an

atmosphere of the sick" (Lottman, *Albert Camus,* 139). Cf. *CA1,* 24, where Camus reflects on his enforced departure for the Massif Central: "What awaits me in the Alps is, together with loneliness and the idea that I shall be there to look after myself, the *awareness* of my illness."

25. According to Herbert Lottman, Camus's elder brother Lucien "remembered that their mother *had been frightened* [my italics] by the first attack of coughing blood. There had been *buckets* of it" (Lottman, *Albert Camus,* 45). Although Lucien may here be defending members of his family against their depiction in his brother's published writings—there appears to have been no love lost between the two men (cf. *PH,* 77 nb; *FM,* 61 nb)—these two differing testimonies on the issue of Camus's tuberculosis cast a shadow of doubt over the authenticity of the aforementioned citation from the unpublished "Fragment."

26. Marcia Weis, *The Lyrical Essays of Albert Camus: "Une Longue Fidélité"* (Quebec: Sherbrooke, 1976), 85.

27. However, worthy of special mention are the penetrating psychoanalytical readings of the mother/son relationship in Camus, undertaken by Alain Costes in *Albert Camus ou la parole manquante: étude psychanalytique,* Collection Science de l'Homme (Paris: Payot, 1973); and Jean Gassin in *L'Univers symbolique d'Albert Camus: essai d'interprétation psychanalytique* (Paris: Minard, 1981). To these titles may be added Kirsteen H. R. Anderson's "La Première Femme: The Mother's Resurrection in the Work of Camus and Irigaray," *French Studies* 56 (2002): 29–43; and the chapter entitled "Mothers and Sons" in Rizzuto's *Camus: Love and Sexuality,* 110–39, where the mother/son relationship in *The First Man* is comprehensively examined. Also worthy of note in this latter connection is Geraldine F. Montgomery, "La mère sacrée dans *Le Premier Homme,*" in *AC20,* 63–86. Cf. *CA2,* 91: "I loved my mother with despair. I have always loved her with despair."

28. McCarthy, *Camus,* 19.

29. Jacques Lemarchand, "Les images que l'on regarde au soir de la mort d'un ami," *Le Figaro littéraire,* January 9, 1960, 1; and cf. Maria Casarès, *Résidente privilégiée* (Paris: Fayard, 1980), 235.

30. As he observes in correspondence with Marguerite Dobrenn and Jeanne Sicard dated July 22, 1936, "each time I realize that I am an invalid, I recognize just how far I am from what I would like to be" (Todd, *Albert Camus, une vie,* 112). See also n23 above; and cf. Viggiani, "Notes pour le futur biographe d'Albert Camus," 209; and Lottman, *Albert Camus,* 45, 443.

31. Two of the *Youthful Writings* (of which more presently), written in 1933, bear out Camus's as yet raw and unrefined response to human mortality. In "In the Presence of the Dead," his awareness of the issue finds expression in highly emotive language (*PC,* 227–28; *YW,* 200–201), a position which, in "Losing a Loved One," is effectively canceled out by his determination to dissolve the question of suffering on the private scale into the composition of the metaphysical condition in general (*PC,* 232–33; *YW,* 205–6).

32. Gassin, *L'Univers symbolique d'Albert Camus,* 158.

33. A later entry highlights Camus's *need* to write to answer an inner call: "I must write as I must swim, because my body demands it" (*CA1,* 6). Incidentally, between 1934 and 1936—according to Jacqueline Lévi-Valensi—Camus planned to write an autobiographical novel in an attempt to discover "the true meaning of life" referred to in the *Carnets* (Jacqueline Lévi-Valensi, "L'Entrée d'Albert Camus en politique," in *Camus et la politique: Actes du colloque de Nanterre, 5–7 juin 1985,* ed. Jeanyves Guérin [Paris: L'Harmattan, 1986], 140; and cf. by the same writer, "La relation au réel dans le roman camusien," in *OFOO,* 153–85).

Although never completed, some of the sketches for that autobiographical project would be incorporated into the composition of *Betwixt and Between.*

34. It is worth recalling that Camus later highlighted André de Richaud's *La Douleur* (1931) as a work instrumental to alerting him to the perception of literature as a window on reality (*E,* 1117–18; *SEN,* 173–74).

35. Davison, *Camus,* 78. For this critic, the idea of indifference highlighted here carries echoes of Dostoevskian serenity, in that it is seen to originate "not from insensitivity but from [a] feeling of accord with creation," 78.

36. Pseudonym of Gabriel Randon de Saint-Amand (1867–1933), Rictus was a versatile French poet, dramatist and novelist whose works eloquently express the atmosphere of Parisian low-life in the late nineteenth century.

37. Although a literary commentary in nature, this early essay explores a theme underscoring Camus's own childhood—social hardship—and so is worthy of scrutiny here. Indeed, Carl Viggiani points out that the decision to write this formative work is, in part, attributable to Camus's own proletarian and poverty-stricken origins (Carl A. Viggiani, "Albert Camus' first publications," *Modern Language Notes* 75 [1960]: 594).

38. Paul Viallaneix, "Le Premier Camus," in *PC,* 30; *YW,* 21. Camus's mature reflections on artistic creation and the role of the intellectual as a social critic can be found in the fourth chapter of *The Rebel* entitled "Rebellion and Art" (*E,* 655–80; *TR,* 219–42) and his acceptance speech upon receiving the 1957 Nobel Prize for Literature (*E,* 1065–96; *RRD,* 193–98).

39. Later, in *The Rebel,* Camus defines art as "an activity which exalts and denies *simultaneously*" (*TR,* 219; my italics), and he deems this tension "between yes and no" as fundamental to the artistic quest for meaning and purpose in an absurd universe. A similar balance between affirmation and negation does not yet figure in Camus's views on art as expressed in his youthful writings, where artistic creation is essentially a device by which to escape (rather than come to terms with) the rigors of reality. Cf. Jacqueline Lévi-Valensi, "Roman, mesure et démesure," in *Albert Camus: les Extrêmes et l'équilibre; Actes du colloque de Keele, 25–27 mars 1993,* ed. David H. Walker (Amsterdam: Rodopi, 1994), 245–59.

40. The dichotomy of the social and metaphysical spheres of thought is particularly apparent in relation to justice. The issue of metaphysical justice is difficult to grasp, since there is a clear distinction between, on the one hand, so-called "metaphysical" injustice and, on the other hand, sociopolitical injustice. The former, associated with the universal nature of certain *a priori* "unjust" features of the world such as human suffering and mortality, is on a completely different epistemological basis to the latter, which is associated with contingent adversity within society. While it is possible to redress social and political injustice by reforms, the same can clearly not be said in relation to the abstract issue of mortality, over which the human individual has no control whatever. Metaphysical justice, therefore, is something of a misnomer, in the sense that human beings are, and will forever remain, unable to transcend the boundaries governing their condition. As I hope to show, the association between the metaphysical and social realms is, for the Camus of the formative years currently under consideration, rather unclear.

41. Interestingly, in "God's Dialogue with his Soul," a text written in the same year as his essay on Rictus—1932—Camus offers, from a divine perspective, a rather ironic response to outbursts such as that of Rictus's Poor Man: "What to do? What to believe? There is nothing. Ah! I am going to tell people that. I want to see them suffer, too. There is nothing. You should no longer believe. You should no longer hope. I hurl at you the certainty of nothingness. Receive it, make a robe

of it, and let the folds fall artfully. And march forward, proud to be the first ones" (*YW,* 208; translation amended). Camus's later rejection of the dogma of Christian transcendence appears in embryo in these remarks.

42. It may reasonably be argued that even in his later acclaimed works, Camus remains either unable or unwilling to make the necessary philosophical distinction between the social and metaphysical domains. In *The Plague,* notably, he uses the image of the plague to symbolize both metaphysical *and* sociopolitical injustice, without attempting to distinguish between the two: see *C2,* 67–72, especially 72; *CA2,* 31–35, especially 35; cf. *C2,* 50; *CA2,* 23; and the writer's correspondence (dated January 14, 1948) with Mme Albert Rioux, quoted in Todd, *Albert Camus, une vie,* 331. For pertinent studies of the pestilence's symbolic status, see John Cruickshank, *Albert Camus and the Literature of Revolt* (Westport, Connecticut: Greenwood Press, 1978), 166–82; and Philip Thody, *Albert Camus: 1913–1960* (London: Hamish Hamilton, 1961), 93–115.

43. Paul Henderickx, "Justice, amour et liberté dans la pensée d'Albert Camus," *Marche Romance-Liège* 14 (1964): 79.

44. Cf. below, chapter 5, 119–124.

45. Cf. below, chapter 7, 172–80.

Chapter 2. Realization

1. See, for instance, Charles-Robert Ageron, *Les Algériens musulmans et la France, 1871–1919* (Paris: PUF, 1968), 1:3–55.

2. The issue of political rights deserves special mention here. Although Moslem men were given voting power in 1919 (partly in recognition of their contribution to the struggle against Germany during the First World War), there remained an unequal representation within the Algerian Assembly between Moslem and European delegates. Moslem women, moreover, would only be politically franchised in 1958 (Alf Andrew Heggoy, "Algerian Women and the Right to Vote: Some Colonial Anomalies," *Muslim World* 64 [1974]: 228–35; and, cf. by the same writer, "Cultural Disrespect: European and Algerian Views on Women in Colonial and Independent Algeria," *Muslim World* 62 [1972]: 323–34).

3. Under French tutelage, Algeria was divided into three distinct zones, the overall effect of which was to transfer Algerian landownership to the French state and the colonists. The *communes de plein exercice* were predominantly European areas, with legislative councils (run on the French model) allowing administrative organization of all public services. The *communes mixtes* were regions with few Europeans and, accordingly, they enjoyed reduced organizational authority. The Arab territories consisted of those remaining areas where Arabs alone lived: these belts were placed under French military rule.

4. Ferhat Abbas, *Guerre et révolution d'Algérie: la nuit coloniale* (Paris: Julliard, 1962), 24–25. Peter Dunwoodie observes that "within one hundred years, European ownership—whether State or private—had been imposed on approximately 7.7 million hectares, or 40 percent of the territory" (Peter Dunwoodie, *Writing French Algeria* [Oxford: Clarendon Press, 1998], 18).

5. Parker, *Albert Camus: The Artist in the Arena,* 4.

6. Lottman uses the testimonies of Amar Ouzegane and Yves Bourgeois as a basis for his comments. Lottman, *Albert Camus,* 56.

7. Ibid. Cf. Charles-Robert Ageron, *Histoire de l'Algérie contemporaine: 1871–1954* (Paris: PUF, 1979), 2:350: "In plain language, *Ikdam* . . . declared itself

against French imperialism and for the independence and unity of the three North African countries."

8. Lottman, *Albert Camus,* 57. Olivier Todd reports that "the teachers and *lycéens* of a liberal tendency around Camus were sensitive to the injustices done to the Moslem masses" (Todd, *Albert Camus, une vie,* 49–50). Such sympathies doubtless played a key role in Camus's own sensitivity in respect of the indigenous race of Algerians. The biographer also submits that Robert Jaussaud and Claude de Fréminville, two of Camus's contemporaries, "urged Camus to become aware of social problems beyond Algiers" (59).

9. It is worth noting that in *The First Man,* Jacques and Pierre are among the boys, "most of whom were Arab" (*FM,* 172) who, because of their family circumstances, exercise the right to free school breakfasts. Todd reports that, in Louis Germain's primary school class in which the boy Albert himself figured, out of thirty-three children, there were just three Arab pupils (Todd, *Albert Camus, une vie,* 31; and cf., 774n.20).

10. Jules Roy, *La Guerre d'Algérie* (Paris: Julliard, 1960), 20.

11. Jules Roy, "'Depuis l'indépendance de l'Algérie-je suis un sans-patrie,'" *Le Figaro littéraire,* February 5–11, 1968, 20. The theme of being "without a homeland" is inherent in much of Roy's own work: see, for instance, Jules Roy, *Les chevaux du soleil* (Paris: Grasset, 1980), and Jules Roy, *Étranger pour mes frères* (Paris: Stock, 1982). For an account of the ambivalence surrounding Roy's relationship with Algeria, see Catharine Savage Brosman, "Les Frères ennemis: Jules Roy et l'Algérie," *French Review* 56 (1983): 579–87. And, for a reassessment of Camus's haunting presence in Roy's work, see Jeannine Hayat, *Jules Roy: ombre et présence d'Albert Camus* (Paris: Lettres Modernes Minard, 2000).

12. Grenier, *Albert Camus (Souvenirs),* 170. Jean Guéhenno, "Une Pureté éclatante," *Le Figaro littéraire,* January 9, 1960, 1.

13. See McCarthy, *Camus,* 25.

14. Lottman, *Albert Camus,* 170.

15. Cf. Camus's response to Claude de Fréminville's charge that he is more an intellectual than a humanist: "if only you knew how much I love people. . . . How much I am touched by old housekeepers who feel distressed because they have been mistreated, or by workers who drink with me in the cafes of Belcourt" (correspondence dated January 16, 1935, quoted in Todd, *Albert Camus, une vie,* 71).

16. Jules Roy, preface to *L'Opéra fabuleux,* by Gabriel Audisio (Paris: Julliard, 1970), 12. Cf. Max-Pol Fouchet, *Un jour, je m'en souviens: mémoire parlée* (Paris: Mercure de France, 1969), 25.

17. As Camus explains to Marguerite Dobrenn and Jeanne Sicard in correspondence dating from around August 24, 1937, "I belong to the intellectual proletariat" (quoted in Todd, *Albert Camus, une vie,* 158). Later, in the *Carnets,* he refers to "French workers" as "the only ones with whom I feel at home, that I want to get to know and 'live with'. They are like me" (*CA2,* 14; translation amended). Cf. McCarthy, *Camus,* 25: "Camus was a left-winger from the moment he first thought about politics. . . . To be a left-winger meant that he was committed to intangible but emotionally-charged things like justice and freedom. More important, it was an instinctive choice which allowed him to assert his working-class upbringing and his dislike of the rich colonials."

18. I have adopted here the wording of Jacqueline Lévi-Valensi, who bases this expression on her interviews with many of Camus's contemporaries (Lévi-Valensi, "L'Entrée d'Albert Camus en politique," 140). Cf. Lottman, *Albert Camus,* 92–94; and Todd, *Albert Camus, une vie,* 82–83, 86–87.

19. Lottman, *Albert Camus,* 86.
20. Jacqueline Lévi-Valensi, "L'Engagement culturel," in *AC5,* 87.
21. Quoted in ibid.
22. Writing over a decade after her remarks in "L'Engagement culturel," (see note 20 above), Lévi-Valensi herself has second thoughts about the identity of the reviewer of Malraux's speech (ibid., 151n29). Curiously, Todd fails to mention this later change of heart in his discussion of the matter (Todd, *Albert Camus, une vie,* 98).
23. Quoted in Todd, *Albert Camus, une vie,* 95.
24. Ibid.
25. Anne Durand, *Le Cas Albert Camus.* Collection Célébrités d'Aujourd'hui 3 (Paris: Hachette, 1961), 63.
26. Worthy of special mention is Parker's pioneering *Albert Camus: The Artist in the Arena,* which remains to this day one of the best expositions of Camus's political situation. To this should be added Fred H. Willhoite Jr.'s *Beyond Nihilism: Albert Camus's Contribution to Political Thought* (Baton Rouge: Louisiana State University Press, 1968); and Jeanyves Guérin's more recent *Albert Camus: portrait de l'artiste en citoyen,* both of which provide rigorous analyses of Camus's politics.
27. A remark reportedly made in response to a question put to Camus by a Kabyle in Stockholm at the time of the Nobel Honors of 1957 (quoted in Claire Paulhan, ed., *Jean Grenier: Carnets 1944–1971* [Paris: Seghers, 1991], 468).
28. Jonathan H. King, ed., *Albert Camus: Selected Political Writings* (London: Methuen, 1981), 3. For an interesting *mise au point* of Camus's political legacy, see Jeanyves Guérin, "Les hommes politiques français lecteurs de Camus," in Guérin, ed., *Camus et la politique: Actes du Colloque de Nanterre, 5–7 juin 1985* (Paris: L'Harmattan, 1986), 19–29; and cf., by the same writer, "Actualité de la politique camusienne," in Walker, ed., *Albert Camus: les Extrêmes et l'équilibre,* 103–14.
29. Quoted in Todd, *Albert Camus, une vie,* 68.
30. The chronology of Camus's adherence to the PCF is difficult to pin down; Lévi-Valensi, basing her remarks on extensive research including interviews with many of Camus's contemporaries, puts the date to be "at the latest, the second fortnight of September 1935; at the earliest, between 21 and 30 August 1935" (Lévi-Valensi, "L'Entrée d'Albert Camus en politque," 137).
31. Lottman, *Albert Camus,* 79 (my italics). See the extracts from undated correspondence (but evidently from 1935) with Claude de Fréminville as quoted in Todd, *Albert Camus, une vie,* 89.
32. It is worth recalling that even though he himself remained suspicious of political commitment, Grenier actively encouraged Camus to join forces with the PCF in Algeria (Lottman, *Albert Camus,* 81–82; cf. Grenier, *Albert Camus: Souvenirs,* 35–46). His teacher's support enabled Camus—at least in the short term—to overcome his own personal misgivings about becoming politically active (*Corr,* 22–23).
33. See below, chapter 7.
34. Viggiani, "Notes pour le futur biographe d'Albert Camus," 211 (my italics).
35. Cf. the "ode to Blum," quoted in Todd, *Albert Camus, une vie,* 96. For a thorough treatment of the Popular Front initiative more generally, see Georges Lefranc, *Histoire du Front Populaire, 1934–1938* (Paris: Payot, 1965).
36. Philip Thody, "Albert Camus, 1913–1960," in *The Politics of Twentieth-*

Century Novelists, ed. Georges A. Panichas (New York: Apollo, 1974), 192–93. "For the intellectuals," Thody goes on to acknowledge, "the appeal of communism was even stronger. It offered an apparently comprehensive philosophy, capable of giving fruitful and interesting results when applied to history, art, and literature, as well as to economic and social questions" (ibid., 193). For a full assessment of communism's intellectual credentials, see, for instance, Max Adereth, *The French Communist Party: A Critical History, 1920–84; From Comintern to "the Colours of France"* (Manchester, UK: Manchester University Press, 1984); and Philippe Buton, *Communisme: une utopie en sursis? Les logiques d'un système* (Paris: Larousse, 2001).

37. At the time, the French Communist Party in Algeria was a rather insignificant body. Lottman reports that there were barely one hundred active members in Algiers and that "it was a tour de force for its leaders to make up a list of thirty-five candidates at election time" (Lottman, *Albert Camus,* 92).

38. For an elucidation of the "Arabization" of internal politics in Algeria during this period, see René Gallissot, *Maghreb, Algérie, classe et nation* (Paris: Arcantère, 1987). Cf. Lottman, *Albert Camus,* 147–60; and Todd, *Albert Camus, une vie,* 144–52.

39. Quoted in Lévi-Valensi, "L'Entrée d'Albert Camus en politique," 139.

40. Quoted in Claudie Broyelle and Jacques Broyelle, *Les Illusions retrouvées: Sartre a toujours raison contre Camus* (Paris: Grasset, 1982), 201.

41. Transcribed from Ouzegane's testimony in *Un homme, une ville: Albert Camus à Alger,* 3, "La justice et la mere."

42. Writing against the backdrop of the Algerian War in 1958, Camus publicly dismissed the notion of Algerian independence as "a conception springing wholly from emotion" (*RRD,* 104). Cf. below, chapter 8, 185–96. This "change" in attitude between the Camus of the 1930s and the Camus of the 1950s in respect of Algeria can, Ouzegane claims, be explained by the fact that following his departure from the PCF in mid-1937, the erstwhile militant Camus lost touch with the more revolutionary elements of Arab nationalism and moderated his own stance thereof accordingly (*Un homme, une ville: Albert Camus à Alger,* 3, "La justice et la mere."). Ouzegane is obviously speaking here from a partisan perspective and, as such, his remarks must be treated with caution. My own view on the matter is that while Camus was, as we shall see, broadly sympathetic to the Arab cause, he would not go so far as to support political independence for Algeria which, in the mid-1930s, was actually an anachronism. There is no evidence (other than Ouzegane's anecdotal information) to support the view that Camus's communist allegiance is predicated on anything other than his intuitive belief in the existence of moral values that he now brings to bear in the quest for general human betterment in Algeria.

43. Remarks transcribed from Mathieu Bénézet and Annie Douel, "Albert Camus, les années 'Combat': naissance d'un engagement, naissance de 'Combat,'" *Juste Camus, Camus le Juste,* originally broadcast on *France Culture* on November 25, 2002, http://www.radiofrance.fr/chaines/france-culture2/.

44. Cf. Camus's remark from 1957, quoted in Roger Grenier et al., *À Albert Camus, ses Amis du Livre* (Paris: Gallimard, 1962), 53: "If I have been a Communist, I have never been a Marxist"; and the oft-quoted rejoinder, during Camus's 1948 polemic with Emmanuel [d'Astier de la] Vigerie: "I did not learn about freedom in Marx, that's true. I learnt it in poverty" (*E,* 357). Camus's 1948 preface to Louis Guilloux's *La Maison du Peuple* (*E,* 1111–15) likewise acknowledges the lessons to be learned from "the school of necessity" (*E,* 1112).

45. Interestingly, Camus's critique of Hegelian historical determinism in *The Rebel* appears in embryo here. Cf. below, chapter 7, 162–64. Quoted in *FC,* 1:20–21. The square brackets indicate phrases which are crossed out in the original manuscript.

46. Fouchet, *Un jour, je m'en souviens,* 15.

47. See below, chapter 4.

48. Viggiani, "Notes pour le futur biographe d'Albert Camus," 211. Cf. *Corr,* 180: "I was responsible for recruiting Arab militants and for getting them brought back to a nationalist organization (L'Étoile nord-africaine, which was destined to become the PPA). I did so and these militant Arabs became my friends."

49. Brée, *Camus and Sartre,* 127–28.

50. Sensing growing unease in the province, Blum dissolved the ENA in an attempt to control the anticolonial mentality, an action which provoked further Arab aggression toward the French. Messali Hadj immediately established the *Parti du Peuple Algérien* (PPA) as a successor to the ENA with a mandate for "neither assimilation nor separation, but emancipation" (Lottman, *Albert Camus,* 154), while the wider struggle for Arab nationalism continued as a clandestine campaign.

51. For a full assessment of the implications of the PCF's change of direction in respect of Algeria, see Jacob Moneta, *Le PCF et le problème algérien, 1920–1965* (Paris: Maspero, 1971); and Emmanuel Sivan, *Communisme et nationalisme algérien, 1920–1962* (Paris: Presses de la Fondation Nationale des Sciences Politiques, 1976).

52. Notable exceptions were Marguerite Dobrenn, Claude de Fréminville, and Jeanne Sicard, all of whom followed Camus's lead and relinquished their membership of the party (Todd, *Albert Camus, une vie,* 151).

53. See Viggiani, "Notes pour le futur biographe d'Albert Camus," 212; and cf. Lottman, *Albert Camus,* 155–59.

54. Durand, *Le Cas Albert Camus,* 42.

55. Parker, *Albert Camus: The Artist in the Arena,* 12.

56. Lévi-Valensi, "L'Entrée d'Albert Camus en politique," 138.

57. Camus's celebratory thoughts on the theater are usefully summarized in "Why do I do theater?" (1959) (*TRN,* 1720–28) and the 1958 interviews granted to *France-Soir* and *Paris-Théâtre* (*TRN,* 1712–19). For informed assessments of Camus and the theater, see Ilona Coombs, *Camus: homme de théâtre* (Paris: Nizet, 1968); Edward Freeman, *The Theatre of Albert Camus: A Critical Study* (London: Methuen, 1971); and Raymond Gay-Crosier, *Les Envers d'un échec.* Also of interest is "Albert Camus, homme de théâtre," *Juste Camus, Camus le Juste,* originally broadcast on *France Culture* on November 26, 2002, http://www.radiofrance.fr/chaines/france-culture2/.

58. See Lottman, *Albert Camus,* 127–36; and McCarthy, *Camus,* 71–104. I shall have cause to return to the "Maison de la Culture" in chapter 7, when Camus's "pensée de midi" is in question (cf. below, 258 note 68).

59. Quoted in Germaine Brée, "Albert Camus et le *Théâtre de l'Équipe,*" *French Review* 22 (1949): 227. It is not unreasonable to assume that, as principal founder of the troupe, Camus himself was responsible for writing this manifesto.

60. The full sequence of plays produced by the *Théâtre du Travail* reads as follows: first, Camus's own adaptation of Malraux's *An Age of Oppression* (staged in January 1936); secondly, the collaborative venture *Revolt in Asturias* (originally due for performance in May 1936 but which, as a result of local censorship, was published instead by Edmond Charlot "for the Friends of the *Théâtre du Travail*" [*TRN,* 397]); thirdly, Maxime Gorki's *The Lower Depths* (November 1936);

fourthly, Ramón Sender's *The Secret* (December 1936); fifthly, Camus's own adaptation of Aeschylus's *Prometheus Bound* (March 1937); sixthly, Ben Jonson's *The Silent Woman* (March 1937); seventhly, Georges Courteline's *Article 330* (April 1937); and, finally, Pushkin's *Don Juan* (May 1937).

61. Durand, *Le Cas Albert Camus,* 49.

62. André Malraux, *Le Temps du mépris* (Paris: Gallimard, 1935).

63. John J. Michalczyk, "Camus and Malraux: A Staged Version of *Le Temps du mépris,*" *French Review* 50 (1976): 105.

64. Quoted in Lévi-Valensi, "L'Engagement culturel," 104n9, 90, 89.

65. Ibid., 90.

66. See also Todd, *Albert Camus, une vie,* 122–24.

67. See, in particular, Teodosio Vertone, "Albert Camus: l'Espagnol," *Cahiers d'Études Romanes* 12 (1987): 240–66; Jacqueline Lévi-Valensi, "Réalité et symbole de l'Espagne dans l'œuvre de Camus," in *AC1,* 149–78; and, by the same writer, "Camus et L'Espagne," in *Espagne et Algérie au XX*[e] *siècle: contacts culturels et création littéraire,* ed. J. Déjeux and D. H. Pageaux (Paris: L'Harmattan, 1985), 141–57.

68. Roger Quilliot, private correspondence with author, April 13, 1994.

69. Cf. Viggiani, "Notes pour le futur biographe d'Albert Camus," 214. Quoted in Lottman, *Albert Camus,* 170–71. Cf. Todd, *Albert Camus, une vie,* 111–12, 128.

70. It is worth recalling that the main reason why Blum refused to aid the republican cause in Spain was the delicate domestic situation in France at the time. Haunted by the nightmare of civil war in France springing from the ideological and social divisions reinforced by the Popular Front's victory, the French Premier resisted calls to send arms to Spain in what, for many on the contemporary left, amounted to a flagrant betrayal of France's democratic duty to fight fascism.

71. Quoted in Parker, *Albert Camus: The Artist in the Arena,* 173. I have adopted here Parker's translation, 10. See also *FC,* 2:597–609.

72. Philippe Vanney, "La démocratie à l'épreuve des relations internationales: reconnaissance et ingérence," *Équinoxe* 13 (1996): 37–49.

73. Walter Langlois, "Rumblings out of Spain: French Writers and the Asturian Revolt, 1934–36," *MLN* 95 (1980): 913. See also, by the same author, "Camus et le sens de la révolte asturienne," in *Albert Camus 1980: Second International Conference, February 21–23 1980, The University of Florida, Gainesville,* ed. Raymond Gay-Crosier (Gainesville: University Presses of Florida, 1980), 163–78.

74. Lévi-Valensi, "L'Entrée d'Albert Camus en politique," 147.

75. Lottman, *Albert Camus,* 101.

76. Cited in a communiqué for the play and originally published in *La Lutte sociale* of March 15–31, 1936, quoted in Lévi-Valensi, "L'Engagement culturel," 90–91.

77. Sicard explains to Quilliot that Alfred Poignant drafted the radio announcements, Yves Bourgeois the cross-examination in act 4, herself the scenes depicting the cabinet of ministers; the remainder was apparently the product of Camus's labor (*TRN,* 1853n).

78. See, for instance, Gay-Crosier, *Les Envers d'un échec,* 41–53; and Carl A. Viggiani, "Camus in 1936: The Beginnings of a Career," *Symposium* 12 (1958): 7–18.

79. See, for instance, Lottman, *Albert Camus,* 102–3.

80. Letter (dated Easter 1936) to Jeanne Sicard and Marguerite Dobrenn, quoted in Todd, *Albert Camus, une vie,* 125.

81. Originally published in *La Lutte sociale,* April 15–30, 1936, quoted in Lott-

man, *Albert Camus,* 103. While the ban remained in place, later productions such as Sender's *The Secret* and *Spain 34* (an abridged version of *Revolt in Asturias*) enabled Camus to continue to use the theater as a vehicle for communicating his antifascist morality.

82. Lévi-Valensi, "L'Entrée d'Albert Camus en politique," 147.

83. Following Camus's departure from the PCF, the *Théâtre du Travail* was disbanded and replaced by the *Théâtre de l'Équipe,* "with neither political nor religious bias" (*TRN,* 1692).

Chapter 3. Consolidating the Concern

1. I wish to acknowledge the rigorous research undertaken by André Abbou and the late Jacqueline Lévi-Valensi and published in the two volumes comprising *Fragments d'un combat* (*FC*). Commendable in so far as they collect and annotate the majority of Camus's early journalism and inasmuch as they situate these writings in their contemporary sociopolitical context, these two sources will be drawn on heavily throughout the next three chapters.

2. For a useful conspectus of the Algerian press at the time, see George Thomas Kurian, ed., *World Press Encyclopedia* (London: Mansell, 1982), 2:1063–65. Cf. *FC,* 1:140–41; and Todd, *Albert Camus, une vie,* 784n8. For a thorough assessment of the historical development of *Alger républicain,* see, for instance, Todd, *Albert Camus, une vie,* 171–83; and Lottman, *Albert Camus,* 186–203.

3. In accordance with Blum's political alliance, this "daily paper of the Popular Front, that is to say of democracy" (*FC,* 1:34) supported the idea of coalition in its drive to put public interest before political predisposition: "*Alger républicain* . . . defends only the public interest. Its political programme will be strictly that of the popular assembly in which all parties and organizations participated upon its foundation" (*FC,* 1:39).

4. Cited during an intervention in a round-table discussion on "Camus journaliste," quoted in Lionel Dubois, ed., *Les trois guerres d'Albert Camus: Actes du Colloque International de Poitiers, 4–5–6 mai 1995* (Poitiers: Éditions du Pont-Neuf, 1995), 53. Cf. Marie-Louise Audin, "Camus: journaliste-écrivain?," *Cahiers de l'Association Internationale des Études Françaises* 48 (1996): 129–47; and Roland Grossman, "Camus, journaliste," *Revue de l'Académie Nationale de Metz* (1996): 237–53.

5. John Rawls, "Justice as Fairness," in *Philosophy, Politics and Society: Second Series,* ed. Peter Laslett and W. G. Runciman (Oxford: Blackwell, 1962), 139.

6. Ronald Dworkin, *Taking Rights Seriously,* 2nd ed. (London: Duckworth, 1978), 199.

7. Ibid., 273.

8. Germaine Brée, *Camus* (New Brunswick: Rutgers University Press, 1959), 28.

9. Jacqueline Lévi-Valensi, "La Condition sociale en Algérie," in *AC5,* 19.

10. Parker, *Albert Camus: The Artist in the Arena,* 33. Roger Quilliot, "Albert Camus's Algeria," in *Camus: A Collection of Critical Essays,* ed. Germaine Brée (Englewood Cliffs, NJ: Prenticehall, 1962), 41.

11. Cf. Neil Macmaster, "Patterns of Emigration, 1905–1954: 'Kabyles' and 'Arabs,' " in *French and Algerian Identities from Colonial Times to the Present: A Century of Interaction,* ed. Alec G. Hargreaves and Michael J. Heffernan (Lampeter: Edwin Mellen, 1993), 21–38.

12. José Lenzini, *L'Algérie de Camus* (Aix-en-Provence: Edisud, 1987), 11.

13. In his treatment of the Kabyle crisis, Frison-Roche plays down the significance of the region's specific difficulties by situating them within the international demographic context (*FC,* 1:274). One feels that the journalist is thinking of Camus specifically when he writes: "I do not share the opinion of certain people; France has done great and noble things in Kabylia and, to deny such an obvious fact, you would have to put your hands over your eyes and persist in seeing in everything only the worst side of things" (*FC,* 1:275).

14. Parker, *Albert Camus: The Artist in the Arena,* 34.

15. It is worth recalling that while wage increases were agreed for French workers with the Matignon agreements of June 1936, there remained a huge discrepancy between the benefits enjoyed by the indigenous and nonindigenous communities of Algeria (cf. *FC,* 1:229–38). Camus is under no illusions as to the motives behind such clear injustice, compounded by the rising cost of living, deeming the matter "a conscious politics of sabotage" (*FC,* 1:231). Highlighting in the Kabyle inquiry "the unjustifiable length of the working day" (*FC,* 1:297), he likewise observes that "exploitation alone is the cause of the low salaries" (*FC,* 1:298). Camus's concern for socioeconomic justice is here all the more outspoken because it is deliberately being undermined by fellow human beings putting political self-interest before moral responsibility.

16. Cf. below, chapter 4.

17. Quoted in Ouahiba Hamouda, *Albert Camus à l'épreuve d'"Alger républicain"* (Algiers: Office des Publications Universitaires, 1991), 49.

18. It has to be said, however, that Camus's response to the social injustice resulting from *sexual* discrimination is, at best, marginal. (We may note in passing Camus's general self-centered treatment of women in his private life and the notable absence of convincing female characters in much of his imaginative writing.) The whole question of Camus's racial and sexual politics is explored in Christine Margerrison, "'Ces Forces obscures de l'âme': Woman, Race and Origins in the Imaginative Writings of Albert Camus" (Ph.D. diss., University of Lancaster, 1998). For a more general assessment of the (often haunting) feminine presence in Camus's work, see Geraldine F. Montgomery, *Noces pour femme seule: le féminin et le sacré dans l'œuvre d'Albert Camus* (Amsterdam: Rodopi, 2004).

19. Cf. below, chapter 6, 132–41, and chapter 8, 197–201.

20. François Mauriac, *Œuvres complètes* (Paris: Fayant, n.d.), 2:536.

21. Raymond Lebègue, ed. *Robert Garnier, Les Juifves, Bradamante, Poésies diverses* (Paris: Les Belles Lettres, 1975), 59. Douglas Bush, ed. *Milton: Poetical Works* (London: Oxford University Press, 1969), 400.

22. Tuzun, "Les positions sociales et politiques d'Albert Camus," 9.

23. Exposing the ongoing problems in his homeland for the metropolitan French readership of *Combat* in May–June 1945, Camus once again highlights the corruption behind grain distribution, a practice exacerbated by racial discrimination, since "throughout Algeria, the share allocated to natives is less than that granted to Europeans" (*E,* 948).

24. The mayor Rozis was a staunch supporter of Édouard Daladier, whose hard-line policies and decree laws were introduced in an attempt to redress the grave economic and political situation following the demise of the French Popular Front. Although Camus campaigned against Daladier's regime, perceiving it as inherently undemocratic (*FC,* 2:731) in the style of "trainee dictators" (*FC,* 1:233), Jeanyves Guérin is right to point out that Daladier remained "a staunch republican and, while not a socialist, did not have the smugness for fascism that Camus ascribes to him" (Guérin, *Albert Camus: portrait de l'artiste en citoyen,* 140).

25. The Blum-Viollette Bill was an assimilationist set of proposals, debated in 1936, which intended to increase social equality between the indigenous and non-indigenous communities of Algeria by according local Moslems enhanced political rights. It remained unimplemented, however. Cf. below, chapter 4, 93–97.

The *Office du Blé* was created by the Popular Front in August 1936 as an agency intending to guarantee cost-effective prices for grain crops cultivated within Algeria's Moslem communities. However, falling victim to bad harvests and a colonial backlash, it had lost much of its powers by 1939.

26. Secretary-general of the trades unionist movement in Algiers, Zittel was persecuted by Rozis for his alleged role in organizing municipal protests that threatened to undermine the mayor's own authority. However, the charges made against Zittel were—and remained—unfounded (*FC,* 1:168–70).

The strike referred to here is that called for November 30, 1938, by the *Confédération Générale du Travail* (CGT) in protest of Daladier's hard-line government but which was largely ignored by workers fearful of the consequences. Interestingly, the idea of "limit" (fundamental to the later *The Rebel*) appears in embryo in Camus's exposition of Rozis's municipal misrule. Transgressing what is deemed morally and politically acceptable behavior, the mayor's breach of authority is usefully formulated in terms of his going beyond the boundaries of what actions can be justified between human beings.

27. André Abbou, "Variations du discours polémique," in *AC5,* 112.

28. Lévi-Valensi, "La Condition sociale en Algérie," 26–27.

29. As Raymond Gay-Crosier notes, "the theatrical trial in which Meursault . . . receives the death penalty offers a satiric version of the institutionalized form of the judicial process carried out by a society that has no doubts about its fundamental values" (Raymond Gay-Crosier, *Literary Masterpieces: "The Stranger,"* vol. 8 [Farmington Hills: Gale Group, 2002], 3).

30. Salas, *Albert Camus: la juste révolte,* 17.

31. This extract from Hodent's autobiography *Des Charognards sur un homme* (1939) is quoted in McCarthy, *Camus,* 117.

32. It is worthy of note that *Alger républicain* was the only newspaper to cover the Hodent trial, so scandalous were its revelations about local administrative procedure. It is also interesting to observe that, following the writer's death, Hodent himself paid eloquent tribute to Camus, whose "thirst for justice and independence" had, in Hodent's view, contributed significantly to his eventual acquittal: "I owe everything to he who is no longer here, but nothing is forgotten" (remarks taken from a letter dated January 6, 1960, from Hodent to Francine Camus, quoted in *FC,* 2:542). Cf. Salas, *Albert Camus: la juste révolte,* 21–23.

33. What Camus is referring to here is the inconsistency of evidence, the unsubstantiated accusations and the use of false testimonies for incriminating purposes, all of which make up what he refers to as "the incredible arbitrariness which rules in certain regions of Algeria" (*FC,* 2:375) and which "prevails over basic rules of justice and fairness" (*FC,* 2:386).

34. Salas, *Albert Camus: la juste révolte,* 20.

35. Just as *Alger républicain* was the only newspaper to cover the Hodent trial, so it was alone in exposing the political scandal at the heart of the case of the supposed arsonists.

36. The memory of his experience aboard *Le Martinière* would remain with Camus in both the short term—cf. the reference in the *Carnets* dated December 15, 1938 (*CA1,* 60)—and the long term. To judge from an entry dated December 1954, he was at that time thinking of writing a short story based on his earlier article (*C3,* 148).

37. Abbou, "Combat pour la justice," 49.

38. Christine Margerrison, "Albert Camus and 'Ces femmes qu'on raie de l'humanité': Sexual Politics in the Colonial Arena," *French Cultural Studies* 10 (1999): 217–30.

39. Ibid., 229.

40. It is worth noting in passing that the need to maintain a basic moral standard even (or especially) in morally contentious circumstances is further in evidence in *The First Man.* In the throes of the Moroccan War, Jacques Cormery's father cannot condone the inhumane killing of one of his comrades on the ground that it oversteps the mark of what is morally acceptable in war: "But Cormery had shouted as if crazed with anger: 'No, a man doesn't let himself do that kind of thing! That's what makes a man, or otherwise'" (*FM,* 52). In the course of a discussion on *The First Man* broadcast on *France Culture* on November 23, 2002, Maurice Weyembergh highlights the link between these remarks and the Camusian notion of "moderation," http://www.radiofrance.fr/chaines/france-culture2/. Cf. J. S. T. Garfitt, "Le Premier homm[ag]e: Grounding history in love," in *Constructing Memories: Camus, Algeria and "Le Premier Homme,"* eds. Peter Dunwoodie and Edward J. Hughes, *Stirling French Publications* 6 (1998): 1–8.

41. For instance, conspiring to pervert the course of justice, evidenced by conflicting medical findings (*FC,* 2:518–19); the absurd logic of the confession ("if the accused cries out, 'I didn't say that willingly', his reply is 'Proof that you said it is that you said it'" [*FC,* 2:518–19]); and the use of police brutality to induce incriminating information (*FC,* 2:516).

42. Parker, *Albert Camus: The Artist in the Arena,* 14.

43. Abbou, "Combat pour la justice," 37.

44. Thody, *Albert Camus,* 11–12.

Chapter 4. The Challenge of Colonialism

1. Quoted in *Un homme, une ville: Albert Camus à Alger,* 3, "La justice et la mere."

2. It should be recalled that Ouzegane's own nationalist prejudices almost certainly colored his views on the nature of Camus's political commitment in the mid-1930s. Sartre later judged Algeria to be "the clearest and most intelligible example of the colonial system" (Jean-Paul Sartre, "Le colonialisme est un système," in his *Situations V: colonialisme et néo-colonialisme* [Paris: Gallimard, 1964], 27). He also insisted that "it is not true that there may be good colonists and others who may be malicious: there are colonists, that's all" (27). Calling for the unconditional liberation of Algeria from her imperial chains, Sartre wrote an incisive preface (reprinted in *Situations V,* 167–93) to Frantz Fanon's *Les damnés de la terre* (Paris: Maspero, 1961), a book advocating the removal of (French) colonialism by all necessary means. It is also worth recalling that Sartre twice would be targeted by the ultranationalist *Organisation Armée Secrète* (OAS) following his public support for the FLN during the Algerian War. For a useful overview of the differing anticolonial perspectives of Sartre and Camus, see Azzedine Haddour, "The Camus-Sartre Debate and the Colonial Question in Algeria," in *Francophone Postcolonial Studies: A Critical Introduction,* ed. Charles Forsdick and David Murphy (London: Arnold, 2003), 66–76. As Camus acknowledges, the *pied-noir* community in what, in *The First Man,* he refers to as "this country of immigration" (*FM,* 158), was a veritable (European) melting pot: "The French of Algeria are a bastard race, made

up of unforeseen mixtures. Spaniards and Alsatians, Italians, Maltese, Jews and Greeks have come together there. As in America this brutal interbreeding has had happy results" (*SEN,* 133). In the history of French colonial discourse, Louis Bertrand's *Méditerranée latine,* heralded by his seminal *Le Sang des races* (Paris: Ollendorf, 1899), relocates Algeria from the subject of an orientalist gaze to one of a new people-in-the-making. See Dunwoodie, *Writing French Algeria,* 83–108.

3. In his 1958 "Avant-Propos" to *Actuelles III* (*RRD,* 81–90), Camus writes of how his paternal grandparents—deemed Alsatians—had arrived in Algeria in 1871 (*RRD,* 86). However, as Herbert Lottman has shown, Camus's antecedents on his father's side were from Bordeaux, *not* Alsace; his mother was of Spanish descent. And his family actually arrived in Algeria a generation earlier than Camus himself supposed (Lottman, *Albert Camus,* 8–13). We may also point out in passing that in *The First Man,* the old Veillard, driven out of Algeria by the impulses of the racially bigoted *gros colons* (*FM,* 138–42), exemplifies the experience of those who, like Camus and his family, "lived through the Algerian calamity as a personal tragedy" (*RRD,* 96). Cf. Nancy Wood, "Colonial Nostalgia and *Le Premier Homme,*" *French Cultural Studies* 9 (1998): 181: "Camus indeed comes perilously close to pleading the case of the *colon* as the dispossessed, the victim of a historical injustice."

4. Tarrow, *Exile from the Kingdom,* 63

5. Sprintzen, *Camus,* 279.

6. J. L. Loubet del Bayle, "Albert Camus et la politique," *Annales de l'Université des Sciences sociales de Toulouse* 26 (1978): 527; and cf. *EX,* 17.

7. Cf. Jacqueline Lévi-Valensi's commentary, in *CAC,* 53–66.

8. It should perhaps be recalled here that, following his expulsion from Algeria in early 1940, Camus *faute de mieux* worked for several months on *Paris-Soir,* the most powerful right-wing newspaper in France at that time where the "despicable shopgirl mentality" (*CA1,* 101; translation amended) was much in evidence. Camus's duties were mainly concerned with the page layouts on the newspaper. For accounts of Camus's stint at *Paris-Soir* (deemed "Pourri Soir" ["Corrupt Evening"] by its many detractors), see, for instance, Lottman, *Albert Camus,* 218–30; and McCarthy, *Camus,* 166–69.

9. Nicola Chiaromonte, "Albert Camus and Moderation," *Partisan Review* 15 (1948): 1145. Later, explaining to Jean Daniel why he chose to return to the profession by writing for *L'Express,* Camus remarks that "journalism has always appeared to me to be the nicest form of commitment, provided however that everything can be said" (quoted in *EX,* 20). But cf. note 10 below.

10. It is worthy of note that Camus would later be highly critical of his own experience of journalism because of his apparent inability to adapt to the demands of the profession: "I have . . . never been happy with my work as a journalist: 1st because it demands a speedy implementation which always bothers me and which for me means the virtually constant impossibility of reviewing my thinking; 2nd because I hate having enemies and as journalistic arguments invariably end up there. For me it is never-ending pain" (quoted in Grenier et al., *À Albert Camus, ses amis du livre,* 47). It is useful to situate such comments in the context of Pascal Pia's contention that "for Camus, journalism had never been the result of a choice, but just an accident" (Pascal Pia, "D'*Alger républicain* à *Combat,*" *Magazine littéraire* 276 [1990]: 38), a view reiterated by Camus himself (cf. Abdelkader Djemaï's intervention in "Camus journaliste," in Dubois, ed., *Les trois guerres d'Albert Camus,* 42). Of course, Camus received no formal journalistic training and so it should come as no surprise that he would find the profession especially demanding.

11. This aspect of Camus is comprehensively explored by David H. Walker, *Outrage and Insight: Modern French Writers and the "Fait Divers"* (Oxford: Berg, 1995), 139–53.

12. David H. Walker, "Albert Camus devant les méfaits de l'Europe," in *Albert Camus et l'Europe: Actes du colloque de Strasbourg, 9 et 10 novembre 1990,* ed. André Abbou (Paris: Ofil, 1995) [np].

13. Tarrow, *Exile from the Kingdom,* 203n3. In *Les Aventures de la liberté: une histoire subjective des intellectuels* (Paris: Grasset, 1991), 472, Lévy deems Camus's Kabyle series "the most damning indictment of French colonialism."

14. Cf. Roger Frison-Roche's series published in *La Dépêche algérienne* from June 8 to June 17, 1939, to which reference was made in the preceding chapter.

15. A fictional representation of Camus's dilemma here over anticolonial sentiment and his own *pied-noir* status appears in *The Plague.* Commissioned by "one of the leading Paris dailies" to undertake a fact-finding mission "on the living conditions prevailing amongst the Arab population and . . . on their sanitary conditions," Rambert discusses with Rieux whether a "statement of the facts without paltering with the truth" would be appropriate under the circumstances. Both agree that such would be "unfounded" in the light of the newspaper's political (i.e. colonial) standing (*TRN,* 1226; *TP,* 12; translation amended). For a full assessment of the intertextual parallels between Camus's fictional and nonfictional exposés of the Arab problem, see Hamouda, *Albert Camus à l'épreuve d'"Alger républicain,"* 99–103.

16. Campaigning on a platform of religious consciousness in the view that Algeria could only be liberated from colonial domination by returning to the first principles of Islam, this movement was one of several set up to voice growing nationalist sentiment in the province during the interwar years. Another such organization was *L'Étoile nord-africaine* (ENA), established by the nationalist extremist Messali Hadj in 1926. But cf. note 26 below.

The case of El Okbi still intrigues today, as Olivier Todd records: "To date, the case has not been totally cleared up. Mohamed Lebjaoui (former leader of the FLN) explained in 1970 that El Okbi was guilty. Amar Ouzegane, in his correspondence with Charles Poncet, does not agree" (Todd, *Albert Camus, une vie,* 787n7). Cf. *FC,* 2:547–50.

17. Cf. Paul F. Smets, *Camus dans le premier silence . . . et au delà suivi de Albert Camus: chroniqueur judiciaire à "Alger-Républicain" en 1939* (Brussels: Goemaere, 1985), 169: "He [Camus] remains outside, nervous, sceptical, as if he didn't manage to express his deep conviction, as if the dice appeared loaded to him."

18. According to the editors of *Fragments d'un combat,* Camus "was perhaps not the most qualified to disentangle the politico-religious threads knotted around the crime" (*FC,* 2:543); such perceived ignorance may well have played a part in the impersonal stance adopted by Camus in chronicling the El Okbi affair. Indeed, the passion driving other aspects of his *chronique judiciaire,* as charted in the previous chapter, remains conspicuously absent in Camus's account of that particular case. It is for this reason that I have chosen not to dwell on the El Okbi proceedings here.

19. *The Outsider* exploits to full dramatic effect the expediency of the colonial justice system to which El Okbi is himself subjected. Others—most notably, Azzedine Haddour and Alec Hargreaves—have shown how, in the 1942 work, Camus (consciously?) manipulates the sympathy of the reader away from the victim of crime (i.e. the murdered Arab) toward the victim of arbitrary justice (i.e.

Meursault) to reinforce in the *récit* the feeling of a miscarriage of justice. See Haddour, "The Other as an Outsider in a Univocal Discourse," 79–97; and Alec G. Hargreaves, "History and Ethnicity in the Reception of *L'Étranger,*" in *Camus's "L'Étranger": Fifty Years On,* 2nd ed., ed. Adèle King (New York: St. Martin's Press, 1994), 101–12. For a more general examination of the Algerian dimension to Camus's work, see Christiane Chaulet-Achour, *Albert Camus, Alger: "L'Étranger" et autres récits* (Biarritz: Atlantica, 1998); and, for an account of the ongoing resonances of Camus in modern Algerian circles, see, by the same writer, "Camus et l'Algérie des années 90," *Europe* 77 (1999): 167–77. As Chaulet-Achour notes, "the obstinacy of Algerian writers from all backgrounds to come back to Camus, with either enthusiasm or condemnation, compels us to think about his 'aura'" (170).

20. Cf. below, chapter 8, 191–96.

21. Camus would describe himself in these terms at the time of the Nobel Honors in 1957: see Gabriel Audisio, "La leçon des écrivains nord-africains," *Combat,* October 24, 1957, 7. There is an engaging discussion of Camus as an Algerian writer and the tensions at issue during "Les Révoltes d'Albert Camus," broadcast on *France Culture* on November 23, 2002, http://www.radiofrance.fr/chaines/france-culture2/.

22. A photograph depicting "a Kabyle *and* a European, with happy faces but apart from one another" (Todd, *Albert Camus, une vie,* 195) reinforces the image of racial tolerance projected by Camus in his concluding remarks to the survey.

23. Admittedly, in his quest for "clear-sighted and concerted policies" (*FC,* 1:335), whereby "the shocking destitution of this country would see its end and also its reward" (*FC,* 1:332), Camus spotlights the notion of self-government for the region—but *not* that of independence—in his belief that "if anyone can improve the fate of the Kabyles, it is first of all the Kabyles themselves" (*FC,* 1:320). However, the fact remains that, in concluding his inquiry, Camus substitutes the language of abstraction for that of pragmatic reformism.

24. For a lucid elaboration of Camus's "resistance to history" in his tendency to bypass colonial reality, see Edward J. Hughes, *Writing Marginality in Modern French Literature: From Loti to Genet* (Cambridge: Cambridge University Press, 2001), 102–34; and cf. Haddour, *Colonial Myths,* 113–54.

25. I am mindful that in cases such as the Hodent affair and the so-called "Auribeau Arsonists," as discussed in chapter 3 above where injustices are perpetrated by fellow human beings eager to put (political) self-interest before moral responsibility, Camus waives these professional restraints and becomes completely partisan to the cause of civil rights. However, this piecemeal concern on behalf of the victims of colonial injustice does not invalidate my contention that the mature Camus remains incapable of criticizing colonialism as such. It is perhaps worth recalling here the remark from "Misery in Kabylia," which constitutes the foundation-stone of Camus's moral mandate in this, and other, aspects: "it is that on any occasion, progress is made every time a political problem is replaced by a human problem" (*FC,* 1:335).

26. It is worth noting here that while sporadic incidents of nationalist unease had formed part of Algerian history ever since the province's conquest by the French, the notion of an Algerian nation was an anachronistic one at the time. In 1936, Ferhat Abbas memorably remarked that he was not prepared to die for the "Algerian nation," because such an idea did not exist (Charles-André Julien, *L'Afrique du Nord en marche* [Paris: Julliard, 1972], 100). Rather, the prevailing philosophy of the period to which the majority of Algerians subscribed was that of

Franco-Arab assimilation, a policy in reality amounting to little more than colonial subjugation. For a comprehensive account of the assimilationist project in French colonial history, see Raymond F. Betts, *Assimilation and Association in French Colonial Theory, 1840–1914* (New York: Columbia University Press, 1961).

27. For a good overview of the Blum-Viollette initiative, see, for instance, David C. Gordon, *The Passing of French Algeria* (London: Oxford University Press, 1966), 34–48. The proposals outlined in the bill were not new; indeed, similar ideas had been expressed as far back as 1897 by Pierre Paul Leroy-Beaulieu (Hubert Gourdon et al., "Histoire idéologique de la période: à propos de l'assimilation," *Revue algérienne des sciences juridiques, économiques et politiques* 11 [1974]: 46n38).

28. Quoted in Alistair Horne, *A Savage War of Peace: Algeria, 1954–1962* (London: Penguin, 1985), 41.

29. According to Herbert Lottman, on April 26, 1936, Camus delivered a speech, organized under the auspices of the *Maison de la Culture,* entitled "Intellectuals and the Viollette Bill" (Lottman, *Albert Camus,* 132).

30. Alec G. Hargreaves, "Caught in the Middle: The Liberal Dilemma in the Algerian War," *Nottingham French Studies* 25 (1986): 80.

31. Cf. Roger Quilliot, "Un texte retrouvé d'Albert Camus," *Bulletin d'Information de la Société des Études Camusiennes* 32 (1994): 6: "The day when Europeans will stop considering Arabs as a quaint and incomprehensible people, the day when Arabs will stop mistaking Europeans for the police which sometimes represent them, that day the world will be a friendlier place." The text from which these remarks are taken was delivered to an audience in Paris in November 1946.

32. In "Misery in Kabylia" and in the spirit of these remarks, Camus calls for the removal of "the artificial barrier dividing European education from indigenous education," a task that is deemed crucial if "at the same school, two kinds of people made to understand one another will begin to get to know one another" (*FC,* 1:314). School syllabuses in Algeria—as Camus's own experience, expressed in *The First Man,* testifies (*FM,* 112–13)—were conditioned by those in force in metropolitan France. Precious little time was devoted to the teaching of Algerian education proper. In the words of Edward Hughes, "the images of France made available to Cormery through his schooling fuel a self-congratulatory exoticism" (Hughes, *Writing Marginality in Modern French Literature,* 124). Cf. Todd, *Albert Camus, une vie,* 39–40.

33. See Alec G. Hargreaves, "Camus and the Colonial Question in Algeria," *Muslim World* 77 (1987): 164–74.

34. It was, of course, in their own interests that the French colonists fought to maintain the unequal power differential underpinning the status quo in Algeria. Only by ensuring that the *colonisés* remained ideologically disfranchised and economically dependent on the mother country could the *colonisateurs* retain their own privileged status in the province. As the Tunisian Jew Albert Memmi, representing a people colonized by the French, puts it, "the colonial relationship chained the Colonizer and the Colonized in a kind of implacable dependence" (Albert Memmi, *Portrait du Colonisé précédé de Portrait du Colonisateur* [Paris: Payot, 1973], 12). See, too, Edward Said's seminal *Orientalism* (New York: Pantheon, 1978).

35. Actually, as Hargreaves points out, "contrary to what was stated here, widespread disillusionment with the idea of assimilation among Algerian Muslims predated the 1948 elections, as Camus had himself reported [cf. *E,* 952–53] in 1945" (Hargreaves, "Camus and the Colonial Question in Algeria," 168).

36. Admittedly, some 65 000 indigenous Algerians would eventually be accredited with French citizenship by means of the "Edict of March 7, 1944," which Camus cautiously welcomed (*E,* 952). However, that initiative amounted to a token gesture on the part of a colonial authority sensing the rumblings of a possible nationalist insurrection in the province. Responding to nationalist sentiment by such half-hearted measures exposes just how wide the gulf had become by the mid-1940s between *colonisateur* and *colonisé* in Algeria. The articles of the "Ordonnance" are cited by Gourdon et al., "Histoire idéologique de la période," 72–74.

37. Quoted in Emmanuel Roblès, "La marque du soleil et de la misère," in *Camus,* ed. René-Marill Albérès, Pierre de Boisdeffre, Jean Daniel, Pierre Gascar, Morvan Lebesque, André Parinaud, Emmanuel Roblès, Jules Roy, and Pierre-Henri Simon, Collection Génies et Réalités (Paris: Hachette, 1964), 66.

38. For a thorough treatment of this crucial phase in Algerian history, see, in particular, Ageron, *Histoire de l'Algérie contemporaine,* 2:545–601; and Mahfoud Kaddache, *Histoire du nationalisme algérien: question nationale et politique algérienne, 1919–1951* (Algiers: SNED, 1980), 2:601–734.

39. Cf. Camus's remark in *Méditerranée-Afrique du Nord* 1 (June 1939): "The only means of producing a fair solution to this painful issue is to show here that face of France which many Algerians persist in believing is the true one. What we need are not martyrs, but free and respected citizens. The rise in Algerian nationalism is brought about by persecutions for which it is being pursued. It will no longer have any point, on the other hand, when injustice disappears from this country" (*FC,* 2:528–29).

40. Cf. Ageron, *Histoire de l'Algérie contemporaine,* 2:359–61. Hargreaves, "Camus and the Colonial Question in Algeria," 169. Although by adopting this attitude Camus continues to champion the cause of Franco-Arab assimilation, he also campaigned publicly on behalf of PPA activists "detained . . . for having expressed their opinion freely" (*FC,* 2:591), a reference to the ability—here denied—to voice dissent as a fundamental component of the democratic right to freedom of expression. See *FC,* 2:530–31; and cf. ibid., 574–78. By the same token, in a text attributed to Camus by Jacqueline Lévi-Valensi and André Abbou (*FC,* 2:579–84), he speaks out "against an unjust interpretation of the Régnier Decree" (*FC,* 2:575–76) in the case of Priaud and Bouhali, convicted "for inciting demonstrations or disturbance against French sovereignty" (*FC,* 2:581).

41. Parker, *Albert Camus: The Artist in the Arena,* 100–1.

42. Salas, *Albert Camus: la juste révolte,* 73.

43. Hargreaves, "Camus and the Colonial Question in Algeria," 169.

44. Raymond Aron, *Mémoires: 50 ans de réflexion politique* (Paris: Julliard, 1983), 379; Albert Memmi, "Camus ou le colonisateur de bonne volonté," *La Nef* 14 (1957): 95–96.

45. Hargreaves, "Camus and the Colonial Question in Algeria," 164.

46. Set "in the interior of the country" (*FM,* 6; translation amended), the opening chapter of *The First Man* highlights the devastation of a country starved of civilization: "The smell of scorched grass, or, suddenly, the strong odour of manure, was all that suggested they were passing by land under cultivation" (*FM,* 5). This is compared with the civilized nature of France, viewed in terms of "the meadows and fields of a land that for centuries had been cultivated" (*FM,* 16).

47. Mouloud Feraoun, *Lettres à ses amis* (Paris: Seuil, 1969), 203–4; and cf. by the same writer, "La source de nos communs malheurs (Lettre à Albert Camus)," *Preuves* 91 (1958): 72–75.

48. Haddour, "The Other as an Outsider," 160–62.

49. Ibid., 124. See, too, Azzedine Haddour, *Colonial Myths: History and Narrative,* which provides a thorough investigation of the (Algerian) colonial experience through works of both *pied-noir* writers (notably, Camus, Emmanuel Roblès, and Jean Pélégri) and Algerian writers (Mohammed Dib, Mouloud Feraoun, and Jean Amrouche).

50. It is worth recalling here that Camus endorses Abbas's 1944 *Manifeste du Peuple Algérien,* which called for the creation of an autonomous—but not independent—multicultural Algerian state, linked to France by federal ties. The project would secure for Algeria its own constitution, civil liberties for its citizens and parliamentary representation. Camus devotes a whole article to that initiative in his 1945 series (*E,* 954–57). By the same token, he welcomed as "sensible and humane" (*CAC,* 529) the communist-inspired proposals of the *Amis de la Démocratie,* which demanded the extension of the "Edict of March 7, 1944" (cf. note 36 above), together with an expansion of civil rights for Algeria's indigenous Moslems.

51. While in view of his general distrust of the colonist mentality, Camus's conciliatory attitude here toward the French colonial authorities may appear puzzling, one must agree with Emmett Parker when he contends that this campaign to secure financial assistance stems from "a practical realization that invective and a partisan political approach to the problem would carry less weight in high administrative circles in metropolitan France, from which source, he well knew, any reform movement had to come" (Parker, *Albert Camus: The Artist in the Arena,* 35). Clearly predicated on pragmatic realism, Camus's stance is in keeping with his underlying engagement with justice not to allow practical objectives to be marred by theoretical deliberations.

52. Paul Siblot and Jean-Louis Planche, "Le 8 mai 1945: éléments pour une analyse des positions de Camus face au nationalisme algérien," in Guérin, ed., *Camus et la politique,* 170.

53. Responding in *Combat* to another ongoing colonial conflict—that ravaging Indochina—Camus likewise posits that justice can be done only if France projects to the international community the image of a nation willing to temper its colonial politics with moral understanding: "Justice, complete justice, that is our victory. Indochina will be with us if France is the first to give it democracy and freedom at the same time. But if we hesitate once, it will be with anyone who is against us" (*CAC,* 467).

54. These remarks should be read in the context of Camus's call, in the postwar period, for an international code of justice, "based on the equality and cooperation of people" and by which "economic wealth will be shared out among everyone" (*CAC,* 576). Cf. below, chapter 6, 145–50.

55. Lev Braun, *Witness of Decline: Albert Camus Moralist of the Absurd* (Rutherford: Fairleigh Dickenson University Press, 1974), 219. As Azzedine Haddour rightly points out, the call for the democratic reformation of the colonies under the aegis of the *Union française* is "*ipso facto* contradictory: the era of colonialism should end but France's imperialism must remain" (Haddour, "The Other as an Outsider," 216). What Haddour refers to as "the vampire of imperialism" (169) is inherently unable to embrace the notion of cultural pluralism sought after by Camus in his quest for colonial compatibility.

56. Conor Cruise O'Brien, *Camus* (London: Fontana / Collins, 1970).

57. Ibid., 9–14, 46–49. Curiously, this "racialist" reading of Camus only emerged some twenty years after the original publication of *The Outsider.* Neither Camus himself nor his early critics were, as far as we can ascertain, amenable to

such interpretations. One is reminded here of a passage from "Jonas or the artist at work" (from *Exile and the Kingdom* [1957]), anachronistic in nature when viewed in the context of Camus's own posthumous reception: "Jonas's disciples explained to him at length what he had painted, and why. In this way Jonas discovered in his work many intentions that rather surprised him, and a host of things he hadn't put there" (*EK,* 94).

O'Brien, *Camus,* 12.

58. O'Brien, *Camus,* 12.

59. Henri Kréa, "Le Malentendu algérien," *France Observateur,* January 5, 1961, 16. Cf. Pierre Nora, "Pour une autre explication de *L'Étranger,*" *France Observateur,* January 5, 1961, 16–17; Said, *Culture and Imperialism,* 204–24; and—for a contrary view—Parker, *Albert Camus: The Artist in the Arena,* 44–45.

60. Cf. McCarthy, *Camus,* 120: "[Camus] could not perceive that the colonial system was a matter of domination and could be changed only by a power struggle."

O'Brien, *Camus,* 13–14.

61. As Camus confides to Jean Grenier in January 1956, he "would have stayed there [Algeria] if he had not been expelled" in early 1940, upon the collapse of *Le Soir républicain* (Paulhan, ed., *Jean Grenier, Carnets: 1944–1971,* 177).

62. Quoted in *Bulletin d'Information de la Société des Études Camusiennes* 27 (1992): 21.

63. See Elaine Showalter, "Significant life, absurd death," *Sunday Times,* October 12, 1997, Books section, 10.

64. A well-documented account of these traumatic events is provided in Radouane Ainad-Tabet, *Le 8 mai 1945 en Algérie* (Algiers: Office des Publications Universitaires, 1985). See also Siblot and Planche, "Le 8 mai 1945"; and cf. Lottman, *Albert Camus,* 353–56. The number of lives lost during the episode remains to this day a bone of contention between French and Algerian historians. The most conservative of French estimates puts the figure of *indigènes* killed in the region of 8000–9000, with French losses amounting to several hundred. However, "official" statistics record the number of Algerian fatalities to be as many as 75000, maybe more (Siblot and Planche, "Le 8 mai 1945," 158–59).

65. What Camus himself later refers to as "the comfortable indifference of the press" (*EX,* 74) *vis-à-vis* the 1945 events—*Combat* was one in only a small handful of newspapers in the metropolis to report the French reprisals—gives the lie to the notion of the mother country's supposed moral accountability.

66. Abbas, *La Nuit coloniale,* 27.

67. Cf. *E,* 958: "The massacres at Guelma and Sétif have provoked a deep and indignant resentment among the French Algerians. The repression which followed has developed a feeling of fear and hostility within the Arab masses. In this climate, a political initiative which would be at the same time firm and democratic sees its chances of success reduced." In the light of such remarks, I cannot agree with Haddour when he writes that "Camus's blindness to the oppression and injustice of the French colonial system leads him to *ignore* the political dimensions of the 1945 crisis" (Haddour, "The Other as an Outsider," 125; my italics).

68. Siblot and Planche, "Le 8 mai, 1945," 165.

69. Following the ferocious French reprisals in Madagascar in March 1947, Camus once again denounced the notion of racial superiority as a betrayal of the moral mandate of the mother country (*E,* 322–23). However, Alec Hargreaves is right to point out that "his [Camus's] claim that France had traditionally been exempt from racial prejudice implies quite astonishing blindness on his part to the

basic facts of French colonization, notably in Algeria" (Hargreaves, "Camus and the Colonial Question in Algeria," 174).

70. Granted the turn of events, it will come as no surprise that Camus chose not to include in his 1958 *Actuelles III* the editorial from which these remarks are taken. Cf. Hargreaves, "Camus and the Colonial Question in Algeria," 167–68.

71. Bertrand Jakobiak, "Camus le colonisateur sublimé," *Souffles* 12 (1968): 25. Jakobiak goes on to argue, with some plausibility, that the figure of Cottard in *The Plague* represents a psychological projection of a "conniving, ashamed and evasive Camus" (27) who is unable to escape from his colonial persona. For his part, David Walker considers many of Camus's fictional characters to be "haunted . . . by a feeling of guilt which seems to be the inevitable patrimony of every European" (Walker, "Albert Camus devant les méfaits de l'Europe.")

Chapter 5. War

1. However, the colonial question to which, as we have seen, Camus is also susceptible is representative of the wider forces of history which now begin to impact on his general concern for justice in the sociopolitical domain.

2. Thody, *Albert Camus, 1913–1960,* 28.

3. Ibid. Although Thody is right to highlight the changing nature of the context in which Camus's concern for sociopolitical justice would henceforth be situated, it is not true to imply that, in comparison with Europe, Algeria is a land removed from philosophy and ideology. For a thorough examination of issues relating to colonial ideology, see Dunwoodie, *Writing French Algeria.*

4. Cf. Camus's correspondence with Blanche Balain, dated August 1939: "You tell me: you are a combatant. But it is quite the opposite. For left-wing parties sicken me (those of the right are contemptible and mediocre). And in reality I am all alone in what I am doing. Injustices disgust me. Not in themselves. But because they are the work of irresponsibility and baseness. So I protest individually. . . . And I look no further. Don't, then, associate me with politics and political activism" (quoted in Monique Baréa, ed., *Albert Camus: 1913–1960; Bibliothèque de l'Université de Nice, 8–14 mai 1980 et Bibliothèque Publique d'Information, Centre Georges Pompidou, 25 mars—4 mai 1981* [Aix-en-Provence: Edisud, 1981], 38).

5. Quoted in Todd, *Albert Camus, une vie,* 184.

6. The fact that this highly despairing article was published some two weeks after the original declaration of war strongly suggests that, in the interim, Camus—doubtless out of desperation—was willing himself not to believe that peace had finally been ravaged by war.

7. Parker, *Albert Camus: The Artist in the Arena,* 52–53.

8. Steve Robson, "Albert Camus: The Man behind the Myth," in *Autobiography and the Existential Self: Studies in Modern French Writing,* eds. Terry Keefe and Edmund Smyth (Liverpool: Liverpool University Press, 1995), 114.

9. Jean-Marc Morjean, "Camus ou le prix des mots (juin 1940—août 1944)," in *La Littérature française sous l'Occupation: Actes du Colloque de Reims (30 septembre—1er et 2 octobre 1981),* ed. Yves Ménager (Reims: Presses Universitaires de Reims, 1989), 31.

10. Parker, *Albert Camus: The Artist in the Arena,* 54.

11. See "Letter to a young Englishman on the state of mind of the French nation," signed "Jean Mersault" and published in *Le Soir républicain* on December

23, 1939 (*FC,* 2:759–60); and the four clandestine *Letters to a German Friend,* composed between mid-1943 and mid-1944 and published openly after the war (*E,* 213–43; *RRD,* 1–24).

12. Steve Robson is right to suggest that the later *Letters to a German Friend* (of which more later) provides a further *public* platform on which to conduct this fictional encounter between despair and lucidity (Robson, "Albert Camus," 119).

13. *The Myth* was, in the words of Roger Grenier, "the fruit of a long maturation" (Roger Grenier, *Albert Camus: soleil et ombre* [Paris: Gallimard, 1987], 107). Notes in the *Carnets* referring to a work in the vein of Camus's "Essay on the Absurd" date back to May 1936 (*C1,* 39; *CA1,* 14); an entry from February 21, 1941 (*C1,* 224; *CA1,* 107) finally announces the completion of the book.

14. A noteworthy exception is Alain Costes, who interprets the work in terms of personal psychotherapy (Costes, *Albert Camus ou la parole manquante,* 106, 108, 135).

15. In a preliminary note to his work, Camus makes clear that his objective is not to explain an "absurd philosophy" (*MS,* 10), but to describe an "absurd sensitivity" (*MS,* 10). Accordingly, his attitude in *The Myth* is primarily that of the involved individual who is interested in emotional as well as intellectual reactions to the so-called "intellectual malady" (*MS,* 10).

16. It is interesting to note that, in so far as *The Myth of Sisyphus* is concerned with (in)justice at all, it is neither a social nor political configuration of the concept, but a metaphysical one. Indeed, the complete absence therein of references to the contemporary international events makes *The Myth* a conspicuously *apolitical* volume. Camus especially criticizes Chestov and Kierkegaard for evading what he deems the facts of the absurd via the leap of faith (*E,* 122–28; *MS,* 35–43).

17. I shall have more to say on revolt and its role in relation to Camus's quest for moral equilibrium in revolutionary action in chapter 7, when *The Rebel* is in question.

18. There is no need to emphasize that Sisyphus represents, for Camus, a paradigm of the absurd predicament. In total lucidity and devoid of all hope, the mythological figure is considered "superior to his fate" (*MS,* 109) and "stronger than his rock" (*MS,* 109). His is an obstinate happiness in maintaining an interminable protest and struggle in the face of defeat. It is useful to consider Camus's reconstruction of the Sisyphus legend as a representation of the "myth" of metaphysical injustice.

19. Henry Amer, "Le Mythe de Sisyphe," *NRF* 8 (1960): 490.

20. Cruickshank, *Albert Camus and the Literature of Revolt,* 88.

21. Cf. below, chapter 7, 170–72.

22. As we shall see, there is a tendency throughout his moral deliberations for Camus to think in somewhat vague and abstract terms without actually identifying to what he is referring.

23. "Preparing the fruit" (*FC,* 2:738–40), originally published in *La Tunisie française* in January 1941. The text appeared in modified form in 1954 under the title "The Almond Trees," one of the pieces comprising *Summer* (*E,* 833–37; *SEN,* 125–27).

24. One practical manifestation of this new-found realism is Camus's decision to volunteer for the French Army (from which he was refused on medical grounds). Cf. *Corr,* 38–39; and Todd, *Albert Camus, une vie,* 252. Implicit in a contemporary *Carnets* entry is Camus's sense of guilt in being, within his establishment comprising 44 men, "the only one left" (*CA1,* 79).

25. Unlike Camus himself, Clamence in *The Fall* would not partake in the Resistance, believing it to be insincere and romantic (*TRN,* 1538–39; *TF,* 89–91).

Written by Camus and Pia sometime after November 21, 1939, "Profession of Faith" was one of the many pieces that fell victim to the imposition of military censorship on *Alger républicain* in July 1939. It is interesting to note in passing that Camus remained sensitive to the issue of censorship. Writing under the pseudonym of "Zaks" on October 14, he highlights that in the French Constitution, freedom of the press was "an individual right necessary for all members of society, an essential means of education, training and of expressing knowledge and opinion and therefore one of the essential components of democratic government" (*FC,* 2:748). Such stands in stark contrast with what he deems "the odious German system" (*FC,* 2:747), whereby the right to free expression is emphatically denied.

Also to be noted here is the clear textual parallel with the earlier *Carnets* entry: see p. 105 above.

26. Attributing material is an inexact science in a context where pseudonyms prevail (see *FC,* 2:714). In what follows, in cases where his own byline does not appear, I shall be drawing on articles from the newspaper which the informed editors of *Fragments d'un combat* claim to be the work of Camus.

It is noteworthy that Hitler's authoritarian rule was not the only manifestation of what Camus deems an abuse of political power. On April 25, 1939, he does not shirk highlighting a similar trait in democratic states, evidenced by recent history: "I believe that, today, a certain amount of courage is needed to dare to say that there is *also* an imperialism within democracies. Many amongst us used to know that. Almost everyone has forgotten it. And yet peoples' destinies are inseparable and we can be certain that the appetite for power inflames the appetite for power, that hatred incites hatred, that imperialism gives rise to imperialism and that the treaty of Versailles is the spiritual father of the Munich agreement" (*FC,* 2:625–26; and cf. *FC,* 2:643–44).

27. In a series of articles on "The national socialist ideology" published in *Le Soir républicain* between October 6 and 11, 1939, a specialist in public law, René Capitant, points up the philosophy's inherent injustice inasmuch as it represents "the antithesis of individualism" (*FC,* 2:654). The whole question of Camus's attitude toward self-reliance and particularism is explored in Shaoyi Wu, "Individualisme altruiste chez Albert Camus," in Dubois, ed., *Albert Camus entre la misère et le soleil,* 94–105.

28. "If we do not want to be defeated by Hitler, it is because we *want* freedom, because we are *convinced* that it brings to people more options, strengths, possibilities, values and joys than servitude does. So let us not flag; let us not hand over our public life to a system similar to or just like hitlerism; let us defend ourselves against authoritarianism!" (*FC,* 2:758).

29. Although, of course, on a different scale entirely, Camus's earlier indictment of the mayor Rozis, the "hostile mayor . . . who stifles the Republic under his kisses" (*FC,* 2:677–78), was also based on the idea of the abuse of power so tellingly manifested by Hitler. There is continuity, as well as progression, in Camus's moral thinking here.

30. Quoted in Nicola Chiaromonte, "Albert Camus: In Memoriam," in Brée, ed., *Camus: A Collection of Critical Essays,* 15.

31. Cf. Camus's correspondence with Blanche Balain, dated November 11, 1939: "This war is not inevitable. It could have been avoided, *it still can be at any time.* . . . And even if this war became just, it would not need to be full of hatred" (*Corres,* xivn1; my italics; and cf. Todd, *Albert Camus, une vie,* 212). In an interview with Balain, Patrick McCarthy reports that Camus's resistance to the hostilities was based on personal psychology: "To submit to the war was like submitting to tuberculosis" (McCarthy, *Camus,* 125). See also King, ed., *Albert Camus,* 8.

32. Thus, he dismisses as a "lethal solution" the notion of a peace based on the enforced enslavement of the German people by Britain and France (*FC,* 2:650). And he makes clear that, were the democratic infrastructures of France and/or other Allied nations to face a military threat, then a military response would be a morally justified response (*FC,* 2:643–44). This last statement would be borne out by Camus's later wartime writings such as the *Letters to a German Friend.*

33. Quoted in Abbou, "Combat pour la justice," 40 (my italics).

34. Chiaromonte, "Albert Camus and Moderation," 1145 (my italics).

35. It is worth recalling that throughout this period, Camus supports the idea of "an international conference where governments would come after having given up their national selfishness" (*FC,* 2:629). He does so in his firm belief—reminiscent of the mentality behind his celebrated Kabyle reports—that "the humanity of a people . . . is reasserted by speaking to them in a humane language" (*FC,* 2:629). There are, of course, strong overtones here of Camus's appeal for a civilian truce which he delivered in Algiers in 1956. See below, chapter 8, 191–96; and cf. Philippe Vanney, "Quelques remarques sur l'idée de trêve dans l'œuvre politique d'Albert Camus," in Walker, ed., *Albert Camus,* 115–28.

36. As we shall discover in chapter 6, how best to realize a social order guaranteeing individual autonomy would be one of Camus's principal moral preoccupations in the postwar period.

37. It is worthy of note that Camus formulates his idea of a "Society of People," leading to a new world order, in terms of values and principles underpinning the *French* Constitution (*FC,* 2:651). As such, it is *prima facie* contradictory that in *The Outsider,* where Camus is concerned with the consequences of imposing metropolitan French cultural values on to an "Algerian" conscience, he should cast a critical light on the mother country's perceived moral stature. Meursault's verdict is delivered by a (presumedly) French Algerian jury "in a *spirit of justice*" (*TO,* 88; my italics), and he subsequently receives the sentence of "decapitation in some public place *in the name of the French people*" (*TO,* 107; translation amended; my italics). These remarks attest to an encroachment, in the name of justice, of Algerian moral conduct by French bureaucratic machinery. On reflection, however, it becomes apparent that what Camus is actually criticizing in *The Outsider* is *not* France's entrenched ideal of justice, based on glorious republican tradition, but its systematized legal processes, considered suspect. Curiously, Camus works from the assumption that these two seemingly opposing issues can in fact coexist.

38. Cf. below, chapter 6, 145–50.

39. In his 1945 "Remark on Revolt," Camus deems such a quest "the only question which seems of some importance" (*E,* 1695–96) in a world conditioned by the absurd. See, too, *C2,* 123; *CA2,* 62.

40. Quoted in Grenier, *Albert Camus: soleil et ombre,* 105–6. In *The Myth,* Camus is at pains to point out that he perceives the absurd as a point of departure for moral deliberation (cf. *E,* 97, 109; *MS,* 10, 22). See also "The Enigma" (1950), which similarly seeks to "play down" the emphasis of Camus's treatment of the Absurd *per se* (*E,* 859–66; *SEN,* 141–46).

41. Worthy of special mention is Cruickshank's *Albert Camus and the Literature of Revolt,* which remains to this day one of the best expositions of Camus's absurd cycle and his concomitant ideas on revolt.

42. Admittedly, the concept of revolt in *The Myth* lacks cogent formulation. Only in his later "Remark on Revolt," as a result of his own wartime experience, would Camus be in a position to clarify the philosophy and advocate revolt as a moral value.

43. Thody, *Albert Camus,* 50 (my italics).

44. Cf. Camus's recognition of collective endeavor in his section on the conqueror in *The Myth,* where he acknowledges being "on the side of the struggle" (*MS,* 81–82).

45. Laurent Martin, "Camus et la guerre 1939–45," in Dubois, ed., *Les trois guerres d'Albert Camus,* 93.

46. Such is the crux of Camus's response to Roland Barthes who, in "*La Peste:* annales d'une épidémie ou roman de la solitude," *Club* (1955): 4–13, criticizes the 1947 *chronique* for being too far removed from historical reality. See *TRN,* 1973–74 for the full text of Camus's reply. For a good analysis of the historical "situation" of *The Plague,* see Guérin, *Albert Camus: portrait de l'artiste en citoyen,* 63–82.

47. Viggiani, "Notes pour le futur biographe d'Albert Camus," 215.

48. Quoted in Guérin, ed., *Camus et la politique,* 134. It is interesting to point out in passing that Mathieu, in Sartre's *Iron in the Soul* (*La Mort dans l'âme* [Paris: Gallimard, 1949], 55–56), undergoes a similar experience to that of Camus reported here.

49. It is worthy of note that Georges Didier's cogent understanding of nationhood in *The First Man* stands in stark contrast to Cormery's ignorance over the issue (*PH,* 190–92; *FM,* 161–63). Didier, through whom Jacques learns "what it was to be a middle-class French family" (*FM,* 162), is representative of a culture totally alien to his friend, who "felt . . . to be of another species, with no past, no family home" (*FM,* 163).

50. It will be useful to recall the biographical milestones of this crucial period. As *persona non grata* in the province following the collapse of *Le Soir républicain* in early 1940, Camus was forced to flee Algeria and—on Pascal Pia's initiative—eventually found work at *Paris-Soir* in metropolitan France, where he stayed until the end of the year. Subsequently, after a rather frustrating time teaching in Oran, a relapse would compel him to return to France to substitute the clean air of the Massif Central for the sultry heat of the Mediterranean. The Allied landings in Algeria on November 8, 1942, meant that, for the remainder of the war, he found himself effectively imprisoned in the *hexagone.* For a full assessment of these events, see, for instance, chapters 17, 18, 21, and 22 of Lottman, *Albert Camus.*

51. Quoted in McCarthy, *Camus,* 174.

52. One is reminded here of Camus's remark in his retrospective preface to *Betwixt and Between:* "Though I was born poor, in a working-class area, I did not know what real misery was like until I saw our cold suburbs. Even extreme Arab poverty cannot be compared to it, since the weather is so different" (*SEN,* 19).

53. "Thus make separation into the main theme of the novel" (*CA2,* 39).

"Hostile to the past, impatient of the present, and cheated of the future, we were much like those whom human justice, or hatred, forces to live behind prison bars" (*TP,* 62; translation amended).

54. McCarthy, *Camus,* 175–76. Although, according to Poncet, Camus did become involved in some clandestine activities while in Oran in 1941 (*E,* 1458; cf. Todd, *Albert Camus, une vie,* 796n7), we should not necessarily deduce from this that he was—or could be—an active member of the French Resistance at that time. For her part, Jacqueline Lévi-Valensi has recently highlighted the Algiers-based branch of the *Combat* organization and suggests that this was not unknown to Camus (*CAC,* 28–31). Be that as it may, one should treat with caution Camus's own recollection that he joined forces with the Resistance movement upon reading, in Lyons, of the death of the influential communist leader Gabriel Péri, who was

murdered by the German militia on December 19, 1941 (*E,* 356). It is now well-known that Camus was in Oran at that time, not Lyons.

55. Quoted in Jacques Hardré, "Camus dans la résistance," *French Review* 37 (1964): 649. Cf. Camus's remark in private correspondence from Septemer 1944: "Six weeks ago, I was nearly arrested and disappeared from public life" (quoted in *CAC,* 39).

56. Leynaud, to whom Camus dedicates his *Letters to a German Friend,* was murdered by German militiamen in June 1944 for his instrumental role in the French Resistance. His death affected Camus considerably: "in thirty years, the death of someone has never had such an impact on me" (*E,* 1477).

57. Parker, *Albert Camus: The Artist in the Arena,* 109.

58. King, ed., *Albert Camus: Selected Political Writings,* 12.

59. As well as the internal rivalries that riddled the Resistance long before the Liberation, there is also the question of German reprisals, on which Camus remains noticeably silent.

60. Simone de Beauvoir's *The Blood of Others* (*Le Sang des autres* [Paris: Gallimard, 1945])—a work which, unlike Camus's own wartime novel *The Plague, does* examine the moral dilemmas of the Resistance—is a splendid fictional representation of this spirit of unity. Camus recognized this, reportedly calling Beauvoir's book "a fraternal book" (Simone de Beauvoir, *La Force de l'âge* [Paris: Gallimard, 1960], 644). (Conversely, in *The Mandarins* [1954], Beauvoir goes on to depict the disintegration of the Resistance's collective ethos which occurred in postwar France: cf. below, chapter 6, 241 note 1.)

61. "À Guerre totale, Résistance totale." *Combat clandestin,* March 1944. I would suggest that this editorial was the work of Camus on the grounds that its style and rallying characteristics are very much like those underscoring the *Letters to a German Friend,* of which more in a moment. Jacqueline Lévi-Valensi confirms this view when she remarks that "the attribution to Camus of this article is more than probable" (*CAC,* 121 n1).

62. Grand, in *The Plague,* embodies similar logic in his unhesitating decision to join the sanitary squads: "'Why, *that's* not difficult! Plague is here and we've got to make a stand, that's obvious. Ah, I only wish everything were as simple!'" (*TP,* 112). Camus's example of the schoolmaster should also be read in this light (*TRN,* 1327; *TP,* 111).

63. Correspondence with Francine Camus dated August 31, 1944, quoted in Todd, *Albert Camus, une vie,* 365. See, too, *CAC,* 18.

64. It hardly needs saying that echoes of this reasoning appear in *The Plague* through Rambert. While this character is initially the victim of an overwhelming sense of alienation, he eventually acknowledges the need to fight the pestilence ravaging Oran and, in so doing, he engages in a process of self-discovery (*TRN,* 1389; *TP,* 170). A parallel may be drawn here with Jean Blomart from Beauvoir's *The Blood of Others,* who similarly acknowledges the impossibility of abstaining from action in certain extreme situations. Both Rambert and Blomart bear witness to the very Camusian idea that "the unique greatness of human beings is to fight against that which outstrips them" (*FC,* 2:736).

65. Parker, *Albert Camus: The Artist in the Arena,* 109.

66. Ibid., 111–12.

67. For an engaging account of how Camus reappropriates the discourse of Europe (notably in the third of the *Letters*) from a fascistic vision to one of unity and fraternity as a way of revitalizing the resistance myth, see John Oswald, "Reappropriating Europe: Albert Camus's wartime Europeanism," *Modern & Contemporary France* 9 (2001): 483–93.

68. For an elaboration of the epistolary qualities of the *Letters,* together with an examination of wartime correspondence from Bernanos and Saint-Exupéry, see Hiroshi Mino, "'Lettres' de Guerre: Bernanos, Saint-Exupéry et Camus," in *AC19,* 171–87. More generally, Brigitte Sändig provides a useful conspectus of the reception of Camus's work in the GDR, in "Réception de l'œuvre de Camus en R.D.A.," in *AC18,* 39–60.

69. "Appel," *Combat,* December 1941. Cf. *Combat*'s motto: "In war as in peace, the final word is with those who never give up" (quoted in Todd, *Albert Camus, une vie,* 343). See, too, *CAC,* 25 (and cf. *CAC,* 26–27), where Jacqueline Lévi-Valensi cites a declaration from De Gaulle himself which was published in *Combat* in May 1942.

70. *Caligula* (the original 1941 rendering of which is less politicized than the definitive version [see *CAL*]) gives dramatic expression to this confrontation. Chéréa's moral integrity counters the emperor's moral impoverishment, but both share a similar mindset (*TRN,* 76–81; *CP,* 45–49).

71. This idea of a "detour" is mentioned in the first two of the *Letters* to highlight the notion of the Allied nations being forced to sacrifice their "regard for truth" in responding to, and ultimately defeating, the nihilism of Nazism (*E,* 223, 227; *RRD,* 7, 10). As Camus puts it in his opening epistle, "we had to overcome our weakness for humankind, the image we had formed of a peaceful destiny, . . . we had to stifle our passion for friendship" (*RRD,* 7; translation amended).

Nietzsche's paean to the *Übermensch,* a philosophy massively misconstrued by German imperialists, was ingloriously incorporated into Nazi ideology, while Heidegger openly supported Hitler and the cause of the Third Reich. Camus, on the other hand, "love[s] [his] country too much to be a nationalist" (*RRD,* 3) as a testimony to his resolve not to allow his own quest for justice to be blinded by politico-ideological prejudice. Cf. Frantz Favre, "L'idée de l'Europe chez Nietzsche et Camus," in Abbou, ed., *Albert Camus et l'Europe.*

72. Cf. Camus's indictment of his adversary in the fourth letter: "I am fighting you because your logic is as criminal as your heart" (*RRD,* 22).

73. Cf. Camus's remarks from contemporary correspondence with Guy Dumur: "We must be pessimistic as far as the Human Condition is concerned, but optimistic as far as people are concerned" (*E,* 1669); "You are always alone when you desert people because only people can be companions for people. . . . I suppose that we have to choose: either solitude with God or history with people" (*E,* 1670).

74. Camus makes the point convincingly in *Combat:* "We did not have any taste for hatred and we had the idea of justice. That is why we wondered whether justice was with us" (*CAC,* 185). Earlier, in a harrowing editorial attributed to Camus highlighting the cold-blooded murder of eighty-six Frenchmen by the German militia, attention is drawn to the French being "vaccinated against horror" (*CAC,* 129). This view would be reiterated in a lecture at Columbia University in March 1946, when Camus highlights what he calls "the passion for justice that animates all Frenchmen" (Camus, "The Human Crisis," in *AC5,* 176; and cf. Lottman, *Albert Camus,* 390). The *Obermann* epigraph to the fourth of the *Letters to a German Friend* (*E,* 239; *RRD,* 20) and the Nietzschean epigraph in *Actuelles* (*E,* 249) are also worth noting in this context.

75. Ginestier, *Pour connaître la pensée de Camus,* 163.

76. Brée, *Camus,* 216.

77. Cf. *CAC,* 186: "we tell you to regret nothing. It was better to perish with justice than to triumph with injustice. And we have done so, so that through our patience and our honor, we have won at the same time as justice itself."

78. This statement once again highlights Camus's tendency to associate socio-political (ephemeral) injustice with metaphysical (eternal) injustice.

79. "'Nous savons bien . . . ,'" *Combat,* May 8, 1945. Although neither Quilliot nor Lévi-Valensi attributes this article to Camus, it does not seem unreasonable to do so given the importance it attaches to the ideal of justice, a principle which, as we have seen, underscores Camus's wartime morality.

80. Thomas Landon Thorson, "Albert Camus and the Rights of Man," *Ethics* 74 (1964): 288.

81. Cf. McCarthy, *Camus,* 204: "Today these articles are almost unreadable, not because their topicality has faded but because Camus's moral impulse made him simplistic and dogmatic. This is moralizing rather than moral thinking."

82. It is worth noting that in respect of the events of August 1945, Camus's was a rare voice of contempt amid the general euphoria of the occasion in many western quarters. Cf. Simone Debout, "Sartre et Camus face à Hiroshima," *Esprit* (January 1998): 151–58.

Chapter 6. From Resistance to Revolution

1. Mention may usefully be made here of Sartre's inability to complete his wartime tetralogy because of the changing nature of the postwar situation in France. Significantly, he considered Beauvoir's *The Mandarins* (1954), a book begun in 1949 portraying the disillusionment of French intellectuals in the aftermath of the hostilities, to be the real sequel to his own *Roads to Freedom* [*Les Chemins de la liberté*] (Jean-Paul Sartre, *Œuvres romanesques,* ed. Michel Contat et al., Bibliothèque de La Pléiade [Paris: Gallimard, 1981], 1878–82); and cf. Sartre's own "Sartre par Sartre," in his *Situations IX* (Paris: Gallimard, 1972), 101.

2. Camus, "The Human Crisis," 161. Cf. Rieux's remark to Rambert in *The Plague* as the disease finally recedes: "'Courage! It's up to you *now* to prove you're right'" (*TP,* 244). See also Lottman, *Albert Camus,* 332.

3. A few days later, Camus writes of revolution that "it is not inevitably about the guillotine and machine guns, or rather it is about machine guns when necessary" (*E,* 1527). "Revolutions," then—as that now envisaged for France would hopefully demonstrate—do not necessarily entail violent insurrection for Camus. Cf. his comment in "Neither Victims nor Executioners," first published in *Combat* in November 1946, by which time France's *révolution manquée* was apparent: "1789 and 1917 are still dates, but they are no longer models" (*E,* 339). For a useful conspectus of Camus's thoughts of reconciling politics with morality, see "Le *Combat* d'un guerrier," *Juste Camus, Camus le Juste,* originally broadcast on *France Culture* on November 28, 2002, http://www.radiofrance.fr/chaines/france-culture2/.

4. It seems that Camus was keen to exploit the possible comparison with Saint-Just, as the latter's name now appeared frequently in *Combat.* However, he would later regret any such association when, in *The Rebel,* Camus accuses Saint-Just of introducing Rousseau's ideas on human betterment into the historical process, thereby paving the way for Marxist historical determinism (*E,* 521–40; *TR,* 82–102).

5. Camus, of course, was not alone in his view of a national renaissance for postwar France; the ideal crossed the political divide. Thus, while De Gaulle frequently used words such as "revive," "renovation," and "reconstruction" in his vision of postwar society (Charles De Gaulle, *Lettres, Notes et Carnets: mai 1945–*

juin 1951 [Paris: Plon, 1984], 62, 65, 92, 130, 139), Maurice Thorez, speaking on Radio Moscow on August 24, 1944, highlighted what he called "a real revival of France" (Maurice Thorez, *Œuvres choisies en trois volumes, II: 1938–1950* [Paris: Éditions Sociales, 1966], 290). Cf. Michael Kelly, "*Révolution, Renaissance, Redressement:* Representations of Historical Change in Post-War France," in *Reconstructing the Past: Representations of the Fascist Era in Post-War European Culture,* ed. Graham Bartram et al. (Keele: Keele University Press, 1996), 32–48.

6. For a full assessment of the latter concept in Camus's thinking, see, in particular, Germain-Paul Gelinas, *La Liberté dans l'œuvre d'Albert Camus* (Fribourg: Éditions Universitaires, 1965); and cf. Joseph Hermet, *À la rencontre d'Albert Camus: le dur chemin de la liberté* (Paris: Beauchesne, 1990).

7. Pierre-Henri Simon, *Témoins de l'homme: la condition humaine dans la littérature contemporaine,* 5th ed. (Paris: Armand Colin, 1963), 191. See also in this connection, Georges Goedert, *Albert Camus et la question du bonheur* (Luxembourg: Édi-Centre, 1969).

8. See Bentham, *"A Fragment on Government."*

9. In philosophical terms, absolutes of morality can only exist beyond the realm of "impure" human experience and must therefore be limited to metaphysical or divine beliefs. As we shall see later, Camus's polemic with Mauriac over the purge in France would pit "absolute" divine values against "relative" human ones.

10. Thus, in his coverage of the Hodent case for *Alger républicain* in February 1939, Camus had stated that "freedom is only a part of justice" (*FC,* 2:369) while, in keeping with the formulation of the concept in *Combat* as "a superior principle" (*E,* 276), he had responded to the moral nihilism of his German friend with "a fierce love of justice" (*RRD,* 21).

11. Camus is, however, under no illusions as to the difficulties that such a task entails, noting that "the Scandinavian democracies alone are closest to the necessary reconciliation" (*E,* 1528). He would later (1951) support the British Labour Leader Clement Attlee, against Churchill, out of similar respect for British socialism (John Cocking, trans., "Britain after the Election: Two French Views," *Listener,* November 22, 1951, 871–73). That he is now preoccupied with the relationship between justice and freedom as mutually opposing absolute concepts is also apparent from the aforementioned *Carnets* entry, anticipating *The Rebel* (*C2,* 123; *CA2,* 62).

12. Camus, preoccupied with politics "in spite of [him]self" (*CA2,* 140), distrusted all political systems, as we have seen. He would later concede that "there is perhaps no good political system, but democracy is most certainly the least bad" (*E,* 319; cf. *E,* 1582). Later, as we shall see, Camus advocates the idea of an international democracy to offset the insecurity posed by the *politique des blocs.*

13. Quoted in Jeanyves Guérin, "Camus devant le socialisme," in *OFOO,* 347.

14. The SFIO, we recall, had voted for Pétain in the summer of 1940.

15. Cf. Roger Quilliot, "Autour d'Albert Camus et du problème socialiste," *La Revue socialiste* 20 (1948): 342–52; and Guérin, "Camus devant le socialisme."

16. Paul Edwards, ed., *The Encyclopedia of Philosophy* (London: Collier-Macmillan, 1967), 4:299.

17. See chapter 4 of Mill's *On Liberty* (1854) ("Of the Limits to the Authority of Society over the Individual"), 131–49.

18. For an assessment of the "Justice as Desert" mentality from a legal perspective, see, for instance, Sadurski, *Giving Desert its Due.*

19. Ibid.,116.

20. The purge in France has been thoroughly documented and it is not my inten-

tion here to engage in discussions which have been expertly provided elsewhere: see, for instance, Pierre Assouline, *L'Épuration des intellectuels: 1944–1945* (Brussels: Complexe, 1985); Antony Beevor and Artemis Cooper, *Paris after the Liberation: 1944–1949* (London: Hamish Hamilton, 1994), 88–101, 179–96; Tony Judt, *Past Imperfect. French Intellectuals: 1944–1956* (Los Angeles and Berkeley: University of California Press, 1992), 45–74; and Herbert R. Lottman, *The People's Anger: Justice and Revenge in Post-Liberation France* (London: Hutchinson, 1986). Rather, my aim will be to assess how the moral dilemmas raised by the purge manifest themselves in Camus's own ethics and thereby demonstrate some of the further anguish now underlying his concern for justice.

21. Of doubtful authorship, this editorial from April 1944 draws on extremely colorful language in its call for the repulsion of French traitors: "The rotten branches of a tree cannot stay attached to it. They must be torn off, crushed and thrown to the ground" (*CAC,* 128).

22. On September 9, 1944, *Les Lettres françaises* thus published a manifesto signed by French intellectuals, calling for the "just punishment of impostors and traitors" (quoted in Guérin, *Albert Camus: portrait de l'artiste en citoyen,* 44). See also André Nouschi et al., *La France de 1940 à nos jours,* rev. ed. (Paris: Nathan, 1988), 23–24.

23. Jacqueline Lévi-Valensi comments that this is a "possible article [written by Camus]. The title, certain expressions and themes make this text attributable without certainty" (*CAC,* 145n1).

24. The issue of judgment is an important Camusian theme, not least in the 1956 masterpiece. Cf. *C3,* 115: "What human beings endure with the most difficulty is to be judged." See also *C2,* 201; *CA2,* 103; and Lottman, *Albert Camus,* 428.

25. Judt, *Past Imperfect,* 73.

26. Susan Mary Patten, quoted in Beevor and Cooper, *Paris after the Liberation,* 181.

27. Quoted in Annie Cohen-Solal, *Sartre: 1905–1980* (Paris: Gallimard, 1985), 290.

28. François Mauriac, "Justice," *Le Figaro,* December 12, 1944, quoted in Guérin, *Albert Camus: portrait de l'artiste en citoyen,* 46.

29. Ibid.

30. François Mauriac, *Blocs-Notes, 1952–1957* (Paris: Flammarion, 1959), 387.

31. Henry Becque, *Œuvres complètes* (Paris: Crès, 1926), 7:112.

32. As Alfred Grosser reminds us, as well as the purge in France, the ongoing "Algerian problem" also looms large in Camus's contemporary moral preoccupations (see Alfred Grosser, "Camus, la politique et les fondements de la morale," in *Camus et le premier "Combat," 1944–1947: Colloque de Paris X-Nanterre,* ed. Jeanyves Guérin [La Garenne-Colombes: Européennes Erasmus, 1990], 135–41). There too, as here in the case of the purge, the standard of justice assumes an almost mythical status by virtue of its association with "the one and indivisible France."

33. In "Misery in Kabylia" for instance, he states that "I do not believe that charity is a pointless sentiment. But I do think that in some cases its results are and so what is needed instead are constructive policies for better living conditions" (*FC,* 1:291). Cf. Henri Gouhier, ed., *Nicolas de Malebranche: Œuvres complètes* (Paris: Librairie Philosophique J. Vrin, 1966), 11:213: "we must always dispense justice before exercising charity."

34. For an informed discussion of the polemic, see, for instance, McCarthy,

Camus, 198–223; and Guérin, *Albert Camus: portrait de l'artsite en citoyen,* 43–62.

35. François Mauriac, *Mémoires politiques* (Paris: Grasset, 1967), 269.

36. Cf. East, *Albert Camus, ou l'homme à la recherche d'une morale,* 57. The idea that God (even if He exists) is powerless to influence human affairs (here, the apportionment of justice) brings to mind Orestes's diatribe to Jupiter in Sartre's *The Flies* (1943): "You are the king of the Gods, Jupiter, the king of rocks and stars, the king of waves of the sea. But you are not the king of human beings" (Jean-Paul Sartre, *Huis clos* suivi de *Les Mouches,* Collection Folio [Paris: Gallimard, 1947], 234).

37. Cf. *E,* 271: "Christianity in its essence (and that is its paradoxical greatness) is a doctrine of injustice. It is based on the sacrifice of the innocent and the acceptance of this sacrifice." For a contrary view of Camus's intellectual relationship with Christianity, see François Chavanes, *Albert Camus: un message d'espoir* (Paris: Cerf, 1996); and cf. Joseph Hermet, *Albert Camus et le christianisme* (Paris: Beauchesne, 1976).

38. Salas, *Albert Camus: la juste révolte,* 12.

39. As Minister of the Interior at the time of the first executions of French hostages by the Nazis, Pucheu had played an instrumental role in turning the German Gestapo into an efficient police force. Cf. Nouschi, *La France de 1940 à nos jours,* 17.

40. "Justice de la France," *Les Lettres françaises* 15 (1944), quoted in Roger Grenier, *Album Camus,* Bibliothèque de La Pléiade (Paris: Gallimard, 1982), 174.

41. "La Machine à sous," *Combat,* January 6, 1945; and cf. "La justice des autres," (also signed "Suétone") *Combat,* January 11, 1945. Ironically, it would take the trial of Pétain himself in July 1945 for Camus publicly to concede the failure of the purge. Writing in *Combat* on August 30, he thus states that "it is from now on certain that the purge in France has not only failed but is also discredited" (*E,* 289). In that same article (which, notably, Camus would include in *Actuelles*), he categorically condemns the arbitrary and disproportionate nature of sentencing in the name of justice. Curiously, however, he appears to forget his own earlier propensity toward retributivism when he comments that, for it to have succeeded, the purge needed to have been undertaken "*without* a mentality of vengeance" (*E,* 290; my italics).

42. For more on Brasillach, see, for instance, Jacques Isorni, *Le Procès de Robert Brasillach (19 janvier 1945)* (Paris: Flammarion, 1946); and David L. Schalk, *The Spectrum of Political Engagement* (Princeton: Princeton University Press, 1979), 76–109.

43. In so doing, he joined, notably, Paul Valéry, Paul Claudel and Jean Anouilh. For their part, however, neither Sartre nor Beauvoir would appendage their names to Mauriac's petition (Beauvoir, *La Forces des choses,* 1:36–38). It is worth mentioning here Beauvoir's "Eye for an Eye" ["Œil pour œil,"] *Les Temps modernes* 1 (October 1945–February 1946): 813–30. In that essay, the author deems "spontaneous" revenge a morally justifiable course of action (cf. *The Blood of Others*), but maintains that society, acting through institutional processes of justice, could never sanction revenge on the part of private individuals. Occurring as it did after the Liberation of France, the Brasillach affair was removed from the "extreme situation" of war and so it is not a little surprising that Beauvoir was not prepared to support Brasillach's case now that the time for "spontaneous" revenge had passed.

44. Quoted in *Bulletin d'Information de la Société des Études Camusiennes* 15 (1987): 8. For an interesting *mise à jour* of the points of divergence *and conver-*

gence between Brasillach and Camus, see Peter Tame, "Robert Brasillach et Albert Camus," *Études* 34 (1989): 20–47. Camus would also intervene in other contentious cases, most notably on behalf of the fascist Lucien Rebatet, whose violently antisemitic *Debris* (1942) became a bestseller in France during the Occupation (*E,* 1886–87; cf. Todd, *Albert Camus, une vie,* 375). Condemned to death in 1946, Rebatet was reprieved and, while in prison, wrote a novel entitled *Two Standards* (1952).

45. It is worthy of note that in *Actuelles II,* Camus publishes a series of articles and interviews under the heading "Justice and Hatred" as testimony to the ongoing nature of the problem of intolerance identified here (cf. *E,* 715–27).

46. Camus levels similar criticism against what he calls "the French ministers responsible for policies which cover Tunisia with blood" (*E,* 789) following further nationalist unrest in January 1952.

47. Julien Benda, ed., *Jean de La Bruyère: Œuvres complètes,* Bibliothèque de La Pléiade (Paris: Gallimard, 1951), 421.

48. Todd, *Albert Camus, une vie,* 371.

49. Guérin, *Albert Camus: portrait de l'artiste en citoyen,* 274.

50. Camus erroneously dates that meeting as taking place in 1948 (*E,* 371; *RRD,* 49). Actually, it took place in 1947 (Todd, *Albert Camus, une vie,* 799n34).

51. Both *State of Siege* (1948) and *The Just Assassins* (1950) would be cast from this mindset.

52. Quoted in Paulhan, ed., *Jean Grenier: Carnets 1944–1971,* 47.

53. Lottman reports that Simone Weil's *The Need for Roots [L'Enracinement*] (1949) influenced Camus greatly in his views on violence in relation to revolutionary justice (Lottman, *Albert Camus,* 374). Cf. *E,* 1699–1702.

54. Camus, "The Human Crisis," 161. For a full assessment of Camus's transatlantic tour, see Lottman, *Albert Camus,* 376–95; Todd, *Albert Camus, une vie,* 399–415; and Fernande Bartfeld, "Le voyage de Camus en Amérique du Nord," in *AC19,* 203–29.

55. Camus is still undecided as late as August 1946 as to which of the two titles to choose: see his letter to Patricia Blake dated August 21, 1946, quoted in Todd, *Albert Camus, une vie,* 417.

56. For a good overview of Camus's preoccupation with violence in works from this period, see Jeanyves Guérin, "L'urgence et la limite: essai sur la violence dans l'œuvre de Camus," *Hebrew University Studies in Literature and the Arts* 20 (1993): 7–26.

57. Quoted in Paulhan, ed., *Jean Grenier: Carnets 1944–1971,* 47.

58. While Jeanyves Guérin sees in Tarrou's confession "an obvious intertext with [*Neither Victims nor Executioners*]" (Guérin, *Albert Camus: portrait de l'artiste en citoyen,* 79; and cf. by the same writer, "Jalons pour une lecture politique de *La Peste,*" *Roman 20–50* 2 [1986]: 7–25), David Walker seems right to suggest that Camus wrote the scene depicting Tarrou's life story *before* the original publication of "Neither Victims nor Executioners" in *Combat* in November 1946 (David H. Walker, "In and Out of History: Albert Camus," *French Cultural Studies* 8 [1997]: 107). It is also interesting to note that by Camus's own admission, Tarrou is a further representation of his own "temptations" (*SEN,* 144), as already noted (see his letter to Pierre Borel dated October 15, 1948, quoted in Todd, *Albert Camus, une vie,* 419). For a very insightful study of *The Plague* as a response to what he calls "a kind of inner demand," see André Abbou, "Sous le soleil du père et de l'histoire: dialogue avec un mythe personnel fondateur dans *La Peste,*" *Europe* 77 (1999): 104–18.

59. It will be recalled that as a revolutionary terrorist, Tarrou had himself perpetrated murder in his aim to "square accounts with that poor blind 'owl'" (*TP,* 204; cf. *Corr,* 141) he once witnessed in a public tribunal.

60. It is worth noting that upon its original publication in *Combat* in November 1946, this series of articles highlighting the dangers of political absolutism would pass almost unnoticed. (Significantly, Camus once more records his "torment" [*CA2,* 94] while writing the pieces.) Only when the articles reappeared in *Caliban* a year later amidst revelations of Stalinist crimes would they provoke a polemic with French communist intellectuals, spearheaded by Vigerie. That Camus understood the pertinence of the series is clear by his decision to publish it for a third time in *Actuelles* in 1950.

These ideas are also given dramatic expression in *State of Siege,* in which The Plague wields power and death in the name of "silence, order and *absolute justice*" (*TRN,* 229–30; my italics), that is, total oppression, or state terrorism: "it is the Plague which is the State" (*TRN,* 222, 228–30). In that play, human autonomy is rendered redundant by the ruthless "rules" (*TRN,* 221), "organization" (*TRN,* 228) and "logical pleasures" (*TRN,* 229) by which political power is manifested and the citizens of Cadix controlled. As the Choir puts it, "we used to be a people and here we are now a mass!" (*TRN,* 248). Cf. Camus's "Response to Gabriel Marcel" (*E,* 389–96).

61. In 1944, Camus rejected anticommunism since to agree to it was implicitly to support right-wing politics. He agreed with the PC that a socialist transformation was needed in postwar France, but disagreed on the means by which to achieve this. (Specifically, he rejects the ideal of historical determinism [*E,* 272–75; and cf. Parker, 119–24]). For a thorough account of Camus's standing in the former Soviet Union, see Evguéni Kouchkine, "Réception de l'œuvre de Camus en U.R.S.S.," in *AC18,* 7–37.

62. Harold Wardman, *Jean-Paul Sartre: The Evolution of his Thought and Art* (Lewiston: Edwin Mellen, 1992), 236. Significantly, *Les Temps modernes* (the contemporary mouthpiece of the French left) would wait until January 1950 before addressing the issue of Stalin's punitive labor camps: cf. Maurice Merleau-Ponty and Jean-Paul Sartre, "Les jours de notre vie," *Les Temps modernes* 51 (1950): 1153–68.

Jeanyves Guérin cites a letter to Emmanuel Mounier in which Camus once again highlights the morally indefensible nature of the Soviet concentration camps (Guérin, *Albert Camus: portrait de l'artiste en citoyen,* 106–7). Cf. Maurice Weyembergh, "L'obsession du clos et le thème des camps," in *OFOO,* 361–75. For a comprehensive account of the Soviet forced labor system, see Edwin Bacon, *The Gulag at War: Stalin's Forced Labour System in the Light of the Archives* (London: Macmillan, 1995).

63. Lottman, *Albert Camus,* 413.

64. We do well to recall here Camus's polemic with Maurice Merleau-Ponty who, in *Humanism and Terror: Essay on the Communist Problem* [*Humanisme et Terreur: essai sur le problème communiste,* rev. ed. (1947; repr. Paris: Gallimard, 1980)], argues that violence (deemed intrinsic to political power) can be excused as a means by which to realize "a future of humanism" (116). Camus accuses Merleau-Ponty of justifying Stalinist atrocities in adopting such a stance. Cf. Maurice Weyembergh, "Merleau-Ponty et Camus: *Humanisme et Terreur* et 'Ni victimes ni bourreaux,'" *Annales de l'Institut de Philosophie. L'Université Libre de Bruxelles* (1971): 53–99. Incidentally, Merleau-Ponty's growing disillusionment with communism would lead, in 1955, to his break with an increasingly committed

Sartre: cf. the letters detailing that rupture in *Magazine littéraire* 320 (1994): 67–86.

65. Camus was intellectually obsessed with the Russian revolutionaries of 1905. In *The Rebel,* he considers the example of the "exceptional souls" (*TRN,* 1834) portrayed in *The Just Assassins* as an effective counterblast to the many manifestations of revolutionary fervor analyzed in that book "where rebellion cuts itself from its roots and abstains from any concrete morality" (*TR,* 101; translation amended; cf. *TR,* 133–42). Championing *The Just Assassins,* Jeanyves Guérin notes: "Rare are, in fact, literary works which have highlighted the issue of terrorist choice with such intensity" (Guérin, "L'urgence et la limite," 11). For an engaging discussion of the moral questions at issue in the play, consult "Camus et le terrorisme," *Juste Camus, Camus le Juste,* originally broadcast on *France Culture* on November 23, 2002, http://www.radiofrance.fr/chaines/france-culture2/.

66. The nihilist Nada in *State of Siege* similarly puts political ideology before human morality (*TRN,* 238, 244–45).

The tension between love and justice is well to the fore both in *State of Siege* and *The Just Assassins.* In the former, love is outlawed in the interests of organized efficiency (*TRN,* 260); in the latter, Dora posits that sentiments of love are incompatible with the pursuit of justice (*TRN,* 351, 355; *CP,* 150, 153). Cf. Rizzuto, *Camus,* 99–109. See also *E,* 873–74; *SEN,* 152; and below, chapter 8, 193–94.

67. Yanek (Stepan's antithesis) noticeably lacks discipline. An unorthodox terrorist in his view that "all poetry is revolutionary" (*CP,* 125) (as against Stepan's conviction that "only bombs are revolutionary" [*CP,* 125], Kaliayev is a revolutionary romantic who finds pleasure in disguising himself (*TRN,* 315–16; *CP,* 127–28) and who changes the agreed entrance signal (*TRN,* 314; *CP,* 127). To Stepan's totalitarian psychology, Kaliayev counters "terrorist sensitivity" (*TRN,* 1831).

68. For an account of the contribution of France to the so-called New World Order in the postwar period, see Andrew Williams, "France and the New World Order, 1940–1947," *Modern & Contemporary France* 8 (2002): 191–202.

69. See Jeanyves Guérin, "L'Europe dans la pensée et l'œuvre de Camus," in *Albert Camus: textes réunis à l'occasion du 25e anniversaire de la mort de l'écrivain,* ed. Paul F. Smets (Brussels: Éditions de l'Université de Bruxelles, 1985), 57–70; and Jean Sarocchi, "L'Europe: exil ou royaume?," *Littératures* 26 (1992): 154–86. To these titles may be added the 1990 Strasbourg conference, Abbou, ed., *Albert Camus et l'Europe,* the papers from which provide a useful overview of Camus's situation in relation to Europe.

70. Walker, "In and Out of History," 107.

71. This is not an altogether new idea for Camus who, we recall, initially responded to the outbreak of the Second World War by campaigning for international fraternity in a new "Society of People." Nor is it a uniquely Camusian proposition, since in 1945 representatives of the League of Nations met in San Francisco to set up the new United Nations as an organization whose remit it was and still remains to preserve world peace.

72. France's own *révolution manquée* would highlight the limitations of national government (cf. *E,* 339). Much in keeping with the spirit of these remarks, Camus supports Garry Davis who, tearing up his American passport in September 1948, proclaimed himself a citizen of the world, even though the mainstream opinion was to dismiss such a gesture as naïve idealism (*E,* 1589–94; cf. *E,* 1698).

73. Cf. below, chapter 8, 197–202.

74. Todd, *Albert Camus, une vie,* 463, 805n34.

75. "Notre Espagne," part of a dossier entitled "Soutien à l'Espagne républicaine" comprising manuscripts, correspondence and (unpublished) articles testifying to Camus's lifelong concern for justice in the Spanish connection (Paris, *L'Institution Mémoires de l'Édition Contemporaine* [L'IMEC], Fonds Albert Camus, B4 [1–11(1), 3]. At the time of writing, this indispensable archive was in the process of relocating to Aix-en-Provence.

76. See Jean-Paul Sartre, "Présentation," *Les Temps modernes* 1 (October 1945—February 1946): 1–21; and cf. Max Adereth, *Commitment in Modern French Literature: A Brief Study of littérature engagée in the Works of Péguy, Aragon and Sartre* (London: Gollancz, 1967), especially 127–71.

77. Although himself not an active member of the RDR (which would soon find its political neutrality compromised by a pro-American stance), Camus would notably speak alongside Sartre and David Rousset (who, with Gérard Rosenthal, had founded the movement in 1948) at a peace rally at the Salle Pleyel in Paris in late 1948. (Camus would retain the text of that speech in *Actuelles* [*E,* 397–406]). For a useful discussion of the RDR, see, in particular, Michel-Antoine Burnier, *Les Existentialistes et la politique* (Paris: Gallimard, 1966), 63–75; and cf. Sartre's own account in "Merleau-Ponty vivant," in his *Situations IV* (Paris: Gallimard, 1964), 223–25.

78. Quoted in Gilbert Walusinski, "Camus et les Groupes de Liaison Internationale," *La Quinzaine littéraire,* March 1–15, 1979, 22. Cf. Philippe Vanney, "Par dessus les frontières, des îlots de résistance: Camus et les Groupes de Liaison Internationale," *Bulletin d'Études françaises* 30 (1999): 155–89.

79. Walusinski cites a letter dated July 12, 1950, in which Camus voices his continuing support for the *Groupes,* even though the outbreak of the Korean War heightened tensions between East and West, thereby threatening all such initiatives (Walusinski, "Camus et les Groupes de Liaison Internationale," 23).

80. Jean-Paul Sartre, "Réponse à Albert Camus," *Les Temps modernes* 82 (1952): 345–46.

Chapter 7. *The Rebel* or "an attempt to understand the time I live in"

1. Maurice Nadeau, "Les Livres: Albert Camus et la révolte," *Combat,* November 8, 1951, 7.

2. Georges Bataille, "Le Temps de la révolte, (I)," *Critique* 7 (1951): 1019. Auguste Viatte, "Albert Camus devant l'athéisme," *La Revue de l'Université Laval* 6 (1952): 642. Robert Greer Cohn, "The True Camus," *French Review* 60 (1986): 36.

3. Pierre Hervé, "La Révolte camuse," *La Nouvelle Critique* 35 (1952): 74. Francis Jeanson, "Albert Camus ou l'âme révoltée," *Les Temps modernes* 79 (1952): 2090. McCarthy, *Camus,* 248. At a recent conference in Aix-en-Provence commemorating the fiftieth anniversary of the publication of *The Rebel,* Jeannine Verdès-Leroux highlights the excellent reception of the work upon its first appearance. The critical reviews of, most notably, *L'Humanité* and *Les Temps modernes* (which appeared in January and May 1952 respectively) should, Verdès-Leroux suggests, be read in the light of this initial impact. See Franck Planeille, "Autour du cinquantième anniversaire de la publication de *L'Homme révolté:* les 26 et 27

octobre 2001 à Aix-en-Provence," *Bulletin d'Information de la Société des Études Camusiennes* 20 (2002): 5.

4. Detailed notes for the book appear increasingly in Camus's *Carnets* from late-1942 onward, while Quilliot gives chapter and verse on the rigorous research undertaken in connection with the study, the original plan of which was extremely ambitious in scope (*E,* 1622–26). It is also worth noting that *The Rebel* marks a veritable watershed in Camus's intellectual intensity (see, for instance, *C2,* 324, 345; *CA2,* 167, 177; and cf. *E,* 1627). His self-imposed asceticism while drafting the work (cf. *E,* 1635, *C2,* 263; *CA2,* 135) likewise attests to the personal commitment he accords the project.

However, elsewhere, Camus expresses considerable doubt as to the quality of what he labels "the object of so much effort" (*E,* 1635). Indeed, to judge from private correspondence with his wife dated March 8, 1951, he is prone to write off the book even before its publication: "I would have liked for this book to have made a decisive step for myself and for many people with me with whom I feel united. If successful, this book, in its way, could have mastered this moment in time, could have announced potential. You see that my ambition was not slim. But I really doubt whether I have succeeded" (quoted in Todd, *Albert Camus, une vie,* 535). A "failed great book" indeed.

5. See Albert Camus, "Le Meurtre et l'Absurde," *Empédocle* 1 (1949): 19–27.

6. Albert Camus, "Lautréamont et la banalité," *Cahiers du Sud* 33 (1951): 399–404. Albert Camus, "Nietzsche et le nihilisme," *Les Temps modernes* 7 (1951): 193–208.

7. Actually, the dichotomy between Hellenism and Historicism on which *The Rebel* pivots is already to the fore in Camus's inaugural lecture, delivered in February 1938 in honor of the Algiers *Maison de la Culture* (*E,* 1321–27). A contemporary *Carnets* entry suggests that even at that time, Camus was reflecting on the "spirit of revolution" (*CA1,* 47–48) at the heart of the 1951 work. Cf. Jacqueline Lévi-Valensi and Jeanyves Guérin, "Camus et l'idée de révolution," *Les Cahiers de Fontenay* 63–64 (1991): 221–41. It is also worth drawing attention to Camus's *diplôme d'études supérieures,* written in 1936, which examines the transition from Hellenism to Christianity through a study of Plotinus and Augustine (*E,* 1224–1313). Judging from an entry in the *Carnets* (*C2,* 342; *CA2,* 176), while completing *The Rebel,* Camus was considering a reassessment of that thesis in relation to Nemesis, the ancient goddess of justice in the sense of Greek *mesura.*

8. Dubois et al., "Camus journaliste," 49.

9. Gay-Crosier, *Les Envers d'un échec,* 166.

10. We shall see later that the Hellenist-inspired "pensée de midi," which Camus espouses by way of a response to the frenzy of revolutionary nihilism explored in his study, does not lend itself very easily to pragmatic application.

11. For a thorough examination of the work in the context of contemporary European history, see Denis Charbit, "*L'Homme révolté:* grandeur et servitude de la fonction intellectuelle," in *AC19,* 11–53. Camus calls his work "a stand on current affairs" (*E,* 729) and "an attempt to understand the time I live in" (*TR,* 11). Philip Thody remembers seeing *The Rebel* for sale in November 1951 with the words "This is an attempt to understand the time I live in" printed on a wrapper around the cover (private correspondence with author, April 9, 1999). Cf. Camus's more detailed explanation in "Defense of *The Rebel,*" a bid to rationalize his thinking following the furor of the book's publication but which he would leave unpublished: "I would not have written *The Rebel* if, in the 1940s, I hadn't found myself

faced with people whose schemes and actions I could not understand. To put it briefly, I could not understand that people could torture others without stopping to look at them" (*E,* 1702). This admission does not invalidate the claim that *The Rebel* is essentially a theoretical formulation of justice as a revolutionary problematic and, as such, is distinct from Camus's other nonfictional writings dealing with (social and political) justice so far examined in this book.

12. The figure of Prometheus, "revolutionary ideal" (*CA1,* 81), long since interests Camus who, in March 1937, staged Aeschylus's *Prometheus Bound* as one of the productions of the *Théâtre du Travail.* In addition, as well as being the subject of the 1946 "Prometheus in Hell," the mythological figure also lends his name to the second cycle of Camus's *œuvre,* with *The Rebel* as its centerpiece, as noted in the *Carnets* (*C2,* 328; *CA2,* 168). For a useful discussion of the status of Prometheus in Camus's thinking, see Germaine Brée, "Avatars of Prometheus: A Shifting Camusian Image," in *Mythology in French Literature,* ed. Philip Crant, French Literature Series III (Columbia: University of South Carolina, College of Humanities and Social Sciences, Department of Foreign Languages and Literatures, 1976), 138–48. For a more general commentary on Camus's use of the myth, see Monique Crochet, *Les Mythes dans l'œuvre de Camus* (Paris: Éditions Universitaires, 1973).

13. Two pioneering commentaries on this work are: George Blin, "Albert Camus et l'idée de révolte," *Fontaine* 53 (1946): 109–17; and Philip Thody, "Albert Camus and 'La Remarque sur la révolte,'" *French Studies* 10 (1956): 335–38. Despite the passage of time, these articles remain invaluable reference points.

14. It is worth pausing for a moment to consider the structure of Camus's work, since the three hugely disproportionate sections of *The Rebel* ("Metaphysical Rebellion" ["La Révolte métaphysique"] (comprising seventy-eight pages in the Pléiade edition); "Historical Rebellion" ["La Révolte historique"] (one hundred forty pages); and "Rebellion and Art" ["Révolte et Art"] (twenty-five pages)) indicate, at the very least, an unbalanced methodological approach. It is significant that Camus is reported to have expressed a preference for the chapter on artistic revolt (Todd, *Albert Camus, une vie,* 557), the concise nature of which suggests that he was more at ease there than, say, in the section on historical revolt. Indeed, the length of the latter section disguises, perhaps, a more acute anxiety on the writer's part to get his ideas across. (Camus, it should be remembered, was not a trained historian.) Fernande Bartfeld highlights Camus's "concern not to separate moral and philosophical preoccupations from aesthetic thought" in texts contemporaneous with the writing of *The Rebel* (Fernande Bartfeld, "Camus en 1945–1946: autour de quelques textes peu connus," *Europe* 77 [1999]: 57–58). For his part, Edouard Morot-Sir offers some further interesting thoughts on the structure of the book in "*L'Homme révolté:* entre non et oui," in *AC12,* 35–64. At this juncture, it is useful to point out that in what follows, my main objective—in accordance with the terms of reference of the present study—will be to offer, through the lens of justice, an assessment of the "problematic" section detailing historical revolt, although this task will also involve drawing on material from the chapter dealing with metaphysical revolt. An analysis of "Rebellion and Art" is beyond the scope of this book. However, I have already had cause to touch on that section in an earlier discussion of Camus's views on art (cf. above, chapter 1, 38–41).

15. Hegel's dialectical logic finds expression in the pioneering *Phenomenology of Spirit* (1807), in which he argues that all human relations can be reduced to the alliance between the master (domination) and the slave (submission) in the mutual struggle for recognition. For Hegel, both master and slave each strive for epistemo-

logical autonomy in relation to the other, so that interdependence is a crucial feature of the struggle for supremacy. However, Nietzsche, whose opposition between "good and bad" (master and slave) finds expression in incipient form in *The Gay Science* (1882) and then again in *On the Genealogy of Morality* (1887), breaks with Hegelian dialectics and sides with the master in his exposition of a system of values which defends the right of the strong to overcome the weak.

16. Maurice Weyembergh, "Révolte et ressentiment," in *AC12,* 65–82.

17. Thody, *Albert Camus: 1913–1960,* 136. Eric Werner has usefully demonstrated how in *The Rebel,* Camus draws on Hegelian reasoning to first illustrate and then reject the idea of historical determinism (Eric Werner, *De la violence au totalitarisme: essai sur la pensée de Camus et de Sartre* [Paris: Calmann-Lévy, 1972], 81–97). As a matter of interest, Camus first speaks publicly of Hegel's dialectical logic in "The Human Crisis," a lecture delivered to an audience at Columbia University in March 1946. He incorporates the Hegelian leitmotiv of that speech into the introductory chapter of the 1951 work (cf. Camus, "The Human Crisis," 165–66; and *E,* 415; *TR,* 13).

18. Anthony Bower's English translation of *The Rebel* (*TR*) is riddled with inaccuracies, as Konrad Bieber has rightly pointed out (see Konrad Bieber, "*Tradut-tore, traditore:* la réception problématique de 'L'Homme révolté' aux États-Unis," in *AC19,* 143–48). However, in this study, I will continue to make references to the Bower text, making amendments to the translation as and when deemed necessary.

19. There is continuity in Camus's thinking between *The Myth of Sisyphus* and *The Rebel,* in that in both works he points up the notion of "tension" as an ideal attitude to, respectively, the Absurd and Revolt. As we shall see later, the idea of "equivalence," inextricably bound up with that of "tension" and already well to the fore in Camus's pursuit of a dialogic ethic incorporating both justice and freedom, will be further developed in his quest for an "ethical justification of justice."

20. For an interesting reading of the short story "The Silent Men" as a fictionalization of Camus's theory of revolt and of the problem of maintaining an ethical balance between affirmation and negation it entails, see Jill Capstick, "Mastery or Slavery: The Ethics of Revolt in Camus's 'Les Muets,'" *Modern & Contemporary France* 11 (2003): 453–62. As this critic perceptively remarks, "Camus's fictional representation of the *pensée de midi* in Yvars can be seen to reveal the intrinsic difficulty of a relativistic approach to revolt which shrinks back from the inevitability of ethical failure" (461).

21. Interestingly, Camus appears to take a slightly different stance in his formulations on revolt and revolution in *Combat* in September 1944 by comparison with the ideas conceptualized in the "Remark" the following year. Indeed, in *Combat,* there is no "yes" in the Resistance's "purity of total refusal" (*E,* 1526) although, in the 1945 work, Camus insists that the rebel "says at the same time *yes* and *no*" (*E,* 1682). It is also interesting to note the puzzling nature of Camus's reference to "concerted action" in *Combat* by which he defines "the moment of revolution" (*E,* 1526). The Resistance—perhaps as opposed to "resistance"—is certainly "concerted action," although he associates the notion of revolt (*not* revolution) with the clandestine organization. One suspects that the distinction Camus is groping for here is that between, on the one hand, negative (socially and politically) destructive action—"concerted" or not—and, on the other hand, (social and political) construction or reconstruction.

22. Cf. *E,* 1709: "in order to reject organized terror and policing, revolution needs to keep intact the principle of revolt which gave birth to it, as revolt itself needs a revolutionary direction in order to find a body and a truth. Each, in the

end, is the limit of the other." Camus draws on similar phraseology in his 1953 preface to Alfred Rosmer's *Moscow in Lenin's Days* (*E,* 789).

23. Philip Thody, private correspondence with author, April 9, 1999. I would like to take this opportunity to thank the late Professor Thody for his useful information pertaining to the original publication of *The Rebel* in general.

24. Although a full account of Camus's interest in metaphysical revolt falls beyond the remit of the present study, it is essential to mention the issue here inasmuch as it represents, in his eyes, the spiritual impulse for historical revolt and the source of revolutionary justice.

25. In *The Plague,* Rieux rejects Paneloux's compassionate response to the death of the child Othon with the conviction that "until my dying day I shall refuse to love a scheme of things in which children are put to torture" (*TP,* 178). This view is reiterated in "The Unbeliever and Christians"(1947), where Camus speaks in his own name of the suffering of the innocent (*E,* 372; *RRD,* 50).

26. In accordance with Camus's claim that "the rebel defies more than he denies" (*TR,* 31), the question of God's existence is no longer an issue for Karamazov, who refuses to accept *any* justification for innocent suffering: "Ivan incarnates the refusal of salvation. Faith leads to immortal life, but faith presumes the acceptance of the mystery and of evil and resignation to injustice. . . . Under these conditions, even if eternal life existed, Ivan would refuse it" (*TR,* 51). However, when infected with nihilistic logic, Ivan's revolt against the divine order itself becomes a source of injustice, with far-reaching consequences in terms of twentieth-century political tyranny.

27. That Camus considers Dostoevsky (principally, though not exclusively, through the character of Ivan Karamazov) to be the true prophet of twentieth-century political nihilism and totalitarianism is further borne out by comments he makes in *Spectacles* in 1958: "For a long time we believed that Marx was the prophet of the 20th Century. We now know that his prophecy misfired. And we discover that the true prophet was Dostoevsky. He prophesied the reign of the Grand Inquisitors and the triumph of power over justice" (*TRN,* 1891). For a full assessment of the significance of Dostoevsky's rebels in the crystallization of Camus's understanding of revolutionary nihilism, see chapters 7 and 8 of Ray Davison's excellent *Camus: The Challenge of Dostoevsky,* 116–60.

28. The seminal role played by the German philosopher in Camus's thinking has already been noted. Cf. William E. Duvall, "The Nietzsche Temptation in the Thought of Albert Camus," *History of European Ideas* 11 (1989): 955–62; and Frantz Favre, "Quand Camus lisait Nietzsche," in *AC20,* 197–206. Portraits of both Nietzsche and Dostoevsky adorned the walls of Camus's flat on the rue de Chanaleilles in Paris (Lottman, *Albert Camus,* 580).

29. A further noteworthy example of how moral absolutism engenders tyranny and injustice is provided by Camus's reading of Sade (*E,* 447–57; *TR,* 32–43). For Camus, Sade's deification of desire, born of unfettered freedom, is seen to instill psychological servitude in a "fortress republic" (*TR,* 39). There is nothing in Sade's scheme to counterbalance the demand for freedom: no notion of justice enters his thinking, with the result that injustice pervades it. For a full assessment of Camus's interpretation of the marquis, see Raymond Gay-Crosier, "Camus et Sade: une relation ambiguë," *Zeitschrift für Französische Sprache und Literatur* 98 (1988): 166–73.

30. However, the parallel Camus makes between metaphysical and historical revolt fails to take into account a fundamental difference separating the two spheres (a criticism which, as we saw in chapter 1, can also be levelled against the Camus

of *The Plague*). Whereas the former allows human beings to fight together against the "unjust" divine order and thereby provide the potential for a unity of solidarity—an idea later formulated in "Reflections on the Guillotine" (*E,* 1056; *RRD,* 158)—the latter does not. Indeed, the idea of historical revolt appears to preclude absolute human solidarity and so compromises the neo-Cartesian postulate, "I *rebel*—therefore *we* exist" (*TR,* 28) on which Camus bases his ethic of revolt.

31. To the question of whether justice is either innate in human consciousness or a concept arising from social conventions, Rousseau posits the latter in his notion of social utopia. Saint-Just applied Rousseau's general will to the Revolution in France. Thus, contrary to what had occurred under the *ancien régime,* laws were reestablished under the revolutionaries to reflect the general will. However, the influence of the *Social Contract* on the French revolutionary consciousness has almost certainly been overstated: "Actually," notes Suzanne Hélein-Koss, "bibliographical investigations and statistics conducted in recent years reveal that the *Social Contract* was read very little before 1789. Admittedly, 'Rousseauism' existed before the Revolution, but then it was a question of a personal and moral cult based on the reading of the *New Heloise* and *Emile,* not on the reading of the *Social Contract* which was considered too abstract and too difficult" (Suzanne Hélein-Koss, "Albert Camus et le 'Contrat social,'" *Studies on Voltaire and the Eighteenth Century* 161 [1976]: 180). More to the point, Camus's own reading of Rousseau is questionable and noticeably selective. By pointing up the significance of what he calls "The New Gospel" as a precursor of such collective ideologies as Marxism, Leninism, and Stalinism (*E,* 523–26; *TR,* 84–87), he arguably distorts the *Social Contract* to suit the main line of argument advanced in *The Rebel.* In so doing, he fails to account for some striking points of convergence—not least as regards how best to reconcile the contradictory demands of justice and freedom—between his own moral position and that of his eighteenth-century predecessor. Two articles which should be noted concerning Camus's selective treatment of Rousseau are: Jorn Schosler, "Rousseau, Camus et le nihilisme: sur l'actualité de Rousseau," *Orbis Litterarum* 40 (1985): 97–110; and the aforementioned title by Hélein-Koss. The latter is particularly severe in highlighting Camus's (mis)use of Rousseau's ideas to reinforce his own argument, but the critic's approach is justified since it raises the whole issue of Camus's conceptual expediency in *The Rebel.* As Roger Quilliot observes in his comments on the research underpinning the book, "Camus read, read very much, not to know such and such an author better, but to find the confirmation of his argument" (*E,* 1624). In his infamous "Response to Albert Camus," Sartre would be more incriminating in his criticism of Camus's *modus operandi:* "what a habit you have of not going back to sources. . . . You hate conceptual difficulty and declare in haste that there is nothing to understand in order to avoid in advance the reproach of not having understood" (Sartre, "Réponse à Albert Camus," 344).

32. Susan Dunn, "Camus and Louis XVI: An Elegy for the Martyred King," *French Review* 62 (1989): 1034. Dunn argues that Camus was more attracted to the myth than to the reality of monarchy: "It is only in the idealistic context of a search which ultimately transcended political reality that he resuscitated the memory of the French monarchy. . . . Grace, the fundamental principle of monarchy, represented for Camus the ethical potential of politics" (1036, 1039). As the critic acknowledges, Camus's interpretation of divine kingship in *The Rebel* needs to be read in the context of his ongoing pursuit "to introduce the language of morality into the duties of politics" (*E,* 274).

33. Later, in his "Reflections on the Guillotine" (1957), Camus further rein-

forces the conviction that justice devoid of compassion is morally indefensible: "if justice has any meaning in this world, it means nothing but the recognition of . . . solidarity; it cannot, by its very essence, divorce itself from compassion" (*RRD,* 154). Cf. below, chapter 8, 197–200.

34. Denis Charbit also highlights the equally curious absence in *The Rebel* of an analysis of colonialism and Nazism, both of which justify violence as a means to an end, an issue increasingly anathema to Camus (Denis Charbit, "*L'Homme révolté:* grandeur et servitude de la fonction intellectuelle," in *AC19,* 33–35, 36, and 53n14.)

35. It has to be said that Camus's reading of Hegel (and Marx) in *The Rebel* smacks of oversimplification and misrepresentation. As was noted earlier in respect of his (mis)use of Rousseau (cf. note 31 above), Camus's questionable interpretations of Hegel's and Marx's respective historicisms appear more as reinforcements of his own thesis and less as an objective account of the ideologies at issue.

36. Hegel's historicism is comprehensively explored in J. Sibree, trans., *Hegel: The Philosophy of History* (New York: Dover, 1956). For useful elucidations of the ideas at issue see, for instance, George Dennis O'Brien, *Hegel on Reason and History: A Contemporary Interpretation* (Chicago: University of Chicago Press, 1975); Joseph McCarney, *Hegel on History* (London: Routledge, 2000); and Roger Scruton et al., *German Philosophers* (Oxford: Oxford University Press, 1997), 123–38.

37. McCarney, *Hegel on History,* 206–7. Cf., 215: "Because all shall be well; that is to say, the 'all' that is presupposed, or implied, by the achievement of freedom, all is already well here and now. . . . Things in general, one might say, are as they ought to be because they are on the way to being what they ought to be. Their present state is wholly appropriate to their place in the overall pattern."

38. Pisarev began the process of intellectual terrorism in his pursuit of political expediency; Bakunin—anticipating Lenin—hoped to see a dictatorship that alone would create freedom for all Russia (a totalitarian scheme requiring absolute submission to the revolutionary government); and Netchaev sets the scene for all subsequent totalitarian regimes in his total sacrifice to the revolutionary cause: "The revolutionary is a man condemned in advance. He must have neither emotional relationships nor objects or loved ones. He should even cast off his own name. Every part of him should be concentrated in one single passion: the revolution" (*TR,* 129; translation amended).

39. Actually, as Dora acknowledges in *The Just Assassins,* this balance is not an absolute one, since "throwing the bomb and then climbing the scaffold, . . . that's giving one's life twice . . . so we give more than we take" (*CP,* 133).

40. Jean Sarocchi, "Les Fureurs adolescents," in Walker, ed., *Albert Camus: les Extrêmes et l'équilibre,* 11.

41. Willhoite, *Beyond Nihilism,* 158. Cruickshank, *Albert Camus and the Literature of Revolt,* 107–8.

42. Jean-Jacques Brochier, *Albert Camus: philosophe pour classes terminales* (Paris: Balland, 1979), 27.

43. "Le Temps des Meurtriers," a lecture delivered by Camus on July 23, 1949, during his visit to Latin America (June—August 1949), quoted in Fernande Bartfeld, *Albert Camus: voyageur et conférencier; Le voyage en Amérique du Sud,* Archives Albert Camus 7 (Paris: Lettres Modernes, 1995), 69.

44. It is almost as if "The Fastidious Assassins" represent, for Camus, the moment of "revolt" rather than "revolution," or of "resistance" rather than "reconstruction."

45. For engaging discussions of Camus's somewhat dubious claims about Marxism, see Wolfgang Klein, "Des révolutionnaires cyniques? Camus sur Hegel, Marx et Lénine," in *AC15,* 123–51; Eveline Pisier and Pierre Bouretz, "Camus et le marxisme," in Guérin, ed., *Camus et la politique,* 269–80; and Bruce K. Ward, "Prometheus or Cain? Albert Camus's account of the western quest for justice," *Faith and Philosophy* 8 (1991): 193–213.

46. Quoted in Grenier, ed., *À Albert Camus, ses amis du livre,* 53.

47. Not surprisingly, Camus also gives short shrift to the inheritors of Marxist theory—Lenin and Stalin—who take the idea of unconditional allegiance to the state to its extremes. Lenin, "passionate lover of justice" (*TR,* 198), predicates his revolutionary vision on a philosophy of state imperialism which "contrives the acceptance of injustice, crime, and falsehood by the promise of a miracle" (*TR,* 199). Such logic would be enshrined under Stalin in his punitive system of forced labor. See Charbit, "*L'Homme révolté:* grandeur et servitude de la fonction intellectuelle," 35–39.

48. Maurice Weyembergh, "A. Camus et K. Popper: la critique de l'historisme et de l'historicisme," in *AC9,* 43–63. K. R. Popper, *The Open Society and its Enemies,* vol. 1, *The Spell of Plato,* rev. ed. (1945; repr., London: Routledge & Kegan Paul, 1966), 2. Both Popper and Camus denounce the Marxist revolutionary prophecy as dictatorship of the state and conclude that a "politics of moderation," implemented through democratic reform, must be allowed to prevail if politically progressive thought is to be rescued from nihilism and tyranny.

49. Quoted in David McLellan, *Marx* (Glasgow: Fontana / Collins, 1975), 28.

50. Ibid., 65; and cf. Scruton et al, *German Philosophers,* 156–61.

51. Although warmly received by right-wing critics, the book was largely derided by the contemporary (pro-Marxist) left. It is worth noting the details of the notorious controversy following the publication of the book between Camus and *Les Temps modernes,* that Michel Contat and Michel Rybalka deem "doubtless one of the great moments of French intellectual life in the postwar period" (Michel Contat and Michel Rybalka, eds., *Les Écrits de Sartre* [Paris: Gallimard, 1970], 251): Francis Jeanson, "Albert Camus ou l'âme révoltée," *Les Temps modernes* 79 (1952): 2070–90; Albert Camus, "Lettre au Directeur des *Temps modernes,*" *Les Temps modernes* 82 (1952): 317–33, reprinted as "Revolt and Servitude," in *E,* 754–74; Jean-Paul Sartre, "Réponse à Albert Camus," *Les Temps modernes* 82 (1952): 334–53, reprinted in Jean-Paul Sartre, *Situations IV* (Paris: Gallimard, 1964), 90–125; and Francis Jeanson, "Pour tout vous dire," *Les Temps modernes* 82 (1952): 354–83. English translations of these articles are available in David A. Sprintzen and Adrian van den Hoven, eds., *Sartre and Camus: A Historic Confrontation* (Amherst, N.Y.: Humanity Books, 2004), which also contains essays on the encounter written from both "Camusian" and "Sartrean" perspectives. It would be presumptuous to claim to be able to further the understanding of this polemic, the details of which have been expertly assimilated by, among others, Georges Bataille, "L'Affaire de *L'Homme révolté,*" *Critique* 8 (1952): 1077–81; André Blanchet, "La vie littéraire: la querelle Sartre-Camus," *Études* 85 (1952): 238–46; and Pierre de Boisdeffre, "La fin d'une amitié: Sartre contre Camus," *La Revue Libre* 1 (1952): 51–57. The legacy of the controversy has also been explored by Bernard Murchland, "Sartre and Camus: The Anatomy of a Quarrel," in *Choice of Action: The French Existentialists on the Political Front Line,* trans. Bernard Murchland (New York: Random House, 1968), 175–96; Ian Birchill, "Camus contre Sartre: quarante ans plus tard," in Walker, ed., *Albert Camus: les Extrêmes et l'équilibre,* 129–50; and, more recently, Ronald Aronson, *Camus and Sartre: The*

Story of a Friendship and the Quarrel that Ended It (Chicago: University of Chicago Press, 2004). Todd, too, provides a useful conspectus of this, and other, polemics surrounding *The Rebel* in *Albert Camus, une vie,* 555–72. To these titles should be added Jonathan H. King's "Sartre-Camus: The Quarrel as Biography," *French Cultural Studies* 5 (1994): 39–56, that offers an interesting alternative interpretation of the polemic from the perspective of Sartrean biographical diagnosis.

52. Sunil Khilnani, *Arguing Revolution: The Intellectual Left in Postwar France* (Newhaven, CT: Yale University Press, 1993), 61–62. Sartre's biographer notes that "he wrote these texts mechanically, grabbing them with all the violence of his hatred for the bourgeoisie" (Cohen-Solal, *Sartre: 1905–1980,* 432).

The essay was subsequently reprinted in Sartre's *Situations VI: problèmes du marxisme, I* (Paris: Gallimard, 1964), 80–384.

53. Sartre's uneasy alliance with Communism and Marxism is comprehensively examined by Max Adereth in "Sartre and Communism," *Journal of European Studies* 17 (1987): 1–48. As he would observe in 1961, "anyone opposed to Communism is a cur, I am not going outside that and will never do so" (Jean-Paul Sartre, "Merleau-Ponty vivant," in his *Situations IV* [Paris: Gallimard, 1964], 248–49).

54. As he puts it in his missive to Sartre, "my book does not deny history (a negation that would be senseless) but just examines the attitude that aims at making history into an absolute. So it isn't history that is rejected, but a frame of mind in relation to history" (*E,* 762; cf. *E,* 351; and *Corr,* 116). For a full account of Camus's engagement with history as a process of evolution, see Françoise Trageser-Rebetez, "Paradigme cyclique dans la philosophie camusienne de l'Histoire," in *AC19,* 55–89. Jean-Paul Sartre, "La nationalisation de la littérature," *Les Temps modernes* 1 (October 1945–February 1946): 200.

55. As he tells his erstwhile companion in what jars with Camus's own terminology, "you have become the victim of a dreary excessiveness which conceals your inner difficulties and that you call, I believe, Mediterranean moderation," (Sartre, "Réponse à Albert Camus," 334, 345).

56. Ibid.

57. Arlette Elkaïm-Sartre, ed., *Jean-Paul Sartre: Critique de la raison dialectique précédé de Questions de méthode,* vol. 1, rev. ed. (1960; repr. Paris: Gallimard, 1985). The ideas articulated in this voluminous work first find concrete expression in "Materialism and Revolution," a series of articles published by Sartre in *Les Temps modernes* in 1946, at which point Camus was preparing his own—entirely different—intellectual history of revolution.

Although in his "Response to Albert Camus," Sartre does not dwell on Marxist historical materialism as such, a revealing footnote makes his fundamentally pro-Marxist stance clear: "I do not have to defend Marx's ideas but allow me to tell you that the dilemma in which you claim to enclose them (either his 'prophecies' are true or Marxism is only a manual) overlooks the whole Marxist philosophy and everything which for me (who is not a Marxist) constitutes its deep truth" (Sartre, "Réponse à Albert Camus," 343n1). However, it is worth noting that Sartre would break all ties he had with Marxism shortly before his death; his attempt in the *Critique* to revitalize Marxism through existentialism would end in failure.

58. L'IMEC, f. AC. "Correspondance: Lecteurs de *Combat* (1944–47)."

59. Quoted in Todd, *Albert Camus, une vie,* 557.

60. Quoted in a letter Camus addresses to Jean Gillibert dated July 19, 1952, quoted in *Revue d'Histoire du Théâtre* 12 (1960): 355.

61. It is worth recalling that a yearning for intellectual regeneration in the wake

of *The Rebel*'s publication is a recurrent theme in Camus's notebooks and correspondence from the time (see *C2,* 324, 343, 345; *CA2,* 167, 176, 177; and *E,* 1627). Cf. Charbit, "*L'Homme révolté:* grandeur et servitude de la fonction intellectuelle," 25: "*The Rebel* . . . is a book of heartbreak and indignation. However it is from this critical but not joyful assumption that it is then possible to conceive of a future revival."

62. I am mindful of the distinction between "confession" and "therapy," since the former may or may not be an attempt at the latter. Purging himself of his earlier moral idealism at the time of the purge is one possible motive behind *The Rebel,* but Camus also seems to have needed some kind of recognition of his ideas.

63. See note 9 above.

64. Cruickshank, *Albert Camus and the Literature of Revolt,* 116. According to Dr Jacques Ménétrier (who was treating Camus's tuberculosis at the time of the composition of the work and who prescribed his patient a series of minerals), "the final pages of [*The Rebel*], a hymn to life seemingly unrelated to the earlier sections of the book, were the work of a rejuvenated patient prepared to live once more" (quoted in Lottman, *Albert Camus,* 485). This evidence, although anecdotal, puts another interesting gloss on the view that, in one sense, *The Rebel* is a very therapeutic book. Interestingly, Camus himself draws on medicinal phraseology in a comment on the structure of the work (*E,* 752). Jacques Chabot offers a reading of *The First Man*—itself a highly therapeutic work—through the lens of *la pensée solaire,* so that Camus's unfinished autobiographical project becomes a vehicle for fleshing out the ethical potential of authentic revolt (Jacques Chabot, "La mémoire des pauvres," *Roman 20–50* 27 [1999]: 65–76).

65. Raymond Gay-Crosier, "La révolte génératrice et régénératrice," in *OFOO,* 130.

66. However, in his quest for "an ethical justification of justice" by which to respond to modern revolutionary nihilism, Camus does not rule out the possibility of finding the "answer" in a Christian-based humanism. Indeed, during the composition of *The Rebel,* would he not confide to the *Carnets*—in a borrowing from the Catholic philosopher Jacques Maritain—that "'Sainthood is also a revolt: it involves refusing things as they are. It means taking upon oneself the grief of the world'" (*CA2,* 154)? I am not suggesting that Camus himself was about to become a "born again Christian"; on the contrary, although he welcomed "the usefulness of the dialogue between believer and unbeliever" (*RRD,* 49), Camus maintained that he felt "closer to the values of the ancient world than to Christian ones" (*E,* 1343; cf. *C2,* 233; *CA2,* 120; and *E,* 380, 1615). Nevertheless, we may note in passing that despite his own different mindset, Camus retained an intellectual respect for Saint Augustine—like himself a son of the Mediterranean (cf. *E,* 1342)—whose Manicheanism seemed to offer a solution to the problem of evil. (Paneloux's sermons in *The Plague* may usefully be examined through the optic of Augustinian thought.) For a comparative account of Camus's dialog and debate with Saint Augustine, see Paul Archambault, *Camus's Hellenic Sources* (Chapel Hill: University of North Carolina Press, 1972), 137–67. For more on Camus's contemplation of Christian ethics as a possible antidote to the modern crisis, see Ward, "Prometheus or Cain?"; and cf. by the same writer, "The Recovery of Helen: Albert Camus's attempt to restore the Greek idea of nature," *Dionysius* 14 (1990): 169–94. The latter article, which will inform parts of the present discussion, offers a comprehensive account of Camus's bid to find in the Hellenic vision a remedy for the revolutionary excesses of modernity.

67. See, in particular, Archambault, *Camus's Hellenic Sources;* and François

Bousquet, *Camus le Méditerranéen, Camus l'Ancien* (Sherbrooke: Naaman, 1977). Camus organizes the three "cycles" of his work around, chronologically, the Greek myths of Sisyphus, Prometheus, and Nemesis (*C2,* 328; *CA2,* 168) in accordance with his concession that "the world in which I am most *at ease:* Greek myth" (*CA2,* 163). It is worth recalling that in April 1955, Camus finally traveled to Greece (the outbreak of the Second World War had prevented him from taking on a similar voyage in September 1939). His correspondence and notebooks from the time attest to the personal value he derives from this pilgrimage to the cradle of (Mediterranean) civilization. As he explains to Jean Grenier in a letter dated May 6, 1955, "I needed . . . Greece and this really strong feeling of space that it gives me. Like a prisoner and who suddenly finds himself on a bare mountain which stands out in the middle of the sky. Yes, I can breathe" (*Corr,* 200).

68. See, for instance, G. S. Kirk and J. E. Raven, *The Presocratic Philosophers* (Cambridge: Cambridge University Press, 1957); and Jonathan Barnes, *Early Greek Philosophy* (London: Penguin, 1987).

The idea of a "Mediterranean enlightenment," we recall, provided the intellectual impetus of *L'École d'Alger,* a movement launched in the mid-1930s by Gabriel Audisio offering an alternative configuration of colonial coexistence to that supported by the *Algérianistes* (see chapters 4 and 5 of Peter Dunwoodie's *Writing French Algeria,* 125–217). Speaking in February 1937 in honor of the Algiers-based "Maison de la Culture," where one discovers the roots of "la pensée de midi," Camus himself champions Mediterranean collectivism as a means by which to transcend racial antagonism (*E,* 1321–27). Accordingly, to posit, as Camus does in *The Rebel,* "la pensée de midi" as an antidote to the moral crisis portrayed in what the writer himself deems "a study of *the ideological aspect* of revolutions" (*E,* 759; my italics) smacks of inconsistency, since it is itself grounded in the ideology of "Mediterraneanism." For an engaging account of how Camus engenders the myth of Mediterraneanism throughout his lifetime, see Ray Davison, "Mythologizing the Mediterranean: The Case of Albert Camus," *Journal of Mediterranean Studies* 10 (2000): 77–92.

69. Salas, *Albert Camus: la juste révolte,* 106.

70. Cf. *SEN,* 90: "if there is a sin against life, it lies perhaps less in despairing of it than in hoping for another life, and evading the implacable grandeur of the one we have." "O my soul, do not aspire to immortal life, but exhaust the limits of the possible" (*MS,* 3; cf. *CA1,* 95).

71. The emphasis here on the idea of "living justice" recalls Kaliayev's moral imperative: "I love those who are alive today who walk on the same earth as I do. It is for them that I am fighting. . . . I shall not strike my brothers in the face for the sake of some unknown, distant city. I refuse to add to the living injustice around me for the sake of a dead justice" (*CP,* 143; translation amended).

72. It is interesting to note that in his rejection of justice and freedom as moral absolutes, Camus levels criticism at (Soviet) communism and (American) capitalism which is both theoretical *and* historical in nature. Not only does he raise the classic theoretical question of whether the end justifies the means, but he also disputes the justification of the ends themselves of what, in Camus's eyes, are two radically opposed, yet equally sinister, political ideologies. As he observes during an interview with *La Patrie mondiale* in December 1948, "imperialisms are like twins, they grow together and cannot live without one another" (*E,* 1587; cf. Todd, *Albert Camus, une vie,* 748).

73. Raymond Gay-Crosier, "Les enjeux de la pensée de midi," in Fernande Bartfeld and David Ohana, eds., "Albert Camus: parcours méditerranéens," *Perspectives: Revue de l'Université Hébraïque de Jérusalem* 5 (1998): 98.

74. In "On the Future of Tragedy," a speech delivered in Athens in 1955 (*TRN,* 1701–11; *SEN,* 192–203), Camus likewise spotlights "limit" as "the constant theme of classical tragedy" (*SEN,* 196). He maintains that the essence of tragedy, originating from "the genius of Greece" (*SEN,* 203), lies in the tension between opposing forces "each of which wears the double mask of good and evil" (*SEN,* 197). It is in Sophocles, Camus submits, that the equilibrium between human assertiveness and divine forces reaches its zenith. As we shall presently discover, the idea of maintaining a balanced tension between opposites is a further crucial factor in Camus's ethical understanding of justice.

75. One noteworthy example of this idea in practice is Camus's 1956 "Appeal for a Civilian Truce in Algeria" by which, as we shall discover in the following chapter, he attempts to humanize political confrontation. However, the failure of that initiative points up what are considerable internal weaknesses in Camus's moral philosophy of "limit." For instance, on what ethical criteria (besides the rather imprecise notion of "human identity" [*TR,* 250]) is the notion to be based? How does one determine which actions transgress the proposed limitation? Who or what implements the philosophy? And what penalties are to be imposed in the event of the boundary being breached? On such crucial issues, Camus remains largely silent.

76. Thomas H. Warren, "On the Mistranslation of 'La Mesure' in Camus's Political Thought," *Journal of the History of Philosophy* 1 (1992): 123–30. Warren takes issue with the fact that in the only English edition of *The Rebel* currently in print *la mesure* is, according to this critic, erroneously translated as "moderation." He highlights, with just cause, "the stultifying implications of applying 'moderation' to the other values Camus defends, such as freedom, justice, and love" (130). *Sophrosyne* connotes not "moderation," Warren argues, but ideas such as "measuredness," "limit," "harmony," and "proportion." This interpretation is in keeping with the notion of "tension" which, as we shall presently confirm, is fundamental to Camus's moral position.

77. See Walker, ed., *Albert Camus: les Extrêmes et l'équilibre.*

78. Noteworthy examples include: *Nuptials,* where the idea of equivalence is inherent in remarks such as "this *marriage* between ruins and springtime" (*SEN,* 70; my italics); "the *nuptials* between human beings and the earth" (*SEN,* 90; translation amended; my italics); and "what is happiness except *the simple harmony* between human beings and the life they lead?" (*SEN,* 98; translation amended; my italics); *The Myth of Sisyphus,* where a balanced tension sustains "this confrontation between the human need and the unreasonable silence of the world" (*MS,* 32); *Letters to a German Friend,* where Camus pursues "*a just equilibrium* between sacrifice and a longing for happiness, between the sword and the spirit" (*RRD,* 19; translation amended; my italics); *The Just Assassins,* where a moral equilibrium is reached through the concept of "redemptive death"; and the retrospective preface to *Betwixt and Between,* where Camus envisages a future work—*The First Man*—characterized by "the admirable silence of a mother and the effort of a man to *rediscover a justice* or a love which *matches* this silence" (*SEN,* 26; my italics).

79. Ward, "The Recovery of Helen," 184–86. Hazel E. Barnes, "Balance and tension in the Philosophy of Camus," *Personalist* 41 (1960): 434.

Heraclitus, whose presence (albeit implicit) underscores Camus's general predilection for antithetical ideas, was a philosopher who posited that the apparent unity and stability of the world conceals a tension of opposites, measured and controlled by reason (*Logos*) or its physical manifestation, fire (see Kirk & Raven, *The Preso-*

cratic Philosophers, 182–215). It is said that Hegelian dialectics owe much to Heraclitean reasoning.

80. Ward, "Recovery of Helen," 188.

81. It is ironic that a culture which is apparently predicated on the principle of *la mesure* fails to preserve an appropriate balance between human freedom and social equality in its own interpersonal morality.

82. See note 7 above; and cf. Agnès Spiquel, "Némésis, une 'pensée de midi'?," in Bartfeld and Ohana, eds., "Albert Camus: parcours méditerranéens," 199–212. See also Grenier, *Albert Camus (Souvenirs),* 133–37 and Paulhan, ed., *Jean Grenier: Carnets 1944–1971,* 111. Herbert Lottman reports that shortly before his death, Camus was assembling a series of notes with the title "For Nemesis," a reference to the long-planned work which, according to Robert Cérésol, Camus deemed "'my return to pre-Socratism'" (Lottman, *Albert Camus,* 656–57). It is no coincidence that in the summer of 1959, Camus informed Claude Vigée of his longing to return to Greece for spiritual inspiration (Claude Vigée, "De *Noces* à 'La Femme adultère': la quête de la lumière cachée dans la pensée d'Albert Camus," in Bartfeld and Ohana, eds., "Albert Camus: parcours méditerranéens," 227). A substantial dossier, "Némésis," is deposited at L'IMEC (f. AC. GO7 [8–14]).

83. Cf. Ward, "Recovery of Helen," 183: "Even in ancient Greece, Nemesis would appear to have been a relatively vague and abstract figure, more a moral symbol than an individualized deity. It is perhaps this very lack of concreteness which makes her appeal to Camus as the personification of an idea which, in the latter part of his life, he was striving to articulate in a form worthy of it." See, too, Crochet, *Les Mythes dans l'œuvre de Camus,* 79–87.

For contemporary critical accounts of *The Rebel,* see, in particular, Albert Béguin, "*L'Homme révolté* d'Albert Camus," *Études* 272 (1952): 48–60; and Roger Dadoun, "Albert Camus le méditerranéen: le rêve de la lumière et le complexe du clair-obscur," *Simoun* 3 (1952): 42–47.

84. Ian Birchall, "The Labourism of Sisyphus: Albert Camus and revolutionary syndicalism," *Journal of European Studies* 20 (1990): 151. Exploring what he perceives as his subject's "peculiar blend of pragmatic reformism and revolutionary syndicalism" (160), Birchall provides a comprehensive assessment of Camus's lifelong leanings toward libertarian socialism, which appear to be in contradiction with his popular image as a man whose politics are fundamentally those of a moderate social democrat. For further elucidations of Camus's "syndicalist sympathies," see Peter Dunwoodie, "Albert Camus and the Anarchist Alternative," *Australian Journal of French Studies* 30 (1993): 84–103; and Raymond Gay-Crosier, "L'Anarchisme mesuré de Camus," *Symposium* 24 (1970): 243–53. For an exploration of Camus's anarchist allegiances in his imaginative works, see Roger Dadoun, "Albert Camus: fondations d'anarchie," in Guérin, ed., *Camus et la politique,* 257–67. The "origins" of such a disposition may reasonably be traced to Camus's uncle, the butcher Gustave Acault, who "had been a militant anarchist in the Belle Époque of anarchy" (Grenier, *Albert Camus [Souvenirs],* 76).

85. Quoted in Roger Quilliot, *La Mer et les prisons: essais sur Albert Camus,* rev. ed. (Paris: Gallimard, 1970), 242n26. See Cocking, trans., "Britain after the Election."

86. Cf. below, chapter 8, 181–85.

87. In the remaining section of his speech, Camus goes on to highlight that "separating freedom from justice is tantamount to separating culture and labour" (*RRD,* 70), a state of affairs that he deems "the epitome of social sin" (*RRD,* 70).

He submits that preserving the link between economic labor and intellectual freedom best serves the interests of justice. Cf. *EX,* 133–36.

88. In the light of events in eastern Europe during the latter half of the twentieth century, *The Rebel* has come to be considered a work of political foresight by many critics, especially in respect of its anti-Marxist message. See, for instance, Bertrand Poirot-Delpech, "Justice pour Camus," *Le Monde,* August 5, 1977, 11; and Pisier and Bouretz, "Camus et le marxisme." However, not surprisingly, Camus remains largely out of favor in the former Soviet Union: see Isabelle Cielens, "La réception d'Albert Camus en Lettonie sous l'occupation soviétique," in Abbou, ed., *Albert Camus et l'Europe.* Brée, *Camus,* 55.

89. As Lottman reports, "there is indisputable evidence that Jeanson's review in Sartre's magazine surprised, shocked, and pained Camus, no matter how inevitable it may seem to the observer removed from it in time. If in retrospect the split between Camus and the Sartrians also appears inevitable, somehow it was not so to Camus, who at the time took the event as a disappointed lover might; he was clearly reacting to an unexpected blow" (Lottman, *Albert Camus,* 502). Cf. Beauvoir, *La Force des choses,* 1:353–55; and Paulhan, ed., *Jean Grenier: Carnets 1944–1971,* 123–24.

Although, as we have seen, it is possible to read *The Rebel* as confessional therapy, Clamence's "calculated confession"—an attempt to claim superiority over others by self-accusation—is based on a totally different mindset to that in force in the essay. Clamence lusts for power over others and—unlike Camus, who genuinely "confesses" in *The Rebel* in order to cleanse his earlier misguided idealism—uses his false avowal to win power over others. In a sense, Clamence represents the subconscious residue of the psychological impact upon Camus made by the hostile reception of *The Rebel.* Camus genuinely confessed, but it was badly received; Clamence's confession is not genuine and, if well received, actually deceives and enslaves others. Viewed in this perspective, the bad press which *The Rebel* receives more than counteracts any therapeutic effect that the book might accord Camus personally. For a reading of *The Fall* in the light of (the polemic of) *The Rebel,* see Warren Tucker, "*La Chute:* voie du salut terrestre," *French Review* 43 (1970): 737–44. And, for an engaging account of the rhetoric of seduction in *The Fall,* see Jean Sarocchi, "Clamence séducteur?," *Europe* 77 (1999): 119–31.

One need only look to the "Letters on Revolt," a series of polemical pieces defending the arguments advanced in *The Rebel* and which Camus deems fit to include in *Actuelles II,* for further confirmation of the value he accords the work (*E,* 729–74).

90. Quoted in Todd, *Albert Camus, une vie,* 573.

Chapter 8. Crisis and Reappraisal

1. Self-doubt and disillusionment are recurrent themes in Camus's contemporary correspondence and notebooks: see, for instance, his letter of November 22, 1951, addressed to Maria Casarès, quoted in Todd, *Albert Camus, une vie,* 557; and cf. *C3,* 30, 30–31, 32, 42, 43, 44, 50, 59, 60–61, 75–77, 80. In July 1954, Camus would confide to Roger Quilliot that he had been unable to work at all during the preceding six months due to pressing personal problems (Lottman, *Albert Camus,* 531, 537).

2. Carl A. Viggiani, "Fall and Exile: Camus, 1956–1958," in Gay-Crosier, ed., *Albert Camus 1980,* 269.

3. Cf. Jeanyves Guérin, "Camus, homme de gauche," *Revue Politique et Parlementaire* (March–April 1988): 76–83.

4. Camus explains to Jean Grenier that "The Renegade" is essentially the story of "the intellectual turned Communist . . . , the intellectual who ends up by adoring the religion of evil" (quoted in Paulhan, ed., *Jean Grenier,* 197–98). *The Fall* offers a satirical portrayal of left-wing intellectuals as Camus now sees them. Cf. Parker, *Albert Camus: The Artist in the Arena,* 160.

5. See Jean-Paul Sartre, "Le Fantôme de Staline," *Les Temps modernes* 12 (July 1956–January 1957): 577–696. Cf. *E,* 1772: "When a worker, somewhere in the world, raises his bare fists in front of a tank and shouts that he is not a slave, what are we then if we remain indifferent?"

Cf. *E,* 1777: "these people having risen up, having had enough humiliation and having been assassinated, I would despise myself for risking the slightest reservation and for expressing before their sacrifice anything other than my respect and absolute solidarity."

For a useful *mise au point* of Camus's reception in Hungary, see Andor Horváth, "'Restituer Dieu à lui-même': lectures hongroises d'Albert Camus," in *AC20,* 133–47.

6. However, Camus's antitotalitarianism goes *some* way toward defending him against charges of self-contradiction here, since it is arguable that French rule in Algeria was not totalitarian in nature. There may well still be contradictions in his attitude to "colonialism" but, as we saw in chapter 4, colonialism as such poses insoluable questions for Camus.

7. Martin was already exonerated by the time Sartre's pamphlet on the affair was finally published (Jean-Paul Sartre, *L'Affaire Henri Martin* [Paris: Gallimard, 1953]).

8. It is worth noting that Camus was equally dismissive of political extremism on both the right and left in France although, as we saw in the preceding chapter, he was especially concerned with Marxist-Leninists whose quest for absolute justice he deems a formula for tyranny. One noteworthy manifestation of right-wing absolutism to which Camus was very acutely sensitive is Francoism, his invectives against which were now given added urgency following the admission, in June 1952, of the Spanish dictator to UNESCO (cf. the dossier established by Roger Quilliot in *E,* 1789–1816; *EX,* 101–4; EX, 122–24; and *EX,* 181–85).

9. As Camus puts it in the second of his acceptance speeches at the time of the Nobel Honors in 1957, the artist, "engaged in the business of his/her time," is conditioned by "an obligatory military service" (*E,* 1079).

10. See, for instance, Cobban, *History of Modern France,* 3:210–26.

11. Founded in May 1953 by Jean-Jacques Servan-Schreiber, *L'Express* was cast from a broadly anticolonialist mold, but actually welcomed a range of political perspectives. Along with Camus, François Mauriac and André Malraux were notable bylines. Camus's contributions (collected and annotated by Paul Smets in Cahiers Albert 6 [*EX*]) deal primarily, but not exclusively, with the issue of the Algerian War.

12. I shall return later to the notion of "true justice" raised by these remarks.

13. Camus hopes (in vain) that Mendès-France would lead a constitution in which trade unions played a role in socioeconomic policy-making decisions (*EX,* 108–10). Although himself not a socialist and so perhaps not an "obvious" candidate for Camus to support, Mendès-France, campaigning on a liberal reformist ticket, represented "for the time being the only chance of improvement and progress for our society" (*EX,* 146). And, as Camus explains in private correspondence

with Charles Poncet dated December 7, 1955, the Radical leader's reformative plans including free elections for what was envisaged as a revamped French Algeria rendered him "the only one able to launch solutions which suit us and which respect equally the rights of Arabs and those of the French" (quoted in Yves Courrière, "Camus devant la Guerre d'Algérie," *Le Figaro littéraire* [June 2–8, 1969]: 11). Given the magnitude of these hopes, it is not surprising that Camus could not disguise his disappointment when the election results confirmed the collapse of Mendès-France's proposed republican alliance (*EX,* 153). In the event, the task of forming the new administration would fall to Guy Mollet who, according to Jean Daniel, "Camus felt would bring no good to Algeria" (Lottman, *Albert Camus,* 558). It is no coincidence that Camus left *L'Express* soon after the defeat of Mendès-France (Jean Daniel, "Parlons de lui," *L'Express,* January 7, 1960, 29).

14. Unlike Sartre, of course, who, in "The Communists and Peace," declared his allegiance to the proletariat and his faith in Marxist-Leninism by which he hoped to see the liberation of the working classes from capitalist oppression. Cf. Adereth, "Sartre and Communism."

15. Cf. Grenier, *Albert Camus,* 53.

16. Taken from Hargreaves's entry, "Algerian War," in *The New Oxford Companion to Literature in French,* ed. Peter France (Oxford: Clarendon Press, 1995), 22. Among the myriad of publications on the Algerian Civil War, see, in particular, the four volumes of Yves Courrière, *La Guerre d'Algérie,* (Paris: Fayard, 1968–71), especially vol. 2, *Le Temps des léopards* (1969); and Alistair Horne, *Savage War of Peace.* To these titles may be added Philip Dine's *Images of the Algerian War: French Fiction and Film, 1954–92* (Oxford: Clarendon Press, 1994), that provides a seminal account of literary and cinematic representations of the Algerian crisis.

17. See Cobban, *History of Modern France,* 3:221–26. It is important to remember that, unlike France's other former colonies, Algeria consisted of French-styled *départements,* so that the mother country could not abandon the province without at the same time triggering considerable constitutional changes. While laws passed in Paris were by no means automatically implemented in the province, the myth of *Algérie française* ensured that Franco-Arab assimilation remained the prevailing philosophy until the idea of a self-governing *Algérie algérienne* became a realistic prospect for local nationalists. Cf. Loughlin, "Algerian War," 149–60.

18. Cf. Michael Walzer, "Commitment and Social Criticism: Camus's Algerian War," *Dissent* (Fall 1984): 424–32. See also James D. Le Sueur, *Uncivil War: Intellectuals and Identity Politics during the Decolonization of Algeria* (Philadelphia: University of Philadelphia Press, 2001), especially 87–127; and Philip Dine, "Fighting and writing the war without a name: polemics and the French-Algerian conflict," *Aurifex* 2 (2002), http://www.goldsmiths.ac.uk/aurifex/issue2/dine.html. While other *pied-noir* liberals such as Jean Pélégri and Jules Roy came to accept Algerian independence as inevitable, Camus remained torn over his homeland.

19. Walzer, "Commitment and Social Criticism,"424.

20. Private correspondence with Charles Poncet dated September 25, 1955, quoted in Courrière, "Camus devant la Guerre d'Algérie," 10. In *Actuelles III* (1958), Camus gathers a collection of his articles from *L'Express* dealing with the issue under the telling subheading of "Algeria torn" (*E,* 967–88). We may also point out in passing that Camus's psychological trauma in respect of Algeria finds potent expression in Daru's suffocating alienation at the end of "The Guest" (written in 1954), the most pessimistic of the stories collected in *Exile and the Kingdom* (*TRN,* 1623; *ER,* 81–82). It is also interesting to note that problems of Franco-Arab

relations in Algeria are in evidence in four of the six stories contained in the 1957 work; a fifth deals with European/non-European relations in Brazil. For more on this last observation, see Mary L. Pratt, "Mapping Ideology: Gide, Camus, and Algeria," *College Literature* 8 (1981): 158–74. And, for an engaging account of Camus's conflicting desires in the face of alterity at issue in "The Guest," see Jill Beer, "*Le Regard:* Face to Face in Albert Camus's 'L'Hôte'," *French Studies* 56 (2002): 179–92.

21. Cf. Camus's description of himself as "a French Algerian writer" at the time of the 1957 Nobel Honors, as noted in chapter 4 above. Poignantly, Camus's torn loyalties over Algeria even pervaded his own family situation, judging from his wife's remark to Jean Grenier on August 13, 1960: "Catherine wants to keep the house at Lourmarin and says that her country is still France; for Jean, it is Algeria" (quoted in Paulhan, ed., *Jean Grenier, Carnets: 1944–1971,* 323).

22. Denis Charbit, "Camus et l'épreuve algérienne," in Bartfeld and Ohana, eds., "Albert Camus," 180.

23. Edward J. Hughes, "Albert Camus, *The First Man,* trans. David Hapgood," *Times Literary Supplement,* (November 23, 1995): 23.

24. Cf. Dunwoodie, *Writing French Algeria,* 242: "There is no doubt that the topoi of loss of memory and anonymity that are insistently foregrounded in *The First Man* are to be read not as pure negatives but as the vehicles of a protest against the injustice which condemned the majority of the Algerian population (Muslim and European) to live in poverty and 'leave no trace of their passage.'" See also, by the same writer, "Re-writing settlement"; and, by Edward J. Hughes, "'Tranquillement monstrueux,'" 33–41 and 21–32 respectively. For a seminal account of the psychological situation of the *pied-noir* community more generally, see Pierre Nora, *Les Français d'Algérie* (Paris: Julliard, 1961).

25. Abbas, *La Nuit coloniale,* 14. One is reminded here of Nietzsche's comment on the Melian Dialogue in book 5 of Thucydides's *History of the Peloponnesian War:* the idea that justice only becomes an issue when relationships can no longer be settled purely on a basis of force (*A Nietzsche Reader,* ed. and trans. R. J. Hollingdale [Harmondsworth: Penguin, 1977], 74–75). Although we now know that Camus read Thucydides while preparing *The Plague* (cf. Archambault, *Camus's Hellenic Sources,* 54–60), there is no evidence to suggest that he noted Nietzsche's reflection on the origin of justice.

26. Camus's refusal to speak out against the use of torture following revelations made in Henri Alleg's *La Question* (Paris: Minuit, 1958) and Pierre-Henri Simon's *Contre la torture* (Paris: Seuil, 1957) would further make him a political pariah on the French left: see, for instance, Beauvoir, *La Force des choses,* 2:144–45. By contrast, in "Le colonialisme est un système" (47), Sartre's parallel between the torture used by the French and that used *on* the French by Nazis during the Second World War reopened many old wounds. There have been a number of recent publications in France reexamining the issue of the French Army's use of torture during the Algerian War: for a useful conspectus, see Jo McCormack, "Torture during the Algerian war," *Modern & Contemporary France* 10 (2002): 392–95. And, for a revealing account of the ongoing resonances of the subject, see Neil Macmaster, "The torture controversy (1998–2002): toward a 'new history' of the Algerian war?," *Modern & Contemporary France* 10 (2002): 449–59.

27. Jeanyves Guérin, *Albert Camus: portrait de l'artiste en citoyen,* 254.

28. See Horne, *Savage War of Peace,* 535–63. For an insightful account of the legacy of the Algerian War examined through the lens of recent Algerian history, see Benjamin Stora, "Algérie: les retours de la mémoire de la guerre d'indépendance," *Modern & Contemporary France* 10 (2002): 461–73.

29. "Essays in negotiation" is how Michael Walzer describes *Actuelles III,* Camus's collection of writings dealing with the Algerian problem from 1939, "when almost no one in France was interested in that country" (*RRD,* 81), to 1958, "when everyone talks about it" (*RRD,* 81) (Walzer, "Commitment and Social Criticism," 425).

30. Henceforth, Camus felt increasingly separated from Daniel who was now moving away from the idea of an *Algérie française* toward that of an *Algérie algérienne.* However, whatever their differences on the Algerian question, Camus remained sympathetic to Daniel's situation: "For me, it is enough for me to understand, reading you, that like me you are torn" (private correspondence from Camus to Daniel, quoted in the latter's "Parlons de lui," 29). Quoted in Jean Daniel, "Une patrie algérienne, deux peuples," *Études méditerranéennes* 7 (1960): 21.

31. For Camus, such decrees were inherently undemocratic and, as such, politically unjust.

32. Todd, *Albert Camus, une vie,* 723, 724–25. Cf. Roger Quilliot, "Le Premier Camus," in *AC18,* 125: "if he, Camus, had by chance to stop being at home in Algeria, where he owned neither land nor house, with just his roots and reasons for living, he preferred to leave France, that was not his country."

33. Following the collapse of his hopes for a diplomatic solution to the crisis, Camus concedes to Mouloud Feraoun in April 1958 his wish for "a truer future, I mean a future where we will be separated neither by injustice [colonialism] nor justice [independence]" (quoted in Mouloud Feraoun, "Au-dessus des haines," *Simoun* 8 [1960]: 19). There is also a tacit recognition that justice is on the side of those campaigning for an Algerian independence in Camus's notorious mother/justice declaration of December 1957, more of which later.

34. Lottman, *Albert Camus,* 624.

35. Robert Mallet, "Présence à la vie, étranger à la mort (Pages de journal)," *Nouvelle Revue Française* 8 (1960): 440.

36. Cf. Camus's incredibly naïve confidence to Jean Grenier dated July 1, 1955: "The Algerians (Arabs) are mistaken to believe that they can win. Indo-China was provided with fresh supplies by Russia and China. Algeria is isolated. Besides, the Moslems of Algeria are sensitive to the charm of France" (quoted in Paulhan, ed., *Jean Grenier: Carnets 1944–1971,* 164). See also Jean Daniel's testimony in *Bulletin d'Information de la Société des Études Camusiennes* 32 (1994): 10.

37. Hargreaves, "Camus and the Colonial Question in Algeria," 173.

38. Examining the impact of Franco-Arab fraternity in *The First Man,* Christiane Chaulet-Achour notes that in Camus's unfinished autobiographical novel, "the two communities involved remain at best observing one another and at worst in conflict" (Christiane Chaulet-Achour, "L'autre autochtone dans *Le Premier Homme* d'Albert Camus," *Roman 20–50* 27 [1999]: 25).

39. This initiative, that advocated a Franco-Arab federation for Algeria to be established within the political framework of the *Union française,* was, in Camus's eyes, "particularly adapted to Algerian realities and likely to satisfy the need for justice and freedom by all the communities" (*RRD,* 108). The proposals included a new French parliament divided into two sections, the second of which would consist of mainly Moslem representatives. However, the plan was predictably rejected by the French Algerian community, a failure that, in the words of Patrick McCarthy, would leave Camus "a broken man" (McCarthy, *Camus,* 302).

40. Michèle and Claude Duchet, "Inactuelles III, ou le juste et l'Algérie," *La Nouvelle Critique* 10 (1958): 152.

41. This commentary from Camus on the "civilian truce," reportedly made in

conversation with a group of Algerian colleagues, is quoted in Yves Courrière, "Albert Camus devant la Guerre d'Algérie, II. 1956: l'échec de la trêve civile," *Le Figaro littéraire,* June 9–15, 1969, 11. For a thorough account of the appeal, see Emmanuel Roblès, *Albert Camus et la trêve civile* (Philadelphia: Celfan Edition Monographs, 1988).

42. Judging from a remark made to Suzon Publicani-Varnier, Camus is under no illusions as to the likely outcome of the "Appeal": "I have been asked to speak, I couldn't refuse to do so but I knew that it would be pointless" (quoted in *Bulletin d'Information de la Société des Études Camusiennes* 39 [1996]: 21). Cf. Camus's correspondence to Charles Poncet dated September 25, 1955, and January 12, 1956, quoted in Courrière, "Camus devant la Guerre d'Algérie," 10, 11. For Edward Hughes, Camus's retreat into sentimentalism "may be read as a sublimation of colonialist guilt" (Hughes, *Writing Marginality in Modern French Literature,* 131).

43. The ongoing political problems in contemporary Algeria have recently occasioned a reconsideration of initiatives such as Camus's "Appeal": see Benjamin Stora, "Deuxième Guerre algérienne? Les habits anciens des combattants," *Les Temps modernes* 580 (January–February 1995): 242–61.

44. To judge from Camus's endorsement of Mozart's leitmotivs (cf. *E,* 1923), the revolutionary quest for freedom, too, is subject to the respect for the human individual: "His work, widespread throughout, permanent source of fresh joy and *controlled freedom,* justifies the human ambition, in spite of misfortune and discouragement and, still today, inspires at the same time our resistance and our hope" (*EX,* 177; my italics).

45. Cf. Camus's correspondence with Jean Sénac dated February 10, 1957, quoted in Todd, *Albert Camus, une vie,* 674: "My position has not varied on this matter and if I can understand and admire the combatant of a liberation, I only have disgust in front of the killer of women and children." See also "Camus et le terrorisme," originally broadcast on *France Culture* on November 23, 2002, http://www.radiofrance.fr/chaines/france-culture2/.

46. Hargreaves, "Caught in the Middle," 80. It is worth noting here that when, in his writings on the Algerian problem, Camus refers to the French Algerian community, he consistently uses the subject pronoun "we," with its connotations of community and belonging, and "you," with its suggestion of alienation and difference, when specifying the indigenous race of Algerians. This observation was first recorded by Jean Daniel (see Jules Roy, "La tragédie algérienne," in Roy et al., *Camus,* Collection Génies et Réalités, 204).

47. Jean Sarocchi, *Camus,* Collection Philosophes (Paris: PUF, 1968), 48.

48. Cf. Jeanyves Guérin, "Noces de sang: Camus," *Esprit* 94–95 (1984): 147–55.

49. Such had been the driving force of Camus's Mediterraneanism, now overpowered by historical reality. Cf. Davison, "Mythologizing the Mediterranean," 89.

50. For an incisive reading of *Exile and the Kingdom* from the perspective of divided communities, see Salas, *Albert Camus: la juste révolte,* 105–13.

51. Cited in correspondence from Camus to Charles Poncet dated January 29, 1956, quoted in Courrière, "Albert Camus devant la Guerre d'Algérie, II," 13. Walzer, "Commitment and Social Criticism," 430. Cf. Kenneth J. Harrow, "Albert Camus and the Algerian Dilemma," *Journal of Modern Literature* 2 (1971–72): 147: "Camus could not forget the Arabs, nor his French Algerian family and compatriots, and so he chose the same silence as his mother's as the only viable expres-

sion for an impossible love." Harrow's remark puts another interesting gloss on Camus's Stockholm declaration. See also Feraoun, "Au-dessus des haines"; and Le Sueur, *Uncivil War,* 109–17.

52. Quoted in Todd, *Albert Camus, une vie,* 634–35. Cf. Camus's letter dated February 10, 1956, addressed to Jean Gillibert, quoted in *Revue d'Histoire du Théâtre* 12 (1960): 359.

53. Steve Andrew Robson, "Albert Camus: les raisons de lutter" (master's thesis, University of Keele, 1992), 164–65. Cf. by the same author "Albert Camus: The Man behind the Myth."

54. Hughes, *"Le Premier Homme" / "La Peste,"* 26.

For a well-documented account of the psychological resonances in *The First Man* of Camus's Algerian crisis, see Paul Merlo, "Les derniers mots du *Premier Homme* de Camus," in *AC18,* 83–100. Equally noteworthy is "*Le Premier Homme* et la guerre d'Algérie," *Roman 20–50* 27 (1999): 7–15, in which Jeanyves Guérin examines some of the echoes of the contemporary events in Algeria in Camus's autobiographical project.

55. Lottman, *Albert Camus,* 651. Cf. Edward Hughes's evaluation of Camus's unfinished novel as one marking "a confidently literal and unapologetic return to origins" (Hughes, *Writing Marginality in Modern French Literature,* 122). For a reading of *The First Man* from a colonial perspective, highlighting Camus's quest for an understanding of the first French settlers of Algeria, see Nancy Wood, "Colonial nostalgia and *Le Premier Homme.*" More generally, Jeanyves Guérin examines the ways in which Camus's unfinished autobiographical novel responds to his political reading of the Algerian crisis in "Des *Chroniques algériennes* au *Premier Homme:* pour une lecture politique du dernier roman de Camus," *Esprit* 211 (1995): 5–16.

56. It will be recalled from chapter 1 that in spite of his poverty-stricken origins, Camus always maintained that his formative experience in Algeria—"the childhood from which he had never recovered" (*FM,* 33)—had been a happy one. A sense of harmony with nature offsets any sense of disharmony surrounding Camus's personal circumstances: "Poverty, first of all, was never a misfortune for me: it was radiant with sunlight" (*SEN,* 18). Cf. Camus's correspondence with Marguerite Dobrenn dated November 17, 1959, quoted in Todd, *Albert Camus, une vie,* 743: "I have changed hairstyles. I have gone back to the one of the happy years in Algiers, which has at least made me feel younger."

The theater is also important in this regard. Between 1953 and 1959, Camus would adapt six plays as well as staging his own *Caligula* for the 1957 Festival d'Angers (see, for instance, Freeman, *Theatre of Albert Camus,* 119–47). That he discovers here a new lease of life is apparent in Camus's contemporary notebooks and correspondence: "Angers festival ended. Happy tiredness. Life, wonderful life, its injustice, its majesty, its passion, its struggles, life is starting again. Still strength to love everything and to create everything" (*C3,* 203; cf. *C3,* 207–8; and *Corr,* 213). It is worth noting that, in an ironic twist of fate, on the very day of his demise—January 4, 1960—Camus's ambition to direct his own theatrical outfit in Paris was finally set to be realized (Todd, *Albert Camus, une vie,* 753).

57. Such is how Camus describes *The First Man* to Jean Grenier in 1957 (Grenier, *Albert Camus: Souvenirs,* 179).

58. The term "pilgrimage to the source" ["pèlerinage aux sources"] is borrowed from a chapter in Roger Quilliot's seminal *La Mer et les prisons,* 249–58. Tantamount to this notion of "returning to one's roots" is an attempt to understand one's situation from a different perspective to that of the present moment as a way

of moving forward. A *Carnets* entry dated October 17, 1957, detailing Camus's frame of mind upon his elevation to the status of Nobel laureate, conveniently sums up the distance between his past (happiness) and present (unhappiness): "Nobel Prize. Strange feeling of depression and melancholy. When I was 20, poor and plain, I knew real splendor. My mother" (*C3,* 214). As Quilliot notes, "as if automatically, Camus sought refuge in his childhood" (*E,* 1894). The metaphor of the escaped prisoner in *The First Man* as Jacques makes his way from France back to the land of his birth provides a poignant illustration of this psychological healing process (*PH,* 44; *FM,* 33).

59. For a useful *mise au point* of the three "cycles" of Camus's work, see Arnaud Corbic, *Camus: l'absurde, la révolte, l'amour* (Paris: Éditions de l'Atelier / Éditions Ouvrières, 2003). For a more focused account of the intertextual parallels between *The First Man* and *Exile and the Kingdom,* see Yosei Matsumoto, "L'ombre portée par *Le Premier Homme* sur *L'Exil et le royaume,*" in *AC20,* 87–101.

60. Jean Sarocchi, *Le Dernier Camus ou "Le Premier Homme"* (Paris: Nizet, 1995), 164.

61. "Reflections on the Guillotine" was published simultaneously in the June and July 1957 issues of *La Nouvelle Revue Française* and (along with Arthur Koestler's acclaimed "Reflections on the Gallows") in *Reflections on Capital Punishment* [*Réflexions sur la peine capitale*] (Paris: Calmann-Lévy, 1957). Camus's text is reprinted in *E,* 1019–64; *RRD,* 125–65.

62. Stemming from an incident in the life of Camus's own father (*E,* 1021; *RRD,* 127), that the writer subsequently incorporates into *The Outsider* (*TRN,* 1203; *TO,* 109), *The Plague* (*TRN,* 1411–29; *TP,* 192–210) and *The First Man* (*PH,* 79–81; *FM,* 63–64), the protest against the death penalty is one of the main themes of Camus's work and a key aspect of his concern for social justice. Among the many interventions he makes against the death penalty figure campaigns in defense of condemned Greek and Iranian intellectuals (*E,* 1765–66), as well as the many cases contested privately. In addition, it is useful to recall the intellectual investment Camus accords the issue both during and after his polemic with Mauriac over the purge in France. For a good overview of Camus's preoccupation with capital punishment, see Paul F. Smets, *Le Combat pour l'abolition de la peine de mort: Hugo, Koestler, Camus, d'autres: textes, prétextes et paratextes* (Brussels: Académie royale de Belgique, 2003).

63. A notable exception is "On Camus and Capital Punishment," *Modern Age* 2 (1958): 298–306, in which Thomas Molnar argues that "Camus' idea of justice is tinged with sentimentality, and it fails to distinguish between a generalized and hazy *guilt-feeling* . . . and the moral and legal concept of individual responsibility" (300). However, Molnar's critical stance does not do justice to the subtlety and intellectual honesty of Camus's moral position in respect of capital punishment.

64. Patrick Henry, "Camus on Capital Punishment," *Midwest Quarterly* 16 (1974–75): 366.

65. Willhoite, *Beyond Nihilism,* 145.

66. Philippe Vanney, "Le partage de la souffrance: Camus et le débat traditionnel sur la peine de mort," *Bulletin d'Études Françaises* 32 (2001): 95. See, too, by the same author, "Camus contre le droit de mort de l'État," *Bulletin d'Études Françaises* 34 (2003): 49–73. I am indebted to this writer for sending me copies of each of these insightful studies.

67. Although "Reflections on the Guillotine" is a fundamental component of Camus's intellectual "pilgrimage to the source" in the wake of the "civilian truce" fiasco, this essay can also usefully be situated in the context of the ongoing crisis

in Algeria, where the French government reserved the right to use capital punishment by which to mete out justice for convicted Algerian militants. For more on this perspective of the 1957 work, see Le Sueur, *Uncivil War,* 104–8.

68. Mention may also usefully be made here of Camus's private interventions on behalf of indicted Arab nationalists such as Ben Saddok (a member of the FLN who was tried in December 1957 for allegedly killing a retrograde Arab) and Amar Ouzegane (tried in January 1959 for his instrumental role in the FLN) and—in a rare *public* intervention—his support for Jean de Maisonseul, arrested in May 1956 for his alleged FLN sympathies (*E,* 1001–8). This is not to imply that Camus did not associate himself with such interventions prior to joining *L'Express* (cf. *EX,* 16–17). Rather, in the wake of the failure of the "civilian truce" initiative, Camus increasingly reverts to his "person-to-person" response to perceived injustice (as opposed to his objective to find a wholesale solution to the Algerian crisis through rational means). Cf. *C3,* 238.

69. There is a clear parallel to be drawn here with *The Fall,* that, similarly undermining universal claims of justice, "reveals justice as a complex and self-flattering illusion" (O'Brien, *Camus,* 84). Like Camus, Clamence becomes disillusioned in his concern for justice and—contrary to the actions of Camus himself—subsequently abandons all of his former values in his quest for moral enslavement. It is interesting to read the 1956 masterpiece in relation to Camus's "temptations" (*SEN,* 144) spotlighted in "The Enigma" so that, in one sense, the work can be read as a subconscious formulation of Camus's own crisis of conscience following his failure to convince with regard to Algeria. Cf. Robson, "Man behind the Myth," 122–23.

70. Following the undue sensationalism in the press concerning the case of Eugen Weidmann (a self-confessed serial killer arrested in December 1937, tried in April 1939 and executed at Versailles in June of the same year), all subsequent capital punishments in France would be conducted "hors de la vue du public" ["out of public view"] in accordance with the *décret-loi* of June 24, 1939 (cf. *Réflexions sur la peine capitale,* 223). Publicity of the Weidmann case was widespread and, notably, was taken up by *Alger républicain* for which Camus himself was working at the time. See chapter 7 of Walker's *Outrage and Insight.*

Far from meting out institutionalized justice, Camus contends, capital punishment is a tool of private vengeance that not only "adds to death a rule, a . . . premeditation . . . , an organization, in short" (*RRD,* 143), but also inflicts upon the family of the offender "an excess of suffering that punishes them beyond all justice" (*RRD,* 146).

Camus's perception of capital punishment as "an unsatisfactory justice" (*RRD,* 150) derives from the view that society, in whose name the death penalty is carried out, lacks the moral authority to mete out irreparable justice that "breaks the human community united against death" (*RRD,* 160; translation amended). Society, after all, is never innocent of the crimes its members commit. Camus cites statistics showing the extent to which social problems such as poor housing and the abuse of alcohol contribute to the prevalence of violent crime (*E,* 1044–45; *RRD,* 148).

71. In *The Outsider,* Meursault represents the prototype of the prisoner condemned by the "implacable machinery" (*TO,* 107) of the state judiciary.

72. Abolitionists across the world share Camus's view that the death penalty breaches the United Nations Universal Declaration of Human Rights because it denies the right to life and the right not to be tortured or subjected to any cruel or degrading punishment. See Paul Donovan, "Imposing the Ultimate Penalty,"

Guardian, Guardian Education, April 18, 1995, 10–11. For a useful historical conspectus of capital punishment in France (finally abolished by Mitterrand in September 1981), see *Réflexions sur la peine capitale,* 181–226; and cf. Robert Badinter, *L'Abolition* (Paris: Fayard, 2000).

73. As he reportedly remarks during a press conference at Stockholm on December 9, 1957, "it's . . . the novel of my maturity, if you like. In consequence, I attach more sentimental value to it than to other books" (quoted in Lottman, *Albert Camus,* 615).

Cf. Camus's remark in conversation with Jean de Maionseul in late summer 1959: "I have written only one third of my works. I am starting them in earnest with this book" (quoted in Todd, *Albert Camus, une vie,* 744).

74. Quoted in ibid., 752.

75. See Christy Lawrence, "*Le Premier Homme:* l'aube de Némésis," in *AC20,* 33–61.

Conclusion

1. Quoted in Todd, *Albert Camus, une vie,* 377.

2. Doubrovsky, "La Morale d'Albert Camus," *Preuves* 116 (1960): 40.

3. It hardly needs emphasizing that his own experience of sport (and, one might add, that of theater [*TRN,* 1724]) as a young man in Algeria furnishes Camus with what he later recalls as "all I know about ethics" (*RRD,* 172). In his "final interview," Camus defines the "moral lessons" he derives from sport as "the faithful obedience to a game rule defined jointly and accepted freely" (*E,* 1925). For a useful overview of the dynamics of sport in the realm of the political, see Philip Dine, "Un héroïsme problématique: le sport, la littérature et la Guerre d'Algérie," *Europe* 806–7 (1996): 177–85.

4. As Rienhold Niebuhr reminds us, "man's capacity for justice makes democracy possible, but man's inclination to injustice makes democracy necessary" (Rienhold Niebuhr, *The Children of Light and the Children of Darkness: A Vindication of Democracy and a Critique of Its Traditional Defenders* [London: Nisbet, 1945], vi).

5. McCarthy, *Camus,* 328.

6. A recent international and interdisciplinary conference held in Paris, "Albert Camus in the 21st Century," explored the ongoing resonances of Camus at the start of the new millennium. A publication of these proceedings is planned.

7. Elie Wiesel, "L'Homme de Conscience," *Europe* 77 (1999): 9.

8. Cruickshank, *Albert Camus and the Literature of Revolt,* 224.

9. Beaunier, ed., *Les Carnets de Joseph Joubert,* 2:772.

10. Cited in correspondence dating from between 1950 and 1952, quoted in Todd, *Albert Camus, une vie,* 545.

Bibliography

Primary Sources

Fictional and Theatrical Works by Camus:

Caligula: version de 1941 suivi de La Poétique du premier "Caligula." Edited by A. James Arnold. Cahiers Albert Camus 4. Paris: Gallimard, 1984.

The Collected Plays of Albert Camus. Translated by Stuart Gilbert, Henry Jones and Justin O'Brien. London: Hamish Hamilton, 1965.

Exile and the Kingdom. Translated by Justin O'Brien. Harmondsworth: Penguin Books, 1974.

The Fall. Translated by Justin O'Brien. Harmondsworth: Penguin Books, 1986.

The First Man. Translated by David Hapgood. London: Hamish Hamilton, 1995.

La Mort heureuse. Edited by Jean Sarocchi. Cahiers Albert Camus 1. Paris: Gallimard, 1971.

The Outsider. Translated by Stuart Gilbert. Harmondsworth: Penguin Books, 1975.

Le Premier Homme. Cahiers Albert Camus 7. Paris: Gallimard, 1994.

The Plague. Translated by Stuart Gilbert. Harmondsworth: Penguin Books, 1960.

Théâtre, Récits, Nouvelles. Edited by Roger Quilliot. Bibliothèque de La Pléiade. Paris: Gallimard, 1962.

Nonfictional Writings by Camus: Published Material

Albert Camus: éditorialiste à "L'Express," mai 1955–février 1956. Edited by Paul F. Smets. Cahiers Albert Camus 6. Paris: Gallimard, 1987.

Albert Camus / Pascal Pia: Correspondance, 1939–1947. Edited by Yves Marc Ajchenbaum. Paris: Fayard / Gallimard, 2000.

"Britain after the Election: Two French Views." Translated by John Cocking. *Listener,* November 22, 1951, 871–73.

Camus à "Combat": éditoriaux et articles d'Albert Camus, 1944–1947. Edited by Jacqueline Lévi-Valensi. Paris: Gallimard, 2002.

Carnets: 1935–1942. Translated by Philip Thody. London: Hamish Hamilton, 1963.

Carnets: 1942–1951. Translated by Philip Thody. London: Hamish Hamilton, 1966.

The Rebel. Translated by Anthony Bower. Harmondsworth: Penguin Books, 1971.

Carnets I: mai 1935–février 1942. Paris: Gallimard, 1962.

Carnets II: janvier 1942–mars 1951. Paris: Gallimard, 1964.

Carnets III: mars 1951–décembre 1959. Paris: Gallimard, 1989.

Correspondance Albert Camus / Jean Grenier, 1932–1960. Edited by Marguerite Dobrenn. Paris: Gallimard, 1981.

Essais. Edited by R. Quilliot and L. Faucon. Bibliothèque de La Pléiade. Paris: Gallimard, 1965.

The First Camus / Youthful Writings. Translated by Ellen Conroy Kennedy. London: Hamish Hamilton, 1977.

Fragments d'un combat 1938–1940: "Alger républicain," "Le Soir républicain." Edited by André Abbou and Jacqueline Lévi-Valensi. Cahiers Albert Camus 3. 2 vols. Paris: Gallimard, 1978.

A Happy Death. Translated by Richard Howard. London: Hamish Hamilton, 1972.

"The Human Crisis." *Twice a Year* (1946): 19–33; repr. in *Albert Camus, 5: "Journalisme et politique: l'entrée dans l'histoire (1938–1940)."* Edited by Brian T. Fitch. La Revue des Lettres Modernes 315–22. Paris: Lettres Modernes, 1972. (The original French edition of this lecture is now lost; however, it has recently been retranslated by Jean-Marie Laclavetine in *NRF* 516 [1996]: 6–29.)

Journaux de voyage, 1946–1949. Edited by Roger Quilliot. Paris: Gallimard, 1978.

Manifesto of the "Groupes de Liaison Internationale" (1948), quoted in Walusinski, Gilbert. "Camus et les Groupes de Liaison Internationale." *La Quinzaine littéraire,* March 1–15, 1979, 22.

The Myth of Sisyphus. Translated by Justin O'Brien. Harmondsworth: Penguin Books, 1988.

Le premier Camus suivi de Écrits de jeunesse d'Albert Camus. Edited by Paul Viallaneix. Cahiers Albert Camus 2. Paris: Gallimard, 1973. (Consisting of: "Un nouveau Verlaine"; "Jehan Rictus: Le Poète de la misère"; "La Philosophie du siècle"; "Essai sur la musique"; "Intuitions": "Délires"; "Incertitude"; "La volonté de mensonge"; "Souhait"; "Retour sur moi-même"; "Notes de lecture"; "La Maison mauresque"; "Le courage"; "Méditerranée"; "Devant la morte"; "Perte de l'être aimé"; "Dialogue de Dieu avec son âme"; "Contradictions"; "L'Hôpital du quartier pauvre"; "L'Art dans la communion"; "Le Livre de Mélusine": "Conte pour des enfants trop tristes"; "Le Rêve de la fée"; "Les Barques"; and "Les Voix du quartier pauvre.")

Resistance, Rebellion and Death. Translated by Justin O'Brien. London: Hamish Hamilton, 1961.

Selected Essays and Notebooks. Edited and translated by Philip Thody. Harmondsworth: Penguin Books, 1979.

"Un texte retrouvé d'Albert Camus." *Bulletin d'Information de la Société des Études Camusiennes* 32 (1994): 4–6. (Consists of a text of a speech delivered at the Maison de la Chimie in Paris on November 18, 1946.)

Unpublished Material

The Fonds Albert Camus, Centre de Documentation Albert Camus, Aix-en-Provence:

"Correspondance: Lecteurs de *L'Express* (1955–56)." A4 (2); "Dossiers Politiques: Lettres sur *L'Homme révolté.*" B3 (11); "*Les Justes:* Pièces annexes, photos, programmes." A3 (2); "Némesis." GO7 (8–14); "Pour *Actuelles IV.*"

DO6; "Réflexions de G. Tezenas à propos de *L'Homme révolté*." February 26, 1952. GO7 (15); "Soutien à l'Espagne républicaine." B4 (1–11) (Comprising manuscripts; correspondence; accounts of, and responses to, Camus's interventions on behalf of Spanish republican prisoners and exiles).

Secondary Sources

Biography and Bibliography:

Alden, Douglas W., and Richard A. Brooks. *A Critical Bibliography of French Literature*. 6 vols. Syracuse: Syracuse University Press, 1980.

Fitch, Brian T. *Essai de bibliographie des études en langue française consacrées à Albert Camus (1937–1962)*. Calepins de Bibliographie 1. Paris: Lettres Modernes Minard, 1965.

Fitch, Brian T., and Peter C. Hoy. *Essai de bibliographie des études en langue française consacrées à Albert Camus (1937–1970)*. Calepins de Bibliographie 1 (3). Paris: Lettres Modernes Minard, 1972.

France, Peter, ed. *The New Oxford Companion to Literature in French*. Oxford: Clarendon Press, 1995.

Gay-Crosier, Raymond, ed. http://www.clas.ufl.edu/users/gaycros/Bibliog.htm. (A regularly updated on-line bibliography).

Harvey, Sir Paul, and J. E. Heseltine, eds. *The Oxford Companion to French Literature*. Oxford: Oxford University Press, 1959.

Hoy, Peter C., ed. *Camus in English: An Annotated Bibliography of Albert Camus's Contributions to English and American Periodicals and Newspapers*. Wymondham: Brewhouse Press, 1968.

Lottman, Herbert R. *Albert Camus: A Biography*. London: Weidenfeld and Nicolson, 1979.

McCarthy, Patrick. *Camus: A Critical Study of his Life and Work*. London: Hamish Hamilton, 1982.

Roeming, Robert F. ed. *Camus: A Bibliography*. 15th ed. Wisconsin-Milwaukee: University of Wisconsin Computing Services Division, 2000. (Comprises 4 microfiches: by far, the most comprehensive bibliography on Camus, detailing material published in 34 different languages.)

Todd, Olivier. *Albert Camus, une vie*. Biographies NRF Gallimard. Paris: Gallimard / Olivier Todd, 1996.

Critical Works and Articles on Camus:

Abbou, André, ed. *Albert Camus et l'Europe: Actes du colloque de Strasbourg, 9–10 novembre 1990*. Paris: L'Ofil, 1995.

———. "Combat pour la justice." In *Albert Camus, 5: "Journalisme et politique: l'entrée dans l'histoire, 1938–1940."* Edited by Brian T. Fitch. La Revue des Lettres Modernes, 315–22. Paris: Lettres Modernes, 1972.

———. "Sous le soleil du père et de l'histoire: dialogue avec un mythe personnel fondateur dans *La Peste*." *Europe* 77 (1999): 104–18.

———. "Une ligne de demarcation."*Les Nouvelles littéraires,* January 10–17, 1980, 18–19.

———. "Variations du discours polémique." In *Albert Camus, 5: "Journalisme et politique: l'entrée dans l'histoire, 1938–1940."* Edited by Brian T. Fitch. La Revue des Lettres Modernes, 315–22. Paris: Lettres Modernes, 1972.

Abdel, Lionel. "Albert Camus: Moralist of Feeling." *Commentary* 31 (1961): 172–75.

———. "Letters from Paris: Impressions and Conversations." *Partisan Review* 16 (1949): 395–99.

Abecassis, Jack I. "Camus's Pulp Fiction." *MLN* 112 (1997): 625–40.

Aciman, André. "From Alexandria." *MLN* 112 (1997): 683–97.

Adams, Robert M. "Adventurer in Morality." *Nation* 188 (1959): 412–13.

Aho, James. "Suffering, Redemption and Violence: Albert Camus and the Sociology of Violence." *Rendezvous* 9 (1974): 51–62.

Aiken, Henry David. "The Revolt against Ideology." *Commentary* 37 (1964): 29–39.

Akeroyd, Richard H. *The Spiritual Quest of Albert Camus.* Tuscaloosa, Alabama: Portals Press, 1976.

Albérès, René-Marill. "Albert Camus dans son siècle: témoin et étranger." *La Table Ronde* 146 (1960): 9–15.

———. "Le Prix Nobel." In *Camus,* edited by René-Marill Albérès, Pierre de Boisdeffre, Jean Daniel, Pierre Gascar, Morvan Lebesque, André Parinaud, Emmanuel Roblès, Jules Roy, and Pierre-Henri Simon. Paris: Hachette, 1964.

Albes, Wolf. *Jean Brune et Albert Camus: deux écrivains pieds-noirs face au drame de l'Algérie française.* Friedberg: Edition Atlantis, 1999.

Alter, André. "De *Caligula* aux *Justes:* de l'absurde à la justice." *Revue d'Histoire du Théâtre* 12 (1960): 321–36.

Altschuler, Georges. "Albert Camus: journaliste du *Combat* de la clandestinité au *Combat* de la Libération." *École et la vie* 7 (1960): 29–30.

Amash, Paul J. "The Choice of an Arab in *L'Étranger.*" *Romance Notes* 9 (1967): 6–7.

Amer, Henry. "Le Mythe de Sisyphe." *NRF* 8 (1960): 487–90.

Amette, Jacques-Pierre. "Un étranger dans Paris." *Le Point,* August 14–20, 1993, 52–53.

Amiot, Anne-Marie. "Interférences Dada / Camus." In *Albert Camus: les Extrêmes et l'équilibre; Actes du colloque de Keele, 25–27 mars 1993,* edited by David H. Walker. Amsterdam: Rodopi, 1994.

———. "Un romantisme corrigé, 'entre oui et non'." *Europe,* 77 (1999): 76–89.

Amiot, Anne-Marie, and F. Mattéi, eds. *Albert Camus et la philosophie.* Paris: PUF, 1997.

Anderson, Abraham. "*L'Homme révolté* and 'Le Renégat.'" In *Albert Camus, "L'Exil et le royaume": The Third Decade,* edited by Anthony Rizzuto. Toronto: Paratexte, 1988.

Anderson, Kirsteen H. R. "Justification and Happiness in Camus's *La Mort heureuse.*" *Forum for Modern Language Studies* 20 (1984): 228–46.

———. "La première femme: the mother's resurrection in the work of Camus and Irigaray." *French Studies* 56 (2002): 29–43.

Añón, Maria-José. "Albert Camus: le droit entre la révolte et la justice." In *Albert Camus, 14: "le texte et ses langages,"* edited by Raymond Gay-Crosier. La Revue des Lettres Modernes, 985–92. Paris: Minard, 1991.

"A Movement of Resistance." *TLS,* November 17, 1950, 734.

"A Practising Rebel: Albert Camus's *The Rebel.*" *TLS,* December 18, 1953, 809–10.

"Albert Camus." *TLS,* January 8, 1960, 13–14.

"Albert Camus: plus actuel que jamais." *Bulletin Gallimard* 392 (1992): 7.

"An Ethical Realist among the Radicals." *TLS,* March 12, 1971, 288.

"Beyond Contradiction." *TLS,* October 12, 1973, 1252.

"Death of a Rebel." *New Republic,* January 18, 1960, 6.

"Generally Right, Always Defeated." *TLS,* August 25, 1966, 762.

"Grandes études: le destin de Camus." *Magazine littéraire,* 3 (1967): 6–14.

"La Polémique Sartre-Camus." *Le Figaro littéraire,* September 13, 1952, 4.

Antonini, Giacomo. "Albert Camus et l'Italie." *NRF* 8 (1960): 563–67.

Apter, Emily. "Out of Character: Camus's French Algerian Subjects." *MLN* 112 (1997): 499–516.

Archambault, Paul. "Camus in Purgatory: Some Recent Scholarship." *Papers on Language and Literature* 9 (1973): 95–110.

———. *Camus's Hellenic Sources.* Chapel Hill: University of North Carolina Press, 1972.

Armel, Aliette. "L'Homme révolté aujourd'hui." *Magazine littéraire* 276 (1990): 46–47.

Arnold, A. James. "Camus: lecteur de Nietzsche." In *Albert Camus, 9: "la pensée de Camus,"* edited by Raymond Gay-Crosier. La Revue des Lettres Modernes, 565–69. Paris: Lettres Modernes Minard, 1979.

———. "La Poétique du premier Caligula." In *Caligula: version de 1941 suivi de La Poétique du premier "Caligula,"* edited by A. James Arnold. Cahiers Albert Camus 4. Paris: Gallimard, 1984.

Aronson, Ronald. *Camus and Sartre: The Story of a Friendship and the Quarrel that Ended It.* Chicago: University of Chicago Press, 2004.

———. "Sartre, Camus, and the *Caliban* Articles." *Sartre Studies International* 7 (2001): 1–7.

d'Astier de la Vigerie, Emmanuel. "Arrachez la victime aux bourreaux." *Caliban* 15 (1948): 12–17.

d'Astorg, Bertrand. "Encore Camus." *Esprit* 15 (1949): 168–70.

———. "L'Homme engagé: de *La Peste* ou d'un nouvel humanitarisme." *Esprit* 16 (1947): 615–21.

Atanassov, Francine, Jacqueline Baisharski, Francisco Belard, Sarah Ben Chaabane, Lionel Dubois, Margaret Gray, Viviane Girault, Adèle King, Geraldine Montgomery, Suzanne Popkin and Neelima Talwar. "La place de la femme dans l'œuvre de Camus." In *Albert Camus entre la misère et le soleil: Actes du Colloque international de Poitiers, 29–30–31 mai 1997,* edited by Lionel Dubois. Poitiers: Éditions du Pont-Neuf, 1997.

Audin, Marie-Louise. "Camus: journaliste-écrivain?" *Cahiers de l'Association Internationale des Études Françaises* 48 (1996): 129–47.

———. "Mais aux plus doués il faut un initiateur." In *Albert Camus: parcours méditerranéens,* edited by Fernande Bartfeld and David Ohana. Vol. 5 of *Perspectives: Revue de l'Université Hébraïque de Jérusalem* (1998): 55–71.

Ayer, A. J. "Novelist-Philosophers, VIII: Albert Camus." *Horizon* 13 (1946): 155–68.

Baciu, Virginia. "Albert Camus et la condamnation à mort." *Studia Universitatis Babes-Bolyai (Philologia)* 17 (1972): 111–21.

Bailey, Anthony. "The Isolated Man." *Commonweal,* October 25, 1957, 91–93.

Baishanski, Jacqueline. *L'Orient dans la pensée du jeune Camus: "L'Étranger," un nouvel évangile?* Paris: Lettres Modernes Minard, 2002.

Barbier, Christophe. "Camus et la politique." *Le Point,* August 14–20, 1993, 55.

———. "Interview: Roger Quilliot." *Le Point,* August 14–20, 1993, 56.

———. "Pour une éthique en politique." *Le Point,* August 14–20, 1993, 56.

Baréa, Monique, ed. *Albert Camus: 1913–1960; Bibliothèque de l'Université de Nice, 8–14 mai 1980 et Bibliothèque Publique d'Information, Centre Georges Pompidou, 25 mars–4 mai 1981.* Aix-en-Provence: Edisud, 1981.

Barilier, Etienne. "La Création corrigée." In *Albert Camus: œuvre fermée, œuvre ouverte? Actes du colloque du Cerisy-la-Salle, juin 1982,* edited by Raymond Gay-Crosier and Jacqueline Lévi-Valensi. Cahiers Albert Camus 5. Paris: Gallimard, 1985.

Barnes, Hazel E. "Balance and Tension in the Philosophy of Camus." *Personalist* 41 (1960): 433–47.

Barret-Kriegel, Blandine. "Camus et la démocratie." In *Camus et la politique: Actes du colloque de Nanterre, 5–7 juin 1985,* edited by Jeanyves Guérin. Paris: L'Harmattan, 1986.

Bartfeld, Fernande. *Albert Camus: voyageur et conférencier. Le voyage en Amérique du Sud.* Archives Albert Camus 7. Paris: Lettres Modernes, 1995.

———. "Anti-Méditerranée et lyrisme de l'exil." In *Albert Camus: parcours méditerranéens,* edited by Fernande Bartfeld and David Ohana. Vol 5 of *Perspectives: Revue de l'Université Hébraïque de Jérusalem* (1998): 213–25.

———. "Camus en 1945–1946: autour de quelques textes peu connus." *Europe* 77 (1999): 48–58.

———. "Camus et le 'Mythe du Christ.'" *L'Information littéraire* 19 (1967): 100–6.

———. "La confession et son effet tragique chez Camus." *Hebrew University Studies in Literature* 12 (1984): 116–29.

———. *L'Effet tragique: essai sur le tragique dans l'œuvre de Camus.* Paris-Geneva: Champion-Slatkine, 1988.

———. "Le Monologue séducteur de *La Chute.*" In *Albert Camus, 13: "études comparatives,"* edited by Raymond Gay-Crosier. La Revue des Lettres Modernes, 904–10. Paris: Lettres Modernes Minard, 1989.

———. "Présentation." In *Albert Camus: parcours méditerranéens,* edited by Fernande Bartfeld and David Ohana. Vol. 5 of *Perspectives: Revue de l'Université Hébraïque de Jérusalem* (1998).

———. "Le voyage de Camus en Amérique du Nord," in *Albert Camus, 19: "'L'Homme révolté' cinquante ans après."* Edited by Raymond Gay-Crosier. Paris: Lettres Modernes Minard, 2001.

Barthes, Roland. "*L'Étranger:* roman solaire." *Club* 12 (1954): 6–7.

———. "*La Peste:* annales d'une épidémie ou roman de la solitude." *Club* (1955): 4–13.

Basset, Guy. "Camus à *Combat:* note de lecture." *Bulletin d'Information de la Société des Études Camusiennes* 66 (2003): 41.

Bataille, Georges. "L'Affaire de *L'Homme révolté.*" *Critique* 8 (1952): 1077–81.

———. "Le Temps de la révolte (I)." *Critique* 7 (1951): 1019–27.

———. "Le Temps de la révolte (II)." *Critique* 8 (1952): 29–41.

Becker, Jean-Jacques. "Albert Camus et la politique à la Libération." In *Camus et la politique: Actes du colloque de Nanterre, 5–7 juin 1985,* edited by Jeanyves Guérin. Paris: L'Harmattan, 1986.

Beer, Jill. "*Le Regard:* Face to Face in Albert Camus's 'L'Hôte.'" *French Studies* 56 (2002): 179–92.

Begue, Louise. "Camus, Albert: 'Le Mythe de Sisyphe.'" *French Review* 20 (1946): 72–73.

Béguin, Albert. "*L'Homme révolté* d'Albert Camus." *Études* 272 (1952): 48–60.

Beigbeder, Marc. "Le monde n'est pas absurde." *Esprit* 13 (1945): 415–19.

Berl, Emmanuel. "Les images, la justice, à l'épreuve." *La Table Ronde* 149 (1960): 181–83.

———. "Lettre à Albert Camus sur l'imposture et sur la discorde." *La Table Ronde* 103–4 (1956): 301–6.

Bernard, Jacqueline Mme. "The Background of *The Plague:* Camus's Experience in the French Resistance." *Kentucky Romance Quarterly* 14 (1967): 165–73.

Bernard, Marc. "La contradiction d'Albert Camus." *NRF* 8 (1960): 594–96.

Berne-Joffroy, André. "Le silence d'Albert Camus." *NRF* 8 (1960): 597–99.

Bertman, Martin A. "Camus: From Indifference to Commitment." *Revue de l'Université d'Ottawa* 40 (1970): 284–89.

Bespaloff, Rachel. "Le monde du condamné à mort." *Esprit* 18 (1950): 1–26.

Bessière, Jean. "Orwell et Camus: histoire, communauté et écriture." In *Camus et la politique: Actes du colloque de Nanterre, 5–7 juin 1985,* edited by Jeanyves Guérin. Paris: L'Harmattan, 1986.

Bieber, Konrad. "The Rebellion of a Humanist." *Yale Review* 43 (1954): 473–75.

———. "*Traduttore, traditore:* la réception problématique de 'L'Homme révolté' aux États-Unis." In *Albert Camus, 19· "'L'Homme révolté': cinquante ans après."* Edited by Raymond Gay-Crosier. Paris: Lettres Modernes Minard, 2001.

Biermez, Jean. "Camus et le Non-Agir." *NRF* 498–99 (1994): 173–81.

Birchall, Ian. "Camus contre Sartre: quarante ans plus tard." In *Albert Camus: les Extrêmes et l'équilibre; Actes du colloque de Keele, 25–27 mars 1993,* edited by David H. Walker. Amsterdam: Rodopi, 1994.

———. "The Labourism of Sisyphus: Albert Camus and revolutionary syndicalism." *Journal of European Studies* 20 (1990): 135–65.

Black, Moishe. "Camus's 'L'Hôte' as a Ritual of Hospitality." *Nottingham French Studies* 28 (1989): 39–52.

———. "'Non récupérable'—Camus et Max Jacob." In *Les trois guerres d'Albert Camus: Actes du Colloque International de Poitiers, 4–5–6 mai 1995.* Edited by Lionel Dubois. Poitiers: Éditions du Pont-Neuf, 1995.

Blanchard, Marc. "Before Ethics: Camus's *Pudeur.*" *MLN* 112 (1997): 666–82.

Blanchet, André. "*L'Homme révolté* d'Albert Camus." *Études.* 85 (1952): 48–60.

———. "La vie littéraire: la querelle Sartre-Camus." *Études* 85 (1952): 238–46.

Blanzat, Jean. "Première rencontre." *NRF* 8 (1960): 427–31.

Blin, Georges. "Albert Camus et l'idée de révolte." *Fontaine* 53 (1946): 109–17.

Bloch-Michel, Jean. "Albert Camus et la nostalgie de l'innocence." *Preuves* 110 (1960): 3–9.

Blondeau, Marie-Thérèse. "Colloque *Camus et la politique,* Nanterre, 5–6–7 juin 1985." *Bulletin d'Information de la Société des Études Camusiennes* 10 (1985): 4–13.

———. "Colloque *Camus et le premier 'Combat.'*" *Bulletin d'Information de la Société des Études Camusiennes* 16 (1987–88): 4–11.

———. "Colloque International 'Albert Camus et L'Europe': Strasbourg, 9 et 10 novembre 1990." *Bulletin d'Information de la Société des Études Camusiennes* 22 (1991): 1–12.

———. "Colloques passés: Amiens (31 mai–2 juin 1988)." *Bulletin d'Information de la Société des Études Camusiennes* 18 (1988): 2–16.

———. "Compte-rendu du colloque international *'L'Étranger', cinquante ans après,* Amiens, 11–12 décembre 1992." *Bulletin d'Information de la Société des Études Camusiennes* 29 (1993): 7–12.

Bloom, Harold, ed. *Albert Camus.* Modern Critical Views. New York: Chelsea House, 1989.

Boisdeffre, Pierre de. "Camus et son destin." In *Camus,* edited by René-Marill Albérès, Pierre de Boisdeffre, Jean Daniel, Pierre Gascar, Morvan Lebesque, André Parinaud, Emmanuel Roblès, Jules Roy, and Pierre-Henri Simon. Collection Génies et Réalités. Paris: Hachette, 1964.

———. "L'évolution spirituelle d'Albert Camus." *Ecclesia* 101 (1957): 107–12.

———. "La fin d'une amitié: Sartre contre Camus." *La Revue Libre* 1 (1952): 51–57.

Boisdeffre, Pierre de, and Monique Difrane. "Camus 1980." *La Revue des Deux Mondes* (1980): 86–96.

Bonnier, Henry. *Albert Camus ou la force d'être: essai.* Lyons: Vitte, 1959.

Boone, Danièle. *Camus.* Paris: Veyrier, 1987.

Bott, François. "Grandes études: le destin de Camus." *Magazine littéraire* 3 (1967): 6–14.

Bourboune, Mourad, and Jules Roy. "Camus, l'Algérie au cœur." *Les Nouvelles littéraires* 55 (1978): 4–5.

Bourel, Dominique. "Albert Camus, Martin Buber et la Méditerranée." In *Albert Camus: parcours méditerranéens,* edited by Fernande Bartfeld and David Ohana. Vol 5 of *Perspectives: Revue de l'Université Hébraïque de Jérusalem* (1998): 147–55.

Bousquet, François. *Camus le Méditerranéen, Camus l'Ancien.* Sherbrooke: Naaman, 1977.

Bouzar, Wadi. "Brève histoire d'une déception: Camus et l'Algérie." *Revue Celfan / Celfan Review* 4 (1985): 36–40.

Braun, Lev. *Witness of Decline. Albert Camus: Moralist of the Absurd.* Rutherford, Fairleigh Dickinson University Press, 1974.

Brée, Germaine. *Albert Camus.* New York: Columbia University Press, 1964.

———. "Albert Camus et le *Théâtre de L'Équipe.*" *French Review* 22 (1949): 225–29.

———. "Avatars of Prometheus: A Shifting Camusian Image." In *Mythology in French Literature,* edited by Philip Crant. French Literature Series III. South Carolina: University of South Carolina, College of Humanities and Social Sciences, Department of Foreign Languages and Literatures, 1976.

———. *Camus.* New Brunswick: Rutgers University Press, 1959.

———, ed. *Camus: A Collection of Critical Essays.* Englewood Cliffs, NJ: Prentice Hall, 1962.

———. *Camus and Sartre: Crisis and Commitment.* London: Calder & Boyars, 1974.

———. "Climates of the Mind. Albert Camus: 1936–1940," in *Critical Essays on Albert Camus.* Edited by Bettina L. Knapp. Boston: Hall, 1988.

Breton, André, and Aimé Patrie. "Dialogue entre André Breton et Aimé Patrie à propos de *L'Homme révolté* d'Albert Camus." *Arts* 333 (1951): 1, 3.

Brisville, Jean-Claude. *Camus.* La Bibliothèque idéale. Paris: Gallimard, 1959.

Brochier, Jean-Jacques. *Albert Camus: philosophe pour classes terminales.* Paris: Balland, 1979.

———. "Camus, mythe et réalité." *Magazine littéraire* 67–68 (1972): 9.

Brody, Ervin C. "Camus Thirty Years Later: His Relevance to our Days." *Literary Review: An International Journal of Contemporary Writing* 35 (1991): 124–33.

Brombert, Victor. "Camus and the Novel of the 'Absurd.'" *Yale French Studies* 1 (1948): 119–23.

Bronner, Stephen Eric. *Albert Camus. The Thinker, the Artist, the Man.* New York: Franklin Watts, 1996.

Brown, James W. *"Sensing," "Seeing," "Saying" in Camus's "Noces": A Meditative Essay.* Amsterdam: Rodopi, 2004.

Broyelle, Jacques, and Claudie Broyelle. *Les Illusions retrouvées: Sartre a toujours raison contre Camus.* Paris: Grasset, 1982.

Brua, Edmond. "Moment." *Simoun* 8 (1960): 44.

Bruckberger, R. L. "Une Image radieuse." *NRF* 8 (1960): 515–21.

Brunswic, Anne, and Catherine Argand, eds. "Les écrivains du bac: Camus au zénith." *Lire* 186 (1991): 121–34.

Buffard-Moret, Brigitte. "'La mémoire du cœur': approche stylistique du *Premier Homme* d'Albert Camus." *Roman 20–50* 27 (1999): 53–64.

Cabaud, Jacques. "Albert Camus et Simone Weil." *Kentucky Romance Quarterly* 21 (1974): 383–94.

Callen, Tony. "A Double First from Scotland." *Modern & Contemporary France* n.s., 4 (1996): 100–2.

Camelin, Colette. "La guerre dans *Le Premier Homme* d'Albert Camus." *Roman 20–50* 27 (1999): 77–87.

Camus, Catherine. "Editor's Note." In Albert Camus, *The First Man,* translated by David Hapgood. London: Hamish Hamilton, 1995.

Camus, Catherine, Pierre Le Baut, Olivier Corpet, Pascale Delahaye, Antoine Gallimard, Robert Gallimard, Roger Grenier, Jacqueline Lévi-Valensi, and Bertrand Poirot-Delpech. "Albert Camus: *Le Premier Homme.*" *Bulletin d'Information de la Société des Études Camusiennes* 33 (1994): 15–19.

Capstick, Jill. "Mastery or Slavery: The Ethics of Revolt in Camus's 'Les Muets.'" *Modern & Contemporary France* 11 (2003): 453–62.

Carroll, David. "Camus's Algeria: Birthrights, Colonial Injustice, and the Fiction of a French-Algerian People." *MLN* 112 (1997): 517–49.

Cassagne, Ines de. "Tension et équilibre des extrêmes dans l'idéal classique de Camus," in *Albert Camus: les Extrêmes et l'équilibre; Actes du colloque de Keele, 25–27 mars 1993.* Edited by David H. Walker. Amsterdam: Rodopi, 1994.

Castex, Pierre-Georges. "Les contradictions d'Albert Camus." *Le Français dans le monde* 5 (1966): 6–10.

Caussat, P. "Le prélude d'une pensée: 'Métaphysique chrétienne et néoplatonisme'." In *Albert Camus et la philosophie,* edited by A.M. Amiot and F. Mattéi. Paris: PUF, 1997.

Cela, Camila José. "Écrit sur la mort d'Albert Camus et à la lumière de son flambeau." *NRF* 8 (1960): 556–58.

Centore, F. F. "Camus, Pascal and the Absurd." *New Scholasticism* 54 (1980): 46–59.

Cervera, Gilles. "Un écrit primal." *Magazine littéraire* 322 (1994): 61–62.

Chabot, Jacques. "La mémoire des pauvres." *Roman 20–50* 27 (1999): 65–76.

Champigny, Robert Jean. "Esthétique et Morale." In *Albert Camus, 9: "la pensée de Camus,"* edited by Raymond Gay-Crosier. La Revue des Lettres Modernes, 565–69. Paris: Lettres Modernes Minard, 1979.

———. *Humanism and Human Racism.* The Hague: Mouton, 1972.

———. "Suffering and Death." *Symposium* 24 (1970): 197–205.

———. "Un jugement personnel," in *Camus 1970: Colloque organisé sous les auspices du Département des Langues et Littératures romanes de l'université de Floride (Gainesville) les 29 et 30 janvier 1970.* Edited by Raymond Gay-Crosier. Sherbrooke: CELEF, 1970.

Charbit, Denis. "Camus et l'épreuve algérienne." In *Albert Camus: parcours méditerranéens,* edited by Fernande Bartfeld and David Ohana. Vol 5 of *Perspectives: Revue de l'Université Hébraïque de Jérusalem* (1998): 157–81.

———. "*L'Homme révolté:* grandeur et servitude de la fonction intellectuelle." In *Albert Camus, 19: "'L'Homme révolté': cinquante ans après,"* edited by Raymond Gay-Crosier. Paris: Lettres Modernes Minard, 2001.

Chaulet-Achour, Christiane. *Albert Camus, Alger: "L'Étranger" et autres récits.* Biarritz: Atlantica, 1998.

———. "L'autre autochtone dans *Le Premier Homme* d'Albert Camus." *Roman 20–50* 27 (1999): 17–29.

———. "Camus et l'Algérie des années 90." *Europe* 77 (1999): 167–77.

Chavanes, François. *Albert Camus: "Il faut vivre maintenant"; Questions posées au christianisme par l'œuvre d'Albert Camus.* Paris: Cerf, 1990.

———. *Albert Camus: un message d'espoir.* Paris: Cerf, 1996.

———. "L'apport d'Albert Camus dans le domaine de l'éthique et la nouvelle Europe," in *Albert Camus et l'Europe: Actes du colloque de Strasbourg, 9 et 10 novembre 1990.* Edited by André Abbou. Paris: Ofil, 1995.

———. "Influence de la Guerre d'Algérie sur la pensée d'Albert Camus." *Études* (September 1992): 235–44.

Chelfi, Mustapha. "Les beignets de la rue Bab-Azoun." *Le Nouvel Observateur,* June 9–15, 1994, 12.

Chiaromonte, Nicola. "Albert Camus and Moderation." *Partisan Review* 15 (1948): 1142–45.

———. "Albert Camus: In Memoriam." In *Camus: A Collection of Critical Essays.* Edited by Germaine Brée. Englewood Cliffs, NJ: Prenticehall, 1962.

———. "Paris Letter." *Partisan Review* 17 (1950): 707–14.

Chife, Aloy. "Agonie au Golgotha: l'image de l'homme dans l'œuvre de Camus." In *Les trois guerres d'Albert Camus: Actes du Colloque International de Poitiers, 4–5–6 mai 1995.* Edited by Lionel Dubois. Poitiers: Éditions du Pont-Neuf, 1995.

Christensen, Peter G. "Camus and Savinkov: Examining the Problems of Terrorism." *Scottish Slavonic Review* (Autumn 1993): 33–51.

Chumbley, Robert. "La mythologie personnelle de Camus." In *Albert Camus entre la misère et le soleil: Actes du Colloque international de Poitiers, 29–30–31 mai 1997.* Edited by Lionel Dubois. Poitiers: Éditions du Pont-Neuf, 1997.

Cielens, Isabelle. "La réception d'Albert Camus en Lettonie sous l'occupation soviétique." In *Albert Camus et l'Europe: Actes du colloque de Stasbourg, 9–10 novembre 1990,* edited by André Abbou. Paris: L'Ofil, 1995.

———. "La réception de Camus en Lettonie." In *Albert Camus, 20: "'Le Premier homme' en perspective."* Edited by Raymond Gay-Crosier. Paris: Lettres Modernes Minard, 2004.

Clayton, A. J. *Étapes d'un itinéraire spirituel: Albert Camus de 1937 à 1944.* Paris: Lettres Modernes, 1971.

Clot, René-Jean. "Camus." *Simoun* 8 (1960): 29–33.

Cocking, John. "The Idea of Promethean Revolt." *Listener,* July 10, 1952, 63–64.

Cohen-Solal, Annie. "Camus, Sartre and the Algerian War." *Journal of European Studies* 28 (1998): 43–50.

Cohn, Yehuda L. "Les sources bibliques dans l'œuvre d'Albert Camus." In *Albert Camus: parcours méditerranéens,* edited by Fernande Bartfeld and David Ohana. Vol 5 of *Perspectives: Revue de l'Université Hébraïque de Jérusalem* (1998): 45–54.

Conilh, Jean. "Albert Camus: L'Exil sans royaume." *Esprit* 26 (1958): 529–43.

———. "Albert Camus: L'Exil sans royaume (II)." *Esprit* 26 (1958): 673–92.

Constable, E. L. "Shame." *MLN* 112 (1997): 641–65.

Coombs, Ilona. *Camus: homme de théâtre.* Paris: Nizet, 1968.

Corbic, Arnaud. *Camus: l'absurde, la révolte, l'amour.* Paris: Éditions de l'Atelier / Éditions Ouvrières, 2003.

Cordes, Alfred. *The Descent of the Doves: Camus's Journey to the Spirit.* Washington, DC: University Presses of America, 1980.

Costes, Alain. *Albert Camus ou la parole manquante: étude psychanalytique.* Collection Science de L'Homme. Paris: Payot, 1973.

Cote, Nicolas M. "Albert Camus et l'existence de Dieu." *Culture* 20 (1959): 268–81.

Cottle, Michaela Voss. "'And so I tell my Life to myself'. Harmony in Writing: Camus's *Carnets.*" Ph.D. diss., University of North Carolina at Chapel Hill, 1992.

Courcy, Louis de. "Rencontre avec Catherine Camus: un formidable désir d'exister." *Bulletin d'Information de la Société des Études Camusiennes* 66 (2003): 38–40.

Courrière, Yves. "Albert Camus devant la Guerre d'Algérie." *Le Figaro littéraire,* June 2–8, 1969, 8–11.

———. "Albert Camus devant la Guerre d'Algérie, II. 1956: l'échec de la trêve civile." *Le Figaro littéraire,* June 9–15, 1969, 10–13.

Crochet, Monique. *Les Mythes dans l'œuvre de Camus.* Paris: Editions Universitaires, 1973.

Cruickshank, John. *Albert Camus and the Literature of Revolt.* Westport, Conn.: Greenwood Press, 1978.

———. "Variations of the Absurd: Malraux, Camus and Sartre." In *Perspectives on Language and Literature: Essays in Honour of William Mailer,* edited by Michael Dash and Bridget Jones. Mona, Jamaica: Department of French and German, University of the West Indies, 1985.

Cryle, Peter. *Bilan critique: "L'Exil et le royaume" d'Albert Camus: essai d'analyse.* Paris: Lettres Modernes Minard, 1973.

Cunningham, Lawrence S. "Camus on Pacifism and Resistance." *Cistercian Studies* 23 (1988): 225–26.

Curtis, Jerry Lynn. "Camus' Vision of Greatness." *Orbis Litterarum* 29 (1974): 338–54.

———. "Meursault or the Leap of Death." *Rice University Studies* 57 (1971): 41–48.

Dadoun, Roger. "Albert Camus: fondations d'anarchie." In *Camus et la politique: Actes du colloque de Nanterre, 5–7 juin 1985,* edited by Jeanyves Guérin. Paris: L'Harmattan, 1986.

———. "Albert Camus le méditerranéen. Le rêve de la lumière et le complexe du clair-obscur." *Simoun* 3 (1952): 42–47.

Dahlin, Lois. "Entretien avec Francis Ponge, ses rapports avec Camus, Sartre et d'autres." *French Review* 54 (1950): 271–81.

Daix, Pierre. "Un quart de vérité selon Camus." *La Nouvelle Critique* 9 (1957): 144–46.

Dana, Catherine. "Remémoration et commémoration dans *La Peste.*" In *Les trois guerres d'Albert Camus: Actes du Colloque International de Poitiers, 4–5–6 mai 1995,* edited by Lionel Dubois. Poitiers: Éditions du Pont-Neuf, 1995.

Daniel, Jean. "Le bonheur entre Athènes et Jérusalem." In *Albert Camus: parcours méditerranéens,* edited by Fernande Bartfeld and David Ohana. Vol 5 of *Perspectives: Revue de l'Université Hébraïque de Jérusalem* (1998): 13–24.

———. "Camus as journalist." *New Republic,* June 13, 1964, 19–21.

———. "Camus et le terrorisme." *Le Nouvel Observateur,* November 14–20, 2002, 24–27.

———. "Cet étrange recours à Camus." *Le Nouvel Observateur,* November 27, 1978, 84–86.

———. "Le combat pour *Combat.*" In *Camus,* edited by René-Marill Albérès, Pierre de Boisdeffre, Jean Daniel, Pierre Gascar, Morvan Lebesque, André Parinaud, Emmanuel Roblès, Jules Roy, and Pierre-Henri Simon. Collection Génies et Réalités. Paris: Hachette, 1964.

———. "Innocence in Camus and Dostoievsky." In *Camus's "L'Étranger": Fifty Years On.* 2nd ed., edited by Adèle King. New York: St. Martin's Press, 1994.

———. "Parlons de lui. . . ." *L'Express,* January 7, 1960, 27–29.

———. "*Le Premier homme:* la religion, le siècle." *Narcisse* 16 (1996): 9–16.

———. "Une patrie algérienne, deux peuples. . . ." *Études méditerranéennes* 7 (1960): 19–24.

Davis, Colin. "Altericide: Camus, Encounters, Readings." *Forum for Modern Language Studies* 33 (1997): 129–41.

Davison, Ray. *Camus: The Challenge of Dostoevsky.* Exeter: University of Exeter Press, 1997.

———. "L'éloquence philosophique des *Muets.*" In *Albert Camus: les Extrêmes et l'équilibre; Actes du colloque de Keele, 25–27 mars 1993,* edited by David H. Walker. Amsterdam: Rodopi, 1994.

———. "Mythologizing the Mediterranean: The Case of Albert Camus." *Journal of Mediterranean Studies* 10 (2000): 77–92.

Davy, Marie Madeleine. "Camus et Simone Weil." *La Table Ronde* 146 (1960): 137–43.

Debeche, Djamila. "Notre frère Albert Camus." *Simoun* 8 (1960): 40–41.

Debout, Simone. "Sartre et Camus face à Hiroshima." *Esprit* (January 1998): 151–58.

———. "Sartre et Camus, témoins de la liberté." *MLN* 112 (1997): 600–7.

Debray, Pierre. "Albert Camus: *Pied Noir.*" *Aspects de la France,* January 12, 1961, 2.

Dedet, Christian. "Librairie du mois: le groupe algérois." *Esprit* 36 (1968): 930–35.

Defay, Alexandre. "Albert Camus: parcours méditerranéens. Ici et maintenant à Jérusalem." In *Albert Camus: parcours méditerranéens,* edited by Fernande Bartfeld and David Ohana. Vol 5 of *Perspectives: Revue de l'Université Hébraïque de Jérusalem* (1998): 9–12.

Delibes, Miguel. "Albert Camus." *NRF* 8 (1960): 562.

Delpech, L. P. "Albert Camus, tel qu'en lui-même." *La Revue des Deux Mondes* (1971): 63–71.

Desgraupes, Pierre. "Sur Albert Camus." *Poésie 47* 8 (1947): 115–25.

Devismes, M. *La justice selon Albert Camus: discours de M. Devismes; Audience solennelle de rentrée du 16 septembre 1959.* Caen: Cour d'Appel de Caen, 1959.

Di Pilla, Francesco. "Camus en Italie." In *Camus et la politique: Actes du colloque de Nanterre, 5–7 juin 1985.* Edited by Jean-Yves Guérin. Paris: L'Harmattan, 1986.

———. "Remarques sur l'*Algérianité* de Camus." In *Albert Camus: textes réunis par Paul F. Smets à l'occasion du 25e anniversaire de la mort de l'écrivain,* edited by Paul F. Smets. Brussels: Éditions de l'Université de Bruxelles, 1985.

Djemaï, Abdelkader. *Camus à Oran.* Paris: Michalon, 1995.

Domenach, Jean-Marie. "Albert Camus." *Esprit* 28 (1960): 280–83.

Doubrovsky, Serge. "La Morale d'Albert Camus." *Preuves* 116 (1960): 39–49.

Draï, Raphaël. "Étranger à la justice." In *Albert Camus, 16: "L'Étranger": cinquante ans après; Actes du Colloque d'Amiens, 11–12 décembre 1992,* edited by Jacqueline Lévi-Valensi and Raymond Gay-Crosier. La Revue des Lettres Modernes, 1259–65. Paris: Lettres Modernes, 1995.

Drake, David. "Sartre, Camus and the Algerian War." *Sartre Studies International* 5 (1999): 16–32.

Dubois, Lionel. "L'actualité de Camus." In *Albert Camus entre la misère et le soleil. Actes du Colloque international de Poitiers, 29–30–31 mai 1997,* edited by Lionel Dubois. Poitiers: Éditions du Pont-Neuf, 1997.

———. *Albert Camus entre la misère et le soleil. Actes du Colloque international de Poitiers, 29–30–31 mai 1997.* Poitiers, Éditions du Pont-Neuf, 1997.

———. "Le combat d'Albert Camus contre la maladie et la misère." *L'Information littéraire* 4 (1994): 21–23.

———. "Le combat d'Albert Camus contre le confort intellectuel et l''establishment.'" In *Albert Camus entre la misère et le soleil: Actes du Colloque international de Poitiers, 29–30–31 mai 1997,* edited by Lionel Dubois. Poitiers: Éditions du Pont-Neuf, 1997.

———. "Le combat d'Albert Camus contre les totalitarismes." In *Les trois guerres d'Albert Camu: Actes du Colloque International de Poitiers, 4–5–6 mai 1995,* edited by Lionel Dubois. Poitiers: Éditions du Pont-Neuf, 1995.

———. "*Le Premier Homme,* le roman inachevé d'Albert Camus." *French Review* 69 (1996): 556–65.

———. "Les premiers combats d'Albert Camus contre l'injustice sociale." *Lettres Romanes* 54 (2000): 69–76.

———. "Le style camusien révélateur d'une morale," in *Albert Camus entre la misère et le soleil: Actes du Colloque international de Poitiers, 29–30–31 mai 1997.* Edited by Lionel Dubois. Poitiers: Éditions du Pont-Neuf, 1997.

———, ed. *Les trois guerres d'Albert Camus: Actes du Colloque International de Poitiers, 4–5–6 mai 1995.* Poitiers: Éditions du Pont-Neuf, 1995.

Dubois, Lionel, Isabelle Auzanneau, Abdelkader Djemai, Elizabeth Hart, Gäetan Langhade, Michel Maillard, and Laurent Martin. "Camus journaliste." In *Les trois guerres d'Albert Camus: Actes du Colloque International de Poitiers, 4–5–6 mai 1995,* edited by Lionel Dubois. Poitiers: Éditions du Pont-Neuf, 1995.

Dubois, Lionel, Isabelle Auzanneau, Moishe Black, Catherine Dana, Abdelkader Djemai, Gaëtan Langhade, Michelle Laperrousaz, and Michel Maillard. "Camus, le méditerranéen." In *Les trois guerres d'Albert Camus: Actes du Colloque International de Poitiers, 4–5–6 mai 1995,* edited by Lionel Dubois. Poitiers: Éditions du Pont-Neuf, 1995.

Dubois, Lionel, Jacqueline Baishanski, Helene M. Brown, Sarah Chaabane, Viviane Girault, Margaret Gray, and Geraldine F. Montgomery. "Lecture psychanalytique du *Premier Homme.*" In *Albert Camus entre la misère et le soleil: Actes du Colloque international de Poitiers, 29–30–31 mai 1997,* edited by Lionel Dubois. Poitiers: Éditions du Pont-Neuf, 1997.

Duchet, Michèle, and Claude Duchet. "Inactuelles III, ou le juste et l'Algérie." *La Nouvelle Critique* 10 (1958): 145–53.

Duke, Robert H. "An Analysis of Guilt in the Writings of Albert Camus." *Theology and Life* 5 (1962): 227–33.

Dumur, Guy. "Homme d'une génération d'espoir et de souffrance." *Le Figaro littéraire,* January 9, 1960, 5.

———. "Une génération trahie." *NRF* 8 (1960): 568–74.

Dunn, Susan. "Camus and Louis XVI: An Elegy for the Martyred King." *French Review* 62 (1989): 1032–40.

Dunwoodie, Peter. "Albert Camus and the Anarchist Alternative." *Australian Journal of French Studies* 30 (1993): 84–104.

———. "Albert Camus et le viol de la révolte." In *Albert Camus: les Extrêmes et l'équilibre: Actes du colloque de Keele, 25–27 mars 1993,* edited by David H. Walker. Amsterdam: Rodopi, 1994.

———. "Constructing memories: Camus, Algeria and *Le Premier Homme.*" *Bulletin d'Information de la Société des Études Camusiennes* 40 (1996): 25–26.

———. "Hors de combat: Albert Camus et l'art de la polémique." *Les Lettres Romanes* 46 (1992): 213–28.

Dunwoodie, Peter, and Edward J. Hughes. "Les Lectures d'Albert Camus avant la guerre." In *Albert Camus, 7: "Le Théâtre,"* edited by Raymond Gay-Crosier. La Revue des Lettres Modernes, 419–24. Paris: Lettres Modernes Minard, 1975.

———. "Re-writing settlement." In *Constructing Memories: Camus, Algeria and "Le Premier Homme,"* edited by Peter Dunwoodie and Edward J. Hughes. Vol 6 of *Stirling French Publications* (1998): 133–41.

———. *Une Histoire ambivalente: le dialogue Camus-Dostoïevski.* Paris: Nizet, 1996.

———. "Introduction." In *Constructing Memories: Camus, Algeria and "Le Premier Homme,"* edited by Peter Dunwoodie and Edward J. Hughes. Vol 6 of *Stirling French Publications* (1998): v–viii.

Dupuy, René-Jean. "Albert Camus: moraliste politique." In *Hommage à Jean Onimus.* Annales de la Faculté des Lettres et Sciences Humaines de Nice 38. Paris: Les Belles Lettres, 1979.

———. "Camus et Les Droits de l'Homme." In *Camus et la politique: Actes du colloque de Nanterre, 5–7 juin 1985,* edited by Jeanyves Guérin. Paris: L'Harmattan, 1986.

Durand, Anne. *Le Cas Albert Camus.* Collection Célébrités d'Aujourd'hui 3. Paris: Hachette, 1961.

Durfee, Harold A. "Albert Camus and the Ethics of Rebellion." *Journal of Religion* 38 (1958): 29–45.

Duvall, William E. "The Nietzsche Temptation in the Thought of Albert Camus." *History of European Thought* 11 (1989): 955–62.

Dyer, Geoff. *Arendt, Camus and Modern Rebellion.* New Haven, CT: Yale University Press, 1993.

Earl, A. J., "Camus and the Christian Religion." *Modern Languages* 54 (1973): 67–74.

East, Bernard. *Albert Camus, ou l'homme à la recherche d'une morale.* Paris: Cerf, 1984.

Elbaz, André. "Albert Camus: l'Algérien?" *Cahiers de Littérature générale et comparée* 5 (1981): 101–9.

Elbaz, Shlomo. "Camus poète méditerranéen." In *Albert Camus: parcours méditerranéens,* edited by Fernande Bartfeld and David Ohana. Vol. 5 of *Perspectives: Revue de l'Université Hébraïque de Jérusalem* (1998): 235–44.

Erkoreka, Yon. *Albert Camus: tout savoir ou rien.* Montreal: Paulines, 1987.

Erickson, John. "Albert Camus and North Africa: A Discourse of Exteriority." In *Critical Essays on Albert Camus,* edited by Bettina L. Knapp. Boston, Ma.: Hall, 1988.

Espiau de la Maestre, André. "Albert Camus: pèlerin de l'absolu." *Les Lettres romanes,* February 1, 1961, 3–22.

Etiemble, René. "D'une amitié." *NRF* 8 (1960): 461–65.

———. "Peste ou péché?" *Les Temps modernes* 3 (1947): 911–20.

Eubanks, Cecil L., and Peter A. Petrakis. "Reconstructing the World: Albert Camus and the Symbolization of Experience." *Journal of Politics* 61 (1999): 293–312.

Ewald, François. "L'Absurde et la révolte." *Magazine littéraire* 276 (1990): 43–45.

Fauconnier, Bernard. "Camus: une enfance en Algérie." *Magazine littéraire* 322 (1994): 60–61.

———. "Le mystère Camus." *Magazine littéraire* 342 (1996): 126–28.

Favre, Frantz. "Camus et Nietzsche: philosophie et existence." In *Albert Camus, 9: "la pensée de Camus,"* edited by Raymond Gay-Crosier. La Revue des Lettres Modernes 565–69. Paris: Lettres Modernes Minard, 1979.

———. "*L'Étranger* and 'Metaphysical Anxiety.'" In *Camus's "L'Étranger": Fifty Years On.* 2nd ed., edited by Adèle King. New York: St. Martin's Press, 1994.

———. "L'idée de l'Europe chez Nietzsche et Camus." In *Albert Camus et l'Europe: Actes du colloque de Strasbourg, 9 et 10 novembre 1990,* edited by André Abbou. Paris: Ofil, 1995.

———. *Montherlant et Camus: une lignée nietzschéenne.* Archives Albert Camus 8. Paris: Lettres Modernes Minard, 2000.

———. "Quand Camus lisait Nietzsche," in *Albert Camus, 20: "'Le Premier homme' en perspective,"* edited by Raymond Gay-Crosier. La Revue des Lettres Modernes. Paris: Lettres Modernes Minard, 2004.

Felman, Shoshana. "Crisis of Witnessing: Albert Camus's Postwar Writings." *Cardozo Studies in Law and Literature* 3 (1991): 197–242.

Feraoun, Mouloud. "Au-dessus des haines." *Simoun* 8 (1960): 18–19.

———. "Le dernier message." *Preuves* 110 (1960): 21–24.

———. "La source de nos communs malheurs (Lettre à Albert Camus)." *Preuves* 91 (1958): 72–75.

Feibleman, James K. "Camus and the Passion of Humanism." *Kenyon Review* 25 (1963): 281–92.

Fitch, Brian T., ed. *Albert Camus, 1: "autour de 'L'Étranger.'"* La Revue des Lettres Modernes, 170–74. Paris: Lettres Modernes, 1968.

———, ed. *Albert Camus, 2: "langue et langage."* La Revue des Lettres Modernes, 212–16. Paris: Lettres Modernes, 1969.

———, ed. *Albert Camus, 4: "sources et influences."* La Revue des Lettres Modernes, 264–70. Paris: Lettres Modernes, 1971.

———, ed. *Albert Camus, 5: "journalisme et politique. L'Entrée dans l'histoire (1938–1940)."* La Revue des Lettres Modernes, 315–22. Paris: Lettres Modernes, 1972.

———, ed. *Albert Camus, 10: "nouvelles approches."* La Revue des Lettres Modernes, 632–36. Paris: Lettres Modernes Minard, 1982.

———, ed. *Albert Camus, 11: "Camus et la religion."* La Revue des Lettres Modernes, 648–51. Paris: Lettres Modernes Minard, 1982.

———, ed. *Albert Camus, 12: "la révolte en question."* La Revue des Lettres Modernes, 715–19. Paris: Lettres Modernes Minard, 1985.

———. "Des écrivains et des bavards: l'intra-intertextualité camusienne." In *Albert Camus: œuvre fermée, œuvre ouverte? Actes du colloque du Centre Culturel International de Cerisy-la-Salle, juin 1982,* edited by Raymond Gay-Crosier and Jacqueline Lévi-Valensi. Cahiers Albert Camus 5. Paris: Gallimard, 1985.

———. "Narcisse interprète: *La Chute* comme modèle herméneutique," in *Albert Camus, 10: "Nouvelles approches."* Edited by Brian T. Fitch. La Revue des Lettres Modernes, 632–36. Paris: Lettres Modernes Minard, 1982.

Fleming, Richard. "Remarks on the Ethical Conclusion of Camus's *The Rebel.*" *College English Association Critic* 49 (1986–1987): 114–23.

Fletcher, John. "*L'Étranger* and the New Novel." In *Camus's "L'Étranger": Fifty Years On.* 2nd ed. Edited by Adèle King. New York: St. Martin's Press, 1994.

Fleure, Eugène. "Albert Camus devant Simone Weil." *Cahiers Simone Weil* 1 (1978): 10–17.

Fontan, Antonio. "Camus entre le paganisme et le christianisme." *La Table Ronde* 146 (1960): 114–19.

Fortier, Paul A. "Le décor symbolique de 'L'Hôte' d'Albert Camus." *French Review* 46 (1973): 535–42.

Fouchet, Max-Pol. "Camus: mémoire parlée." *Magazine littéraire* 8 (1967): 4–7.

———. "L'Homme du juste milieu: entretien avec Max-Pol Fouchet." *Magazine littéraire* 67–68 (1972): 31–32.

Fraisse, Simone. "De Lucrèce, Camus ou les contradictions de la révolte." *Esprit.* 27 (1959): 437–53.

Frank, Joseph. "Camus and the Algerian War." *Dissent* (Winter 1985): 105–10.

Frank, Waldo. "That Europe May Live . . . *The Rebel.*" *New Republic* 130 (1954): 19–20.

Freeman, Edward. *The Theatre of Albert Camus: A Critical Study.* London: Methuen, 1971.

Fremont, S. C. Laurent. "Albert Camus: Prométhée et le bonheur." *La Revue de l'Université Laval* 19 (1965): 551–63.

Frohock, W. M. "Camus: Image, Influence and Sensibility." *Yale French Studies* 2 (1949): 91–99.

Gadourek, Carina. *Les Innocents et les coupables: essai d'exégèse de l'œuvre d'Albert Camus.* The Hague: Mouton, 1963

Gagnebin, Laurent. *Albert Camus dans sa lumière: essai sur l'évolution de sa pensée.* Lausanne: Cahiers de la Renaissance Vaudoise, 1964.

Gaillard, Pol. *Albert Camus.* Collection Présence Littéraire. Paris: Bordas, 1973.

Galey, Matthieu. "Camus avant Camus." *L'Express,* April 3–9, 1978, 18–19.

Galliani, R. "Camus, *L'Étranger* et les arabes." *Revue de l'Université d'Ottawa* 43 (1973): 436–44.

Garfitt, Toby. "Camus et Grenier." In *Albert Camus: les Extrêmes et l'équilibre; Actes du colloque de Keele, 25–27 mars 1993,* edited by David H. Walker. Amsterdam: Rodopi, 1994.

———. "Le Premier homm[ag]e: Grounding history in love." In *Constructing Memories: Camus, Algeria and "Le Premier Homme,"* edited by Peter Dunwoodie and Edward J. Hughes. Vol 6 of *Stirling French Publications* (1998): 1–8.

Gargan, Edward T. "Revolution and Morale in the Formative Thought of Albert Camus." *Review of Politics* 25 (1963): 483–96.

Garnham, B. G. "Camus, Metaphysical Revolt and Historical Action." *Modern Language Review* 62 (1967): 248–55.

Gascar, Pierre. "Le dernier visage de Camus." In *Camus,* edited by René-Marill Albérès, Pierre de Boisdeffre, Jean Daniel, Pierre Gascar, Morvan Lebesque, André Parinaud, Emmanuel Roblès, Jules Roy, and Pierre-Henri Simon. Collection Génies et Réalités. Paris: Hachette, 1964.

Gassin, Jean. "*La Chute* et le retable de L'Agneau mystique." In *Albert Camus 1980: Second International Conference, February 21–23 1980, The University of Florida, Gainesville,* edited by Raymond Gay-Crosier. Gainesville: University Presses of Florida, 1980.

———. *L'Univers symbolique d'Albert Camus: essai d'interprétation psychanalytique.* Paris: Minard, 1981.

Gaston, Renaud R. "Saint Tarrou, martyr laïque ou Camus et le problème de la sainteté." *Revue de l'Université d'Ottawa* 41 (1971): 322–30.

Gay-Crosier, Raymond, ed. *Albert Camus, 7: "Le Théâtre."* La Revue des Lettres Modernes 419–24. Paris: Lettres Modernes, Minard, 1975.

———, ed. *Albert Camus, 9: "la pensée de Camus."* La Revue des Lettres Modernes, 565–69. Paris: Lettres Modernes Minard, 1979.

———, ed. *Albert Camus, 12: "la révolte en question."* La Revue des Lettres Modernes, 715–19. Paris: Lettres Modernes Minard, 1985.

———, ed. *Albert Camus, 13: "études comparatives."* La Revue des Lettres Modernes, 904–10. Paris: Lettres Modernes Minard, 1989.

———, ed. *Albert Camus, 14: "le texte et ses langages."* La Revue des Lettres Modernes, 985–92. Paris: Lettres Modernes Minard, 1991.

———, ed. *Albert Camus, 15: "textes, intertextes, contextes autour de 'La Chute.'"* La Revue des Lettres Modernes 1123–32. Paris: Lettres Modernes, 1993.

———, ed. *Albert Camus, 16: "'L'Étranger": cinquante ans après'. Actes du Colloque d'Amiens, 11–12 décembre 1992, sous la direction de Jacqueline Lévi-Valensi.* La Revue des Lettres Modernes, 1259–65. Paris: Lettres Modernes, 1995.

———, ed. *Albert Camus, 17: "toujours autour de 'L'Étranger.'"* La Revue des Lettres Modernes 1310–16. Paris: Lettres Modernes Minard, 1996.

———, ed. *Albert Camus, 18: "la réception de l'œuvre de Camus en U.R.S.S. et en R.D.A.."* La Revue des Lettres Modernes, 1472–77. Paris: Lettres Modernes Minard, 1999.

———, ed. *Albert Camus, 19: "'L'Homme révolté': cinquante ans après."* La Revue des Lettres Modernes. Paris: Lettres Modernes Minard, 2001.

———, ed. *Albert Camus, 20: "'Le Premier homme' en perspective."* La Revue des Lettres Modernes. Paris: Lettres Modernes Minard, 2004.

———, ed. *Albert Camus 1980. Second International Conference, February 21–23 1980, The University of Florida, Gainesville.* Gainesville: University Presses of Florida, 1980.

———. "Albert Camus: algérianité et marginalité." *Australian Journal of French Studies* 27 (1990): 283–90.

———. "Albert Camus: pour une culture européenne sans eurocentrisme." *Orbis Litterarum* 50 (1995): 304–19.

———. "L'Anarchisme mesuré de Camus." *Symposium* 24 (1970): 243–53.

———, ed. *Camus 1970: Colloque organisé sous les auspices du Département des Langues et Littératures romanes de l'université de Floride (Gainesville) les 29 et 30 janvier 1970.* Sherbrooke: CELEF, 1970.

———. "Les enjeux de la pensée de midi." In *Albert Camus: parcours méditerranéens,* edited by Fernande Bartfeld and David Ohana. Vol. 5 of *Perspectives: Revue de l'Université Hébraïque de Jérusalem* (1998): 33–108.

———. "Camus et Sade: une relation ambiguë." *Zeitschrift für Französische Sprache und Literatur* 98 (1988): 166–73.

———. *Les Envers d'un échec: étude sur le théâtre d'Albert Camus.* Bibliothèque des Lettres Modernes 10. Paris: Lettres Modernes Minard, 1967.

———. *Literary Masterpieces: "The Stranger."* Vol. 8. Farmington Hills: Gale Group, 2002.

———. "Les Masques de l'impossible: le théâtre de Camus aujourd'hui." *Europe* 77 (1999): 90–103.

———. "Reprise d'une polémique." *Bulletin d'Information de la Société des Études Camusiennes* 43 (1997): 3.

———. "La révolte génératrice et régénératrice." In *Albert Camus: œuvre fermée, œuvre ouverte? Actes du colloque du Centre Culturel International de Cerisy-la-Salle, juin 1982,* edited by Raymond Gay-Crosier and Jacqueline Lévi-Valensi. Cahiers Albert Camus 5. Paris, Gallimard: 1985.

———. "Révolte, souveraineté et jeu chez Bataille et Camus." In *Albert Camus, 12: "la révolte en question."* Edited by Raymond Gay-Crosier. La Revue des Lettres Modernes, 715–19. Paris: Lettres Modernes Minard, 1985.

———. "Un débat universitaire aux U.S.A." *Bulletin d'Information de la Société des Études Camusiennes* 30 (1993): 27–31.

———. "Une fausse attribution: petite clef pour *Révolte dans les Asturies.*" In *Albert Camus, 7: "Le Théâtre."* Edited by Raymond Gay-Crosier. La Revue des Lettres Modernes, 419–24. Paris: Lettres Modernes Minard, 1975.

Gay-Crosier, Raymond, and Jacqueline Lévi-Valensi, eds. *Albert Camus: œuvre fermée, œuvre ouverte? Actes du colloque du Centre Culturel International de Cerisy-la-Salle, juin 1982.* Cahiers Albert Camus 5. Paris: Gallimard, 1985.

Gehrels, Aleida Joanna. "The Concept of Justice in the Fiction of Albert Camus." Ph.D. diss., University of Arizona, 1969.

Gelinas, Germain-Paul. *La Liberté dans l'œuvre d'Albert Camus.* Fribourg: Éditions Universitaires, 1965.

Ginestier, Paul. *Pour connaître la pensée de Camus.* Paris: Bordas, 1964.

Giraud, René. "Camus' Stranger Retried." *PMLA* 79 (1964): 519–33.

Goedert, Georges. *Albert Camus et la question du bonheur.* Luxembourg: Edi-Centre, 1969.

Goldstain, Jacques. "Camus et la Bible." In *Albert Camus, 4: "sources et influences,"* edited by Brian T. Fitch. La Revue des Lettres Modernes, 264–70. Paris: Lettres Modernes, 1971.

Golsan, Richard J. "Spain and the Lessons of History: Albert Camus and the Spanish Civil War." *Romance Quarterly* 38 (1991): 407–16.

Gray, Margaret, Sarah Ben Chaabane, Lionel Dubois, Viviane Girault, Geraldine F. Montgomery, and Neelima Talwar. "L'œuvre de Camus: une lecture à plusieurs niveaux." In *Albert Camus entre la misère et le soleil: Actes du Colloque international de Poitiers, 29–30–31 mai 1997,* edited by Lionel Dubois. Poitiers: Éditions du Pont-Neuf, 1997.

Green, Mary Jean. "Pascalian Motifs in the Thought of Camus." *Stanford French Review* 1 (1977): 229–42.

Greenlee, James W. "Camus' 'Guest': The Inadmissible Complicity." *Studies in Twentieth Century Literature* 2 (1978): 127–39.

Greer Cohn, Robert. "The True Camus." *French Review* 60 (1986): 30–38.

Grégoire, Vincent. "École et souffrance dans les œuvres de Malraux, Sartre, et Camus." *Symposium* 55 (2001): 15–28.

Grenier, Jean. *Albert Camus: Souvenirs.* Paris: Gallimard, 1968.

———. "Un oui, un non, une ligne droite." *Le Figaro littéraire,* October 26, 1957: 1, 5.

Grenier, Roger. "À *Combat.*" *NRF* 8 (1960): 472–75.

———. "Je n'ai jamais rencontré personne qui fasse comme lui confiance à un inconnu." *Le Figaro littéraire,* January 9, 1960, 6.

Grenier, Roger, ed. *À Albert Camus, ses amis du livre.* Paris: Gallimard, 1962.

———. *Albert Camus: soleil et ombre.* Paris: Gallimard, 1987.

———, ed. *Album Camus.* Bibliothèque de La Pléiade. Paris: Gallimard, 1982.

———. "Camus: Sisyphe et les autres." *Magazine littéraire* 298 (1992): 75–76.

———. "Chronologie." *Magazine littéraire* 276 (1990): 20–26.

Grimaud, Michel. "Humanism and the 'White Man's Burden': Camus, Daru, Meursault, and the Arabs." In *Camus's "L'Étranger": Fifty Years On,* 2nd ed., edited by Adèle King. New York: St. Martin's Press, 1994.

Griswold, Charles. "*The Myth of Sisyphus:* A Reconsideration." *Philosophy in Context* 7 (1978): 45–59.

Grobe, Edwin P. "The Psychological Structure of Camus's 'L'Hôte'." *French Review* 40 (1966): 357–67.

Grosser, Alfred. "Camus, la politique et les fondements de la morale." In *Camus et le premier "Combat" (1944–1947): Colloque de Paris X-Nanterre,* edited by Jeanyves Guérin. La Garenne-Colombes: Européennes Erasmus, 1990.

Grossman, Roland. "Camus, journaliste." *Revue de l'Académie Nationale de Metz.* (1996): 237–53.

Groux, Pierre. "*Et on allait souffrir . . .* : imaginaire de l'Allemagne et des Allemands dans *Le Premier Homme."Roman 20–50* 27 (1999): 31–38.

Guéhenno, Jean. "Une Pureté éclatante." *Le Figaro littéraire,* January 9, 1960, 1, 7.

Guérin, Jeanyves. "Actualité de la politique camusienne." In *Albert Camus: les Extrêmes et l'équilibre; Actes du colloque de Keele, 25–27 mars 1993,* edited by David H. Walker. Amsterdam: Rodopi, 1994.

———. "*Albert Camus, les extrêmes et l'équilibre,* Keele University, 25–27 mars 1993." *Bulletin d'Information de la Société des Études Camusiennes* 30 (1993): 25–27.

———. *Albert Camus: portrait de l'artiste en citoyen.* Paris: Bourin, 1993.

———. "Camus, Caligula et les poètes." *Europe* 77 (1999): 67–75.

———. "Camus devant le socialisme." In *Albert Camus: œuvre fermée, œuvre ouverte? Actes du colloque du Centre Culturel International de Cerisy-la-Salle, juin 1982,* edited by Raymond Gay-Crosier and Jacqueline Lévi-Valensi. Cahiers Albert Camus 5. Paris: Gallimard, 1985.

———. "Camus et de Gaulle." *Espoir* (September 1990): 39–45.

———, ed. *Camus et la politique: Actes du Colloque de Nanterre, 5–7 juin 1985.* Paris: L'Harmattan, 1986.

———, ed. *Camus et le premier "Combat" (1944–1947): Colloque de Paris X-Nanterre.* La Garenne-Colombes: Européennes Erasmus, 1990.

———. "Camus et les deux gauches." *Intervention* 7 (1983–1984): 40–47.

———. "Camus face au terrorisme." *Fragmentos* 2 (1987): 39–55.

———. "Camus: homme de gauche." *Revue politique et parlementaire* (March—April 1988): 76–83.

———. "Le colloque Albert Camus aujourd'hui." *Bulletin d'Information de la Société des Études Camusiennes* 31 (1993): 37–39.

———. "Le combat pour les droits de l'homme: l'Europe, la démocratie et le totalitarisme hier et aujourd'hui." In *Albert Camus et l'Europe: Actes du colloque de Srasbourg, 9 et 10 novembre 1990,* edited by André Abbou. Paris: Ofil, 1995.

———. "Conclusion." In *Camus et la politique: Actes du colloque de Nanterre, 5–7 juin 1985,* edited by Jeanyves Guérin. Paris: L'Harmattan, 1986.

———. "Conclusions des débats." In *Camus et le premier "Combat" (1944–1947): Colloque de Paris X-Nanterre.* Edited by Jeanyves Guérin. La Garenne-Colombes: Européennes Erasmus, 1990.

———. "Des *Chroniques algériennes* au *Premier Homme:* pour une lecture politique du dernier roman de Camus." *Esprit* 211 (1995): 5–16.

———. "L'Europe dans la pensée et l'œuvre de Camus." In *Albert Camus: textes réunis à l'occasion du 25*e anniversaire de la mort de l'écrivain, edited by Paul F. Smets. Brussels: Éditions de l'Université de Bruxelles, 1985.

———. "Hommage à Jean Bloch-Michel." *Bulletin d'Information de la Société des Études Camusiennes* 16 (1987–88): 1–3.

———. "Les Hommes politiques français lecteurs de Camus." In *Camus et la politique: Actes du colloque de Nanterre, 5–7 juin 1985.* Edited by Jeanyves Guérin. Paris: L'Harmattan, 1986.

———. "Jalons pour une lecture politique de *La Peste.*" *Roman 20–50* 2 (1986): 7–25.

———. "Justice pour un juste." *Sud* 13 (1983): 220–26.

———. "Malraux et le *Combat* de Camus." *Europe* 67 (1989): 43–49.

———. "Noces de sang: Camus." *Esprit* 94–95 (1984): 147–55.

———. "Le premier *Combat* ou l'aventure d'un intellectuel collectif." In *Camus et le premier "Combat" (1944–1947): Colloque de Paris X-Nanterre.* Edited by Jeanyves Guérin. La Garenne-Colombes: Européennes Erasmus, 1990.

———. "*Le Premier Homme* et la guerre d'Algérie." *Roman 20–50* 27 (1999): 7–15.

———. "La revanche d'Albert Camus." *Le Nouvel Observateur,* June 9–15, 1994, 4–10.

———. "L'urgence et la limite: essai sur la violence dans l'œuvre de Camus." *Hebrew University Studies in Literature and the Arts* 20 (1993): 7–26.

Haddour, Azzedine. "Camus: The Other as an Outsider in a Univocal Discourse." Ph.D. diss., University of Sussex, 1989.

———. "The Camus-Sartre Debate and the Colonial Question in Algeria." In *Francophone Postcolonial Studies: A Critical Introduction,* edited by Charles Forsdick and David Murphy. London: Arnold, 2003.

———. *Colonial Myths: History and Narrative.* Manchester: Manchester University Press, 2000.

Haggis, D. R. *Albert Camus: "La Peste."* Studies in French Literature 9. London: Edward Arnold, 1962.

Hamouda, Ouahiba. *Albert Camus à l'épreuve d'"Alger Républicain."* Algiers: Office des Publications Universitaires, 1991.

Hanna, Thomas. "Albert Camus and the Christian Faith." *Journal of Religion* 36 (1956): 224–33.

———. *The Thought and Art of Albert Camus.* Chicago: Regnery, 1958.

Hadré, Jacques. "Camus dans la résistance." *French Review* 37 (1964): 646–50.

———. "Camus's Thoughts on Christian Metaphysics and Neoplatism." *Studies in Philology* 64 (1967): 97–108.

Hargreaves, Alec G. "Camus and the Colonial Question in Algeria." *Muslim World* 77 (1987): 164–74.

———. "Caught in the Middle: The Liberal Dilemma in the Algerian War." *Nottingham French Studies* 25 (1986): 73–82.

———. "History and Ethnicity in the Reception of *L'Étranger.*" In *Camus's "L'Étranger": Fifty Years On.* 2nd ed. Edited by Adèle King. New York: St. Martin's Press, 1994.

———. "Personnes grammaticales et relations affectives chez Camus." *Revue Celfan / Celfan Review* 4 (1985): 10–17.

Harlow, Barbara. "Camus and Algeria 1985: 'Ne touchez pas à mon pote'." *Revue Celfan / Celfan Review* 4 (1985): 31–35.

Haroutunian, Lulu. "Albert Camus and the White Plague." *MLN* 79 (1964): 311–15.

Harrow, Kenneth J. "Albert Camus and the Algerian Dilemma." *Journal of Modern Literature* 2 (1971–72): 143–47.

Hassine, Juliette. "Camus et Dostoïevski ou l'écriture de l'exil et de la culpabilité." In *Albert Camus, 13: "études comparatives,"* edited by Raymond Gay-Crosier. La Revue des Lettres Modernes, 904–10. Paris: Lettres Modernes Minard, 1989.

Hayat, Jeannine. Jules Roy: ombre et présence d'Albert Camus. Archives des Lettres Modernes, 278. Paris: Lettres Modernes Minard, 2000.

Hélein-Koss, Suzanne. "Albert Camus et le *Contrat social.*" *Studies on Voltaire and the Eighteenth Century* 161 (1976): 165–204.

Hellens, Franz. "Le Mythe chez Albert Camus." *NRF* 8 (1960): 480–86.

Henderickx, Paul. "Justice, amour et liberté dans la pensée d'Albert Camus." *Marche Romance-Liège* 14 (1964): 71–81.

Henein, Georges. "Camus ou les mains propres." *Études méditerranéennes* 7 (1960): 10–16.

Henry, Jean-Robert. "Introduction." In *French and Algerian Identities from Colonial Times to the Present: A Century of Interaction,* edited by Alec G. Hargreaves and Michael J. Heffernan. Lampeter: Edwin Mellen, 1993.

Henry, Patrick. "Camus on Capital Punishment." *Midwest Quarterly* 16 (1974–75): 362–70.

Hermet, Joseph. *À la rencontre d'Albert Camus: le dur chemin de la liberté.* Paris: Beauchesne, 1990.

———. *Albert Camus et le christianisme.* Paris: Beauchesne, 1976.

Hervé, Pierre. "La Révolte camuse." *La Nouvelle Critique* 35 (1952): 66–76.

Hewitt, Nicholas. "*La Chute* et *Les Temps modernes.*" *Essays in French Literature* 10 (1973): 64–81.

Hitchens, Christopher. "Hope Through Despair." *New Statesman,* July 20, 1979, 95

Holter, Karin. "'Le premier homme' devant le livre." *Narcisse* 16 (1996): 67–74.

Hopkins, Patricia Mary. "The Evolution of the Concept of Revolt in the Works of Albert Camus." Ph.D. diss., University of Missouri, Columbia, 1969.

Horváth, Andor. "'Restituer Dieu à lui-même': lectures hongroises d'Albert Camus." In *Albert Camus, 20: 'Le Premier homme' en perspective,"* edited by Raymond Gay-Crosier. La Revue des Lettres Modernes. Paris: Lettres Modernes Minard, 2004.

Hourdin, Georges. *Camus le Juste.* Collection Tout le monde en parle. Paris: Cerf, 1962.

Howells, Valerie. "Camus's narrative strategies in *L'Exil et le royaume.*" Ph.D. diss., University of Wales, Swansea, 1994.

Hoy, Terry. "Albert Camus: The Nature of Political Rebellion." *Western Political Quarterly* 13 (1960): 573–80.

Hughes, Edward J. *Albert Camus: "Le Premier Homme" / "La Peste."* Glasgow Introductory Guides to French Literature 33. Glasgow: University of Glasgow French and German Publications, 1995.

———. Review of *The First Man,* by Albert Camus, translated by David Hapgood." *TLS,* November 23, 1995, 23.

———. "'Tranquillement monstrueux': Violence and kinship in *Le Premier Homme.*" In *Constructing Memories: Camus, Algeria and "Le Premier Homme,"* edited by Peter Dunwoodie and Edward J. Hughes. Vol 6 of *Stirling French Publications* (1998): 21–32.

Hurely, D. F. "Looking for the Arab: Reading the Readings of Camus's 'The Guest.'" *Studies in Short Fiction* 30 (1993): 79–93.

Imbert, Claude. "De *L'Étranger* à *L'Homme révolté.*" *MLN* 112 (1997): 595–99.

Isaac, Jeffrey C. *Arendt, Camus and Modern Rebellion.* New Haven, CT: Yale University Press, 1992.

Jakobiak, Bertrand. "Camus le colonisateur sublimé." *Souffles* 12 (1968): 22–28.

Jeanson, Francis. "Albert Camus ou l'âme révoltée." *Les Temps modernes* 79 (1952): 2070–90.

———. "Pour tout vous dire." *Les Temps modernes* 82 (1952): 354–83.

Jones, Rosemarie. "Perspectives on the Self in Camus's *L'Exil et le royaume.*" In *Moy qui me voy: The Writer and the Self from Montaigne to Leiris,* edited by George Craig and Margaret McGowan. Oxford: Clarendon Press, 1989.

Jonesco, Tony. *Un homme, Camus et le destin ou autour de la mort de Camus.* Paris: Promotion et Édition, 1968.

Joyaux, Georges J. "Albert Camus and North Africa." *Yale French Studies* 25 (1960): 10–19.

Joyeux, Maurice. *Albert Camus ou la révolte sur mesure.* Antony: Groupe Fresnes Antony Fédération Anarchiste, 1984.

Kanters, Robert. "Camus: prince des bien pensants ou de la révolte?" *L'Express* May 3, 1962, 32–33.

———. "Pour et contre Camus: les accélérations de la gloire." *Le Figaro littéraire,* January 5–11, 1970, 11–12.

Kaplan, H. J. "Paris Letter." *Partisan Review* 12 (1945): 473–80.

———. "Paris Letter." *Partisan Review* 13 (1946): 68–74.

Keefe, Terry. "'Heroes of our Time' in Three of the Stories of Camus and Simone de Beauvoir." *Forum for Modern Language Studies* 17 (1981): 39–54.

Kelly, Debra. "'Les Fils du pauvre': Poverty, knowledge and politics. Reading *Le Premier Homme* in the Context of North-African Writing in French." In *Constructing Memories: Camus, Algeria and "Le Premier Homme,"* edited by Peter Dunwoodie and Edward J. Hughes. Vol 6 of *Stirling French Publications* (1998): 155–67.

Kemp, Robert. "*L'Homme révolté.*" *Les Nouvelles littéraires,* November 15, 1951, 2.

Kessous, El Aziz. "Albert Camus et l'honneur de l'homme." *Simoun* 8 (1960): 3–12.

King, Adèle. *Camus.* Edinburgh: Oliver and Boyd, 1964.

———, ed. *Camus's "L'Étranger": Fifty Years On.* 2nd ed. New York: St. Martin's Press, 1994.

———. "Introduction: After Fifty Years, Still a Stranger." In *Camus's "L'Étranger": Fifty Years On,* 2nd ed, edited by Adèle King. New York: St. Martin's Press, 1994.

———. "La révélation de l'amour dans *Le Premier Homme.*" In *Albert Camus entre la misère et le soleil: Actes du Colloque international de Poitiers, 29–30–31 mai 1997.* Edited by Lionel Dubois. Poitiers: Éditions du Pont-Neuf, 1997.

———. "Structure and Meaning in *La Chute.*" *PMLA* 77 (1962): 660–67.

King, Jonathan H., ed. *Albert Camus: Selected Political Writings.* London: Methuen, 1981.

———. "Sartre-Camus: The Quarrel as Biography." *French Cultural Studies* 5 (1994): 39–56.

Klein, Wolfgang. "Des révolutionnaires cyniques? Camus sur Hegel, Marx et Lénine." In *Albert Camus, 15: "textes, intertextes, contextes autour de 'La Chute,'"* edited by Raymond Gay-Crosier. La Revue des Lettres Modernes, 1123–32. Paris: Lettres Modernes, 1993.

Knapp, Bettina L., ed. *Critical Essays on Albert Camus.* Boston: Hall, 1988.

Kouchkine, Evguéni. "Camus et Pasternak." In *Albert Camus et l'Europe: Actes du colloque de Strasbourg, 9 et 10 novembre 1990,* edited by André Abbou. Paris: Ofil, 1995.

———. "Réception de l'œuvre de Camus en U.R.S.S." In *Albert Camus, 18: "la réception de l'œuvre de Camus en U.R.S.S. et en R.D.A.,"* edited by Raymond Gay-Crosier. La Revue des Lettres Modernes 1472–77. Paris: Lettres Modernes Minard, 1999.

Kovac, Nikola. "Camus aurait milité pour l'embargo." *Le Nouvel Observateur,* June 9–15, 1994, 11.

Kréa, Henri. "Le Malentendu algérien." *France Observateur,* January 5, 1961,16.

Kritzman, Lawrence D. "Camus's Curious Humanism or the Intellectual in Exile." *MLN* 112 (1997): 550–75.

Kushnir, Slava M. "Camus et la peine de mort." *Cahiers des Amis de Robert Brasillach* 17 (1972): 48–50.

Kwiatkowski, Jerzy. "Camus en Pologne." In *Camus et la politique: Actes du colloque de Nanterre, 5–7 juin 1985,* edited by Jeanyves Guérin. Paris: L'Harmattan, 1986.

Lafon, Noel. "Albert Camus à *Combat:* de la résistance à la revolution." *La Revue socialiste* 191 (1966): 235–55.

———. "Camus de 1945 à 1947." *La Revue socialiste* 197 (1966): 370–89.

Lalou, René. "Un Témoin de notre époque." *Les Nouvelles littéraires,* January 7, 1960, 8.

Lambert, Richard T. "Albert Camus and the Paradoxes of Expressing a Relativism." *Thought* 56 (1981): 185–98.

Langlois, Walter G. "Camus et le sens de la révolte asturienne." In *Albert Camus 1980: Second International Conference, February 21–23 1980, The University of Florida, Gainesville,* edited by Raymond Gay-Crosier. Gainesville: University Presses of Florida, 1980.

Lannes, Roger. "Vu et entendu à une répétition des *Justes,* la nouvelle pièce de Camus." *Le Figaro littéraire,* December 10, 1949, 8.

Lanoux, Armand. "Une œuvre en débat devant la nouvelle génération: par le ton, par la voix, cet étranger est un ami." *Le Figaro littéraire,* October 26, 1957, 7.

Lapaire, Pierre J. "L'Enfance—limite du terrorisme dans *Les Justes.*" *USF Language Quarterly* 24 (1986): 38–40.

———. "Meurtre et révolte: problème de limites chez Camus." *USF Language Quarterly* 26 (1987): 45–48.

Laperrousaz, Michelle, Isabelle Auzanneau, Moishe Black, Catherine Dana, Abdelkader Djemai, Lionel Dubois, Gaëtan Langhade and Michel Maillard. "Albert Camus et la guerre 1914–18." In *Les trois guerres d'Albert Camus: Actes du Colloque International de Poitiers, 4–5–6 mai 1995,* edited by Lionel Dubois. Poitiers: Éditions du Pont-Neuf, 1995.

Lawrence, Christy. "*Le Premier Homme:* l'aube de Némésis." In *Albert Camus, 20: "'Le Premier homme' en perspective,"* edited by Raymond Gay-Crosier. La Revue des Lettres Modernes. Paris: Lettres Modernes Minard, 2004.

Lazere, Donald. "*The Myth* and *The Rebel:* Diversity and Unity." In *Albert Camus,* edited by Harold Bloom. Modern Critical Views. New York: Chelsea House, 1989.

———. *The Unique Creation of Albert Camus.* New Haven, CT: Yale University Press, 1973.

Le Baut, Pierre. "Exposition / Représentation / Lecture-Spectacle / Rencontre-Débat: *du dernier mot au Premier homme,* Montauban, 21 mars 1991." *Bulletin d'Information de la Société des Études Camusiennes* 22 (1991): 12–13.

———. "Identification de quelques lieux et personnages du *Premier Homme.*" *Bulletin d'Information de la Société des Études Camusiennes* 37 (1995): 35–37.

———. "Nouvelle identification de 'Pierre', l'ami de Jacques Cormery dans *Le Premier Homme.*" *Bulletin d'Information de la Société des Études Camusiennes* 42 (1997): 4–6.

———. "Vers l'identification d'un autre ami d'enfance appelé 'Joseph' dans *Le Premier Homme.*" *Bulletin d'Information de la Société des Études Camusiennes* 37 (1995): 35–37.

———. "Vers une identification partielle de l'ami d'enfance appelé 'Pierre' dans *Le Premier Homme."Bulletin d'Information de la Société des Études Camusiennes* 36 (1995): 5.

Le Clec'h, Guy. "Pour et contre Camus: un classique démodé?" *Le Figaro littéraire,* January 5–11, 1970, 12–13.

Le Foulon, Marie-Laure. "Camus de père en fille." *Télérama,* December 30, 1992, 50–51.

Lebesque, Morvan. *Camus par lui-même.* Écrivains de toujours. Paris: Seuil, 1963.

———. "La Passion pour la scène." In *Camus,* edited by René-Marill Albérès, Pierre de Boisdeffre, Jean Daniel, Pierre Gascar, Morvan Lebesque, André Parinaud, Emmanuel Roblès, Jules Roy, and Pierre-Henri Simon. Collection Génies et Réalités. Paris: Hachette, 1964.

Lecarme, Jacques. "Camus, lecteur des *Mandarins.*" *Bulletin d'Information de la Société des Études Camusiennes* 39 (1996): 4–5.

Leclère, Marie-Françoise. "Camus vu d'Algérie." *Le Point,* August 14–20, 1993, 57.

Leenhardt, Jacques. "Essai sur la morale d'*Actuelles.*" In *Albert Camus: œuvre fermée, œuvre ouverte? Actes du colloque du Centre Culturel International de Cerisy-la-Salle, juin 1982,* edited by Raymond Gay-Crosier and Jacqueline Lévi-Valensi. Cahiers Albert Camus 5. Paris: Gallimard, 1985.

Lemarchand, Jacques. "Les images que l'on regarde au soir de la mort d'un ami." *Le Figaro littéraire,* January 9, 1960, 1, 6.

Lenoir, Thomas. "L'Homme de la semaine: Albert Camus." *L'Express,* June 8, 1956, 12–13.

Lenzini, José. *L'Algérie de Camus.* Aix-en-Provence: Edisud, 1987.

———. "Camus: l'éternel retour à la mer." *Méditerranée-magazine* 2 (1994): 36–41.

Leov, Nola M. "Thalassa, Thalassa: Camus's Use of Imagery in *La Chute.*" *New Zealand Journal of French Studies* 14 (1993): 5–29.

Leroy, Pierre. "La politique dans l'œuvre d'Albert Camus." *La Revue politique et parlementaire* 68 (1966): 61–71.

Lestavel, Jean. "Adieu à Camus." *Vers la vie nouvelle* 1 (1960): 2–3.

Lévi-Valensi, Jacqueline, ed. *Albert Camus et le théâtre: Actes du colloque tenu à Amiens du 31 mai au 2 juin 1988.* Paris: Imec, 1992.

———. "Camus et L'Espagne." In *Espagne et Algérie au XXe siècle: contacts culturels et création littéraire,* edited by J. Déjeux and D. H. Pageaux. Paris: L'Harmattan, 1985.

———. "Camus et le théâtre: quelques faits, quelques questions." In *Albert Camus et le théâtre: Actes du colloque tenu à Amiens du 31 mai au 2 juin 1988,* edited by Jacqueline Lévi-Valensi. Paris: Imec, 1992.

———. *Camus et les critiques de notre temps*. Paris: Garnier, 1970.

———. "Camus journaliste et écrivain au temps de *Combat*." In *Camus et le premier 'Combat' (1944–1947): Colloque de Paris X-Nanterre,* edited by Jeanyves Guérin. La Garenne-Colombes: Européennes Erasmus, 1990.

———. "La Collaboration d'Albert Camus à *Alger républicain* et au *Soir républicain.*" In *Albert Camus, 2: "langue et langage,"* edited by Brian T. Fitch. La Revue des Lettres Modernes, 212–16. Paris: Lettres Modernes, 1969.

———. "La Condition sociale en Algérie." In *Albert Camus, 5: "journalisme et politique: l'entrée dans l'histoire (1938–1940),"* edited by Brian T. Fitch. La Revue des Lettres Modernes, 315–22. Paris: Lettres Modernes, 1972.

———. "L'Engagement culturel." In *Albert Camus, 5: "journalisme et politique: l'entrée dans l'histoire (1938–1940),"* edited by Brian T. Fitch. La Revue des Lettres Modernes 315–22. Paris: Lettres Modernes, 1972.

———. "L'Entrée d'Albert Camus en politique." In *Camus et la politique: Actes du colloque de Nanterre, 5–7 juin 1985,* edited by Jeanyves Guérin. Paris: L'Harmattan, 1986.

———. "L'Europe dans les œuvres de fiction d'Albert Camus: une mythologie ambiguë." In *Albert Camus et l'Europe: Actes du colloque de Srasbourg, 9 et 10 novembre 1990,* edited by André Abbou. Paris: Ofil, 1995.

———, ed. "La Peste" d'Albert Camus. Collection Foliothèque. Paris: Gallimard, 1991.

———. "Réalité et symbole de l'Espagne dans l'œuvre de Camus." In *Albert Camus, 1: "autour de 'L'Étranger,'"* edited by Brian T. Fitch. La Revue des Lettres Modernes, 170–74. Paris: Lettres Modernes, 1968.

———. "La Relation au réel dans le roman camusien." In *Albert Camus: œuvre fermée, œuvre ouverte? Actes du colloque du Centre Culturel International de Cerisy-la-Salle, juin 1982,* edited by Raymond Gay-Crosier and Jacqueline Lévi-Valensi. Cahiers Albert Camus 5. Paris: Gallimard, 1985.

———. "Regards sur l'homme, lecture de l'œuvre." *Europe* 77 (1999): 3–8.

———. "Repères chronologiques." *Europe* 77 (1999): 184–87.

———. "Roman, mesure et démesure." In *Albert Camus: les Extrêmes et l'équilibre; Actes du colloque de Keele, 25–27 mars 1993,* edited by David H. Walker. Amsterdam: Rodopi, 1994.

———. "'Terre faite à mon âme': pour une mythologie du reel." In *Albert Camus: parcours méditerranéens,* edited by Fernande Bartfeld and David Ohana. Vol 5 of *Perspectives: Revue de l'Université Hébraïque de Jérusalem* (1998): 185–97.

Lévi-Valensi, Jacqueline, and Jeanyves Guérin. "Camus et l'idée de révolution." *Les Cahiers de Fontenay* 63–64 (1991): 22?–41.

Little, J. P. "Albert Camus, Simone Weil and Modern Tragedy." *French Studies* 31 (1977): 42–51.

Loesch, Anne. "Il nous a fait pied-noir." *Les Nouvelles littéraires,* January 1, 1970, 7.

Longstaffe, Moya. "La Chute de qui? Meursault, Clamence, et le seul Pascal que nous méritons." In *Albert Camus: les Extrêmes et l'équilibre; Actes du colloque de Keele, 25–27 mars 1993,* edited by David H. Walker. Amsterdam: Rodopi, 1994.

Luppe, Robert de. *Albert Camus.* Paris: Editions Universitaires, 1952.

Lynch, Martha. "Le *je* utopique dans 'Le Renégat.'" In *Albert Camus, 13: "études comparatives,"* edited by Raymond Gay-Crosier. La Revue des Lettres Modernes, 904–10. Paris: Lettres Modernes Minard, 1989.

Macchia, Giovanni. "Camus le Dissident." *Europe* 77 (1999): 12–16.

Madariaga, Salvador de. "L'esprit et le cœur." *NRF* 8 (1960): 539–44.

———. "Un des nôtres." *Preuves* 110 (1960): 10–13.

Madison, M. M. "Albert Camus: Philosopher of Limits." *Modern Fiction Studies* 10 (1964): 223–31.

Mailhot, Laurent. *Camus ou l'imagination du désert.* Montreal: Presses de l'Université de Montreal, 1973.

Maillard, Michel. *Camus.* Les Écrivains balises. Paris: Nathan, 1993.

Majault, Joseph. *Camus: révolte et liberté.* Paris: Centurion, 1965.

Mallet, Robert. "Présent à la vie, étranger à la mort (Pages du journal)." *NRF* 8 (1960): 440–48.

Maquet, Albert. *Albert Camus ou l'invincible été.* Paris: Débresse, 1955.

Marcel, Gabriel. "Albert Camus." *Les Nouvelles littéraires,* January 7, 1960, 1, 8.

Margerrison, Christine. "Albert Camus and 'Ces femmes qu'on raie de l'humanité': Sexual Politics in the Colonial Arena." *French Cultural Studies* 10 (1999): 217–30.

———. "'Ces Forces obscures de l'âme': Woman, Race and Origins in the Imaginative Writings of Albert Camus." Ph.D. diss., University of Lancaster, 1998.

———. "The Dark Continent of Camus's *L'Étranger.*" *French Studies* 55 (2001): 59–73.

Marion, Sylvie. "Memoirs of Oblivion." *THES,* April 22, 1994, 19.

Marissel, André. "Les écrivains algériens s'expliquent . . . une enquête." *Les Nouvelles littéraires,* October 13, 1960, 1, 5.

Marlière, Philippe. "Camus against the tide: Algeria and the intellectual doxa." In *Constructing Memories: Camus, Algeria and "Le Premier Homme,"* edited by Peter Dunwoodie and Edward J. Hughes. Vol 6 of *Stirling French Publications* (1998): 42–54.

Marnham, Patrick. "He was too modest for the rampant Beauvoir." *Literary Review* (October 1997): 13–14.

Marque-Pucheu, Christiane. "Les circonstants dans *Noces* de Camus: des acteurs à part entière." In *Albert Camus entre la misère et le soleil: Actes du Colloque international de Poitiers, 29–30–31 mai 1997,* edited by Lionel Dubois. Poitiers: Éditions du Pont-Neuf, 1997.

Marson, Eric. "Justice and the Obsessed Character in 'Michael Kohlhaas,' *Der Prozess* and *L'Étranger.*" *Seminar* 2 (1966): 21–33.

Martin, Eleanor J. "Camus's Translation of Calderón: *La Dévotion à la croix* and the Ideology of Limits." *Forum for Modern Language Studies* 12 (1976): 329–35.

Martin, Laurent. "Actualité et inactualité d'Albert Camus." In *Les trois guerres d'Albert Camus: Actes du Colloque International de Poitiers, 4–5–6 mai 1995,* edited by Lionel Dubois. Poitiers: Éditions du Pont-Neuf, 1995.

Martin, Marc. "'*Combat*' et la presse de la Libération." In *Camus et le premier "Combat" (1944–1947): Colloque de Paris X-Nanterre,* edited by Jeanyves Guérin. La Garenne-Colombes: Européennes Erasmus, 1990.

Martin du Gard, Roger. "Personne n'est moins dupé, personne plus indépendant." *Le Figaro littéraire,* October 26, 1957, 1.

Martinet, Daniel. "Albert Camus aux Groupes de Liaison Internationale." *Témoins* 8 (1960): 6–7.

Martinet, Gilles. "Les Justes et les autres." *Le Nouvel Observateur,* January 19–25, 1966, 34–35.

Mascolo, Dionys. "Sur deux amis morts." *NRF* 8 (1960): 451–60.

Mason, Haydn T. "Voltaire and Camus." *Romanic Review* 59 (1968): 198–212.

Matala, Marie. "Camus et la Grèce." In *Albert Camus et l'Europe: Actes du colloque de Strasbourg, 9 et 10 novembre 1990,* edited by André Abbou. Paris: Ofil, 1995.

Matsumoto, Yosei. "L'ombre portée par *Le Premier Homme* sur *L'Exil et le royaume.*" In *Albert Camus, 20: "'Le Premier homme' en perspective,"* edited by Raymond Gay-Crosier. La Revue des Lettres Modernes. Paris: Lettres Modernes Minard, 2004.

———. "*Le Premier Homme:* le processes d'élaboration." In *Albert Camus, 20: "'Le Premier homme' en perspective,"* edited by Raymond Gay-Crosier. La Revue des Lettres Modernes. Paris: Lettres Modernes Minard, 2004.

Mauriac, François. "Une jeune voix à laquelle une génération fait écho." *Le Figaro littéraire,* October 26, 1957, 1.

May, William F. "Albert Camus: Political Moralist." *Christianity and Crisis,* November 24, 1958, 165–68.

McBride, Joseph. *Albert Camus: Philosopher and Littérateur.* New York: St. Martin's Press, 1992.

McCann, J. "The Verdict on Meursault." *Nottingham French Studies* 29 (1990): 51–63.

McCarthy, Patrick. "Beyond Morality." *TLS,* September 1, 1989, 954.

———. "Camus, Orwell and Greene: The Impossible Fascination of the Colonised." In *Camus's "L'Étranger": Fifty Years On,* 2nd ed., edited by Adèle King. New York: St. Martin's Press, 1994.

———. "The First Arab in *L'Étranger.*" *Revue Celfan / Celfan Review* 4 (1985): 23–26.

———. "The *Pied-Noir* Story." *TLS,* June 24, 1994, 26.

———. "Up with the Popular Front." *TLS,* October 13, 1978, 1148.

McDermott, John V. "Camus' Daru: Just How Humane?" *Notes on Contemporary Literature* 15 (1985): 11–12.

McLure, Roger. "Autour de la vérité avec Camus, Ayer et le barman." In *Albert Camus: les Extrêmes et l'équilibre; Actes du colloque de Keele, 25–27 mars 1993,* edited by David H. Walker. Amsterdam: Rodopi, 1994.

Méfret, Jean-Pax. "Albert Camus: nos découvertes." *Le Figaro Magazine,* January 21, 1995, 38–46.

Méglio, Ingrid di. "Camus et la religion: antireligiosité et cryptothéologie." In *Albert Camus, 11: "Camus et la religion,"* edited by Brian T. Fitch. La Revue des Lettres Modernes, 648–51. Paris: Lettres Modernes Minard, 1982.

Mélançon, Marcel. *Albert Camus: analyse de sa pensée.* Fribourg: Éditions Universitaires Fribourg, 1976.

Memmi, Albert. "Camus ou le colonisateur de bonne volonté." *La Nef* 14 (1957): 95–96.

Ménard, René. "Albert Camus devant un secret." *NRF* 8 (1960): 608–13.

———. "Albert Camus et la recherche d'une légitimité." *Critique* 14 (1958): 675–89.

Merad, Ghani. "Emmanuel Roblès et Albert Camus: deux grands amis et deux grands écrivains algériens." *Revue Celfan / Celfan Review* 4 (1985): 29–31.

Merlo, Paul. "Les derniers mots du *Premier Homme* de Camus." In *Albert Camus, 18: "la réception de l'œuvre de Camus en U.R.S.S. et en R.D.A.,"* edited by Raymond Gay-Crosier. La Revue des Lettres Modernes, 1472–77. Paris: Lettres Modernes Minard, 1999.

Meto'o, Maxime Pierre. "Les thèmes du bonheur et de la justice dans l'œuvre d'Albert Camus." Ph.D. diss., University of Western Ontario, 1982.

Meyers, Jeffrey. "Camus' *The Fall* and Van Eyck's *The Adoration of the Lamb.*" *Mosaic* 7 (1974): 43–51.

Michalczyk, John J. "Camus and Malraux: A Staged Version of *Le Temps du mépris.*" *French Review* 50 (1976): 102–5.

Miller, Stephen. "The Posthumous Victory of Albert Camus." *Commentary* 70 (1980): 53–58.

Milosz, Czeslaw. "L'Interlocuteur fraternel." *Preuves* 110 (1960): 14–16.

Mimouni, Rachid. "Camus et l'Algérie intégriste." *Le Nouvel Observateur,* June 9–15, 1994, 8.

Mingelgrün, Albert. "Langages et paysages algérois." In *Albert Camus: parcours méditerranéens,* edited by Fernande Bartfeld and David Ohana. Vol. 5 of *Perspectives: Revue de l'Université Hébraïque de Jérusalem* (1998): 85–90.

Mino, Hiroshi. "'Lettres' de Guerre: Bernanos, Saint-Exupéry et Camus." In *Albert Camus, 19: "'L'Homme révolté': cinquante ans après,"* edited by Raymond Gay-Crosier. La Revue des Lettres Modernes. Paris: Lettres Modernes Minard, 2001.

———. "Rieux comme narrateur/narrataire." In *Albert Camus, 18: "la réception de l'œuvre de Camus en U.R.S.S. et en R.D.A.,"* edited by Raymond Gay-Crosier. La Revue des Lettres Modernes, 1472–77. Paris: Lettres Modernes Minard, 1999.

———. *Le silence dans l'œuvre d'Albert Camus.* Paris: Corti, 1987.

Modiano, Patrick. "Je me sens proche de lui." *Les Nouvelles littéraires,* January 1, 1970, 7.

Moeller, Charles. "Albert Camus: The Question of Hope." *Cross Currents* 8 (1958): 172–84.

Mohrt, Michel. "Ethic and Poetry in the Work of Camus." *Yale French Studies* 1 (1948): 113–18.

Moix, Gabrielle. "'L'Enigme' d'Albert Camus." In *Albert Camus, 13: "études comparatives,"* edited by Raymond Gay-Crosier. La Revue des Lettres Modernes, 904–10. Paris: Lettres Modernes Minard, 1989.

Molnar, Thomas. "On Camus and Capital Punishment." *Modern Age* 2 (1958): 298–306.

Montalbetti, Jean. "Camus: écrivain algérien." *Magazine littéraire* 53 (1971): 23–24.

Montgomery, Geraldine F. "La mère sacrée dans *Le Premier Homme.*" In *Albert Camus, 20: "'Le Premier homme' en perspective,"* edited by Raymond Gay-Crosier. La Revue des Lettres Modernes. Paris: Lettres Modernes Minard, 2004.

———. *Noces pour femme seule: le féminin et le sacré dans l'œuvre d'Albert Camus.* Amsterdam: Rodopi, 2004.

Moraly, Yehuda. "Cruauté, peste et création: Camus et Artaud." In *Albert Camus: parcours méditerranéens,* edited by Fernande Bartfeld and David Ohana. Vol. 5 of *Perspectives: Revue de l'Université Hébraïque de Jérusalem* (1998): 73–84.

More, Marcel. "Les Racines métaphysiques de la révolte." *Dieu vivant* 21 (1952): 35–59.

Morjean, Jean-Marc. "Camus ou le prix des mots (juin 1940–août 1944)." In *La Littérature française sous l'Occupation: Actes du colloque de Reims (30 septembre—1er et 2 octobre 1981),* edited by Yves Ménager. Reims: Presses Universitaires de Reims, 1989.

Morot-Sir, Edouard. "Les *Carnets III* d'Albert Camus: aristocratie et folie de la création." *Romance Notes* 31 (1991): 83–98.

———. "*L'Homme révolté:* entre non et oui." In *Albert Camus, 12: "la révolte en question,"* edited by Brian T. Fitch. La Revue des Lettres Modernes, 715–19. Paris: Lettres Modernes Minard, 1985.

Morzewski, Christian. "*Le Premier Homme* ou l'anti-enfance d'un chef." *Roman 20–50* 27 (1999): 89–102.

Mounier, Emmanuel. "Albert Camus ou l'appel des humiliés." *Esprit* 18 (1950): 27–66.

———. "Élégie pour *Combat.*" *Esprit* 18 (1950): 655–57.

Murray, Jack. "Colonial Bodies: Gide's *L'Immoraliste* as an intertext of Camus's *La Femme adultère.*" *Modern Language Quarterly* 52 (1991): 71–85.

Nadeau, Maurice. "Les enfances Camus." *La Quinzaine littéraire,* May 1–5 1994, 9–10.

———. "Passage de Camus." *La Quinzaine littéraire,* March 1–15, 1987, 13–14.

Nagy, Moses M. "The Theatre of Camus: A Stage for Destiny." *Claudel Studies* 9 (1982): 17–25.

Nahas, Hélène. "L'évolution de la pensée d'Albert Camus dans *Actuelles.*" *French Review* 26 (1952): 105–11.

Naudin, Marie. "Hugo et Camus face à la peine capitale." *Revue d'Histoire littéraire de la France* 72 (1972): 264–73.

Négroni, Jean. "Albert Camus et le *Théâtre de l'Équipe.*" *Revue d'Histoire du Théâtre* 12 (1960): 343–49.

Neilson, Frank P. "*The Plague:* Camus's Pro-Fascist Allegory." *Literature and Ideology* 15 (1973): 17–26.

Nicolas, André. *Albert Camus ou le vrai Prométhée.* Paris: Seghers, 1966.

———. *Une philosophie de l'existence: Albert Camus.* Paris: PUF, 1964.

Nora, Pierre. "Pour une autre explication de *L'Étranger.*" *France Observateur,* January 5, 1961, 16–17.

Novello, Samantha. "Du nihilisme aux théocraties totalitaires: *Les Sources et le sens du communisme russe* de Berdiaev dans les *Carnets* de Camus." In *Albert Camus, 20: "'Le Premier homme' en perspective,"* edited by Raymond-Gay-Crosier. La Revue des Lettres Modernes. Paris: Lettres Modernes Minard, 2004.

O'Brien, Conor Cruise. *Camus.* London: Fontana / Collins, 1970.

———. "The Fall." *New Republic,* October 16, 1995, 44.

O'Brien, Justin. "Albert Camus: Militant." In *Camus: A Collection of Critical Essays,* edited by Germaine Brée. Englewood Cliffs, NJ: Prenticehall, 1962.

———. "De Mémoire de francophile américain . . ." *NRF* 8 (1960): 559–61.

———. *Resistance, Rebellion and Death.* New York: Knopf, 1972.

O'Donohoe, Benedict. "L'autodérision chez Sartre et Camus: 'L'Enfance d'un chef' et 'Jonas ou l'artiste au travail'." In *Albert Camus, 19: "'L'Homme révolté': cinquante ans après,"* edited by Raymond Gay-Crosier. La Revue des Lettres Modernes. Paris: Lettres Modernes Minard, 2001.

Oswald, John. "Re-appropriating Europe: Albert Camus's wartime Europeanism." *Modern & Contemporary France* 9 (2001): 483–93.

Ozwald, Thierry. "*Les Lettres à un ami allemand* ou la juste mesure de Camus." *Roman 20/50* 28 (1999): 77–92.

Papamalamis, Dimitris. *Albert Camus et la pensée grecque.* Nancy: Imprimerie Idoux, 1965.

Parinaud, André. "La vie d'un écrivain engagé." In *Camus,* edited by René-Marill Albérès, Pierre de Boisdeffre, Jean Daniel, Pierre Gascar, Morvan Lebesque, André Parinaud, Emmanuel Roblès, Jules Roy, and Pierre-Henri Simon. Collection Génies et Réalités. Paris: Hachette, 1964.

Parish, Richard. "Absurd majesty." *THES,* February 27, 1998, 33.

Parker, Emmett. *Albert Camus: The Artist in the Arena.* Madison: University of Wisconsin Press, 1965.

Pasqua, Hervé. "Albert Camus et le problème du mal." *Les Études philosophiques* 1 (1990): 49–58.

Patocková, Jana. "Camus sur les scènes tchèques dans les années soixante." In *Albert Camus, 20: "'Le Premier homme' en perspective,"* edited by Raymond Gay-Crosier. La Revue des Lettres Modernes. Paris: Lettres Modernes Minard, 2004.

Pauwels, Louis. "Une conversation avec Camus." *Le Figaro Magazine,* January 12, 1980, 10.

Paz, Octavio. "Il pensait que Sartre l'épargnerait." *Le Nouvel Observateur,* June 9–15, 1994, 13.

Pécheur, Jacques. "Camus retrouvé: *Le Premier Homme.*" *Le Français dans le monde* 267 (1994): 12–13.

———. "Camus vu par . . ." *Le Français dans le monde* 270 (1995): 49–50.

Pélégri, Jean. "Jean Pélégri se souvient." *Bulletin d'Information de la Société des Études Camusiennes* 51 (1999): 37.

Perrine, Laurence. "Camus' 'The Guest': A Subtle and Difficult Story." *Studies in Short Fiction* 1 (1963): 52–58.

———. "Daru: Camus' Humane Host." *Notes on Contemporary Literature* 14 (1984): 11–12.

Perros, Georges. "L'Homme fatigué." *NRF* 8 (1960): 614–20.

Peters, Renate. "L'Art, la révolte et l'histoire: 'Le Renégat' et *L'Homme révolté.*" *French Review* 54 (1981): 517–23.

Petit, Pierre. "Tuberculose et sensibilité chez Gide et Camus." *Bulletin des Amis d'André Gide* 9 (1981): 279–92.

Petitbon, Jean-François. "Camus le Méditerranéen." *Revue Générale* (1995): 53–63.

Peyre, Henri. "Camus the Pagan." In *Camus: A Collection of Critical Essays,* edited by Germaine Brée. Englewood Cliffs, NJ: Prenticehall, 1962.

Pia, Pascal. "D'*Alger-Républicain* à *Combat.*" *Magazine littéraire* 276 (1990): 34–38.

Pingaud, Bernard, ed. *"L'Étranger" d'Albert Camus.* Collection Foliothèque. Paris: Gallimard, 1992.

Pisier, Eveline and Pierre Bouretz. "Camus et le marxisme." In *Camus et la politique: Actes du colloque de Nanterre, 5–7 juin 1985,* edited by Jeanyves Guérin. Paris: L'Harmattan, 1986.

Planche, Jean-Louis. "Une jeunesse algéroise: Albert Camus 1914–1940." *Europe* 77 (1999): 17–39.

Planeille, Franck. "Autour du cinquantième anniversaire de la publication de *L'Homme révolté:* les 26 et 27 octobre 2001 à Aix-en-Provence." *Bulletin d'Information de la Société des Études Camusiennes* 20 (2002): 5–6.

———. "Hommes de midi: René Char et Albert Camus." In *Albert Camus, 19: "'L'Homme révolté': cinquante ans après,"* edited by Raymond Gay-Crosier. La Revue des Lettres Modernes. Paris: Lettres Modernes Minard, 2001.

Poncet, Charles. "L'impossible trêve civile." *Magazine littéraire* 276 (1990): 28–31.

Popkin, Suzanne. "*La Peste* et les possibilités du bonheur." In *Albert Camus entre la misère et le soleil: Actes du Colloque international de Poitiers, 29–30–31 mai 1997,* edited by Lionel Dubois. Poitiers: Éditions du Pont-Neuf, 1997.

Poplyansky, Hélène. "The Reception of *L'Étranger* in the Soviet Union." In *Camus's "L'Étranger": Fifty Years On,* 2nd ed., edited by Adèle King. New York: St. Martin's Press, 1994.

Pouillon, Jean. "L'optimisme de Camus." *Les Temps modernes* 3 (1947): 921–29.

Pratt, Mary L. "Mapping Ideology: Gide, Camus, and Algeria." *College Literature* 8 (1981): 158–74.

Quilliot, Roger. "Albert Camus's Algeria." In *Camus: A Collection of Critical Essays,* edited by Germaine Brée. Englewood Cliffs, NJ: Prenticehall, 1962.

———. "L'Algérie d'Albert Camus." *La Revue socialiste* 120 (1958): 121–31.

———. "Autour d'Albert Camus et du problème socialiste." *La Revue socialiste* 20 (1948): 342–52.

———. "Camus: commandeur de l'Ordre de la Libération Espagnole." *La Revue socialiste* 193 (1966): 471–73.

———. "Camus et le socialisme." In *Camus et la politique: Actes du colloque de Nanterre, 5–7 juin 1985,* edited by Jeanyves Guérin. Paris: L'Harmattan, 1986.

———. "Camus's Libertarian Socialism." In *Critical Essays on Albert Camus,* edited by Bettina L. Knapp. Boston: Hall, 1988.

———. "Les jeunes soviétiques peuvent enfin parler de Camus." *Le Figaro littéraire,* November 14, 1963, 1, 18.

———. *La Mer et les prisons: essais sur Albert Camus.* rev. ed. Paris: Gallimard, 1970.

———. "La 'Pléiade.'" In *Albert Camus, 18: "la réception de l'œuvre de Camus en U.R.S.S. et en R.D.A.,"* edited by Raymond Gay-Crosier. La Revue des Lettres Modernes. Paris: Lettres Modernes Minard, 1999.

———. "Le Premier Camus." In *Albert Camus, 18: "la réception de l'œuvre de*

Camus en U.R.S.S. et en R.D.A.," edited by Raymond Gay-Crosier. La Revue des Lettres Modernes, 1472–77. Paris: Lettres Modernes Minard, 1999.

———. "Rencontre du 13 juillet 1954 avec Camus." In *Albert Camus, 18: "la réception de l'œuvre de Camus en U.R.S.S. et en R.D.A.,"* edited by Raymond Gay-Crosier. La Revue des Lettres Modernes, 1472–77. Paris: Lettres Modernes Minard, 1999.

———. "Tombeau d'Albert Camus." *La Revue socialiste* 130 (1960): 175–80.

———. "Un monde ambigu." *Preuves* 110 (1960): 28–38.

Quinn, Renée. "Albert Camus devant le problème algérien." *La Revue des Sciences Humaines* 32 (1967): 613–31.

Racine-Furlaud, Nicole. "Le premier *Combat* de Camus." *Vingtième Siècle* 16 (1987): 110–12.

Ramsey, Warren. "Letters and Comment: Albert Camus on Capital Punishment; his Adaptation of *The Possessed.*" *Yale Review* 48 (1969): 634–40.

Rauhut, Franz. "Du nihilisme à la 'mesure' et à l'amour des hommes." In *Configuration critique d'Albert Camus, II: Camus devant la critique de langue allemande,* edited by R. Thieberger. La Revue des Lettres Modernes, 90–93. Paris: Minard, 1963.

Read, Sir Herbert. Foreword to *The Rebel,* by Albert Camus. Translated by Anthony Bower. London: Hamish Hamilton, 1953.

Reardon, B. M. G. "Albert Camus's Philosophy of Revolt." *Theology* 63 (1960): 236–42.

Reck, Rima Drell. "Albert Camus: The Artist and his Time." *Modern Language Quarterly* 23 (1962): 129–34.

Redfern, W. D. "Camus and Confusion." *Symposium* 20 (1966): 329–42.

Reed, Peter J. "Judges in the Plays of Albert Camus." *Modern Drama* 5 (1962): 47–57.

Reid, David. "The Rains of Empire: Camus in New York." *MLN* 112 (1997): 608–24.

Renard, Jean-Claude. "L'œuvre de Camus en débat devant la nouvelle génération: 'une expérience à laquelle j'adhère—en chrétien.'" *Le Figaro littéraire,* November 2, 1957, 11.

Renaud, Gaston R. "Saint Tarrou: martyr laïque ou Camus et le problème de la sainteté." *Revue de l'Université d'Ottawa* 41 (1971): 322–30.

Rey, Pierre-Louis. "Noms et lieux d'Alger." *Europe* 77 (1999): 40–47.

Rigaud, Jan. "The Depiction of Arabs in *L'Étranger.*" In *Camus's "L'Étranger": Fifty Years On,* 2nd ed., edited by Adèle King. New York: St. Martin's Press, 1994.

Rinaldi, Angelo. "Albert Camus: regrets éternels." *L'Express,* May 5, 1994, 61–62.

Rizzuto, Anthony, ed. *Albert Camus: "L'Exil et le royaume": The Third Decade.* Toronto: Paratexte, 1988.

———. *Camus: Love and Sexuality.* Gainesville: University Press of Florida, 1998.

———. *Camus's Imperial Vision.* Carbondale: Southern Illinois University Press, 1981.

Robin, Maurice. "Albert Camus et la crise de l'homme dans le tiers monde." In

Albert Camus et l'Europe: Actes du colloque de Strasbourg, 9 et 10 novembre 1990, edited by André Abbou. Paris: Ofil, 1995.

———. "Remarques sur l'attitude de Camus face à la guerre d'Algérie." In *Camus et la politique: Actes du colloque de Nanterre, 5–7 juin 1985,* edited by Jeanyves Guérin. Paris: L'Harmattan, 1986.

Roblès, Emmanuel. *Albert Camus et la trêve civile.* Philadelphia: Celfan Edition Monographs, 1988.

———. *Camus: frère de soleil.* Paris: Seuil, 1995.

———. "Camus: Our Youthful Years." In *Camus's "L'Étranger": Fifty Years On,* 2nd ed., edited by Adèle King. New York: St. Martin's Press, 1994.

———. "La marque du soleil et de la misère." In *Camus,* edited by René-Marill Albérès, Pierre de Boisdeffre, Jean Daniel, Pierre Gascar, Morvan Lebesque, André Parinaud, Emmanuel Roblès, Jules Roy, and Pierre-Henri Simon. Collection Génies et Réalités. Paris: Hachette, 1964.

———. "Visages d'Albert Camus." *Simoun* 8 (1960): 13–17.

Robson, Steve. "Albert Camus: The Man behind the Myth." In *Autobiography and the Existential Self: Studies in Modern French Writing,* edited by Terry Keefe and Edmund Smyth. Liverpool: Liverpool University Press, 1995.

Robson, Steven Andrew. "Albert Camus: les raisons de lutter." Master's thesis, University of Keele, 1992.

Rodan, Martin. "La Grèce de Camus: Patrie et patrimoine." In *Albert Camus: parcours méditerranéens,* edited by Fernande Bartfeld and David Ohana. Vol. 5 of *Perspectives: Revue de l'Université Hébraïque de Jérusalem* (1998): 37–44.

Roelens, Maurice. "Un texte, 'son histoire' et l'histoire: 'L'Hôte' d'Albert Camus." *La Revue des Sciences Humaines* 42 (1977): 5–22.

Roeming, Robert F. "The Concept of the Judge-Penitent of Albert Camus." *Transactions of the Wisconsin Academy of Sciences, Arts and Letters* 48 (1959): 143–49.

Rolo, Charles J. "Albert Camus: A Good Man." *Atlantic Monthly* 201 (1958): 27–33.

Roman, Joël. "Histoire et utopie dans 'Ni victimes ni bourreaux.'" In *Camus et le premier "Combat" (1944–1947: Colloque de Paris X-Nanterre),* edited by Jeanyves Guérin. La Garenne-Colombes: Européennes Erasmus, 1990.

Rooke, Constance. "Camus's 'The Guest': The Message on the Blackboard." *Studies in Short Fiction* 14 (1977): 78–81.

Roth, Leon. "A Contemporary Moralist: Albert Camus." *Philosophy* 30 (1955): 291–303.

Rousseaux, André. "Albert Camus et notre espoir." *Le Figaro littéraire,* October 26, 1957, 2.

———. "*L'Homme révolté* d'Albert Camus." *Le Figaro littéraire,* November 17, 1951, 2.

———. "La morale d'Albert Camus." *Le Figaro littéraire,* October 21, 1950, 2.

Roy, Jules. "'Depuis l'indépendance de l'Algérie—je suis un sans-patrie.'" *Le Figaro littéraire,* February 5–11, 1968, 20–21.

———. "La Tragédie algérienne." In *Camus,* edited by René-Marill Albérès, Pierre de Boisdeffre, Jean Daniel, Pierre Gascar, Morvan Lebesque, André Parinaud, Emmanuel Roblès, Jules Roy, and Pierre-Henri Simon. Collection Génies et Réalités. Paris: Hachette, 1964.

———. "Pour et contre Camus: l'homme qui avait une étoile." *Le Figaro littéraire,* January 5–11, 1970, 10–11.

Rubinlicht-Proux, Anne. "*L'Étranger* et le positivisme juridique." In *Albert Camus, 17: "toujours autour de 'L'Étranger,'"* edited by Raymond Gay-Crosier. La Revue des Lettres Modernes, 1310–16. Paris: Lettres Modernes Minard, 1996.

Sabatier, Robert. "L'œuvre de Camus en débat devant la nouvelle génération: 'il livre une bataille contre la peur.'" *Le Figaro littéraire,* October 26, 1957, 11.

Salas, Denis. *Albert Camus: la juste révolte.* Collection Le bien commun. Paris: Michalon, 2002.

Sändig, Brigitte. "La réception de Camus en R. D. A." In *Albert Camus et l'Europe: Actes du colloque de Strasbourg, 9 et 10 novembre 1990,* edited by André Abbou. Paris: Ofil, 1995.

———. "Réception de l'œuvre de Camus en R.D.A." In *Albert Camus, 18: "la réception de l'œuvre de Camus en U.R.S.S. et en R.D.A.,"* edited by Raymond Gay-Crosier. La Revue des Lettres Modernes 1472–77. Paris: Lettres Modernes Minard, 1999.

Sarang, Vilas. "A Brother to the Stranger." In *Camus's "L'Étranger": Fifty Years On,* 2nd ed., edited by Adèle King. New York: St. Martin's Press, 1994.

Sarocchi, Jean. *Camus.* Collection Philosophes. Paris: PUF, 1968.

———. "Camus: juste traître?" *Littératures* 14 (1986): 115–22.

———. "Clamence séducteur?" *Europe* 77 (1999): 119–31.

———. "Compte-rendu du seminaire indo-français des 19, 20 et 21 septembre 1990 au Centre Indien International de New-Delhi sur *Camus et L'Humanisme.*" *Bulletin d'Information de la Société des Études Camusiennes* 23 (1991): 1–7.

———. *Le Dernier Camus ou "Le Premier Homme."* Paris: Nizet, 1995.

———. "L'Europe: exil ou royaume?" *Littératures* 26 (1992): 154–86.

———. "Les Fureurs adolescents." In *Albert Camus: les Extrêmes et l'équilibre; Actes du colloque de Keele, 25–27 mars 1993,* edited by David H. Walker. Amsterdam: Rodopi, 1994.

———. "'La Méditerranée est un songe, monsieur.'" In *Albert Camus: parcours méditerranéens,* edited by Fernande Bartfeld and David Ohana. Vol. 5 of *Perspectives: Revue de l'Université Hébraïque de Jérusalem* (1998): 109–29.

Sartre, Jean-Paul. "Albert Camus." *France Observateur,* January 7, 1960, 17.

———. "Explication de *L'Étranger.*" *Les Cahiers du Sud* 30 (1943): 189–253.

———. "Réponse à Albert Camus." *Les Temps modernes* 82 (1952): 334–53.

Savage Brosman, Catharine. "Strangers and Brothers in the Works of Albert Camus and Jules Roy." In *Camus's "L'Étranger": Fifty Years On,* 2nd ed., edited by Adèle King. New York: St. Martin's Press, 1994.

Scherr Salgado, Raquel. "Memoir at Saint-Brieuc." *MLN* 112 (1997): 576–94.

Schlette, Heinz-Robert. "La critique de la technique chez Camus." In *Albert Camus et l'Europe: Actes du colloque de Strasbourg, 9 et 10 novembre 1990,* edited by André Abbou. Paris: Ofil, 1995.

———. "Remarques sur la réception des idées politiques de Camus en RFA." In *Camus et la politique: Actes du colloque de Nanterre, 5–7 juin 1985,* edited by Jeanyves Guérin. Paris: L'Harmattan, 1986.

Schlumberger, Jean. "À propos de la peine de mort (*Réflexions sur la peine capi-*

tale, par Albert Camus et Arthur Koestler)." *Le Figaro littéraire,* February 8, 1958, 1, 4.

———. "Dans cette lumière . . ." *Le Figaro littéraire,* January 9, 1960, 1.

Schneider, Peter. "Mesure et justice." In *Configuration critique d'Albert Camus, II: Camus devant la critique de langue allemande,* edited by R. Thieberger. La Revue des Lettres Modernes, 90–93. Paris: Minard, 1963.

Schoentjes, Pierre. "*Le Premier Homme* et *L'Acacia*: 'faire voir' le père." *Europe* 77 (1999): 154–66.

Schosler, Jorn. "Rousseau, Camus et le nihilisme: sur l'actualité de Rousseau." *Orbis Litterarum* 40 (1985): 97–110.

Schwartzbrod, Alexandra. "Le mythe décisif." *Libération,* August 10, 1998, 26.

Schwarz, Alfred. "The Limits of Violence: Camus's Tragic View of the Rebel." *Comparative Drama* 4 (1972): 28–39.

Scott, Nathan A. *Albert Camus.* London: Bowes & Bowes, 1962.

Sénard, Jean. "Un certain journaliste." *Le Figaro littéraire,* October 26, 1957, 5.

Sénart, Philippe. "Camus et le juste milieu." *La Table Ronde* 174–75 (1962): 112–15.

Shattuck, Roger. "Guilt, Justice, and Empathy in Melville and Camus." *Partisan Review* 63 (1996): 430–49.

Showalter, Jr., English. *Exiles and Strangers: A Reading of Camus's "Exile and the Kingdom."* Columbus, Ohio: Ohio State University Press, 1984.

Shillony, Helena. "Les traductions de Camus en hébreu." In *Albert Camus: parcours méditerranéens,* edited by Fernande Bartfeld and David Ohana. Vol. 5 of *Perspectives: Revue de l'Université Hébraïque de Jérusalem* (1998): 247–51.

Siblot, Paul, and Jean-Louis Planche. "Le 8 mai 1945: éléments pour une analyse des positions de Camus face au nationalisme algérien." In *Camus et la politique: Actes du colloque de Nanterre, 5–7 juin 1985,* edited by Jeanyves Guérin. Paris: L'Harmattan, 1986.

Simon, Ernest. "Palais de Justice and Poetic Justice in Albert Camus's *The Stranger.*" *Cardoza Studies in Law and Literature* 3 (1991): 111–25.

Simon, John K. "Camus' Kingdom: The Native Host and an Unwanted Guest." *Studies in Short Fiction* 1 (1964): 289–91.

Simon, Pierre-Henri. "Le combat contre les mandarins." In *Camus,* edited by René-Marill Albérès, Pierre de Boisdeffre, Jean Daniel, Pierre Gascar, Morvan Lebesque, André Parinaud, Emmanuel Roblès, Jules Roy, and Pierre-Henri Simon. Collection Génies et Réalités. Paris: Hachette, 1964.

———. *Présence de Camus.* Paris: La Renaissance du Livre, 1962.

Sjursen, Nina. "Beauté et savoir dans la quête de Camus." In *Albert Camus: parcours méditerranéens,* edited by Fernande Bartfeld and David Ohana. Vol. 5 of *Perspectives: Revue de l'Université Hébraïque de Jérusalem* (1998): 27–36.

———. "Colloque Jean Grenier à Cerisy-la-Salle, 1–8 août 1991." *Bulletin d'Information de la Société des Études Camusiennes* 24 (1991): 6–7.

———. "Jeux, justice et amour dans *Le Premier Homme.*" *Narcisse* 16 (1996): 53–65.

———. "Le piège et la démesure." In *Albert Camus et l'Europe: Actes du colloque de Strasbourg, 9 et 10 novembre 1990,* edited by André Abbou. Paris: Ofil, 1995.

Smets, Paul F. *Albert Camus: ce "premier homme."* Brussels: Ceuterick, 1995.

———. "Albert Camus: mort et renaissance." *La Revue générale* 121 (1985): 17–29.

———. *Albert Camus: ses engagements pour la justice et la justesse.* Brussels: Ceuterick, n.d. [1998].

———, ed. *Albert Camus: textes réunis par Paul F. Smets à l'occasion du 25e anniversaire de la mort de l'écrivain.* Brussels: Éditions de l'Université de Bruxelles, 1985.

———. *Camus dans le premier silence . . . et au delà suivi de Albert Camus: chroniqueur judiciaire à "Alger-Républicain" en 1939.* Brussels: Goemaere, 1985.

———. "Camus: éditorialiste à *Combat.*" *La Revue générale* 123 (1987): 3–15.

———. *Le Combat pour l'abolition de la peine de mort: Hugo, Koestler, Camus, d'autres: textes, prétextes et paratextes.* Brussels: Académie royale de Belgique, 2003.

———. "Des *Justes* en hiver." *La Revue générale* 1 (1990): 53–68.

———. "Le juge-pénitent du *Mexico City.*" *La Revue générale* 125 (1989): 71–79.

———. "Lettre ouverte à Olivier Todd, auteur d'*Albert Camus, une vie.*" *La Revue générale* 6–7 (1996): 57–61.

———. *Le Pari européen dans les essais d'Albert Camus.* Brussels: Bruylant, 1991.

———. *Un Testament ambigu: Albert Camu, "La Chute"; Pièces pour un dossier inachevé.* Brussels: Smets, 1988.

Solier, René de. "Sens du journalisme critique." *NRF* 8 (1960): 476–79.

Sperber, Michael A. "Camus' *The Fall:* The Icarus Complex." *American Imago* 36 (1969): 269–80.

Spiquel, Agnès. "Némésis, une 'pensée de midi'?" In *Albert Camus: parcours méditerranéens,* edited by Fernande Bartfeld and David Ohana. Vol. 5 of *Perspectives: Revue de l'Université Hébraïque de Jérusalem* (1998): 199–212.

Spitéri, Gérard. "Parmi les justes?" *Les Nouvelles littéraires,* January 10–17, 1980, 18.

Sponville, André Comte, Laurent Bove, and Patrick Renou. *Albert Camus: de l'absurde à l'amour.* Vénissieux: Paroles de l'Aube, 1995.

Sprintzen, David. *Camus: A Critical Examination.* Philadelphia: Temple University Press, 1988.

———. "Confronting the 21st Century: A Camusian Vision." In *Albert Camus et l'Europe: Actes du colloque de Strasbourg, 9 et 10 novembre 1990,* edited by André Abbou. Paris: Ofil, 1995.

Sprintzen, David A., and Adrian van den Hoven, eds. *Sartre and Camus: A Historic Confrontation.* Amherst, N.Y.: Humanity Books, 2004.

Stéphane, Nelly. "La Mer heureuse." *Europe* 77 (1999): 132–44.

Sterling, Elwyn F. "A Story of Cain: Another Look at 'L'Hôte'." *French Review* 54 (1981): 524–29.

Stockwell, H. C. R. "Albert Camus." *Cambridge Journal* 7 (1954): 690–704.

Stokle, Norman, ed. *Le combat d'Albert Camus.* Quebec: Presses de l'Université Laval, 1970.

Stolarski, Robert. *Camus et la Méditerranée.* Uniwersytet im Adama Mickiewieza W Poznaniu: Poznan, 1979.

Suffert, Georges. "Camus: pas un ride." *Le Point,* January 16, 1984, 117.

Tadashi, Suzuki. "La mère et les mots: une contribution aux études de la genèse de *L'Envers et l'endroit.*" *Journal of Gifu Keizai University* 29 (1995): 203–28.

Tall, Emily. "Correspondence between Albert Camus and Boris Pasternak." *Canadian Slavonic Papers: An Inter-Disciplinary Quarterly devoted to the Soviet Union and Eastern Europe* 22 (1980): 319–37.

———. "Letters of Camus and Pasternak." *Partisan Review* 47 (1980): 195–98.

Tame, Peter. "Robert Brasillach et Albert Camus." *Cahiers des Amis de Brasillach* 34 (1989): 20–47.

Taos, Marguerite. "Hommage à Albert Camus." *Simoun* 8 (1960): 22–24.

Tarrow, Susan. *Exile from the Kingdom: A Political Rereading of Albert Camus.* Tuscaloosa: University of Alabama Press, 1985.

Terrien, Samuel. "Christianity's debt to a modern pagan: Albert Camus (1913–1960)." *Union Seminary Quarterly Review* 15 (1960): 185–94.

Thieberger, R., ed. *Configuration critique d'Albert Camus, II: Camus devant la critique de langue allemande.* La Revue des Lettres Modernes, 90–93. Paris: Lettres Modernes Minard, 1963.

Thody, Philip. *Albert Camus.* Macmillan Modern Novelists. London: Macmillan, 1989.

———. *Albert Camus: 1913–1960.* London: Hamish Hamilton, 1961.

———. "Albert Camus (1913–1960)." In *The Politics of Twentieth-Century Novelists,* edited by George A. Panichas. New York: Apollo, 1974.

———. *Albert Camus: A Study of his Work.* London: Hamish Hamilton, 1957.

———. "Albert Camus and 'La Remarque sur la révolte.'" *French Studies* 10 (1956): 335–38.

———. "Camus et la politique." In *Albert Camus, 2: "langue et langage,"* edited by Brian T. Fitch. La Revue des Lettres Modernes, 212–16. Paris: Lettres Modernes, 1969.

———. "The Great System Builder and the Apostle to the *Pieds-Noirs.*" *THES,* April 19, 1974, 11.

Thorson, Thomas Landon. "Albert Camus and the Rights of Man." *Ethics* 74 (1964): 281–91.

Tillion, Germaine. "Albert Camus et l'Algérie." *Preuves* 91 (1958): 69–72.

———. "Devant le malheur algérien." *Preuves* 110 (1960): 25–27.

Tison, Guillemette. "La culture de l'enfant dans *Le Premier Homme.*" *Roman 20–50* 27 (1999): 39–51.

Todd, Olivier. "Camus and Sartre." In *Camus's "L'Étranger": Fifty Years On,* 2nd ed., edited by Adèle King. New York: St. Martin's Press, 1994.

———. "Pourquoi Camus?" *Europe* 77 (1999): 178–83.

Trageser-Rebetez, Françoise. "Paradigme cyclique dans la philosophie camusienne de l'Histoire." In *Albert Camus, 19: "'L'Homme révolté': cinquante ans après,"* edited by Raymond Gay-Crosier. La Revue des Lettres Modernes. Paris: Lettres Modernes Minard, 2001.

Treil, Claude. *L'Indifférence dans l'œuvre d'Albert Camus.* Quebec: Cosmos, 1971.

Triolet, Elsa. "Qui est cet étranger qui n'est pas d'ici? ou le mythe de la baronne Mélanie." *Poésie 43* 4 (1943): 11–26.

Tucker, Warren. "*La Chute:* voie du salut terrestre." *French Review* 43 (1970): 737–44.

Tuzun, Tanju. "Les positions sociales et politiques d'Albert Camus dans son œuvre." Ph.D. diss., University of Poitiers, 1968.

Ubersfeld, Annie. "Albert Camus ou la métaphysique de la contre-révolution." *La Nouvelle Critique* 10 (1958): 110–30.

Valette-Fondo, Madeleine. "Camus et Artaud." In *Albert Camus et le théâtre: Actes du colloque tenu à Amiens du 31 mai au 2 juin 1988,* edited by Jacqueline Lévi-Valensi. Paris: Imec, 1992.

Van Cauwelaert, Didier. "Le gardien du but de la philosophie." *Le Figaro littéraire,* March 9, 1987, iii, v.

Vanney, Philippe. "Camus contre le droit de mort de l'État." *Bulletin d'Études Françaises* 34 (2003): 49–73.

———. "La démocratie à l'épreuve des relations internationales: reconnaissance et ingérence." *Equinoxe* 13 (1996): 37–49.

———. "Par dessus les frontières, des îlots de résistance. Camus et les Groupes de Liaison Internationale." *Bulletin d'Études Françaises* 30 (1999): 155–89.

———. "Le partage de la souffrance: Camus et le débat traditionnel sur la peine de mort." *Bulletin d'Études Françaises* 32 (2001): 95–120.

———. "Quelques remarques sur l'idée de trêve dans l'œuvre politique d'Albert Camus." In *Albert Camus: les Extrêmes et l'équilibre; Actes du colloque de Keele, 25–27 mars 1993,* edited by David H. Walker. Amsterdam: Rodopi, 1994.

Vasil, Dean. *The Ethical Pragmatism of Albert Camus: Two Studies in the History of Ideas.* New York: Berne, 1985.

Velikovski, Samary. "Camus et l'existentialisme." In *Albert Camus, 12: "la révolte en question,"* edited by Brian T. Fitch. La Revue des Lettres Modernes, 715–19. Paris: Lettres Modernes Minard, 1985.

Vertone, Teodosio. "Albert Camus: l'Espagnol." *Cahiers d'Études Romanes* 12 (1987): 240–66.

———. "La pensée libertaire d'Albert Camus." *L'Arc* 91–92 (1984): 113–18.

———. "La tentation nihiliste et hédoniste du jeune Camus." *Cahiers d'Études Romanes* 6 (1980): 69–82.

Viallaneix, Paul. "Le défi du mal: dialogue avec Albert Camus." *Foi et Vie* (January 1995): 25–34.

———. "Le premier Camus." In *Le premier Camus suivi de Écrits de jeunesse d'Albert Camus.* Cahiers Albert Camus 2. Paris: Gallimard, 1973.

———. "Souvenirs d'un lecteur de *Combat.*" In *Albert Camus: textes réunis par Paul F. Smets à l'occasion du 25e anniversaire de la mort de l'écrivain,* edited by Paul F. Smets. Brussels: Éditions de l'Université de Bruxelles, 1985.

———. "Le testament du *Premier Homme.*" *Equinoxe* 13 (1996): 95–100.

Viatte, Auguste. "Albert Camus devant l'athéisme." *La Revue de l'Université Laval* 6 (1952): 642–47.

Vigée, Claude. "De *Noces* à 'La Femme adultère': la quête de la lumière cachée dans la pensée d'Albert Camus." In *Albert Camus: parcours méditerranéens,* edited by Fernande Bartfeld and David Ohana. Vol. 5 of *Perspectives: Revue de l'Université Hébraïque de Jérusalem* (1998): 227–33.

Viggiani, Carl A. "Albert Camus' first publications." *MLN* 75 (1960): 589–96.
———. "Camus in 1936: The Beginnings of a Career." *Symposium* 12 (1958): 7–18.
———. "Fall and Exile. Camus: 1956–1958." In *Albert Camus 1980: Second International Conference, February 21–23 1980, The University of Florida, Gainesville,* edited by Raymond Gay-Crosier. Gainesville: University Presses of Florida, 1980.
———. "Notes pour le futur biographe d'Albert Camus." In *Albert Camus, 1: "autour de 'L'Étranger,'"* edited by Brian T. Fitch. La Revue des Lettres Modernes, 170–74. Paris: Lettres Modernes, 1968.
Vircondelet, Alain. *Albert Camus: vérité et légendes.* Photographies Collection Catherine et Jean Camus. Paris: Chêne-Hachette Livre, 1998.
Vulor, Ena Cecilia. "The North African Reality in the Work of Albert Camus: Rereading *L'Étranger, La Peste* and *L'Exil et le royaume* from a colonial perspective." Ph.D diss., University of Cornell, 1994.
Walker, David H. "Albert Camus devant les méfaits de l'Europe." In *Albert Camus et l'Europe: Actes du colloque de Strasbourg, 9 et 10 novembre 1990,* edited by André Abbou. Paris: Ofil, 1995.
———., ed. *Albert Camus: "L'Exil et le royaume."* London: Harrap, 1981.
———., ed. *Albert Camus: les Extrêmes et l'équilibre; Actes du colloque de Keele, 25–27 mars 1993.* Amsterdam: Rodopi, 1994.
———. "Albert Camus: les Extrêmes et l'équilibre." In *Albert Camus: les Extrêmes et l'équilibre; Actes du colloque de Keele, 25–27 mars 1993,* edited by David H. Walker. Amsterdam: Rodopi, 1994.
———. "Le criminel chez Camus." In *Albert Camus: les Extrêmes et l'équilibre; Actes du colloque de Keele, 25–27 mars 1993,* edited by David H. Walker. Amsterdam: Rodopi, 1994.
———. "Image, symbole et signification dans 'La Pierre qui pousse.'" In *Albert Camus, 11: "Camus et la religion,"* edited by Brian T. Fitch. La Revue des Lettres Modernes, 648–51. Paris: Lettres Modernes Minard, 1982.
———. "In and Out of History: Albert Camus." *French Cultural Studies* 8 (1997): 103–15.
———. "Knowing the Place For the First Time?" In *Constructing Memories: Camus, Algeria and "Le Premier Homme,"* edited by Peter Dunwoodie and Edward J. Hughes. Vol 6 of *Stirling French Publications* (1998): 19–20.
Walker, Ian H. "The Early Camus: A Reconsideration." *Philosophical Journal* 2 (1965): 91–103.
Walusinski, Gilbert. "Camus and les Groupes de Liaison Internationale." *La Quinzaine littéraire,* March 1–15, 1979: 22–24.
———. "Le combat de Camus." *La Quinzaine littéraire,* April 16, 1978, 9.
Walzer, Michael. "Commitment and Social Criticism: Camus's Algerian War." *Dissent* (Fall 1984): 424–32.
Ward, Bruce K. "Prometheus or Caïn? Albert Camus's Account of the Western Quest for Justice." *Faith and Philosophy* 8 (1991): 193–213.
———. "The Recovery of Helen: Albert Camus's Attempt to Restore the Greek Idea of Nature." *Dionysius* 14 (1990): 169–94.
Wardman, Harold W. "Parody in Camus." *Essays in French Literature* 2 (1965): 15–29.

Warren, Thomas H. "On the Mistranslation of 'La Mesure' in Camus's Political Thought." *Journal of the History of Philosophy* 1 (1992): 123–30.

Weis, Marcia. *The Lyrical Essays of Albert Camus: "Une Longue Fidélité."* Quebec: Sherbrooke, 1976.

Werner, Eric. *De la violence au totalitarisme: essai sur la pensée de Camus et de Sartre.* Paris: Calmann-Lévy, 1972.

Wernicke, Horst. "Mesure et justice: les *Lettres à un ami allemand* de Camus et les *Billets à Francis Curel* de René Char." In *Albert Camus et l'Europe: Actes du colloque de Strasbourg, 9 et 10 novembre 1990,* edited by André Abbou. Paris: Ofil, 1995.

Weyembergh, Maurice. "A. Camus et K. Popper: la critique de l'historisme et de l'historicisme." In *Albert Camus, 9: "la pensée de Camus,"* edited by Raymond Gay-Crosier. La Revue des Lettres Modernes, 565–69. Paris: Lettres Modernes Minard, 1979.

———. "Camus et Nietzsche: évolution d'une affinité." In *Albert Camus 1980: Second International Conference, February 21–23 1980, The University of Florida, Gainesville,* edited by Raymond Gay-Crosier. Gainesville: University Presses of Florida, 1980.

———. "Camus et Saint Augustin." In *Albert Camus: parcours méditerranéens,* edited by Fernande Bartfeld and David Ohana. Vol. 5 of *Perspectives: Revue de l'Université Hébraïque de Jérusalem* (1998): 131–46.

———. "Camus nietzschéen de gauche, Aron marxien de droite?" In *Camus et la politique: Actes du colloque de Nanterre, 5–7 juin 1985,* edited by Jeanyves Guérin. Paris: L'Harmattan, 1986.

———. "Colloque de Berlin: *'Ich revoltiere, also sind wir',* 15–16 juin 1991." *Bulletin d'Information de la Société des Études Camusiennes* 25 (1991): 3–11.

———. "La mémoire du retour et le retour de la mémoire." In *Albert Camus et l'Europe. Actes du colloque de Strasbourg, 9 et 10 novembre 1990,* edited by André Abbou. Paris: Ofil, 1995.

———. "L'obsession du clos et le thème des camps." In *Albert Camus: œuvre fermée, œuvre ouverte? Actes du colloque du Centre International de Cerisy-la-Salle, juin 1982,* edited by Raymond Gay-Crosier and Jacqueline Lévi-Valensi. Cahiers Albert Camus 5. Paris: Gallimard, 1985.

———. "Merleau-Ponty et Camus: *Humanisme et Terreur* et 'Ni victimes ni bourreaux.'" *Annales de L'Institut de Philosophie, L'Université Libre de Bruxelles* (1971): 53–99.

———. "Ni victimes ni bourreaux: continuité ou rupture?" In *Camus et le premier "Combat" (1944–1947): Colloque de Paris X-Nanterre,* edited by Jeanyves Guérin. La Garenne-Colombes: Européennes Erasmus, 1990.

———. "Le Plongeon, la baleine et les piranhas." *Europe* 77 (1999): 145–53.

———. Review of *Camus: portrait de l'artiste en citoyen,* by Jeanyves Guérin." In *Albert Camus, 17: "toujours autour de 'L'Étranger,'"* edited by Raymond Gay-Crosier. La Revue des Lettres Modernes, 1310–16. Paris: Lettres Modernes Minard, 1996.

———. "Révolte et ressentiment." In *Albert Camus, 12: "la révolte en question,"* edited by Raymond Gay-Crosier. La Revue des Lettres Modernes, 715–19. Paris: Lettres Modernes Minard, 1985.

———. "Théâtre et politique chez Albert Camus." In *Albert Camus et le théâtre:*

Actes du colloque tenu à Amiens du 31 mai au 2 juin 1988, edited by Jacqueline Lévi-Valensi. Paris: Imec, 1992.

———. "L'Unité, la totalité et l'énigme ontologique." In *Albert Camus: les Extrêmes et l'équilibre. Actes du colloque de Keele, 25–27 mars 1993,* edited by David H. Walker. Amsterdam: Rodopi, 1994.

Whartenby, H. Allen. "The Interlocutor in *La Chute:* A Key to its Meaning." *PMLA* 83 (1968): 1326–33.

Wiesel, Elie. "L'Homme de Conscience." *Europe* 77 (1999): 9–11.

Wilkinson, Russell, and Chris Mitchell. "'Solitaire et Solidaire'." *Philosophy Now* 14 (1995–96): 24–27.

Willhoite Jr., Fred H. "Albert Camus' Politics of Rebellion." *Western Political Quarterly* 14 (1961): 400–14.

———. *Beyond Nihilism: Albert Camus's Contribution to Political Thought.* Baton Rouge: Louisiana State University Press, 1968.

Williams, James S. *Camus: "La Peste."* Critical Guides to French Texts 128. London: Grant & Cutler, 2000.

Willoquet-Maricondi, Paula. "Correspondance inédite d'Albert Camus." *French Review* 67 (1994): 501–4.

Woelfel, James. *Camus: A Theological Perspective.* Nashville, TN: Abingdon Press, 1975.

Wood, Nancy. "Colonial nostalgia and *Le Premier Homme.*" *French Cultural Studies* 9 (1998): 167–89.

Woolfolk, Alan N. "The Dangers of *Engagement:* Camus's Political Esthetics." *Mosaic* 17 (1984): 59–70.

Wu, Shaoyi. "Individualisme altruiste chez Albert Camus." In *Albert Camus entre la misère et le soleil: Actes du Colloque international de Poitiers, 29–30–31 mai 1997,* edited by Lionel Dubois. Poitiers: Éditions du Pont-Neuf, 1997.

———. "La mise à l'index d'Albert Camus en Chine populaire." In *Les trois guerres d'Albert Camus: Actes du Colloque International de Poitiers, 4–5–6 mai 1995,* edited by Lionel Dubois. Poitiers: Éditions du Pont-Neuf, 1995.

Yalom, Marilyn K. "Albert Camus and the Myth of the Trial." *Modern Language Quarterly* 25 (1964): 434–50.

Yannakakis, Ilias. "Camus et la Tchécaslovaquie." In *Camus et la politique: Actes du colloque de Nanterre, 5–7 juin 1985,* edited by Jeanyves Guérin. Paris: L'Harmattan, 1986.

Zants, Emily. "The Relationship of Judge and Priest in *La Peste.*" *French Review* 37 (1964): 419–25.

Zirem, Youcef. "Entre l'enfer et la raison." *La Nation,* August 15–21, 1995, 21.

Zucker, Richard. "The Happiness of Sisyphus." *Kinesis* 16 (1987): 41–65.

Historical, Literary, and Philosophical Studies:

Abbas, Ferhat. *Guerre et révolution d'Algérie: la nuit coloniale.* Paris: Julliard, 1962.

Addi, Lahouari. "Nationality and Algerian Immigrants in France." In *French and Algerian Identities from Colonial Times to the Present: A Century of Interaction,* edited by Alec G. Hargreaves and Michael J. Heffernan. Lewiston: Edwin Mellen, 1993.

Adereth, Max. *Commitment in Modern French Literature: A Brief Study of "Littérature Engagée" in the Works of Péguy, Aragon, and Sartre.* London: Gollancz, 1967.

———. *The French Communist Party: A Critical History, 1920–84. From Comintern to "The Colours of France."* Manchester: Manchester University Press, 1984.

———. "Sartre and Communism." *Journal of European Studies* 17 (1987): 1–48.

Ageron, Charles-Robert. *Les Algériens musulmans et la France, 1871–1919.* 2 vols. Paris: PUF, 1968.

———. "Les Français devant la guerre civile algérienne." In *La Guerre d'Algérie et les Français,* edited by Jean-Pierre Rioux. Paris: Fayard, 1990.

———. *Histoire de l'Algérie contemporaine, 1871–1954.* 2 vols. Paris: PUF, 1979.

———. Histoire de l'Algérie contemporaine. Collection Que sais-je?. 4th ed. Paris: PUF, 1970.

Ainad-Tabet, Radouane. *Le 8 mai 1945 en Algérie.* Algiers: Office des Publications Universitaires, 1985.

Albérès, René-Marill. Les Hommes traqués. Paris: La Nouvelle Édition, 1953.

———. *La révolte des écrivains d'aujourd'hui.* Paris: Correa, 1949.

Alleg, Henri. *La Question.* Paris: Minuit, 1958.

Amouroux, Henri. *La Grande Histoire des Français sous l'Occupation. Les passions et les haines, avril–décembre 1942.* Paris: Laffont, 1981.

———. *La vie des Français sous l'Occupation.* Paris: Marabout, 1976.

Anderson, Kirsteen H. R. "Imagination and Ideology: Ethical Tensions in Twentieth-Century French Writing." *Modern Language Review* 96 (2001): 47–60.

Anderson, Peter J. *The Global Politics of Power, Justice and Death: An Introduction to International Relations.* London: Routledge, 1996.

Angenot, Marc. *La Parole pamphlétaire.* Paris: Payot, 1982.

Anglès, Auguste. *Circumnavigations: littérature, voyages, politique 1942–1983.* Lyons: Presses Universitaires de Lyon, 1986.

Annas, Julia. *An Introduction to Plato's Republic.* Oxford: Clarendon Press, 1980.

Ansell-Pearson, Keith. *An Introduction to Nietzsche as Political Thinker: The Perfect Nihilist.* Cambridge: Cambridge University Press, 1994.

Aouli, Smaïl, and Ramdane Redjala. "La Kabylie face à la dérive intégriste." *Les Temps modernes* 580 (1995): 196–208.

Arendt, Hannah. *Crises of the Republic* London: Penguin Books, 1973.

Aristotle. *Nicomachean Ethics.* Translated by Terence Irwin. Indianapolis, Indiana: Hackett, 1985.

———. *The Works of Aristotle.* Translated and edited by W. D. Ross. 12 vols. Oxford: Oxford University Press, 1908–15.

Aron, Raymond. *L'Algérie et la République.* Paris: Plon, 1958.

———. "L'éditorialiste." *Commentaire* 8 (1985): 387–96.

———. *Histoire et dialectique de la violence.* Paris: Gallimard, 1973.

———. *Mémoires: 50 ans de réflexion politique.* Paris: Julliard, 1983.

———. *L'Opium des intellectuals.* Paris: Calmann-Lévy, 1955.

———. *La Tragédie algérienne.* Paris: Plon, 1957.

Aron, Robert. *Histoire de l'épuration.* Paris: Fayard, 1975.

———. *Histoire de la Libération de France.* Paris: Fayard, 1959.

Aronson, Ronald. "Sartre and Marxism: A Double Retrospective." *Sartre Studies International* 1 (1995): 21–36.

Aschenbaum, Yves-Marc. *À la vie à la mort: histoire du journal "Combat."* Paris: *Le Monde* Éditions, 1995.

Assouline, Pierre. *L'épuration des intellectuels.* Brussels: Complexe, 1985.

Astier, Pierre A. G. *Écrivains français engagés: la génération littéraire de 1930.* Paris: Debresse, 1978.

Astre, Georges-Albert. *Emmanuel Roblès ou le risque de vivre.* Paris: Grasset, 1987.

Atack, Margaret. *Literature and the French Resistance: Cultural Politics and Narrative Forms, 1940–1950.* Manchester: Manchester University Press, 1989.

Audisio, Gabriel. *Jeunesse de la Méditerranée.* Paris: Gallimard, 1935.

———. *L'Opéra fabuleux.* Paris: Julliard, 1970.

Azéma, Jean-Pierre. "Les enjeux de l'épuration en France." *French Cultural Studies* 5 (1994): 273–79.

Bacon, Edwin. *The Gulag at War: Stalin's Forced Labour System in the Light of the Archives.* London: Macmillan, 1995.

Badinter, Robert. *L'Abolition.* Paris: Fayard, 2000.

Baldwin, James. *The Price of the Ticket: Collected Nonfiction 1948–1985.* London: Joseph, 1985.

Barnes, Jonathan. *Early Greek Philosophy.* London: Penguin Books, 1987.

Baroli, Marc. *Algérie, terre d'espérance (colons et immigrants, 1830–1914).* Paris: Hachette, 1976.

Barrault, Jean-Louis. *Réflexions sur le théâtre.* Paris: Vautrain, 1949.

Bartram, Graham, Maurice Slawinski, and David Steel, eds. *Reconstructing the Past: Representations of the Fascist Era in Post-War European Culture.* Keele: Keele University Press, 1996.

Basset, Guy and Patrick Gallaud. "*Combat* et les enjeux de l'Indochine (1945–1947)." In *Camus et le premier "Combat" (1944–1947): Colloque de Paris X-Nanterre.* Edited by Jeanyves Guérin. La Garenne-Colombes: Européennes Erasmus, 1990.

Beaunier, André, ed. *Les Carnets de Joseph Joubert.* 2 vols. Paris: Gallimard, 1938.

Beauvoir, Simone de. *La Force de l'âge.* Collection Folio. Paris: Gallimard, 1960.

———. *La Force des choses.* Collection Folio. 2 vols. Paris: Gallimard, 1963.

———. *Les Mandarins.* Collection Folio. 2 vols. Paris: Gallimard, 1954.

———. "Œil pour œil." *Les Temps modernes* 1 (October 1945—February 1946): 813–30.

———. *Le Sang des autres.* Paris: Gallimard, 1945.

Becque, Henry. *Œuvres complètes.* 7 vols. Paris: Crès, 1924–26.

Beevor, Antony, and Artemis Cooper. *Paris after the Liberation: 1944–1949.* London: Hamish Hamilton, 1994.

Begag, Azouz. "Les relations France—Algérie vues de la diaspora algérienne." *Modern & Contemporary France* 10 (2002): 475–82.

Belamich, André. *Souvenirs d'Oran.* Collection Méditerranée vivante. Paris: Pézenas, 1995.

Bellanger, Claude, Jacques Godechot, Pierre Guiral, and Fernand Terrou. *Histoire générale de la presse française.* 5 vols. Paris: PUF, 1969–75.

Bentham, Jeremy. *"A Fragment on Government" and "An Introduction to the Principles of Morals and Legislation."* Blackwells Political Texts. Oxford: Blackwell, 1948.

Berkowitz, Peter. *Nietzsche: The Ethics of an Immoralist.* London: Harvard University Press, 1995.

Bertrand, Louis. *Le Sang des races.* Paris: Ollendorf, 1899.

Bertrand de Munoz, Maryse. *La guerre civile espagnole et la littérature française.* Ottawa: Didier, 1972.

Betts, Raymond F. *Assimilation and Association in French Colonial Theory, 1840–1914.* New York: Columbia University Press, 1961.

Bieber, Konrad F. *L'Allemagne vue par les écrivains de la résistance française.* Geneva: Droz, 1954.

———. "Engagement as a Professional Risk." *Yale French Studies* 16 (1955–56): 29–39.

Birchall, Ian H. "Neither Washington nor Moscow? The Rise and Fall of the Rassemblement Démocratique Révolutionnaire." *Journal of European Studies* 29 (1999): 365–404.

Blanchot, Maurice. "Réflexions sur le nihilisme." *NNRF* 2 (1954): 850–59.

———. "Tu peux tuer cet homme." *NNRF* 2 (1954): 1059–69.

Bloch-Michel, Jean. "La peine de mort en France." In *Réflexions sur la peine capitale,* Albert Camus and Arthur Koestler. Paris: Calmann-Lévy, 1957.

Blocker, H. Gene. *The Metaphysics of Absurdity.* Washington, DC: University Press of America, 1979.

Blocker, H. Gene, and Elizabeth H. Smith, eds. *John Rawls' Theory of Social Justice: An Introduction.* Athens: Ohio University Press, 1980.

Bodin, Louis, and Jean Touchard. *Front Populaire, 1936.* Paris: Armand Colin, 1972.

Bonn, Charles. *La Littérature algérienne de langue française et ses lecteurs (Imaginaire et discours d'idées).* Ottawa: Naaman, 1974.

———. "La littérature algérienne francophone serait-elle sortie du face-à-face post-colonial?" *Modern & Contemporary France* 10 (2002): 483–93.

Bosquet, Alain. *Injustice.* Paris: La Table Ronde, 1969.

Bourdet, Claude. "La politique intérieure de la résistance." *Les Temps modernes* 112–13 (1955): 1837–62.

Bouretz, Pierre. "Penser au XXe siècle: la place de l'énigme totalitaire." *Esprit* 218 (1996): 122–39.

Boutefnouchet, M. *La Culture en Algérie: mythe et réalité.* Algiers: SNED, 1982.

Brosman, Catharine Savage. *Art as Testimony: The Works of Jules Roy.* University of Florida Humanities Monographs 62. Gainesville: University of Florida Press, 1989.

———. "Les frères ennemis: Jules Roy et l'Algérie." *French Review* 56 (1982–83): 579–87.

Bruckberger, R. L. *À l'heure où les ombres s'allongent.* Paris: Albin Michel, 1989.

Buchanan, Allen. "Revisability and Rational Choice." *Canadian Journal of Philosophy* 5 (1975): 395–408.

Burnier, Michel-Antoine. *Choice of Action: The French Existentialists on the Political Front Line.* Translated by Bernard Murchland with an additional chapter by Bernard Murchland, "Sartre and Camus—The Anatomy of a Quarrel." New York: Random House, 1968.

———. *Les existentialistes et la politique.* Paris: Gallimard, 1966.

Bush, Douglas, ed. *Milton: Poetical Works.* London: Oxford University Press, 1969.

Buton, Philippe. *Communisme: une utopie en sursis? Les logiques d'un système.* Paris: Larousse, 2001.

Campbell, Tom. *The Left and Rights.* London: Routledge, 1983.

———. *Justice.* London: Macmillan, 1988.

Cardinal, Marie. *Les Pieds-noirs (Algérie: 1920–1954).* Paris: Belfond, 1988.

Casarès, Maria. *Résidente privilégiée.* Paris: Fayard, 1980.

Cau, Jean. *Croquis de mémoire.* Paris: Julliard, 1985.

Caute, David. *Communism and the French Intellectuals, 1914–1960.* London: Deutsch, 1964.

Chafer, Tony and Brian Jenkins, eds. *France: From the Cold War to the New World Order.* London: Macmillan, 1995.

Chauviré, Jacques. *Les Passants.* Paris: Michel, 1961.

Chebel d'Appollonia Ariane. *Histoire politique des intellectuels en France, 1944–1954.* 2 vols. Brussels: Complexe, 1991.

Cobban, Alfred. *A History of Modern France.* 3 vols. London: Penguin Books, 1957–65.

Cohen-Solal, Annie. *Sartre, 1905–1980.* Paris: Gallimard, 1985.

———. "Sartre et la Guerre d'Algérie." In *Camus et la politique: Actes du colloque de Nanterre, 5–7 juin 1985,* edited by Jeanyves Guérin. Paris: L'Harmattan, 1986.

Connellan, Coln. *Why Does Evil Exist? A Philosophical Study of the Contemporary Presentation of the Question.* Hicksville, N.Y.: Exposition Press, 1974.

Contat, Michel, and Michel Rybalka. *Les écrits de Sartre.* Paris: Gallimard, 1970.

Cornick, Martyn. "Living Memory: French Intellectuals and the Experience of Phoney War, 1939–1940." *Journal of European Studies* 27 (1997): 261–80.

Courrière, Yves. *La Guerre d'Algérie.* 4 vols. Paris: Fayard, 1968–71.

Cox, Harvey. *The Secular City: Secularization and Urbanization in Theological Perspective.* London: SCM Press, 1965.

Craig, George, and Margaret McGowan. *Moy qui me voy: The Writer and the Self from Montaigne to Leiris.* Oxford: Clarendon Press, 1989.

Cranston, Maurice. Review of *The Rebel,* by Albert Camus and *Sartre,* by Iris Murdoch. *London Magazine* 1 (1954): 99–102.

Crant, Philip, ed. *French Literature Series, III: Mythology in French Literature.* South Carolina: University of South Carolina College of Humanities and Social Sciences, Department of Foreign Languages and Literatures, 1976.

Cruickshank, John, ed. *French Literature and its Background.* 6 vols. London: Oxford University Press, 1970.

———. *The Novelist as Philosopher. Studies in French Fiction: 1935–1960.* London: Oxford University Press, 1962.

Cryle, Peter. *The Thematics of Commitment: The Tower and the Plain.* Princeton: Princeton University Press, 1985.

Daniel, Jean. *La Blessure suivi de Le Temps qui vient.* Paris: Grasset, 1992.

———. *De Gaulle et l'Algérie.* Paris: Seuil, 1986.

———. *Le temps qui reste: essai d'autobiographie professionnelle.* Paris: Stock, 1973.

———. "La visite à Jean-Paul Sartre." *Les Temps modernes* 46 (1990): 1192–1200.

Danos, J. Gibelin, M. *June '36: Class Struggle and the Popular Front in France.* London: Bookmark, 1986.

Dash, Michael, and Bridget Jones, eds. *Perspectives on Language and Literature: Essays in Honour of William Mailer.* University of the West Indies, Department of French and German. Mona, Jamaica: Department of French and German, University of the West Indies, 1985.

Debû-Bridel, Jacques. *La Résistance intellectuelle.* Paris: Julliard, 1970.

Dejeux, Jean. *Littérature maghrebine de langue française: introduction générale et auteurs* Sherbrooke: Naaman, 1973.

Dejeux, Jean, and D. H. Pageaux, eds. *Espagne et Algérie au XX*[e] *siècle: contacts culturels et création littéraire.* Paris: L'Harmattan, 1985.

Delais, Jeanne. *L'Ami de chaque matin: vie et luttes de Claude Terrien.* Paris: Grasset, 1969.

Delarue, Jacques. *La Tuberculose.* Collection Que sais-je? 15. Paris: PUF, 1972.

Delpech, Jeanine. "Pascal, Proust et l'Algérie: instantané Mohammed Dib." *Les Nouvelles littéraires,* February 7, 1963, 2.

Delporte, Christophe. *Intellectuels et politique: XX*[e] *siècle.* Paris: Casterman-Giunti, 1995.

Depieris, Jean-Louis. *Entretien avec Emmanuel Roblès.* Paris: Seuil, 1967.

Desan, Wilfred. *The Marxism of J. P. Sartre.* New York: Doubleday, 1966.

Desanti, Dominique. *Les Staliniens.* Paris: Marabout, 1980.

Dine, Philip D. "Begging *La Question:* Fresh Insights into the Algerian War." *Modern & Contemporary France* 43 (1990): 58–60.

———. "Fighting and writing the war without a name: polemics and the French-Algerian conflict." *Aurifex* 2 (2002), http://www.goldsmiths.ac.uk/aurifex/issue2/dine.html.

———. "France, Algeria and sport: from colonisation to globalisation." *Modern & Contemporary France* 10 (2002): 495–505.

———. "French Culture and the Algerian War: Mobilizing Icons." *Journal of European Studies* 28 (1998): 51–68.

———. *Images of the Algerian War. French Fiction and Film, 1954–1992.* Oxford: Clarendon Press, 1994.

———. "Reading and Remembering *la Guerre des Mythes*: French Literary Representations of the Algerian War." *Modern & Contemporary France* 2 (1994): 141–49.

———. "Un héroïsme problématique: le sport, la littérature et la Guerre d'Algérie." *Europe* 806–7 (1996): 177–85.

Dostoevsky, Fyodor. *The Brothers Karamazov*. Translated by Larissa Volokhonsky and Richard Pevear. London: Vintage, 1992.

———. *Devils*. Translated and edited by Michael R. Katz. Oxford: Oxford University Press, 1992.

Drake, David. "*Les Temps modernes* and the French war in Indochina." *Journal of European Studies* 28 (1998): 25–41.

Droz, Bernard, and Evelyne Lever. *Histoire de la Guerre d'Algérie, 1954–1962*. Paris: Seuil, 1982.

Dunn, Susan. *The Deaths of Louis XVI: Regicide and the French Political Imagination*. Princeton: Princeton University Press, 1994.

Dunwoodie, Peter. *Writing French Algeria*. Oxford: Clarendon Press, 1998.

Dupuy, Aimé. *L'Algérie dans les lettres d'expression française*. Paris: Éditions Universitaires, 1956.

Dupuy, Jean-Pierre. *Le Sacrifice et l'envie*. Paris: Calmann-Lévy, 1992.

Duron, Jacques-Robert. "Un nouveau mal du siècle." *Renaissances* 16 (1945): 62–69.

Dworkin, Ronald. *Taking Rights Seriously*. 2nd ed. London: Duckworth, 1978.

Eakin, Paul John. *Fictions in Autobiography: Studies in the Art of Self-Inventing*. Princeton, NJ: Princeton University Press, 1985.

Eatwell, Roger. *Fascism: A History*. London: Chatto & Windus, 1995.

Edwards, Paul, ed. *The Encyclopedia of Philosophy*. 8 vols. London: Collier-Macmillan, 1967.

Entrèves, A. P. d', ed. *Aquinas: Selected Political Writings*. Oxford: Blackwell, 1965.

Evans, Martin. "Memories of Resistance to the Algerian War: Janine Cahen, Roger Rey, Denise Barral." *Modern & Contemporary France* n.s., 2 (1994): 165–74.

Everson, Stephen, ed. *Aristotle, The Politics*. Cambridge: Cambridge University Press, 1988.

Ewald, François, ed. "Sartre, Merleau-Ponty: les lettres d'une rupture." Les inédits du *Magazine littéraire*. *Magazine littéraire* 320 (1994): 67–86.

Fanon, Frantz. *Les damnés de la terre*. Paris: Maspero, 1961.

———. *Peau noire, masques blancs*. Paris: Seuil, 1952.

Feraoun, Mouloud. *L'Anniversaire*. Collection Points. Paris: Seuil, 1972.

———. *Les Chemins qui montent*. Paris: Seuil, 1976.

———. *Le Fils du pauvre*. Paris: Seuil, 1982.

———. *Journal, 1955–1962*. Collection Méditerranée. Paris: Seuil, 1962.

———. *Lettres à ses amis*. Paris: Seuil, 1969.

Flood, Christopher, and Hugo Frey. "Questions of Decolonization and Postcolonialism in the Ideology of the French Extreme Right." *Journal of European Studies* 28 (1998): 69–88.

Flynn, Thomas. *Sartre and Marxist Existentialism*. Chicago: University of Chicago Press, 1984.

Fontaine, André. *Histoire de la guerre froide*. Paris: Seuil, 1967.

Fontaine, Jean de La. *Œuvres complètes*. 2 vols. Edited by René Groos and Jacques Schiffrin. Bibliothèque de La Pléiade. Paris: Gallimard, 1954.

Forsdick, Charles, and David Murphy, eds. *Francophone Postcolonial Studies: A Critical Introduction*. London: Arnold, 2003.

Fouchet, Max-Pol. *Les Appels*. Paris: Mercure de France, 1967.

———. *Un jour, je m'en souviens: mémoire parlée*. Paris: Mercure de France, 1969.

Freeman, Ted. "France and the 'First' Cold War: Introduction." *French Cultural Studies* 8 (1997): 1–2.

Friedman, Maurice. *Problematic Rebel: An Image of Modern Man*. New York: Random House, 1963.

———. *To Deny our Nothingness: Contemporary Images of Man*. London: Gollancz, 1967.

Furet, François. *Le Passé d'une illusion: essai sur l'idée communiste au XXe siècle*. Paris: Laffont / Calmann-Lévy, 1995.

Gallissot, René. *Maghreb, Algérie, classe et nation*. Paris: Arcantère, 1987.

———. "Le mixte franco-algérien." *Les Temps modernes* 452–54 (1984): 1707–25.

Garapon, Antoine. *Le Gardien des promesses: le juge et la démocratie*. Paris: Jacob, 1996.

Garnier, Robert. *Les Juifves, Bradamante, Poésies diverses*. Edited by Raymond Lebègue. Paris: Les Belles Lettres, 1975.

Gaulle, Charles de. *Lettres, Notes et Carnets: mai 1945–juin 1951*. Paris: Plon, 1984.

———. *Mémoires de guerre*. 3 vols. Paris: Plon, 1954–59.

Gellner, Ernest. "The Mightier Pen? Edward Said and the Double Standards of Inside-Out Colonialism." *TLS*, February 19, 1993, 3–4.

George, François. "Sartre et moi." *Critique* 582 (1995): 844–57.

Geras, Norman. "The Controversy about Marx and Justice." *New Left Review* 150 (1988): 47–89.

Gide, André. *Journal, 1939–1949: souvenirs*. Bibliothèque de La Pléiade. Paris: Gallimard, 1954.

Gimeno, Paul. "L'animal, l'environnement et la justice selon Rawls." *Critique* 581 (1995): 734–50.

Giroud, Françoise. *Si je mens*. Paris: Stock, 1972.

Glicksberg, Charles I. *The Literature of Commitment*. Lewisburg, PA: Bucknell University Press, 1976.

Goldsmith, J. H. "Paris Letter: The New French Sense of Reality." *Partisan Review* 23 (1956): 81–89.

Golomb, Jacob. *In Search of Authenticity: From Kierkegaard to Camus*. London: Routledge, 1995.

Gordon, David C. *The Passing of French Algeria*. London: Oxford University Press, 1966.

Gorz, André. *Le Socialisme difficile*. Paris: Seuil, 1967.

Gourdon, Hubert, Jean-Robert Henry, and Françoise Henry-Lorcerie. "Histoire idéologique de la période: à propos de l'assimilation." *Revue algérienne des sciences juridiques, économiques et politiques* 11 (1974): 33–59.

Grand, Alexander J. de. *Fascist Italy and Nazi Germany: The "Fascist" Style of Rule: Historical Connections*. London: Routledge, 1995.

Graves, Robert. *Greek Myths*. London: Quality Paperbacks Direct, 1991.

Grenier, Jean. *Essai sur l'esprit d'orthodoxie.* Paris: Gallimard, 1938.

———. *Les îles.* Paris: Gallimard, 1959.

Grenier, Roger. *Pascal Pia ou la tentation du néant.* Paris: Gallimard, 1989.

Grevisse, Maurice. *Le Bon Usage: grammaire française avec des remarques sur la langue française d'aujourd'hui.* 8th ed. Gembloux: Duculot, 1964.

Guedj, Aimé. "Objectivité de l'information et conditionnement de l'opinion publique." *La Nouvelle Critique,* n.s., 53 (1972): 23–29.

Guérin, Daniel. *Quand l'Algérie s'insurgeait, 1954–1962.* Claise: La Pensée Sauvage, 1979.

Haddour, Azzedine. "Algeria and Its History: Colonial Myths and the Forging and Deconstructing of Identity in *Pied-Noir* Literature." In *French and Algerian Identities from Colonial Times to the Present: A Century of Interaction,* edited by Alec G. Hargreaves and Michael J. Heffernan. Lewiston: Edwin Mellen, 1993.

Haffenden, John. "What the Life Leaves out." *TLS,* February 23, 1996, 14–16.

Hanley, David. "From Co-operation to Conflict: the French Political System and the Onset of the Cold War." *French Cultural Studies* 8 (1997): 3–15.

Harbi, Mohammed. *La guerre commence en Algérie.* Brussels: Complexe, 1984.

Hargreaves, Alec G., and Michael J. Heffernan, eds. *French and Algerian Identities from Colonial Times to the Present: A Century of Interaction.* Lewiston: Edwin Mellen, 1993.

Harrington, Michael. *The Accidental Century.* London: Weidenfeld & Nicolson, 1966.

Harris, Geoffrey. "Malraux, Myth, Political Commitment and the Spanish Civil War." *Modern & Contemporary France* 5 (1997): 319–28.

Hegel, Georg Wilheim Friedrich. *The Philosophy of History.* Translated by J. Sibree. New York, Dover, 1956.

Heggoy, Alf Andrew. "Algerian Women and the Right to Vote: Some Colonial Anomalies." *Muslim World* 64 (1974): 228–35.

———. "Cultural Disrespect: European and Algerian Views on Women in Colonial and Independent Algeria." *Muslim World* 62 (1972): 323–34.

———. "Looking Back: The Military and Colonial Policies in French Algeria." *Muslim World* 73 (1983): 57–66.

Hewitt, Nicholas. "1944/1793: la droite intellectuelle et le mythe de la Terreur Rouge." *French Cultural Studies* 5 (1994): 281–92.

Hodges, Lucy. "A Disarming Chap." *THES,* December 8, 1995, 21.

Honderich, Ted, ed. *The Oxford Companion to Philosophy.* Oxford: Oxford University Press, 1995.

Horne, Alistair. *A Savage War of Peace: Algeria, 1954–1962.* London: Penguin Books, 1985.

———. *To Lose a Battle: France, 1940.* London: Macmillan, 1990.

Hubin, D. Clayton. "The Scope of Justice." *Philosophy and Public Affairs* 9 (1979): 3–24.

Hughes, Edward J. *Writing Marginality in Modern French Literature: From Loti to Genet.* Cambridge: Cambridge University Press, 2001.

Ibrahimi, Ahmed Taleb. *De la décolonisation à la révolution culturelle.* Algiers: Société Nationale d'Édition, 1973.

Irwin, Robert. "A War Without a Name." *TLS,* January 19, 1996, 22.

Isorni, Jacques. *Le procès de Robert Brasillach (19 janvier 1945).* Paris: Flammarion, 1946.

Jackson, Gabriel. *The Spanish Republic and the Civil War, 1931–39.* Princeton, NJ: Princeton University Press, 1965.

Jackson, Tommie L. *The Existentialist Fiction of Ayi Kwei Armah, Albert Camus and Jean-Paul Sartre.* Lanham: University Press of America, 1997.

Jacob, Max. *Lettres à un ami. Correspondance: 1922–1937 avec Jean Grenier.* Cognac: Le temps qu'il fait, 1982.

Jacoby, Russel. "Colonial Writers Lost in the Post." *THES,* December 29, 1995, 17.

Jarrett-Kerr, Martin. *The Secular Promise: Christian Presence amid Contemporary Humanism.* London: SCM Press, 1964.

Jeanson, Francis. *Algérie hors-la-loi.* Paris: Seuil, 1955.

———. *La Révolution algérienne.* Milan: Feltrinelli, 1952.

———. *Sartre dans sa vie.* Paris: Seuil, 1974.

———. *Sartre par lui-même.* Paris: Seuil, 1955.

Joubert, Joseph. *Pensées, Jugements et Notations.* 2nd ed. Edited by Rémy Tessonneau. Paris: Corti, 1989.

Judt, Tony. *Marxism and the French Left.* Oxford: Oxford University Press, 1986.

———. *Past Imperfect. French Intellectuals, 1944–1956.* Berkeley and Los Angeles: University of California Press, 1992.

———. "Two Dissenters." *TLS,* January 19, 1996, 4–6.

Julien, Charles-André. *L'Afrique du Nord en marche.* Paris: Julliard, 1952.

Kaddache, Mahfoud. *Histoire du nationalisme algérien: question nationale et politique algérienne, 1919–1951.* 2 vols. Algiers: SNED, 1980–81.

———. *Il y a trente ans, le 8 mai 1945.* Paris: Centenaire, 1975.

Kahéna, N. *Témoignage: de 1954 en Algérie à 2001 en France.* Toulon: Les Presses du Midi, 2001.

Kant, Immanuel. *Metaphysical Elements of Justice.* Library of Liberal Arts. New York: Macmillan, 1965.

Keefe, Terry. "Commitment, Re-commitment and Puzzlement: Aspects of the Cold War in the Fiction of Simone de Beauvoir." *French Cultural Studies* 8 (1997): 127–36.

———. *French Existentialist Fiction: Changing Moral Perspectives.* London: Croom Helm, 1986.

———. "Reconstructing the Occupation: Sartre and Beauvoir." In *Reconstructing the Past: Representations of the Fascist Era in Post-War European Culture,* edited by Graham Bartram, Maurice Slawinski, and David Steel. Keele: Keele University Press, 1996.

Keefe, Terry, and Edmund Smyth, eds. *Autobiography and the Existential Self: Studies in Modern French Writing.* Liverpool: Liverpool University Press, 1995.

Kelly, Michael. "Death at the Liberation: The Cultural Articulation of Death and Suffering in France 1944–47." *French Cultural Studies* 5 (1994): 227–40.

———. "*Révolution, Renaissance, Redressement:* Representations of Historical Change in Post-War France." In *Reconstructing the Past: Representations of the*

Fascist Era in Post-War European Culture, edited by Graham Bartram, Maurice Slawinski, and David Steel. Keele: Keele University Press, 1996.

Kelsen, Hans. *What is Justice? Justice, Law and Politics in the Mirror of Silence: Collected Essays.* Berkeley and Los Angeles: University of California Press, 1971.

Kershaw, Ian. "Retour sur le totalitarisme: le nazisme et le stalinisme dans une perspective comparative." *Esprit* 218 (1996): 101–21.

Khane, Mohammed. "*Le Monde* and the Algerian War during the Fourth Republic." In *French and Algerian Identities from Colonial Times to the Present: A Century of Interaction,* edited by Alec G. Hargreaves and Michael J. Heffernan. Lewiston: Edwin Mellen, 1993.

Khilnani, Sunil. *Arguing Revolution: The Intellectual Left in Postwar France.* Newhaven, CT: Yale University Press, 1993.

King, J. H. "Gabriel Péri and the poetry of commemoration." *Journal of European Studies* 26 (1996): 17–35.

Knight, Amy. "Female Terrorists in the Russian Socialist Revolutionary Party." *Russian Review* 38 (1979): 139–59.

Koestler, Arthur. *Darkness at Noon.* Translated by Daphne Hardy. 1940. Reprint, London: Cape, 1965.

———. *"The Yogi and the Commissar" and Other Essays.* 1945. Reprint, London: Cape, 1960.

Krieger, Murray. *The Tragic Vision.* New York: Holt, 1960.

Kukathas, Chandran, and Philip Pettit. *Rawls's "A Theory of Justice" and Its Critics.* Oxford: Polity Press, 1990.

Kurian, George Thomas, ed. *World Press Encyclopedia.* 2 vols. London: Mansell, 1982.

La Bruyère, Jean. *Œuvres complètes.* Edited by Julien Benda. Bibliothèque de La Pléiade. Paris: Gallimard, 1951.

Lacouture, Jean. *André Malraux.* Paris: Seuil, 1973.

———. *De Gaulle.* 2 vols. Paris: Seuil, 1984.

———. "Le Journalisme nécessaire." *Les Nouvelles littéraires,* March 23–30, 1978, 3.

Langlois, Walter G. "Rumblings out of Spain: French Writers and the Asturian Revolt (1934–36)." *MLN* 95 (1980): 884–921.

Laslett, Peter, and W. G. Runciman, eds. *Philosophy, Politics and Society: Second Series.* Oxford: Blackwell, 1962.

Lazreg, Marnia. *The Emergence of Classes in Algeria: A Study of Colonialism and Socio-Political Change.* Boulder, Colo.: Westview Press, 1976.

Le Guern, Michel, ed. *Blaise Pascal: "Pensées."* Collection Folio. 2 vols. Paris: Gallimard, 1977.

Le Sueur, James D. "Ghost Walking in Algiers? Why Alek Baylee Toumi Resurrected Sartre and de Beauvoir." *Modern & Contemporary France* 10 (2002): 507–17.

———. *Uncivil War: Intellectuals and Identity Politics during the Decolonization of Algeria.* Philadelphia: University of Pennsylvania Press, 2001.

Lebjaoui, Mohamed. *Vérités sur la révolution algérienne.* Paris: Gallimard, 1970.

Leconte, Daniel. *Les "Pieds-Noirs": histoire et portrait d'une communauté.* Paris: Seuil, 1980.

Lefebvre, Denis. *Guy Mollet: le mal aimé.* Paris: Plon, 1992.

Lefranc, Georges. *Histoire du Front Populaire, 1934–1938.* Paris: Payot, 1965.

Lejeune, Philippe. *L'Autobiographie en France.* Paris: Armand Colin, 1971.

———. *Le Pacte autobiographique.* Paris: Seuil, 1975.

———. "Le Pacte autobiographique (bis)." *Poétique* 56 (1983): 416–34.

Lévy, Bernard-Henri. *Les Aventures de la liberté: une histoire subjective des intellectuels.* Paris: Grasset, 1991.

———. *Le siècle de Sartre.* Paris: Grasset, 2000.

Lottman, Herbert R. *The Left Bank: Writers, Artists and Politics from the Popular Front to the Cold War.* London: Heinemann, 1982.

———. *The People's Anger: Justice and Revenge in Post-Liberation France.* London: Hutchinson, 1986.

Loughlin, John P. "The Algerian War and the One and Indivisible French Republic." In *French and Algerian Identities from Colonial Times to the Present: A Century of Interaction,* edited by Alec G. Hargreaves and Michael J. Heffernan. Lewiston: Edwin Mellen, 1993.

Lucas, John. *On Justice.* Oxford: Clarendon Press, 1989.

MacKenzie, John M. *Orientalism: History, Theory and the Arts.* Manchester: Manchester University Press, 1995.

Macmaster, Neil. "Patterns of Emigration, 1905–1954: 'Kabyles' and 'Arabs.'" In *French and Algerian Identities from Colonial Times to the Present: A Century of Interaction,* edited by Alec G. Hargreaves and Michael J. Heffernan. Lewiston: Edwin Mellen, 1993.

———. "The Torture Controversy (1998–2002): Towards a 'New History' of the Algerian War?" *Modern & Contemporary France* 10 (2002): 449–59.

Macworth, Cecily. "Les Coupables." *Twentieth Century* 161 (1957): 459–68.

Malebranche, Nicolas de. *Œuvres complètes.* 20 vols. 1958–66. Edited by Henri Gouhier. Paris: Librairie Philosophique J. Vrin, 1966.

Malraux, André. *La Condition humaine.* Paris: Gallimard, 1933.

———. *L'Espoir.* Paris: Gallimard, 1937.

———. *Le Temps du mépris.* Paris: Gallimard, 1935.

Margadant, Ted Winston. "Camus and Sartre: A Study in Revolt and Revolution on the French Left." M.A. diss., Harvard University, 1962.

Marshall, D. B. *The French Colonial Myth.* New Haven, CT: Yale University Press, 1973.

Martin, Marc. "*Combat* et la presse parisienne de la Libération, ou l'insuccès de la vertu." *Bulletin du Centre d'Histoire de la France* 10 (1989): 25–40.

Martin-Chauffier, Louis. *Algérie: An VII. L'Examen des consciences.* Paris: Julliard, 1961.

———, ed. *François La Rochefoucauld. Œuvres complètes.* Bibliothèque de La Pléiade. Paris: Gallimard, 1964.

Mauriac, François. *Bloc-Notes, 1952–1957.* Paris: Flammarion, 1959.

———. *Mémoires politiques.* Paris: Grasset, 1967.

———. *Œuvres complètes.* 12 vols. Paris: Fayant, n.d.

McCann, Graham. "Off your Marx?" *THES,* April 29, 1994, 15–16.

McCarney, Joseph. *Hegel on history.* London: Routledge, 2000.

McCormack, Jo. "Torture during the Algerian War." *Modern & Contemporary France* 10 (2002): 392–95.

McLellan, David. *Marx.* Glasgow: Fontana / Collins, 1975.

McMillan, James F. *Twentieth-Century France: Politics and Society, 1898–1991.* Rev. ed. London: Edward Arnold, 1993.

Medvedev, Zhores. "The Doctors' Stroke of Luck." *THES,* February 16, 1996, 16.

Memmi, Albert. *Anthologie des écrivains français du Maghreb.* Paris: Présence Africaine, 1969.

———. *Portrait du colonisé précédé de Portrait du colonisateur.* Paris: Payot, 1973.

———. *La Statue de sel.* Collection Folio. Paris: Gallimard, 1966. [Preface by Camus]

Ménager, Yves, ed. *La Littérature française sous l'Occupation: Actes du colloque de Reims, 30 septembre–1er et 2 octobre 1981.* Reims: Presses Universitaires de Reims, 1989.

Merleau-Ponty, Maurice. *Humanisme et Terreur: essai sur le problème communiste.* Collection Idées. 1947. Reprint, Paris: Gallimard, 1980.

Merleau-Ponty, Maurice, and Jean-Paul Sartre. "Les jours de notre vie." *Les Temps modernes* 51 (1950): 1153–68.

Meyer, Nicole. *Catalogue de l'exposition Louis Guilloux organisée à la Bibliothèque Municipale de la ville de Saint-Brieuc, décembre 1978–janvier 1979.* Saint-Brieuc: Bibliothèque municipale, 1978.

Michel, François-Bernard. *Le Souffle coupé (respirer et écrire).* Paris: Gallimard, 1984.

Michel, Henri. *La Libération de Paris.* Paris: Complexe, 1980.

Michel, Henri, and Boris Mirkine-Guétzévitch, eds. *Les idées politiques et sociales de la résistance: Documents clandestins, 1940–1944.* Collection Esprit de la Résistance. Paris: Presses Universitaires, 1954.

Mill, John Stuart. *Utilitarianism, On Liberty and Considerations on Representative Government.* Edited by H. B. Acton. London: Dent, 1972.

Miller, David. *Social Justice.* Oxford: Clarendon Press, 1976.

Mitter, Partha. "Close Encounters with Far Pavilions." *THES,* November 24, 1995, 22.

Moeller, Charles. *La Littérature du XXe siècle et christianisme.* 2 vols. Paris: Casterman, 1953.

Moneta, Jacob. *Le PCF et le problème algérien, 1920–1965.* Paris: Maspero, 1971.

Montaigne. *Œuvres complètes.* Edited by Albert Thibaudet et Maurice Rat. Bibliothèque de La Pléiade. Paris: Gallimard, 1952.

Morin, Violette. *L'écriture de presse.* Paris: Mouton, 1969.

Morris, Jonathan. "Any Room for the Third Way?" *TLS,* December 22, 1995, 25.

Mortimer, Lorraine. "Sweet Finitude: Relative Utopias with Live Inhabitants." *French Cultural Studies* 8 (1997): 147–72.

Nadeau, Maurice. *Graces leur soient rendues: mémoires littéraires.* Paris: Michel, 1990.

Nairn, Tom. "What nations are for." *London Review of Books,* September 8, 1994, 7–8.

Niebuhr, Reinhold. *The Children of Light and the Children of Darkness: A Vindication of Democracry and a Critique of Its Traditional Defenders.* London: Nisbet, 1945.

Nietzsche, Friedrich. *A Nietzsche Reader.* Edited and translated by R. J. Hollingdale. Harmondsworth: Penguin, 1977.

———. *Thus Spoke Zarathustra.* Translated and edited by R. J. Hollingdale. Harmondsworth: Penguin, 1961.

Noiriel, Gérard. *Le creuset français.* Paris: Seuil, 1988.

Nora, Pierre. *Les Français d'Algérie.* Paris: Julliard, 1961.

Nouschi, André. *La naissance du nationalisme algérien.* Paris: Minuit, 1962.

Nouschi, André, Maurice Aqulhon, and Ralph Schor. *La France de 1940 à nos jours.* rev. ed. Paris: Nathan, 1988.

Novick, Peter. *The Resistance versus Vichy: The Purge of Collaborators in Liberated France.* Cambridge: Cambridge University Press, 1968.

Nugent, Neil, and David Lowe. *The Left in France.* London: Macmillan, 1982.

O'Brien, George Dennis. *Hegel on Reason and History: A Contemporary Interpretation.* Chicago: University of Chicago Press, 1975.

Obuchowski, Chester W. "Algeria: The Tortured Conscience." *French Review* 42 (1968): 9–103.

O'Donnell, Donat. "France as the Conscience of Europe." *Listener,* January 20, 1955, 105–6.

Orwell, George. *Hommage to Catalonia.* London: Secker & Warburg, 1959.

Ory, Pascal, and Jean-François Sirinelli. *Les intellectuels en France de l'Affaire Dreyfus à nos jours.* Paris: Armand Colin, 1986.

Ouzegane, Amar. *Le meilleur combat.* Paris: Julliard, 1962.

Panichas, Georges A. *Mansions of the Spirit: Essays in Literature and Religion.* New York: Hawthorn, 1967.

———, ed. *The Politics of Twentieth-Century Novelists.* New York: Apollo, 1974.

Paulhan, Claire, ed. *Jean Grenier: Carnets 1944–1971.* Paris: Seghers, 1991.

Peillon, Vincent. *La Tradition de l'esprit: itinéraire de Maurice Merleau-Ponty.* Paris: Grasset, 1994.

Pélégri, Jean. *Les oliviers de la justice.* Paris: Gallimard, 1959.

Phillips, D. Z. *From Fantasy to Faith: The Philosophy of Religion in Twentieth Century Literature.* London: Macmillan, 1991.

Picard, Raymond, ed. *Racine, Œuvres complètes.* Vol. 1, *Théâtre, Poésies.* Bibliothèque de La Pléiade. Paris: Gallimard, 1950.

Pickles, Dorothy. *Algeria and France: From Colonialism to Cooperation.* London: Methuen, 1963.

Pingaud, Bernard. "L'écriture et la cure." *NRF* 18 (1970): 144–63.

Planchais, Jean, ed. "L'Algérie depuis 1945." *Le Monde: Dossiers et Documents* 203 (1992).

Plato. *The Republic of Plato.* Translated by Allan Bloom. New York: Basic Books, 1968.

Popper, K. R. *The Open Society and its Enemies.* 2 vols. 1945. Reprint, London: Routledge & Kegan Paul, 1966.

Posner, Richard A. *Law and Literature: A Misunderstood Relation.* Cambridge, MA: Harvard University Press, 1988.

Poster, Mark. *Sartre's Marxism.* London: Pluto Press, 1979.

Preston, Paul, ed. *Revolution and War in Spain, 1931–1939.* New York: Methuen, 1984.

———. *The Spanish Civil War, 1936–39.* London: Weidenfeld & Nicolson, 1986.

———. "Strutting into Infamy." *THES,* February 9, 1996, 19.

Ragache, Gilles, and Jean-Robert Ragache. *La vie quotidienne des écrivains et des artistes sous l'Occupation, 1940–1944.* Paris: Hachette, 1988.

Raphael, D. D. *Problems of Political Philosophy.* London: Pall Mall, 1970.

Rawls, John. "Justice as Fairness." In *Philosophy, Politics and Society, Second Series.* Edited by Peter Laslett and W. G. Runciman. Oxford: Blackwell, 1962.

———. *A Theory of Justice.* Oxford: Oxford University Press, 1971.

Reid, M. H., ed. *The Concise Oxford Dictionary of French Literature.* Oxford: University Press, 1976.

Reynolds, D., ed. *The Origins of the Cold War in Europe.* New Haven, CT: Yale University Press, 1994.

Richards, Huw. "Happy with the Reign in Spain." *THES,* November 17, 1995, 15.

Richaud, André de. *La Douleur.* 1931. Reprint, Paris: Grasset, 1988.

Rigby, Brian. "Intellectuals, Education and Culture at the Liberation: The Opposition to 'la culture scolaire.'" *French Cultural Studies* 5 (1994): 241–51.

Rioux, Jean-Pierre. "Camus et la seconde guerre mondiale ou 'rentrons dans l'histoire avec le mépris qui convient.'" In *Camus et la politique: Actes du colloque de Nanterre, 5–7 juin 1985,* edited by Jeanyves Guérin. Paris: L'Harmattan, 1986.

———. *La France de la IVe République.* Paris: Seuil, 1980.

———, ed. *La Guerre d'Algérie et les Français.* Paris: Fayard, 1990.

Rioux, Jean-Pierre, and Jean-François Sirinelli. *La Guerre d'Algérie et les intellectuels français.* Paris: Complexe, 1991.

Roberts, Hugh. "Algeria's Ruinous Impasse and the Honourable Way Out." *International Affairs* 71 (1995): 247–67.

Roblès, Emmanuel. *Les rives du fleuve bleu.* Paris: Seuil, 1990.

Rocard, Michel. *Le cœur à l'ouvrage.* Paris: Jacob, 1987.

Roche, Anne. "Pieds-noirs: le 'retour.'" *Modern & Contemporary France* n.s., 2 (1994): 151–64.

Romains, Jules. *Les hommes de bonne volonté.* 27 vols. Paris: Flammarion, 1958.

Rosfelder, André. *L'Algérie à bâtir.* Algiers: Baconnier, 1959.

Ross, Alf. *On Law and Justice.* London: Steven & Sons, 1958.

Roy, Jules. *Amours barbares.* Paris: Albin Michel, 1993.

———. *Les chevaux du soleil.* Paris: Grasset, 1980.

———. *Étranger à mes frères.* Collection Les Grands Auteurs. Paris: Stock, 1982.

———. *La Guerre d'Algérie.* Paris: Julliard, 1960.

———. *Mémoires barbares.* Paris: Albin Michel, 1989.

———. *Un après-guerre amoureux.* Paris: Albin Michel, 1995.

Rubenstein, Diane. "Publish and Perish: The *Épuration* of French Intellectuals." *Journal of European Studies* 23 (1993): 71–99.

Ryan, Alan. *J. S. Mill.* London: Routledge & Kegan Paul, 1974.

———, ed. *Justice.* Oxford: Oxford University Press, 1993.

Sadurski, Wojciech. *Giving Desert its Due: Social Justice and Legal Theory.* Dordrecht: Reidel, 1985.

Said, Edward. *Culture and Imperialism.* London: Chatto & Windus, 1993.

———. "East Isn't East: The Impending End of the Age of Orientalism." *TLS,* February 3, 1995, 3–6.

———. *Orientalism.* New York: Pantheon, 1978.

———. *The Pen and the Sword: Conversations with David Barsamian.* Edinburgh: AK Press, 1994.

———. "Representing the Colonized: Anthropology's Interlocutors." *Critical Inquiry* 15 (1989): 205–25.

Sartre, Jean-Paul. *L'Affaire Henri Martin.* Paris: Gallimard, 1953.

———. *L'Age de raison.* Collection Folio. Paris: Gallimard, 1945.

———. *Les Carnets de la drôle de guerre: septembre 1939–mars 1940.* Paris: Gallimard, 1995.

———. "Le colonialisme est un système." In Jean-Paul Sartre, *Situations V: colonialisme et néo-colonialisme.* Paris: Gallimard, 1964.

———. "Les Communistes et la paix." In Jean-Paul Sartre, *Situations VI: problèmes du marxisme.* Vol. 1. Paris: Gallimard, 1964.

———. *Critique de la raison dialectique, précédé de Questions de méthode.* Edited by Arlette Elkaïm-Sartre. Vol. 1. 1960. Reprint, Paris: Gallimard, 1985.

———. *Critique de la raison dialectique précédé de Questions de méthode.* Edited by Arlette Elkaïm-Sartre. Vol. 2. Paris: Gallimard, 1985.

———. "Les damnés de la terre." In Jean-Paul Sartre, *Situations V: colonialisme et néo-colonialisme.* Paris: Gallimard, 1964.

———. "Le Fantôme de Staline." *Les Temps modernes* 12 (July 1956–January 1957): 577–696.

———. *Huis clos suivi de Les Mouches.* Collection Folio. Paris: Gallimard, 1947.

———. "Matérialisme et Révolution I." *Les Temps modernes* 1 (June 1946): 1537–63.

———. "Matérialisme et Révolution II." *Les Temps modernes* 1 (July 1946): 1–32.

———. "Merleau-Ponty vivant." In Jean-Paul Sartre, *Situations IV.* Paris: Gallimard, 1964.

———. *La Mort dans l'âme.* Collection Folio. Paris: Gallimard, 1949.

———. *Les Mots.* Collection Folio. Paris: Gallimard, 1964.

———. "La nationalisation de la littérature." *Les Temps modernes* 1 (October 1945–February 1946): 193–211.

———. *Œuvres romanesques.* Edited by George H. Bauer, Michel Contat, Geneviève Idt, and Michel Rybalka. Bibliothèque de La Pléiade. Paris: Gallimard, 1981.

———. "Présentation." *Les Temps modernes* 1 (October 1945–February 1946): 1–21.

———. *Qu'est-ce que la littérature?* Collection Folio. Paris: Gallimard, 1948.

———. *Saint Genet: comédien et martyr.* Paris: Gallimard, 1952.

———. "Sartre par Sartre." In Jean-Paul Sartre, *Situations IX* . Paris: Gallimard, 1972.

———. *Les Séquestrés d'Altona.* Collection Folio. Paris: Gallimard, 1960.

———. *Situations III.* Paris: Gallimard, 1949.

———. *Situations IV.* Paris: Gallimard, 1964.

———. *Situations V: colonialisme et néo-colonialisme.* Paris: Gallimard, 1964.

———. *Situations VI: problèmes du marxisme.* Vol. 1. Paris: Gallimard, 1964.

———. *Situations IX.* Paris: Gallimard, 1972.

———. *Situations X: politique et autobiographique.* Paris: Gallimard, 1976.

———. *Le Sursis.* Collection Folio. Paris: Gallimard, 1972.

Savage Brosman, Catharine. "Les Frères ennemis: Jules Roy et l'Algérie." *French Review* 56 (1983): 579–87.

Savinkov, Boris Viktorovich. *Memoirs of a Terrorist.* Translated by Joseph Shaplen. New York: Albert & Charles Boni, 1931.

Schalk, David L. "Reflections *d'outre-mer* on French Colonialism." *Journal of European Studies* 28 (1998): 5–23.

———. *The Spectrum of Political Engagement.* Princeton, NJ: Princeton University Press, 1979.

Schiffer, Daniel Salvatore. *Grandeur et misère des intellectuels: Histoire critique de l'intelligentsia du XXe siècle.* Paris: Rocher, 1998.

Schmidt, James. *Maurice Merleau-Ponty: Between Phenomenology and Structuralism.* London: Macmillan, 1985.

Scott, Jr., Nathan A. *Mirrors of Man in Existentialism.* London: Collins, 1978.

Scriven, Michael. "Sartre and the Politics of Radio Broadcasting: *La Tribune des Temps modernes,* 1947." *Modern & Contemporary France* 43 (1990): 16–28.

Scruton, Roger, Christopher Janaway, Peter Singer, Michael Tanner, and Keith Thomas. *German Philosophers.* Oxford: Oxford University Press, 1997.

Sheringham, Michael. *French Autobiography: Devices and Desires.* Oxford: Clarendon Press, 1993.

———. "The Hateful Ego." *TLS,* February 23, 1996, 31.

Shields, James G. "The Poujadist Movement: A Faux 'Fascism.'" *Modern & Contemporary France* 8 (2000): 19–34.

Shubert, Adrian. "The Epic Failure: The Asturian Revolution of October 1934." In *Revolution and War in Spain, 1931–1939,* edited by Paul Preston. New York: Methuen, 1984.

Shukman, Harry. "Red Starry Eyes." *THES,* March 8, 1996, 16–17.

Simon, Emile. *Une Métaphysique tragique.* 2nd ed. Collection Espoir. Paris: Gallimard, 1951.

Simon, Pierre-Henri. *Contre la torture.* Paris: Seuil, 1957.

———. *Histoire de la littérature française au XXe siècle, II, 1900–1950.* 7th ed. Paris: Armand Colin, 1963.

———. *L'Homme en procès: Malraux, Sartre, Camus, Saint-Exupery.* Neuchâtel: Baconnière, 1950.

———. *Témoins de l'homme: la condition humaine dans la littérature contemporaine.* 5th ed. Paris: Armand Colin, 1963.

———. *Théâtre et destin: la signification de la renaissance dramatique en France au XXe siècle.* Paris: Armand Colin, 1959.

Sivan, Emmanuel. *Communisme et nationalisme en Algérie, 1920–1962.* Paris: Presses de la Fondation Nationale des Sciences Politiques, 1976.

Smith, Tony. "Idealism and Peoples' War: Sartre on Algeria." *Political Theory* 1 (1973): 426–49.

Solomon, Robert C. *A History of Western Philosophy, 7: Continental Philosophy since 1750; The Rise and Fall of the Self.* Oxford: Oxford University Press, 1988.

Solzhenitsyn, Alexander. *The Gulag Archipelago.* London: Collin / Harvill Press and Fontana, 1974.

Spence, Richard B. *Boris Savinkov: Renegade on the Left.* Columbia: Columbia University Press, 1991.

Stora, Benjamin. "Algérie: les retours de la mémoire de la guerre d'indépendance." *Modern & Contemporary France* 10 (2002): 461–73.

———. "Deuxième Guerre algérienne? Les habits anciens des combatants." *Les Temps modernes* 580 (January-February 1995): 242–61.

———. "Immigrants and Political Activists: Algerian Nationalists in France, 1945–1954." In *French and Algerian Identities from Colonial Times to the Present: A Century of Interaction,* edited by Alec G. Hargreaves and Michael J. Heffernan. Lampeter: Edwin Mellen, 1993.

———. *La Gangrène et l'oubli. La mémoire de la guerre d'Algérie.* Paris: La Découverte, 1991.

———. "La Guerre d'Algérie quarante ans après: connaissances et reconnaissances." *Modern & Contemporary France,* n.s., 2 (1994): 131–39

———. *Les sources du nationalisme algérien.* Paris: L'Harmattan, 1989.

Talbott, John. "Terrorism and the Liberal Dilemma: The Case of the Battle of Algiers." *Contemporary French Civilization* 212 (1978): 177–89.

———. *The War Without a Name: France in Algeria, 1954–1962.* London: Faber & Faber, 1981.

Taleb, Ahmed. *Lettres de prison: 1957–1961.* Algiers: SNED, 1966.

Tannenbaum, Edward R. *The New France.* Chicago: University of Chicago Press, 1961.

Taylor, John. "Abandoning Pacifism: The Case of Sartre (1939–1940)." *Journal of European Studies* 23 (1993): 207–22.

Teyssier, Arnaud. *Histoire politique de la France: la Vᵉ République 1958–1995; de De Gaulle à Chirac.* Paris: Pygmalion / Gérard Watelet, 1995.

Thibaud, Paul and Pierre Vidal-Naquet. "Le combat pour l'indépendance algérienne: une fausse coïncidence." *Esprit* 208 (1995): 142–61.

Thody, Philip. *20th-Century Literature: Critical Issues and Themes.* London: Macmillan, 1996.

Thomson, David. *Democracy in France since 1870.* Oxford: Oxford University Press, 1969.

Thorez, Maurice. *Œuvres choisies en trois volumes, II: 1938–1950.* Paris: Éditions Sociales, 1966.

Thucydides. *The Peloponnesian War,* translated by Rex Warner. London: Penguin Books, 1956.

Tiersky, Ronald. *French Communism, 1920–72.* Columbia: Columbia University Press, 1974.

Tocqueville, A. *De la démocratie en Amérique*. Paris: Garnier / Flammarion, 1981.

Todd, Olivier. "Jean-Paul Sartre on his Autobiography." *Listener,* June 6, 1957, 915–16.

Tomuschat, Christian, ed. *Modern Law of Self-Determination.* London: Nijhoff, 1993.

Touchard, Jean. *La Gauche en France depuis 1900.* Paris: Seuil, 1977.

Tricot, Bernard. *Mémoires.* Paris: Quai Voltaire, 1994.

Tronchon, J. *L'Insurrection malgache en 1947.* Paris: Maspero, 1974.

Vaïsse, Maurice. *Le Putsch d'Alger.* Paris: Complexe, 1983.

Van Parijs, Philippe. *Qu'est-ce qu'une société juste?* Paris: Seuil, 1991.

Verdès-Leroux, Jeannine. *Au Service du parti: le Parti Communiste, les intellectuels et la culture: 1944–1956.* Paris: Fayard / Minuit, 1983.

———. "'*Combat,*' Staline et la Pologne." In *Camus et le premier "Combat," 1944–1947: Colloque de Paris X-Nanterre,* edited by Jeanyves Guérin. La Garenne-Colombes: Européennes Erasmus, 1990.

———. *Le Réveil des somnambules: le Parti Communiste, les intellectuels et la culture, 1956–1985.* Paris: Fayard / Minuit, 1987.

Vichniac, Judith E. "French Socialists and *Droit à la Différence:* A Changing Dynamic." *French Politics and Society* 9 (1991): 40–56.

Vidal-Naquet, Pierre. *La Torture dans la République.* Paris: Minuit, 1972.

Vigée, Claude. *Les Artistes de la faim.* Paris: Calmann-Lévy, 1960.

Viollette, Maurice. *L'Algérie vivra-t-elle? Notes d'un ancien gouverneur général.* Paris: Alcan, 1931.

Walker, David H. "Literature, History and Factidiversiality." *Journal of European Studies* 25 (1995): 35–50.

———. *Outrage and Insight: Modern French Writing and the "fait divers."* Oxford: Berg, 1995.

Walzer, Michael. *Spheres of Justice.* Oxford: Robertson, 1983.

Wardman, H. W. *Jean-Paul Sartre: The Evolution of his Thought and Art.* Lewiston: Edwin Mellen, 1992.

Weber, Eugen. *The Hollow Years: France in the 1930s.* London: Sinclair-Stevenson, 1995.

Webster, Paul and Nicholas Powell. *Saint-Germain-des-Prés.* London: Constable, 1984.

Wicks, Robert. *Modern French Philosophy: From Existentialism to Postmodernism.* Oxford: Oneworld, 2003.

Wilkinson, James D. *The Intellectual Resistance in Europe.* Cambridge, MA: Harvard University Press, 1981.

Williams, Andrew. "France and the New World Order, 1940–1947." *Modern & Contemporary France* 8 (2000): 191–202.

Wilson, Colin. *The Age of Defeat.* London: Gollancz, 1959.

Winock, Michel. *Le siècle des intellectuels.* Paris: Seuil, 1997.

Wollheim, Richard. "Correspondence." *London Magazine* 1 (1954): 72.

———. "The Political Philosophy of Existentialism." *Cambridge Journal* 7 (1953): 3–19.

Wright, Gordon. *France in Modern Times: From the Enlightenment to the Present.* 4th ed. New York: Norton, 1987.

Newspaper Articles

Arban, Dominique. "Albert Camus reçoit le Prix des Critiques." *Combat,* June 14, 1947.

Audisio, Gabriel. "La leçon des écrivains nord-africains." *Combat,* October 24, 1957.

Birmann, Dominique. "Albert Camus a exposé aux étudiants suédois son attitude devant le problème algérien." *Le Monde,* December 14, 1957.

Bosquet, Alain. "Réflexions sur un Prix Nobel." *Combat,* October 24, 1957.

Bosquet, Alain. "Une conscience contre le chaos." *Combat,* January 5, 1960.

Bright, Martin. "A plague on France." *Guardian,* January 12, 1993, Education sections.

———. "The Struggle for Freedom from France." *Guardian,* November 14, 1995, Education section.

———. "Winds of Change in France." *Guardian,* September 19, 1995, Education section.

Broyelle, Jacques and Claudie Broyelle. "Le silence et les mots." *Le Monde,* January 5, 1980.

Clavel, Maurice. "Le meilleur des nôtres." *Combat,* January 5, 1960.

Contat, Michel and Michel Rybalka. "Un entretien avec Jean-Paul Sartre." *Le Monde,* May 14, 1971.

Cournot, Michel. "L'incertitude des terroristes." *Le Monde,* March 15, 1986.

Diéguez, Manuel de. "Idées, situation et postérité d'Albert Camus." *Combat,* January 7, 1960.

Donovan, Paul. "Imposing the Ultimate Penalty." *Guardian,* April 18, 1995, Education section.

Dumur, Guy. "Une lettre de René Char à propos de *La Révolte en question.*" *Combat,* March 3, 1952.

Fouchet, Max-Pol. "Une volonté de bonheur." *Le Matin,* January 4, 1980.

Frappat, Bruno. "Camus." *Le Monde,* January 5, 1985.

Gallo, Max. "L'Étanger de l'intelligentsia: vingt ans après, Camus toujours lu." *Le Matin,* January 4, 1980.

Gaudemar, Antoine de. "This one's had a good start-born in the middle of a move. This is how Albert Camus, alias Jacques Cormery in the novel, was born." *Guardian,* April 16, 1994.

Gaussen, Frédéric. "Il y a vingt-cinq ans mourait Albert Camus: sacré par les professeurs." *Le Monde,* January 6, 1985.

Gittings, John. "Dreams of Peace Shattered." *Guardian,* June 27, 1995, Education section.

Golliet, Pierre. "Le Problème d'Albert Camus." *Le Monde,* January 6, 1961.

Gordimer, Nadine. "Testament of the Word." *Guardian,* June 15, 2002, Review section.

Guicciardi, Elena. "Camus: Primo Uomo," *La Repubblica,* April 7, 1994.

Guppy, Shusha. "Going back to Africa." *Sunday Times,* October 8, 1995, Books section.

Henriot, Emile. *"L'Homme révolté." Le Monde,* December 26, 1951.

Ionesco, Eugène. "La Conscience de l'histoire." *Le Matin,* January 4, 1980.

Jacob, Odile. "Les derniers mots de François Mitterrand." *Le Monde,* April 25, 1996, Weekly edition.

Jannoud, Claude. "Écrivain ou philosophe?" *Le Figaro,* March 9, 1987.

Judt, Tony. "A hero for our times." *Guardian,* November 17, 2001, Review section.

Junqua, Daniel. "La 'Toussaint rouge'." *Le Monde,* November 2, 1974.

Lebesque, Morvan. "Albert Camus l'Algérien." *Le Canard enchaîné,* October 23, 1957.

Leduc, Victor. "Un Bréviaire de la contre-révolution: *L'Homme révolté* d'Albert Camus." *L'Humanité,* January 26, 1952.

Léon, Georges. "*Les Justes* d'Albert Camus: 'Contradictions insurmontées'." *L'Humanité,* January 15, 1966.

Matignon, Renaud. "Camus: L'Homme toujours révolté." *Le Figaro,* January 22, 1980.

Mauriac, François. "Réponse à *Combat.*" *Le Figaro,* October 22–23, 1944.

Morrison, Blake. "A prize worth writing for." *Independent on Sunday,* October 1, 1995, Review sectiion.

Nadeau, Maurice. "Les Livres: Albert Camus et la révolte." *Combat,* November 8, 1951.

Nayeri, Farah. "A skeleton rattles its bones." *Independent,* April 23, 1994.

Newnham, David. "The Politics of Consumption." *Guardian,* April 27, 1996, Weekend section.

Noiville, Florence. "Camus retrouvé." *Le Monde,* April 22, 1994, Books section.

———. "L'Enfance inguérissable d'Albert Camus." *Le Monde,* April 16, 1994.

Norton-Taylor, Richard. "The Ghosts of Nuremberg." *Guardian,* November 28, 1995, Section 2.

Perrier, Jean-Louis. "Le système Nobel." *Le Monde,* October 12, 1995.

Poirot-Delpech, Bertrand. "Camus, genèse d'une exigence." *Le Monde,* February 9, 1996, Books section.

———. "L'enchantement de la mort." *Le Monde,* March 10, 1978.

———. "Griots." *Le Monde,* April 13, 1994.

———. "Il y a trente ans: la mort d'Albert Camus." *Le Monde,* December 31, 1989–January 1, 1990.

———. "Justice pour Camus." *Le Monde,* August 5, 1977.

———. April 14, 1989.

———. December 31, 1989–January 1, 1990.

———. April 13, 1994.

———. April 16, 1994.

———. April 22, 1994, Le Monde des Livres.

———. October 12, 1995, Sélection hebdomadaire.

———. November 23, 1995, Sélection hebdomadaire.

———. February 9, 1996, Le Monde des Livres.

———. April 25, 1996, Sélection hebdomadaire.

New York Times, April 26, 1994.

Observer, October 8, 1995.
———. April 21, 1996, Review section.
Sunday Times, October 8, 1995, Books section.
Times, October 31, 1957.
———. "Solitude du juste." *Le Monde,* March 6, 1987.
———. "La Vérité!" *Le Monde,* April 14, 1989, Books section.
Rawsthorn, Alice. "Camus cult hits France." *Financial Times,* April 30–May 1, 1994, Weekend section.
Riding, Alan. "Camus's last work, a first draft, shows his life and his style." *New York Times,* April 26, 1994.
Rose, David. "Dead Man Stalking." *Observer,* April 21, 1996, Review section.
Rousseaux, André. "L'Homme juste." *Le Figaro,* January 5, 1960.
Roy, Jules. "Il fut mon soleil." *Le Matin,* January 4, 1980.
Sauvage, Léo. "L'Opinion américaine salue en Camus celui qui demande aux hommes de dire oui à la vie de la façon la plus héroïque." *Le Figaro,* January 6, 1960.
Solers, Philippe. "La Vérité morale." *Le Matin,* January 4, 1980.
Strawson, Galen. "Memory, and other luxury goods." *Independent on Sunday,* October 8, 1995, Review section.
Théolleyre, Jean-Marc. "Nuremberg et après." *Le Monde,* November 23, 1995.
Velter, André. "Il y a trente ans: Albert Camus, Prix Nobel de Littérature." *Le Monde,* October 25–26, 1987.
Viansson-Ponte, Pierre. "Au fils de la semaine: Camus et Mauriac à *L'Express.*" *Le Monde,* December 3–4, 1978
Wood, Gaby. "Outsider's dutiful daughter." *Observer,* October 8, 1995.
Wood, James. "Second Childhood." *Guardian,* October 29, 1995, Weekly edition.
Zand, Nicole. "Les voix du massacre." *Le Monde,* November 23, 1995, Weekly edition.

Special Issues of Reviews on Camus

L'Avant-Scène 413–14 (November 1968).
Équinoxe 13 (1996).
Europe 77 (October 1999).
Le Figaro littéraire 5–11 January 1970.
———. March 9, 1987.
Lire 186 (March 1991).
Magazine littéraire 3 (January 1967).
———. 67–68 (September 1972).
———. 276 (April 1990).
Minesota Review 4 (Spring 1964).
MLN 112 (September 1997).
Modern Fiction Studies 10 (Autumn 1964).
Narcisse 16 (1996).

Le Nouvel Observateur June 9–15, 1994.
NRF 8 (March 1960).
Perspectives: Revue de l'Université Hébraïque de Jérusalem 5 (1998).
Phosphore 97 (February 1989).
Le Point August 14–20, 1993.
Preuves 110 (April 1960).
La Revue du Caire 237 (May 1960).
Revue Celfan / Celfan Review 4 (May 1985)
Revue d'Histoire du Théâtre 12 (October–December 1960).
Roman 20/50: Revue d'étude du roman du XXe *siècle* 27 (June 1999).
Simoun 8 (July 1960).
Stirling French Publications 6 (1998).
Symposium 12 (Spring–Fall 1970).
———. 24 (Fall 1970).
La Table Ronde 146 (February 1960)
Yale French Studies 25 (Spring 1960)

La Société des Études Camusiennes

The *Société des Études Camusiennes* was founded in June 1982. In the words of its own manifesto, "the object of this association is to lead and coordinate studies of the work of Albert Camus, to gather and distribute information relative to this work through an *Information Bulletin* and to organize periodic meetings." As of this writing, the President of the Society is Agnès Spiquel (succeeding the late Jacqueline Lévi-Valensi); Vice-Presidents are Raymond Gay-Crosier and Maurice Weyembergh. To date (spring 2006), 77 issues of the *Bulletin d'Information,* an invaluable working tool for the Camus scholar, have been produced.

Audio-Visual Material

Berland, François, Philippe Lejour, and Arnaud Mathon. *Albert Camus: "La Chute."* 3 cassettes. Paris: Livraphone, 1991. [LIV 202]

Interview with Olivier Todd. *Metropolis.* Arte, April 20, 1996. [on Todd's biography of Camus]

Kent, James. *Albert Camus: The Madness of Sincerity. Bookmark,* BBC 2, October 11, 1997.

Maine, Richard. *Imagine Camus Happy.* BBC Radio 3, 1987. [Including contributions from Claude Bourdet, Jean Camus, Jean Daniel, Guy Dumur, Herbert Lottman, Marcel Moussy, René Tavernier, Olivier Todd, and David Walker].

Roy, Jules, and Jean Montalbetti. *Un homme, une ville: Albert Camus à Alger.* 3 cassettes. Paris: Cassettes Radio France, [n.d.]. [1: 'Une jeunesse algérienne'; 2: 'Les racines méditerranéennes'; 3: 'La justice et la mère'] [RF 300].

Roy, Jules, Michaël Lonsdale, and Jean Montalbetti. *Camus: "L'Étranger."* 3 cassettes. Paris: Auvidid, 1986. [Z 104 AD 802]

Vaughan, Paul, and Andy Martin. *Kaleidoscope,* BBC Radio 4, October 10, 1995 [on the English-language translation of *Le Premier Homme*].

Vecchiali, Paul and Claire Clairval. *Albert Camus.* Paris: L'Institut National de L'Audiovisuel (L'INA), 1975.

Wheeler, Charles. *Points of Departure.* BBC Radio 4, April 26, 1996 [on the 1956 Hungarian Uprising].

The following series was also consulted in the preparation of this study:

Juste Camus, Camus le Juste, Broadcast on France Culture, November 2002. (http: //www.radiofrance.fr/chaines/france-culture2/): 1. Achour, Christiane, Catherine Camus, Jean Daniel, Alain Kinkielkraut, Jacqueline Lévi-Valensi, Michel Surya, and Maurice Weyembergh. *Les Révoltes d'Albert Camus.* November 23, 2002. 2. Garapan, Antoine, Jacqueline Lévi-Valensi, and Denis Salas. *Camus et le terrorisme,* November 23, 2002. 3. Bénézet, Mathieu, and Annie Douel. *Albert Camus, les années "Combat,"* November 25–29, 2002 [Lévi-Valensi, Jacqueline. "Naissance d'un engagement, naissance de *Combat*"; Guérin, Jeanyves. "*Combat* ou l'espoir d'une génération"; Ajchenbaum, Yves-Marc. "Albert Camus, Pascal Pia, une amitié contrariée"; Curnier, Jean-Paul. "Le *Combat* d'un guerrier"; and Milner, Jean-Claude. "Du journaliste-critique au règne du Journal."] 4. Attoun, Lucien, Elodie Boublil, Michel Bouquet, Serge Reggiani, Catherine Sellers, and Michel Vinaver. *Albert Camus, homme de théâtre,* November 26, 2002. 5. Fellous, Colette. *"L'Étranger" d'Albert Camus: portrait,* November 29, 2002.

Index